PostgreSQL 9.4 Vol5: Reference

A catalogue record for this book is available from the Hong Kong Public Libraries.

Published in Hong Kong by Samurai Media Limited.

Email: info@samuraimedia.org

ISBN 978-988-8381-35-7

Table of Contents

VI. Reference

The entries in this Reference are meant to provide in reasonable length an authoritative, complete, and formal summary about their respective subjects. More information about the use of PostgreSQL, in narrative, tutorial, or example form, can be found in other parts of this book. See the cross-references listed on each reference page.

The reference entries are also available as traditional "man" pages.

I. SQL Commands

This part contains reference information for the SQL commands supported by PostgreSQL. By "SQL" the language in general is meant; information about the standards conformance and compatibility of each command can be found on the respective reference page.

ABORT

Name

ABORT — abort the current transaction

Synopsis

```
ABORT [ WORK | TRANSACTION ]
```

Description

ABORT rolls back the current transaction and causes all the updates made by the transaction to be discarded. This command is identical in behavior to the standard SQL command ROLLBACK, and is present only for historical reasons.

Parameters

```
WORK
TRANSACTION
```

Optional key words. They have no effect.

Notes

Use COMMIT to successfully terminate a transaction.

Issuing ABORT outside of a transaction block emits a warning and otherwise has no effect.

Examples

To abort all changes:

```
ABORT;
```

Compatibility

This command is a PostgreSQL extension present for historical reasons. ROLLBACK is the equivalent standard SQL command.

See Also

BEGIN, COMMIT, ROLLBACK

ALTER AGGREGATE

Name

ALTER AGGREGATE — change the definition of an aggregate function

Synopsis

```
ALTER AGGREGATE name ( aggregate_signature ) RENAME TO new_name
ALTER AGGREGATE name ( aggregate_signature ) OWNER TO new_owner
ALTER AGGREGATE name ( aggregate_signature ) SET SCHEMA new_schema

where aggregate_signature is:

* |
[ argmode ] [ argname ] argtype [ , ... ] |
[ [ argmode ] [ argname ] argtype [ , ... ] ] ORDER BY [ argmode ] [ argname ] argt
```

Description

ALTER AGGREGATE changes the definition of an aggregate function.

You must own the aggregate function to use ALTER AGGREGATE. To change the schema of an aggregate function, you must also have CREATE privilege on the new schema. To alter the owner, you must also be a direct or indirect member of the new owning role, and that role must have CREATE privilege on the aggregate function's schema. (These restrictions enforce that altering the owner doesn't do anything you couldn't do by dropping and recreating the aggregate function. However, a superuser can alter ownership of any aggregate function anyway.)

Parameters

name

The name (optionally schema-qualified) of an existing aggregate function.

argmode

The mode of an argument: IN or VARIADIC. If omitted, the default is IN.

argname

The name of an argument. Note that ALTER AGGREGATE does not actually pay any attention to argument names, since only the argument data types are needed to determine the aggregate function's identity.

argtype

> An input data type on which the aggregate function operates. To reference a zero-argument aggregate function, write `*` in place of the list of argument specifications. To reference an ordered-set aggregate function, write `ORDER BY` between the direct and aggregated argument specifications.

new_name

> The new name of the aggregate function.

new_owner

> The new owner of the aggregate function.

new_schema

> The new schema for the aggregate function.

Notes

The recommended syntax for referencing an ordered-set aggregate is to write `ORDER BY` between the direct and aggregated argument specifications, in the same style as in CREATE AGGREGATE. However, it will also work to omit `ORDER BY` and just run the direct and aggregated argument specifications into a single list. In this abbreviated form, if `VARIADIC "any"` was used in both the direct and aggregated argument lists, write `VARIADIC "any"` only once.

Examples

To rename the aggregate function `myavg` for type `integer` to `my_average`:

```
ALTER AGGREGATE myavg(integer) RENAME TO my_average;
```

To change the owner of the aggregate function `myavg` for type `integer` to `joe`:

```
ALTER AGGREGATE myavg(integer) OWNER TO joe;
```

To move the ordered-set aggregate `mypercentile` with direct argument of type `float8` and aggregated argument of type `integer` into schema `myschema`:

```
ALTER AGGREGATE mypercentile(float8 ORDER BY integer) SET SCHEMA myschema;
```

This will work too:

```
ALTER AGGREGATE mypercentile(float8, integer) SET SCHEMA myschema;
```

Compatibility

There is no ALTER AGGREGATE statement in the SQL standard.

See Also

CREATE AGGREGATE, DROP AGGREGATE

ALTER COLLATION

Name

ALTER COLLATION — change the definition of a collation

Synopsis

```
ALTER COLLATION name RENAME TO new_name
ALTER COLLATION name OWNER TO new_owner
ALTER COLLATION name SET SCHEMA new_schema
```

Description

ALTER COLLATION changes the definition of a collation.

You must own the collation to use ALTER COLLATION. To alter the owner, you must also be a direct or indirect member of the new owning role, and that role must have CREATE privilege on the collation's schema. (These restrictions enforce that altering the owner doesn't do anything you couldn't do by dropping and recreating the collation. However, a superuser can alter ownership of any collation anyway.)

Parameters

name

> The name (optionally schema-qualified) of an existing collation.

new_name

> The new name of the collation.

new_owner

> The new owner of the collation.

new_schema

> The new schema for the collation.

Examples

To rename the collation de_DE to german:

```
ALTER COLLATION "de_DE" RENAME TO german;
```

To change the owner of the collation en_US to joe:

```
ALTER COLLATION "en_US" OWNER TO joe;
```

Compatibility

There is no `ALTER COLLATION` statement in the SQL standard.

See Also

CREATE COLLATION, DROP COLLATION

```
ALTER COLLATION "en_US" OWNER TO joe;
```

ALTER CONVERSION

Name

ALTER CONVERSION — change the definition of a conversion

Synopsis

```
ALTER CONVERSION name RENAME TO new_name
ALTER CONVERSION name OWNER TO new_owner
ALTER CONVERSION name SET SCHEMA new_schema
```

Description

ALTER CONVERSION changes the definition of a conversion.

You must own the conversion to use ALTER CONVERSION. To alter the owner, you must also be a direct or indirect member of the new owning role, and that role must have CREATE privilege on the conversion's schema. (These restrictions enforce that altering the owner doesn't do anything you couldn't do by dropping and recreating the conversion. However, a superuser can alter ownership of any conversion anyway.)

Parameters

name

The name (optionally schema-qualified) of an existing conversion.

new_name

The new name of the conversion.

new_owner

The new owner of the conversion.

new_schema

The new schema for the conversion.

Examples

To rename the conversion iso_8859_1_to_utf8 to latin1_to_unicode:

```
ALTER CONVERSION iso_8859_1_to_utf8 RENAME TO latin1_to_unicode;
```

To change the owner of the conversion iso_8859_1_to_utf8 to joe:

```
ALTER CONVERSION iso_8859_1_to_utf8 OWNER TO joe;
```

Compatibility

There is no ALTER CONVERSION statement in the SQL standard.

See Also

CREATE CONVERSION, DROP CONVERSION

ALTER DATABASE

Name

ALTER DATABASE — change a database

Synopsis

```
ALTER DATABASE name [ [ WITH ] option [ ... ] ]

where option can be:

    CONNECTION LIMIT connlimit

ALTER DATABASE name RENAME TO new_name

ALTER DATABASE name OWNER TO new_owner

ALTER DATABASE name SET TABLESPACE new_tablespace

ALTER DATABASE name SET configuration_parameter { TO | = } { value | DEFAULT }
ALTER DATABASE name SET configuration_parameter FROM CURRENT
ALTER DATABASE name RESET configuration_parameter
ALTER DATABASE name RESET ALL
```

Description

ALTER DATABASE changes the attributes of a database.

The first form changes certain per-database settings. (See below for details.) Only the database owner or a superuser can change these settings.

The second form changes the name of the database. Only the database owner or a superuser can rename a database; non-superuser owners must also have the CREATEDB privilege. The current database cannot be renamed. (Connect to a different database if you need to do that.)

The third form changes the owner of the database. To alter the owner, you must own the database and also be a direct or indirect member of the new owning role, and you must have the CREATEDB privilege. (Note that superusers have all these privileges automatically.)

The fourth form changes the default tablespace of the database. Only the database owner or a superuser can do this; you must also have create privilege for the new tablespace. This command physically moves any tables or indexes in the database's old default tablespace to the new tablespace. Note that tables and indexes in non-default tablespaces are not affected.

The remaining forms change the session default for a run-time configuration variable for a PostgreSQL database. Whenever a new session is subsequently started in that database, the specified value becomes the session default value. The database-specific default overrides whatever setting is present in postgresql.conf or has been received from the postgres command line. Only the database owner

1281

or a superuser can change the session defaults for a database. Certain variables cannot be set this way, or can only be set by a superuser.

Parameters

name

> The name of the database whose attributes are to be altered.

connlimit

> How many concurrent connections can be made to this database. -1 means no limit.

new_name

> The new name of the database.

new_owner

> The new owner of the database.

new_tablespace

> The new default tablespace of the database.

configuration_parameter
value

> Set this database's session default for the specified configuration parameter to the given value. If *value* is DEFAULT or, equivalently, RESET is used, the database-specific setting is removed, so the system-wide default setting will be inherited in new sessions. Use RESET ALL to clear all database-specific settings. SET FROM CURRENT saves the session's current value of the parameter as the database-specific value.

> See SET and Chapter 18 for more information about allowed parameter names and values.

Notes

It is also possible to tie a session default to a specific role rather than to a database; see ALTER ROLE. Role-specific settings override database-specific ones if there is a conflict.

Examples

To disable index scans by default in the database test:

```
ALTER DATABASE test SET enable_indexscan TO off;
```

Compatibility

The `ALTER DATABASE` statement is a PostgreSQL extension.

See Also

CREATE DATABASE, DROP DATABASE, SET, CREATE TABLESPACE

ALTER DEFAULT PRIVILEGES

Name

ALTER DEFAULT PRIVILEGES — define default access privileges

Synopsis

```
ALTER DEFAULT PRIVILEGES
    [ FOR { ROLE | USER } target_role [, ...] ]
    [ IN SCHEMA schema_name [, ...] ]
    abbreviated_grant_or_revoke

where abbreviated_grant_or_revoke is one of:

GRANT { { SELECT | INSERT | UPDATE | DELETE | TRUNCATE | REFERENCES | TRIGGER }
    [, ...] | ALL [ PRIVILEGES ] }
    ON TABLES
    TO { [ GROUP ] role_name | PUBLIC } [, ...] [ WITH GRANT OPTION ]

GRANT { { USAGE | SELECT | UPDATE }
    [, ...] | ALL [ PRIVILEGES ] }
    ON SEQUENCES
    TO { [ GROUP ] role_name | PUBLIC } [, ...] [ WITH GRANT OPTION ]

GRANT { EXECUTE | ALL [ PRIVILEGES ] }
    ON FUNCTIONS
    TO { [ GROUP ] role_name | PUBLIC } [, ...] [ WITH GRANT OPTION ]

GRANT { USAGE | ALL [ PRIVILEGES ] }
    ON TYPES
    TO { [ GROUP ] role_name | PUBLIC } [, ...] [ WITH GRANT OPTION ]

REVOKE [ GRANT OPTION FOR ]
    { { SELECT | INSERT | UPDATE | DELETE | TRUNCATE | REFERENCES | TRIGGER }
    [, ...] | ALL [ PRIVILEGES ] }
    ON TABLES
    FROM { [ GROUP ] role_name | PUBLIC } [, ...]
    [ CASCADE | RESTRICT ]

REVOKE [ GRANT OPTION FOR ]
    { { USAGE | SELECT | UPDATE }
    [, ...] | ALL [ PRIVILEGES ] }
    ON SEQUENCES
    FROM { [ GROUP ] role_name | PUBLIC } [, ...]
    [ CASCADE | RESTRICT ]

REVOKE [ GRANT OPTION FOR ]
    { EXECUTE | ALL [ PRIVILEGES ] }
    ON FUNCTIONS
    FROM { [ GROUP ] role_name | PUBLIC } [, ...]
```

```
    [ CASCADE | RESTRICT ]

REVOKE [ GRANT OPTION FOR ]
    { USAGE | ALL [ PRIVILEGES ] }
    ON TYPES
    FROM { [ GROUP ] role_name | PUBLIC } [, ...]
    [ CASCADE | RESTRICT ]
```

Description

ALTER DEFAULT PRIVILEGES allows you to set the privileges that will be applied to objects created in the future. (It does not affect privileges assigned to already-existing objects.) Currently, only the privileges for tables (including views and foreign tables), sequences, functions, and types (including domains) can be altered.

You can change default privileges only for objects that will be created by yourself or by roles that you are a member of. The privileges can be set globally (i.e., for all objects created in the current database), or just for objects created in specified schemas. Default privileges that are specified per-schema are added to whatever the global default privileges are for the particular object type.

As explained under GRANT, the default privileges for any object type normally grant all grantable permissions to the object owner, and may grant some privileges to PUBLIC as well. However, this behavior can be changed by altering the global default privileges with ALTER DEFAULT PRIVILEGES.

Parameters

target_role

> The name of an existing role of which the current role is a member. If FOR ROLE is omitted, the current role is assumed.

schema_name

> The name of an existing schema. If specified, the default privileges are altered for objects later created in that schema. If IN SCHEMA is omitted, the global default privileges are altered.

role_name

> The name of an existing role to grant or revoke privileges for. This parameter, and all the other parameters in *abbreviated_grant_or_revoke*, act as described under GRANT or REVOKE, except that one is setting permissions for a whole class of objects rather than specific named objects.

Notes

Use psql's \ddp command to obtain information about existing assignments of default privileges. The meaning of the privilege values is the same as explained for \dp under GRANT.

If you wish to drop a role for which the default privileges have been altered, it is necessary to reverse the changes in its default privileges or use DROP OWNED BY to get rid of the default privileges entry for the role.

Examples

Grant SELECT privilege to everyone for all tables (and views) you subsequently create in schema `myschema`, and allow role `webuser` to INSERT into them too:

```
ALTER DEFAULT PRIVILEGES IN SCHEMA myschema GRANT SELECT ON TABLES TO PUBLIC;
ALTER DEFAULT PRIVILEGES IN SCHEMA myschema GRANT INSERT ON TABLES TO webuser;
```

Undo the above, so that subsequently-created tables won't have any more permissions than normal:

```
ALTER DEFAULT PRIVILEGES IN SCHEMA myschema REVOKE SELECT ON TABLES FROM PUBLIC
ALTER DEFAULT PRIVILEGES IN SCHEMA myschema REVOKE INSERT ON TABLES FROM webuse
```

Remove the public EXECUTE permission that is normally granted on functions, for all functions subsequently created by role `admin`:

```
ALTER DEFAULT PRIVILEGES FOR ROLE admin REVOKE EXECUTE ON FUNCTIONS FROM PUBLIC
```

Compatibility

There is no `ALTER DEFAULT PRIVILEGES` statement in the SQL standard.

See Also

GRANT, REVOKE

ALTER DOMAIN

Name

ALTER DOMAIN — change the definition of a domain

Synopsis

```
ALTER DOMAIN name
    { SET DEFAULT expression | DROP DEFAULT }
ALTER DOMAIN name
    { SET | DROP } NOT NULL
ALTER DOMAIN name
    ADD domain_constraint [ NOT VALID ]
ALTER DOMAIN name
    DROP CONSTRAINT [ IF EXISTS ] constraint_name [ RESTRICT | CASCADE ]
ALTER DOMAIN name
     RENAME CONSTRAINT constraint_name TO new_constraint_name
ALTER DOMAIN name
    VALIDATE CONSTRAINT constraint_name
ALTER DOMAIN name
    OWNER TO new_owner
ALTER DOMAIN name
    RENAME TO new_name
ALTER DOMAIN name
    SET SCHEMA new_schema
```

Description

ALTER DOMAIN changes the definition of an existing domain. There are several sub-forms:

SET/DROP DEFAULT

These forms set or remove the default value for a domain. Note that defaults only apply to subsequent INSERT commands; they do not affect rows already in a table using the domain.

SET/DROP NOT NULL

These forms change whether a domain is marked to allow NULL values or to reject NULL values. You can only SET NOT NULL when the columns using the domain contain no null values.

ADD domain_constraint [NOT VALID]

This form adds a new constraint to a domain using the same syntax as CREATE DOMAIN. When a new constraint is added to a domain, all columns using that domain will be checked against the newly added constraint. These checks can be suppressed by adding the new constraint using the NOT VALID option; the constraint can later be made valid using ALTER DOMAIN ... VALIDATE CONSTRAINT. Newly inserted or updated rows are always checked against all constraints, even those marked NOT VALID. NOT VALID is only accepted for CHECK constraints.

DROP CONSTRAINT [IF EXISTS]

This form drops constraints on a domain. If IF EXISTS is specified and the constraint does not exist, no error is thrown. In this case a notice is issued instead.

RENAME CONSTRAINT

This form changes the name of a constraint on a domain.

VALIDATE CONSTRAINT

This form validates a constraint previously added as NOT VALID, that is, verify that all data in columns using the domain satisfy the specified constraint.

OWNER

This form changes the owner of the domain to the specified user.

RENAME

This form changes the name of the domain.

SET SCHEMA

This form changes the schema of the domain. Any constraints associated with the domain are moved into the new schema as well.

You must own the domain to use ALTER DOMAIN. To change the schema of a domain, you must also have CREATE privilege on the new schema. To alter the owner, you must also be a direct or indirect member of the new owning role, and that role must have CREATE privilege on the domain's schema. (These restrictions enforce that altering the owner doesn't do anything you couldn't do by dropping and recreating the domain. However, a superuser can alter ownership of any domain anyway.)

Parameters

name

The name (possibly schema-qualified) of an existing domain to alter.

domain_constraint

New domain constraint for the domain.

constraint_name

Name of an existing constraint to drop or rename.

NOT VALID

Do not verify existing column data for constraint validity.

CASCADE

Automatically drop objects that depend on the constraint.

RESTRICT

Refuse to drop the constraint if there are any dependent objects. This is the default behavior.

new_name

> The new name for the domain.

new_constraint_name

> The new name for the constraint.

new_owner

> The user name of the new owner of the domain.

new_schema

> The new schema for the domain.

Notes

Currently, ALTER DOMAIN ADD CONSTRAINT and ALTER DOMAIN SET NOT NULL will fail if the named domain or any derived domain is used within a composite-type column of any table in the database. They should eventually be improved to be able to verify the new constraint for such nested columns.

Examples

To add a NOT NULL constraint to a domain:

```
ALTER DOMAIN zipcode SET NOT NULL;
```

To remove a NOT NULL constraint from a domain:

```
ALTER DOMAIN zipcode DROP NOT NULL;
```

To add a check constraint to a domain:

```
ALTER DOMAIN zipcode ADD CONSTRAINT zipchk CHECK (char_length(VALUE) = 5);
```

To remove a check constraint from a domain:

```
ALTER DOMAIN zipcode DROP CONSTRAINT zipchk;
```

To rename a check constraint on a domain:

```
ALTER DOMAIN zipcode RENAME CONSTRAINT zipchk TO zip_check;
```

To move the domain into a different schema:

```
ALTER DOMAIN zipcode SET SCHEMA customers;
```

Compatibility

ALTER DOMAIN conforms to the SQL standard, except for the OWNER, RENAME, SET SCHEMA, and VALIDATE CONSTRAINT variants, which are PostgreSQL extensions. The NOT VALID clause of the ADD CONSTRAINT variant is also a PostgreSQL extension.

See Also

CREATE DOMAIN, DROP DOMAIN

```
ALTER DOMAIN zipcode SET SCHEMA customers;
```

ALTER EVENT TRIGGER

Name

ALTER EVENT TRIGGER — change the definition of an event trigger

Synopsis

```
ALTER EVENT TRIGGER name DISABLE
ALTER EVENT TRIGGER name ENABLE [ REPLICA | ALWAYS ]
ALTER EVENT TRIGGER name OWNER TO new_owner
ALTER EVENT TRIGGER name RENAME TO new_name
```

Description

ALTER EVENT TRIGGER changes properties of an existing event trigger.

You must be superuser to alter an event trigger.

Parameters

name

> The name of an existing trigger to alter.

new_owner

> The user name of the new owner of the event trigger.

new_name

> The new name of the event trigger.

DISABLE/ENABLE [REPLICA | ALWAYS] TRIGGER

> These forms configure the firing of event triggers. A disabled trigger is still known to the system, but is not executed when its triggering event occurs. See also session_replication_role.

Compatibility

There is no ALTER EVENT TRIGGER statement in the SQL standard.

See Also

CREATE EVENT TRIGGER, DROP EVENT TRIGGER

ALTER EXTENSION

Name

ALTER EXTENSION — change the definition of an extension

Synopsis

```
ALTER EXTENSION name UPDATE [ TO new_version ]
ALTER EXTENSION name SET SCHEMA new_schema
ALTER EXTENSION name ADD member_object
ALTER EXTENSION name DROP member_object

where member_object is:

  AGGREGATE aggregate_name ( aggregate_signature ) |
  CAST (source_type AS target_type) |
  COLLATION object_name |
  CONVERSION object_name |
  DOMAIN object_name |
  EVENT TRIGGER object_name |
  FOREIGN DATA WRAPPER object_name |
  FOREIGN TABLE object_name |
  FUNCTION function_name ( [ [ argmode ] [ argname ] argtype [, ...] ] ) ) |
  MATERIALIZED VIEW object_name |
  OPERATOR operator_name (left_type, right_type) |
  OPERATOR CLASS object_name USING index_method |
  OPERATOR FAMILY object_name USING index_method |
  [ PROCEDURAL ] LANGUAGE object_name |
  SCHEMA object_name |
  SEQUENCE object_name |
  SERVER object_name |
  TABLE object_name |
  TEXT SEARCH CONFIGURATION object_name |
  TEXT SEARCH DICTIONARY object_name |
  TEXT SEARCH PARSER object_name |
  TEXT SEARCH TEMPLATE object_name |
  TYPE object_name |
  VIEW object_name

and aggregate_signature is:

* |
[ argmode ] [ argname ] argtype [ , ... ] |
[ [ argmode ] [ argname ] argtype [ , ... ] ] ORDER BY [ argmode ] [ argname ] argt
```

Description

ALTER EXTENSION changes the definition of an installed extension. There are several subforms:

UPDATE

> This form updates the extension to a newer version. The extension must supply a suitable update script (or series of scripts) that can modify the currently-installed version into the requested version.

SET SCHEMA

> This form moves the extension's objects into another schema. The extension has to be *relocatable* for this command to succeed.

ADD *member_object*

> This form adds an existing object to the extension. This is mainly useful in extension update scripts. The object will subsequently be treated as a member of the extension; notably, it can only be dropped by dropping the extension.

DROP *member_object*

> This form removes a member object from the extension. This is mainly useful in extension update scripts. The object is not dropped, only disassociated from the extension.

See Section 35.15 for more information about these operations.

You must own the extension to use ALTER EXTENSION. The ADD/DROP forms require ownership of the added/dropped object as well.

Parameters

name

> The name of an installed extension.

new_version

> The desired new version of the extension. This can be written as either an identifier or a string literal. If not specified, ALTER EXTENSION UPDATE attempts to update to whatever is shown as the default version in the extension's control file.

new_schema

> The new schema for the extension.

object_name
aggregate_name
function_name
operator_name

> The name of an object to be added to or removed from the extension. Names of tables, aggregates, domains, foreign tables, functions, operators, operator classes, operator families, sequences, text search objects, types, and views can be schema-qualified.

source_type

> The name of the source data type of the cast.

target_type

> The name of the target data type of the cast.

argmode

> The mode of a function or aggregate argument: IN, OUT, INOUT, or VARIADIC. If omitted, the default is IN. Note that ALTER EXTENSION does not actually pay any attention to OUT arguments, since only the input arguments are needed to determine the function's identity. So it is sufficient to list the IN, INOUT, and VARIADIC arguments.

argname

> The name of a function or aggregate argument. Note that ALTER EXTENSION does not actually pay any attention to argument names, since only the argument data types are needed to determine the function's identity.

argtype

> The data type of a function or aggregate argument.

left_type
right_type

> The data type(s) of the operator's arguments (optionally schema-qualified). Write NONE for the missing argument of a prefix or postfix operator.

PROCEDURAL

> This is a noise word.

Examples

To update the hstore extension to version 2.0:

```
ALTER EXTENSION hstore UPDATE TO '2.0';
```

To change the schema of the hstore extension to utils:

```
ALTER EXTENSION hstore SET SCHEMA utils;
```

To add an existing function to the hstore extension:

```
ALTER EXTENSION hstore ADD FUNCTION populate_record(anyelement, hstore);
```

Compatibility

ALTER EXTENSION is a PostgreSQL extension.

See Also

CREATE EXTENSION, DROP EXTENSION

ALTER FOREIGN DATA WRAPPER

Name

ALTER FOREIGN DATA WRAPPER — change the definition of a foreign-data wrapper

Synopsis

```
ALTER FOREIGN DATA WRAPPER name
    [ HANDLER handler_function | NO HANDLER ]
    [ VALIDATOR validator_function | NO VALIDATOR ]
    [ OPTIONS ( [ ADD | SET | DROP ] option ['value'] [, ... ]) ]
ALTER FOREIGN DATA WRAPPER name OWNER TO new_owner
ALTER FOREIGN DATA WRAPPER name RENAME TO new_name
```

Description

ALTER FOREIGN DATA WRAPPER changes the definition of a foreign-data wrapper. The first form of the command changes the support functions or the generic options of the foreign-data wrapper (at least one clause is required). The second form changes the owner of the foreign-data wrapper.

Only superusers can alter foreign-data wrappers. Additionally, only superusers can own foreign-data wrappers.

Parameters

name

> The name of an existing foreign-data wrapper.

HANDLER handler_function

> Specifies a new handler function for the foreign-data wrapper.

NO HANDLER

> This is used to specify that the foreign-data wrapper should no longer have a handler function.

> Note that foreign tables that use a foreign-data wrapper with no handler cannot be accessed.

VALIDATOR validator_function

> Specifies a new validator function for the foreign-data wrapper.

> Note that it is possible that pre-existing options of the foreign-data wrapper, or of dependent servers, user mappings, or foreign tables, are invalid according to the new validator. PostgreSQL does not check for this. It is up to the user to make sure that these options are correct before using the modified foreign-data wrapper. However, any options specified in this ALTER FOREIGN DATA WRAPPER command will be checked using the new validator.

```
NO VALIDATOR
```

This is used to specify that the foreign-data wrapper should no longer have a validator function.

```
OPTIONS ( [ ADD | SET | DROP ] option ['value'] [, ... ] )
```

Change options for the foreign-data wrapper. `ADD`, `SET`, and `DROP` specify the action to be performed. `ADD` is assumed if no operation is explicitly specified. Option names must be unique; names and values are also validated using the foreign data wrapper's validator function, if any.

```
new_owner
```

The user name of the new owner of the foreign-data wrapper.

```
new_name
```

The new name for the foreign-data wrapper.

Examples

Change a foreign-data wrapper `dbi`, add option `foo`, drop `bar`:

```
ALTER FOREIGN DATA WRAPPER dbi OPTIONS (ADD foo '1', DROP 'bar');
```

Change the foreign-data wrapper `dbi` validator to `bob.myvalidator`:

```
ALTER FOREIGN DATA WRAPPER dbi VALIDATOR bob.myvalidator;
```

Compatibility

`ALTER FOREIGN DATA WRAPPER` conforms to ISO/IEC 9075-9 (SQL/MED), except that the `HANDLER`, `VALIDATOR`, `OWNER TO`, and `RENAME` clauses are extensions.

See Also

CREATE FOREIGN DATA WRAPPER, DROP FOREIGN DATA WRAPPER

ALTER FOREIGN TABLE

Name

ALTER FOREIGN TABLE — change the definition of a foreign table

Synopsis

```
ALTER FOREIGN TABLE [ IF EXISTS ] name
    action [, ... ]
ALTER FOREIGN TABLE [ IF EXISTS ] name
    RENAME [ COLUMN ] column_name TO new_column_name
ALTER FOREIGN TABLE [ IF EXISTS ] name
    RENAME TO new_name
ALTER FOREIGN TABLE [ IF EXISTS ] name
    SET SCHEMA new_schema

where action is one of:

    ADD [ COLUMN ] column_name data_type [ COLLATE collation ] [ column_constraint
    DROP [ COLUMN ] [ IF EXISTS ] column_name [ RESTRICT | CASCADE ]
    ALTER [ COLUMN ] column_name [ SET DATA ] TYPE data_type
    ALTER [ COLUMN ] column_name SET DEFAULT expression
    ALTER [ COLUMN ] column_name DROP DEFAULT
    ALTER [ COLUMN ] column_name { SET | DROP } NOT NULL
    ALTER [ COLUMN ] column_name SET STATISTICS integer
    ALTER [ COLUMN ] column_name SET ( attribute_option = value [, ... ] )
    ALTER [ COLUMN ] column_name RESET ( attribute_option [, ... ] )
    ALTER [ COLUMN ] column_name OPTIONS ( [ ADD | SET | DROP ] option ['value']
    DISABLE TRIGGER [ trigger_name | ALL | USER ]
    ENABLE TRIGGER [ trigger_name | ALL | USER ]
    ENABLE REPLICA TRIGGER trigger_name
    ENABLE ALWAYS TRIGGER trigger_name
    OWNER TO new_owner
    OPTIONS ( [ ADD | SET | DROP ] option ['value'] [, ... ])
```

Description

ALTER FOREIGN TABLE changes the definition of an existing foreign table. There are several subforms:

ADD COLUMN

> This form adds a new column to the foreign table, using the same syntax as CREATE FOREIGN TABLE. Unlike the case when adding a column to a regular table, nothing happens to the underlying storage: this action simply declares that some new column is now accessible through the foreign table.

DROP COLUMN [IF EXISTS]

This form drops a column from a foreign table. You will need to say CASCADE if anything outside the table depends on the column; for example, views. If IF EXISTS is specified and the column does not exist, no error is thrown. In this case a notice is issued instead.

IF EXISTS

Do not throw an error if the foreign table does not exist. A notice is issued in this case.

SET DATA TYPE

This form changes the type of a column of a foreign table.

SET/DROP DEFAULT

These forms set or remove the default value for a column. Default values only apply in subsequent INSERT or UPDATE commands; they do not cause rows already in the table to change.

SET/DROP NOT NULL

Mark a column as allowing, or not allowing, null values.

SET STATISTICS

This form sets the per-column statistics-gathering target for subsequent ANALYZE operations. See the similar form of **ALTER TABLE** for more details.

SET (*attribute_option* = *value* [, ...])
RESET (*attribute_option* [, ...])

This form sets or resets per-attribute options. See the similar form of **ALTER TABLE** for more details.

DISABLE/ENABLE [REPLICA | ALWAYS] TRIGGER

These forms configure the firing of trigger(s) belonging to the foreign table. See the similar form of **ALTER TABLE** for more details.

OWNER

This form changes the owner of the foreign table to the specified user.

RENAME

The RENAME forms change the name of a foreign table or the name of an individual column in a foreign table.

SET SCHEMA

This form moves the foreign table into another schema.

OPTIONS ([ADD | SET | DROP] *option* ['*value*'] [, ...])

Change options for the foreign table or one of its columns. ADD, SET, and DROP specify the action to be performed. ADD is assumed if no operation is explicitly specified. Duplicate option names are not allowed (although it's OK for a table option and a column option to have the same name). Option names and values are also validated using the foreign data wrapper library.

All the actions except RENAME and SET SCHEMA can be combined into a list of multiple alterations to apply in parallel. For example, it is possible to add several columns and/or alter the type of several columns in a single command.

You must own the table to use ALTER FOREIGN TABLE. To change the schema of a foreign table, you must also have CREATE privilege on the new schema. To alter the owner, you must also be a direct or indirect member of the new owning role, and that role must have CREATE privilege on the table's schema. (These restrictions enforce that altering the owner doesn't do anything you couldn't do by dropping and recreating the table. However, a superuser can alter ownership of any table anyway.) To add a column or alter a column type, you must also have USAGE privilege on the data type.

Parameters

name

The name (possibly schema-qualified) of an existing foreign table to alter.

column_name

Name of a new or existing column.

new_column_name

New name for an existing column.

new_name

New name for the table.

data_type

Data type of the new column, or new data type for an existing column.

CASCADE

Automatically drop objects that depend on the dropped column (for example, views referencing the column).

RESTRICT

Refuse to drop the column if there are any dependent objects. This is the default behavior.

trigger_name

Name of a single trigger to disable or enable.

ALL

Disable or enable all triggers belonging to the foreign table. (This requires superuser privilege if any of the triggers are internally generated triggers. The core system does not add such triggers to foreign tables, but add-on code could do so.)

USER

Disable or enable all triggers belonging to the foreign table except for internally generated triggers.

new_owner

The user name of the new owner of the table.

new_schema

The name of the schema to which the table will be moved.

Notes

The key word COLUMN is noise and can be omitted.

Consistency with the foreign server is not checked when a column is added or removed with ADD COLUMN or DROP COLUMN, a NOT NULL constraint is added, or a column type is changed with SET DATA TYPE. It is the user's responsibility to ensure that the table definition matches the remote side.

Refer to CREATE FOREIGN TABLE for a further description of valid parameters.

Examples

To mark a column as not-null:

```
ALTER FOREIGN TABLE distributors ALTER COLUMN street SET NOT NULL;
```

To change options of a foreign table:

```
ALTER FOREIGN TABLE myschema.distributors OPTIONS (ADD opt1 'value', SET opt2,
```

Compatibility

The forms ADD, DROP, and SET DATA TYPE conform with the SQL standard. The other forms are PostgreSQL extensions of the SQL standard. Also, the ability to specify more than one manipulation in a single ALTER FOREIGN TABLE command is an extension.

ALTER FOREIGN TABLE DROP COLUMN can be used to drop the only column of a foreign table, leaving a zero-column table. This is an extension of SQL, which disallows zero-column foreign tables.

ALTER FUNCTION

Name

ALTER FUNCTION — change the definition of a function

Synopsis

```
ALTER FUNCTION name ( [ [ argmode ] [ argname ] argtype [, ...] ] )
    action [ ... ] [ RESTRICT ]
ALTER FUNCTION name ( [ [ argmode ] [ argname ] argtype [, ...] ] )
    RENAME TO new_name
ALTER FUNCTION name ( [ [ argmode ] [ argname ] argtype [, ...] ] )
    OWNER TO new_owner
ALTER FUNCTION name ( [ [ argmode ] [ argname ] argtype [, ...] ] )
    SET SCHEMA new_schema

where action is one of:

    CALLED ON NULL INPUT | RETURNS NULL ON NULL INPUT | STRICT
    IMMUTABLE | STABLE | VOLATILE | [ NOT ] LEAKPROOF
    [ EXTERNAL ] SECURITY INVOKER | [ EXTERNAL ] SECURITY DEFINER
    COST execution_cost
    ROWS result_rows
    SET configuration_parameter { TO | = } { value | DEFAULT }
    SET configuration_parameter FROM CURRENT
    RESET configuration_parameter
    RESET ALL
```

Description

ALTER FUNCTION changes the definition of a function.

You must own the function to use ALTER FUNCTION. To change a function's schema, you must also have CREATE privilege on the new schema. To alter the owner, you must also be a direct or indirect member of the new owning role, and that role must have CREATE privilege on the function's schema. (These restrictions enforce that altering the owner doesn't do anything you couldn't do by dropping and recreating the function. However, a superuser can alter ownership of any function anyway.)

Parameters

name

The name (optionally schema-qualified) of an existing function.

argmode

> The mode of an argument: IN, OUT, INOUT, or VARIADIC. If omitted, the default is IN. Note that ALTER FUNCTION does not actually pay any attention to OUT arguments, since only the input arguments are needed to determine the function's identity. So it is sufficient to list the IN, INOUT, and VARIADIC arguments.

argname

> The name of an argument. Note that ALTER FUNCTION does not actually pay any attention to argument names, since only the argument data types are needed to determine the function's identity.

argtype

> The data type(s) of the function's arguments (optionally schema-qualified), if any.

new_name

> The new name of the function.

new_owner

> The new owner of the function. Note that if the function is marked SECURITY DEFINER, it will subsequently execute as the new owner.

new_schema

> The new schema for the function.

CALLED ON NULL INPUT
RETURNS NULL ON NULL INPUT
STRICT

> CALLED ON NULL INPUT changes the function so that it will be invoked when some or all of its arguments are null. RETURNS NULL ON NULL INPUT or STRICT changes the function so that it is not invoked if any of its arguments are null; instead, a null result is assumed automatically. See CREATE FUNCTION for more information.

IMMUTABLE
STABLE
VOLATILE

> Change the volatility of the function to the specified setting. See CREATE FUNCTION for details.

[EXTERNAL] SECURITY INVOKER
[EXTERNAL] SECURITY DEFINER

> Change whether the function is a security definer or not. The key word EXTERNAL is ignored for SQL conformance. See CREATE FUNCTION for more information about this capability.

LEAKPROOF

> Change whether the function is considered leakproof or not. See CREATE FUNCTION for more information about this capability.

COST execution_cost

> Change the estimated execution cost of the function. See CREATE FUNCTION for more information.

ROWS *result_rows*

> Change the estimated number of rows returned by a set-returning function. See CREATE FUNC-
> TION for more information.

configuration_parameter
value

> Add or change the assignment to be made to a configuration parameter when the function is called. If
> *value* is DEFAULT or, equivalently, RESET is used, the function-local setting is removed, so that the
> function executes with the value present in its environment. Use RESET ALL to clear all function-
> local settings. SET FROM CURRENT saves the session's current value of the parameter as the value to
> be applied when the function is entered.

> See SET and Chapter 18 for more information about allowed parameter names and values.

RESTRICT

> Ignored for conformance with the SQL standard.

Examples

To rename the function sqrt for type integer to square_root:

ALTER FUNCTION sqrt(integer) RENAME TO square_root;

To change the owner of the function sqrt for type integer to joe:

ALTER FUNCTION sqrt(integer) OWNER TO joe;

To change the schema of the function sqrt for type integer to maths:

ALTER FUNCTION sqrt(integer) SET SCHEMA maths;

To adjust the search path that is automatically set for a function:

ALTER FUNCTION check_password(text) SET search_path = admin, pg_temp;

To disable automatic setting of search_path for a function:

ALTER FUNCTION check_password(text) RESET search_path;

The function will now execute with whatever search path is used by its caller.

Compatibility

This statement is partially compatible with the ALTER FUNCTION statement in the SQL standard. The standard allows more properties of a function to be modified, but does not provide the ability to rename a function, make a function a security definer, attach configuration parameter values to a function, or change the owner, schema, or volatility of a function. The standard also requires the RESTRICT key word, which is optional in PostgreSQL.

See Also

CREATE FUNCTION, DROP FUNCTION

ALTER GROUP

Name

ALTER GROUP — change role name or membership

Synopsis

```
ALTER GROUP group_name ADD USER user_name [, ... ]
ALTER GROUP group_name DROP USER user_name [, ... ]

ALTER GROUP group_name RENAME TO new_name
```

Description

ALTER GROUP changes the attributes of a user group. This is an obsolete command, though still accepted for backwards compatibility, because groups (and users too) have been superseded by the more general concept of roles.

The first two variants add users to a group or remove them from a group. (Any role can play the part of either a "user" or a "group" for this purpose.) These variants are effectively equivalent to granting or revoking membership in the role named as the "group"; so the preferred way to do this is to use GRANT or REVOKE.

The third variant changes the name of the group. This is exactly equivalent to renaming the role with ALTER ROLE.

Parameters

group_name

The name of the group (role) to modify.

user_name

Users (roles) that are to be added to or removed from the group. The users must already exist; ALTER GROUP does not create or drop users.

new_name

The new name of the group.

Examples

Add users to a group:

```
ALTER GROUP staff ADD USER karl, john;
```

Remove a user from a group:

```
ALTER GROUP workers DROP USER beth;
```

Compatibility

There is no ALTER GROUP statement in the SQL standard.

See Also

GRANT, REVOKE, ALTER ROLE

ALTER INDEX

Name

ALTER INDEX — change the definition of an index

Synopsis

```
ALTER INDEX [ IF EXISTS ] name RENAME TO new_name
ALTER INDEX [ IF EXISTS ] name SET TABLESPACE tablespace_name
ALTER INDEX [ IF EXISTS ] name SET ( storage_parameter = value [, ... ] )
ALTER INDEX [ IF EXISTS ] name RESET ( storage_parameter [, ... ] )
ALTER INDEX ALL IN TABLESPACE name [ OWNED BY role_name [, ... ] ]
    SET TABLESPACE new_tablespace [ NOWAIT ]
```

Description

ALTER INDEX changes the definition of an existing index. There are several subforms:

IF EXISTS

Do not throw an error if the index does not exist. A notice is issued in this case.

RENAME

The RENAME form changes the name of the index. There is no effect on the stored data.

SET TABLESPACE

This form changes the index's tablespace to the specified tablespace and moves the data file(s) associated with the index to the new tablespace. To change the tablespace of an index, you must own the index and have CREATE privilege on the new tablespace. All indexes in the current database in a tablespace can be moved by using the ALL IN TABLESPACE form, which will lock all indexes to be moved and then move each one. This form also supports OWNED BY, which will only move indexes owned by the roles specified. If the NOWAIT option is specified then the command will fail if it is unable to acquire all of the locks required immediately. Note that system catalogs will not be moved by this command, use ALTER DATABASE or explicit ALTER INDEX invocations instead if desired. See also CREATE TABLESPACE.

SET (storage_parameter = value [, ...])

This form changes one or more index-method-specific storage parameters for the index. See CREATE INDEX for details on the available parameters. Note that the index contents will not be modified immediately by this command; depending on the parameter you might need to rebuild the index with REINDEX to get the desired effects.

RESET (storage_parameter [, ...])

This form resets one or more index-method-specific storage parameters to their defaults. As with SET, a REINDEX might be needed to update the index entirely.

Parameters

name

> The name (possibly schema-qualified) of an existing index to alter.

new_name

> The new name for the index.

tablespace_name

> The tablespace to which the index will be moved.

storage_parameter

> The name of an index-method-specific storage parameter.

value

> The new value for an index-method-specific storage parameter. This might be a number or a word depending on the parameter.

Notes

These operations are also possible using ALTER TABLE. `ALTER INDEX` is in fact just an alias for the forms of `ALTER TABLE` that apply to indexes.

There was formerly an `ALTER INDEX OWNER` variant, but this is now ignored (with a warning). An index cannot have an owner different from its table's owner. Changing the table's owner automatically changes the index as well.

Changing any part of a system catalog index is not permitted.

Examples

To rename an existing index:

```
ALTER INDEX distributors RENAME TO suppliers;
```

To move an index to a different tablespace:

```
ALTER INDEX distributors SET TABLESPACE fasttablespace;
```

To change an index's fill factor (assuming that the index method supports it):

```
ALTER INDEX distributors SET (fillfactor = 75);
REINDEX INDEX distributors;
```

Compatibility

ALTER INDEX is a PostgreSQL extension.

See Also

CREATE INDEX, REINDEX

ALTER LANGUAGE

Name

ALTER LANGUAGE — change the definition of a procedural language

Synopsis

```
ALTER [ PROCEDURAL ] LANGUAGE name RENAME TO new_name
ALTER [ PROCEDURAL ] LANGUAGE name OWNER TO new_owner
```

Description

ALTER LANGUAGE changes the definition of a procedural language. The only functionality is to rename the language or assign a new owner. You must be superuser or owner of the language to use ALTER LANGUAGE.

Parameters

name

Name of a language

new_name

The new name of the language

new_owner

The new owner of the language

Compatibility

There is no ALTER LANGUAGE statement in the SQL standard.

See Also

CREATE LANGUAGE, DROP LANGUAGE

ALTER LARGE OBJECT

Name

ALTER LARGE OBJECT — change the definition of a large object

Synopsis

ALTER LARGE OBJECT *large_object_oid* OWNER TO *new_owner*

Description

ALTER LARGE OBJECT changes the definition of a large object. The only functionality is to assign a new owner. You must be superuser or owner of the large object to use ALTER LARGE OBJECT.

Parameters

large_object_oid

OID of the large object to be altered

new_owner

The new owner of the large object

Compatibility

There is no ALTER LARGE OBJECT statement in the SQL standard.

See Also

Chapter 32

ALTER MATERIALIZED VIEW

Name

ALTER MATERIALIZED VIEW — change the definition of a materialized view

Synopsis

```
ALTER MATERIALIZED VIEW [ IF EXISTS ] name
    action [, ... ]
ALTER MATERIALIZED VIEW [ IF EXISTS ] name
    RENAME [ COLUMN ] column_name TO new_column_name
ALTER MATERIALIZED VIEW [ IF EXISTS ] name
    RENAME TO new_name
ALTER MATERIALIZED VIEW [ IF EXISTS ] name
    SET SCHEMA new_schema
ALTER MATERIALIZED VIEW ALL IN TABLESPACE name [ OWNED BY role_name [, ... ] ]
    SET TABLESPACE new_tablespace [ NOWAIT ]

where action is one of:

    ALTER [ COLUMN ] column_name SET STATISTICS integer
    ALTER [ COLUMN ] column_name SET ( attribute_option = value [, ... ] )
    ALTER [ COLUMN ] column_name RESET ( attribute_option [, ... ] )
    ALTER [ COLUMN ] column_name SET STORAGE { PLAIN | EXTERNAL | EXTENDED | MAI
    CLUSTER ON index_name
    SET WITHOUT CLUSTER
    SET ( storage_parameter = value [, ... ] )
    RESET ( storage_parameter [, ... ] )
    OWNER TO new_owner
    SET TABLESPACE new_tablespace
```

Description

ALTER MATERIALIZED VIEW changes various auxiliary properties of an existing materialized view.

You must own the materialized view to use ALTER MATERIALIZED VIEW. To change a materialized view's schema, you must also have CREATE privilege on the new schema. To alter the owner, you must also be a direct or indirect member of the new owning role, and that role must have CREATE privilege on the materialized view's schema. (These restrictions enforce that altering the owner doesn't do anything you couldn't do by dropping and recreating the materialized view. However, a superuser can alter ownership of any view anyway.)

The statement subforms and actions available for ALTER MATERIALIZED VIEW are a subset of those available for ALTER TABLE, and have the same meaning when used for materialized views. See the descriptions for ALTER TABLE for details.

Parameters

name

> The name (optionally schema-qualified) of an existing materialized view.

column_name

> Name of a new or existing column.

new_column_name

> New name for an existing column.

new_owner

> The user name of the new owner of the materialized view.

new_name

> The new name for the materialized view.

new_schema

> The new schema for the materialized view.

Examples

To rename the materialized view foo to bar:

```
ALTER MATERIALIZED VIEW foo RENAME TO bar;
```

Compatibility

ALTER MATERIALIZED VIEW is a PostgreSQL extension.

See Also

CREATE MATERIALIZED VIEW, DROP MATERIALIZED VIEW, REFRESH MATERIALIZED VIEW

ALTER OPERATOR

Name

ALTER OPERATOR — change the definition of an operator

Synopsis

```
ALTER OPERATOR name ( { left_type | NONE } , { right_type | NONE } ) OWNER TO new
ALTER OPERATOR name ( { left_type | NONE } , { right_type | NONE } ) SET SCHEMA n
```

Description

ALTER OPERATOR changes the definition of an operator. The only currently available functionality is to change the owner of the operator.

You must own the operator to use ALTER OPERATOR. To alter the owner, you must also be a direct or indirect member of the new owning role, and that role must have CREATE privilege on the operator's schema. (These restrictions enforce that altering the owner doesn't do anything you couldn't do by dropping and recreating the operator. However, a superuser can alter ownership of any operator anyway.)

Parameters

name

The name (optionally schema-qualified) of an existing operator.

left_type

The data type of the operator's left operand; write NONE if the operator has no left operand.

right_type

The data type of the operator's right operand; write NONE if the operator has no right operand.

new_owner

The new owner of the operator.

new_schema

The new schema for the operator.

Examples

Change the owner of a custom operator a @@ b for type text:

```
ALTER OPERATOR @@ (text, text) OWNER TO joe;
```

Compatibility

There is no ALTER OPERATOR statement in the SQL standard.

See Also

CREATE OPERATOR, DROP OPERATOR

ALTER OPERATOR CLASS

Name

ALTER OPERATOR CLASS — change the definition of an operator class

Synopsis

```
ALTER OPERATOR CLASS name USING index_method RENAME TO new_name
ALTER OPERATOR CLASS name USING index_method OWNER TO new_owner
ALTER OPERATOR CLASS name USING index_method SET SCHEMA new_schema
```

Description

ALTER OPERATOR CLASS changes the definition of an operator class.

You must own the operator class to use ALTER OPERATOR CLASS. To alter the owner, you must also be a direct or indirect member of the new owning role, and that role must have CREATE privilege on the operator class's schema. (These restrictions enforce that altering the owner doesn't do anything you couldn't do by dropping and recreating the operator class. However, a superuser can alter ownership of any operator class anyway.)

Parameters

name

The name (optionally schema-qualified) of an existing operator class.

index_method

The name of the index method this operator class is for.

new_name

The new name of the operator class.

new_owner

The new owner of the operator class.

new_schema

The new schema for the operator class.

Compatibility

There is no ALTER OPERATOR CLASS statement in the SQL standard.

See Also

CREATE OPERATOR CLASS, DROP OPERATOR CLASS, ALTER OPERATOR FAMILY

ALTER OPERATOR FAMILY

Name

ALTER OPERATOR FAMILY — change the definition of an operator family

Synopsis

```
ALTER OPERATOR FAMILY name USING index_method ADD
  { OPERATOR strategy_number operator_name ( op_type, op_type ) [ FOR SEARCH | FOR
  | FUNCTION support_number [ ( op_type [ , op_type ] ) ] function_name ( argument_
  } [, ... ]
ALTER OPERATOR FAMILY name USING index_method DROP
  { OPERATOR strategy_number ( op_type [ , op_type ] )
  | FUNCTION support_number ( op_type [ , op_type ] )
  } [, ... ]
ALTER OPERATOR FAMILY name USING index_method RENAME TO new_name
ALTER OPERATOR FAMILY name USING index_method OWNER TO new_owner
ALTER OPERATOR FAMILY name USING index_method SET SCHEMA new_schema
```

Description

ALTER OPERATOR FAMILY changes the definition of an operator family. You can add operators and support functions to the family, remove them from the family, or change the family's name or owner.

When operators and support functions are added to a family with ALTER OPERATOR FAMILY, they are not part of any specific operator class within the family, but are just "loose" within the family. This indicates that these operators and functions are compatible with the family's semantics, but are not required for correct functioning of any specific index. (Operators and functions that are so required should be declared as part of an operator class, instead; see CREATE OPERATOR CLASS.) PostgreSQL will allow loose members of a family to be dropped from the family at any time, but members of an operator class cannot be dropped without dropping the whole class and any indexes that depend on it. Typically, single-data-type operators and functions are part of operator classes because they are needed to support an index on that specific data type, while cross-data-type operators and functions are made loose members of the family.

You must be a superuser to use ALTER OPERATOR FAMILY. (This restriction is made because an erroneous operator family definition could confuse or even crash the server.)

ALTER OPERATOR FAMILY does not presently check whether the operator family definition includes all the operators and functions required by the index method, nor whether the operators and functions form a self-consistent set. It is the user's responsibility to define a valid operator family.

Refer to Section 35.14 for further information.

Parameters

name

 The name (optionally schema-qualified) of an existing operator family.

index_method

 The name of the index method this operator family is for.

strategy_number

 The index method's strategy number for an operator associated with the operator family.

operator_name

 The name (optionally schema-qualified) of an operator associated with the operator family.

op_type

 In an OPERATOR clause, the operand data type(s) of the operator, or NONE to signify a left-unary or right-unary operator. Unlike the comparable syntax in CREATE OPERATOR CLASS, the operand data types must always be specified.

 In an ADD FUNCTION clause, the operand data type(s) the function is intended to support, if different from the input data type(s) of the function. For B-tree comparison functions and hash functions it is not necessary to specify *op_type* since the function's input data type(s) are always the correct ones to use. For B-tree sort support functions and all functions in GiST, SP-GiST and GIN operator classes, it is necessary to specify the operand data type(s) the function is to be used with.

 In a DROP FUNCTION clause, the operand data type(s) the function is intended to support must be specified.

sort_family_name

 The name (optionally schema-qualified) of an existing btree operator family that describes the sort ordering associated with an ordering operator.

 If neither FOR SEARCH nor FOR ORDER BY is specified, FOR SEARCH is the default.

support_number

 The index method's support procedure number for a function associated with the operator family.

function_name

 The name (optionally schema-qualified) of a function that is an index method support procedure for the operator family.

argument_type

 The parameter data type(s) of the function.

new_name

 The new name of the operator family.

new_owner

 The new owner of the operator family.

new_schema

The new schema for the operator family.

The OPERATOR and FUNCTION clauses can appear in any order.

Notes

Notice that the DROP syntax only specifies the "slot" in the operator family, by strategy or support number and input data type(s). The name of the operator or function occupying the slot is not mentioned. Also, for DROP FUNCTION the type(s) to specify are the input data type(s) the function is intended to support; for GiST, SP-GiST and GIN indexes this might have nothing to do with the actual input argument types of the function.

Because the index machinery does not check access permissions on functions before using them, including a function or operator in an operator family is tantamount to granting public execute permission on it. This is usually not an issue for the sorts of functions that are useful in an operator family.

The operators should not be defined by SQL functions. A SQL function is likely to be inlined into the calling query, which will prevent the optimizer from recognizing that the query matches an index.

Before PostgreSQL 8.4, the OPERATOR clause could include a RECHECK option. This is no longer supported because whether an index operator is "lossy" is now determined on-the-fly at run time. This allows efficient handling of cases where an operator might or might not be lossy.

Examples

The following example command adds cross-data-type operators and support functions to an operator family that already contains B-tree operator classes for data types int4 and int2.

```
ALTER OPERATOR FAMILY integer_ops USING btree ADD

  -- int4 vs int2
  OPERATOR 1 < (int4, int2) ,
  OPERATOR 2 <= (int4, int2) ,
  OPERATOR 3 = (int4, int2) ,
  OPERATOR 4 >= (int4, int2) ,
  OPERATOR 5 > (int4, int2) ,
  FUNCTION 1 btint42cmp(int4, int2) ,

  -- int2 vs int4
  OPERATOR 1 < (int2, int4) ,
  OPERATOR 2 <= (int2, int4) ,
  OPERATOR 3 = (int2, int4) ,
  OPERATOR 4 >= (int2, int4) ,
  OPERATOR 5 > (int2, int4) ,
  FUNCTION 1 btint24cmp(int2, int4) ;
```

To remove these entries again:

```
ALTER OPERATOR FAMILY integer_ops USING btree DROP
```

```
-- int4 vs int2
OPERATOR 1 (int4, int2) ,
OPERATOR 2 (int4, int2) ,
OPERATOR 3 (int4, int2) ,
OPERATOR 4 (int4, int2) ,
OPERATOR 5 (int4, int2) ,
FUNCTION 1 (int4, int2) ,

-- int2 vs int4
OPERATOR 1 (int2, int4) ,
OPERATOR 2 (int2, int4) ,
OPERATOR 3 (int2, int4) ,
OPERATOR 4 (int2, int4) ,
OPERATOR 5 (int2, int4) ,
FUNCTION 1 (int2, int4) ;
```

Compatibility

There is no ALTER OPERATOR FAMILY statement in the SQL standard.

See Also

CREATE OPERATOR FAMILY, DROP OPERATOR FAMILY, CREATE OPERATOR CLASS, ALTER OPERATOR CLASS, DROP OPERATOR CLASS

ALTER ROLE

Name

ALTER ROLE — change a database role

Synopsis

```
ALTER ROLE name [ [ WITH ] option [ ... ] ]

where option can be:

    SUPERUSER | NOSUPERUSER
  | CREATEDB | NOCREATEDB
  | CREATEROLE | NOCREATEROLE
  | CREATEUSER | NOCREATEUSER
  | INHERIT | NOINHERIT
  | LOGIN | NOLOGIN
  | REPLICATION | NOREPLICATION
  | CONNECTION LIMIT connlimit
  | [ ENCRYPTED | UNENCRYPTED ] PASSWORD 'password'
  | VALID UNTIL 'timestamp'

ALTER ROLE name RENAME TO new_name

ALTER ROLE name [ IN DATABASE database_name ] SET configuration_parameter { TO | =
ALTER ROLE { name | ALL } [ IN DATABASE database_name ] SET configuration_parameter
ALTER ROLE { name | ALL } [ IN DATABASE database_name ] RESET configuration_parameter
ALTER ROLE { name | ALL } [ IN DATABASE database_name ] RESET ALL
```

Description

ALTER ROLE changes the attributes of a PostgreSQL role.

The first variant of this command listed in the synopsis can change many of the role attributes that can be specified in CREATE ROLE. (All the possible attributes are covered, except that there are no options for adding or removing memberships; use GRANT and REVOKE for that.) Attributes not mentioned in the command retain their previous settings. Database superusers can change any of these settings for any role. Roles having CREATEROLE privilege can change any of these settings, but only for non-superuser and non-replication roles. Ordinary roles can only change their own password.

The second variant changes the name of the role. Database superusers can rename any role. Roles having CREATEROLE privilege can rename non-superuser roles. The current session user cannot be renamed. (Connect as a different user if you need to do that.) Because MD5-encrypted passwords use the role name as cryptographic salt, renaming a role clears its password if the password is MD5-encrypted.

The remaining variants change a role's session default for a configuration variable, either for all databases or, when the IN DATABASE clause is specified, only for sessions in the named database. If ALL is specified instead of a role name, this changes the setting for all roles. Using `ALL` with `IN DATABASE` is effectively the same as using the command `ALTER DATABASE ... SET ...`.

Whenever the role subsequently starts a new session, the specified value becomes the session default, overriding whatever setting is present in `postgresql.conf` or has been received from the `postgres` command line. This only happens at login time; executing SET ROLE or SET SESSION AUTHORIZATION does not cause new configuration values to be set. Settings set for all databases are overridden by database-specific settings attached to a role. Settings for specific databases or specific roles override settings for all roles.

Superusers can change anyone's session defaults. Roles having `CREATEROLE` privilege can change defaults for non-superuser roles. Ordinary roles can only set defaults for themselves. Certain configuration variables cannot be set this way, or can only be set if a superuser issues the command. Only superusers can change a setting for all roles in all databases.

Parameters

name

> The name of the role whose attributes are to be altered.

```
SUPERUSER
NOSUPERUSER
CREATEDB
NOCREATEDB
CREATEROLE
NOCREATEROLE
CREATEUSER
NOCREATEUSER
INHERIT
NOINHERIT
LOGIN
NOLOGIN
REPLICATION
NOREPLICATION
CONNECTION LIMIT connlimit
PASSWORD password
ENCRYPTED
UNENCRYPTED
VALID UNTIL 'timestamp'
```

> These clauses alter attributes originally set by CREATE ROLE. For more information, see the `CREATE ROLE` reference page.

new_name

> The new name of the role.

database_name

> The name of the database the configuration variable should be set in.

`configuration_parameter`
`value`

Set this role's session default for the specified configuration parameter to the given value. If `value` is DEFAULT or, equivalently, RESET is used, the role-specific variable setting is removed, so the role will inherit the system-wide default setting in new sessions. Use RESET ALL to clear all role-specific settings. SET FROM CURRENT saves the session's current value of the parameter as the role-specific value. If IN DATABASE is specified, the configuration parameter is set or removed for the given role and database only.

Role-specific variable settings take effect only at login; SET ROLE and SET SESSION AUTHO-RIZATION do not process role-specific variable settings.

See SET and Chapter 18 for more information about allowed parameter names and values.

Notes

Use CREATE ROLE to add new roles, and DROP ROLE to remove a role.

ALTER ROLE cannot change a role's memberships. Use GRANT and REVOKE to do that.

Caution must be exercised when specifying an unencrypted password with this command. The password will be transmitted to the server in cleartext, and it might also be logged in the client's command history or the server log. psql contains a command \password that can be used to change a role's password without exposing the cleartext password.

It is also possible to tie a session default to a specific database rather than to a role; see ALTER DATABASE. If there is a conflict, database-role-specific settings override role-specific ones, which in turn override database-specific ones.

Examples

Change a role's password:

```
ALTER ROLE davide WITH PASSWORD 'hu8jmn3';
```

Remove a role's password:

```
ALTER ROLE davide WITH PASSWORD NULL;
```

Change a password expiration date, specifying that the password should expire at midday on 4th May 2015 using the time zone which is one hour ahead of UTC:

```
ALTER ROLE chris VALID UNTIL 'May 4 12:00:00 2015 +1';
```

Make a password valid forever:

```
ALTER ROLE fred VALID UNTIL 'infinity';
```

Give a role the ability to create other roles and new databases:

```
ALTER ROLE miriam CREATEROLE CREATEDB;
```

Give a role a non-default setting of the maintenance_work_mem parameter:

```
ALTER ROLE worker_bee SET maintenance_work_mem = 100000;
```

Give a role a non-default, database-specific setting of the client_min_messages parameter:

```
ALTER ROLE fred IN DATABASE devel SET client_min_messages = DEBUG;
```

Compatibility

The ALTER ROLE statement is a PostgreSQL extension.

See Also

CREATE ROLE, DROP ROLE, ALTER DATABASE, SET

ALTER RULE

Name

ALTER RULE — change the definition of a rule

Synopsis

```
ALTER RULE name ON table_name RENAME TO new_name
```

Description

ALTER RULE changes properties of an existing rule. Currently, the only available action is to change the rule's name.

To use ALTER RULE, you must own the table or view that the rule applies to.

Parameters

name

The name of an existing rule to alter.

table_name

The name (optionally schema-qualified) of the table or view that the rule applies to.

new_name

The new name for the rule.

Examples

To rename an existing rule:

```
ALTER RULE notify_all ON emp RENAME TO notify_me;
```

Compatibility

ALTER RULE is a PostgreSQL language extension, as is the entire query rewrite system.

See Also

CREATE RULE, DROP RULE

ALTER SCHEMA

Name

ALTER SCHEMA — change the definition of a schema

Synopsis

```
ALTER SCHEMA name RENAME TO new_name
ALTER SCHEMA name OWNER TO new_owner
```

Description

ALTER SCHEMA changes the definition of a schema.

You must own the schema to use ALTER SCHEMA. To rename a schema you must also have the CREATE privilege for the database. To alter the owner, you must also be a direct or indirect member of the new owning role, and you must have the CREATE privilege for the database. (Note that superusers have all these privileges automatically.)

Parameters

name

The name of an existing schema.

new_name

The new name of the schema. The new name cannot begin with pg_, as such names are reserved for system schemas.

new_owner

The new owner of the schema.

Compatibility

There is no ALTER SCHEMA statement in the SQL standard.

See Also

CREATE SCHEMA, DROP SCHEMA

ALTER SEQUENCE

Name

ALTER SEQUENCE — change the definition of a sequence generator

Synopsis

```
ALTER SEQUENCE [ IF EXISTS ] name [ INCREMENT [ BY ] increment ]
    [ MINVALUE minvalue | NO MINVALUE ] [ MAXVALUE maxvalue | NO MAXVALUE ]
    [ START [ WITH ] start ]
    [ RESTART [ [ WITH ] restart ] ]
    [ CACHE cache ] [ [ NO ] CYCLE ]
    [ OWNED BY { table_name.column_name | NONE } ]
ALTER SEQUENCE [ IF EXISTS ] name OWNER TO new_owner
ALTER SEQUENCE [ IF EXISTS ] name RENAME TO new_name
ALTER SEQUENCE [ IF EXISTS ] name SET SCHEMA new_schema
```

Description

ALTER SEQUENCE changes the parameters of an existing sequence generator. Any parameters not specifically set in the ALTER SEQUENCE command retain their prior settings.

You must own the sequence to use ALTER SEQUENCE. To change a sequence's schema, you must also have CREATE privilege on the new schema. To alter the owner, you must also be a direct or indirect member of the new owning role, and that role must have CREATE privilege on the sequence's schema. (These restrictions enforce that altering the owner doesn't do anything you couldn't do by dropping and recreating the sequence. However, a superuser can alter ownership of any sequence anyway.)

Parameters

name

The name (optionally schema-qualified) of a sequence to be altered.

IF EXISTS

Do not throw an error if the sequence does not exist. A notice is issued in this case.

increment

The clause INCREMENT BY increment is optional. A positive value will make an ascending sequence, a negative one a descending sequence. If unspecified, the old increment value will be maintained.

minvalue
NO MINVALUE

> The optional clause MINVALUE *minvalue* determines the minimum value a sequence can generate. If NO MINVALUE is specified, the defaults of 1 and $-2^{63}-1$ for ascending and descending sequences, respectively, will be used. If neither option is specified, the current minimum value will be maintained.

maxvalue
NO MAXVALUE

> The optional clause MAXVALUE *maxvalue* determines the maximum value for the sequence. If NO MAXVALUE is specified, the defaults are $2^{63}-1$ and -1 for ascending and descending sequences, respectively, will be used. If neither option is specified, the current maximum value will be maintained.

start

> The optional clause START WITH *start* changes the recorded start value of the sequence. This has no effect on the *current* sequence value; it simply sets the value that future ALTER SEQUENCE RESTART commands will use.

restart

> The optional clause RESTART [WITH *restart*] changes the current value of the sequence. This is equivalent to calling the setval function with is_called = false: the specified value will be returned by the *next* call of nextval. Writing RESTART with no *restart* value is equivalent to supplying the start value that was recorded by CREATE SEQUENCE or last set by ALTER SEQUENCE START WITH.

cache

> The clause CACHE *cache* enables sequence numbers to be preallocated and stored in memory for faster access. The minimum value is 1 (only one value can be generated at a time, i.e., no cache). If unspecified, the old cache value will be maintained.

CYCLE

> The optional CYCLE key word can be used to enable the sequence to wrap around when the *maxvalue* or *minvalue* has been reached by an ascending or descending sequence respectively. If the limit is reached, the next number generated will be the *minvalue* or *maxvalue*, respectively.

NO CYCLE

> If the optional NO CYCLE key word is specified, any calls to nextval after the sequence has reached its maximum value will return an error. If neither CYCLE or NO CYCLE are specified, the old cycle behavior will be maintained.

OWNED BY *table_name.column_name*
OWNED BY NONE

> The OWNED BY option causes the sequence to be associated with a specific table column, such that if that column (or its whole table) is dropped, the sequence will be automatically dropped as well. If specified, this association replaces any previously specified association for the sequence. The specified table must have the same owner and be in the same schema as the sequence. Specifying OWNED BY NONE removes any existing association, making the sequence "free-standing".

new_owner

    The user name of the new owner of the sequence.

new_name

    The new name for the sequence.

new_schema

    The new schema for the sequence.

Notes

To avoid blocking of concurrent transactions that obtain numbers from the same sequence, ALTER SEQUENCE's effects on the sequence generation parameters are never rolled back; those changes take effect immediately and are not reversible. However, the OWNED BY, OWNER TO, RENAME TO, and SET SCHEMA clauses cause ordinary catalog updates that can be rolled back.

ALTER SEQUENCE will not immediately affect nextval results in backends, other than the current one, that have preallocated (cached) sequence values. They will use up all cached values prior to noticing the changed sequence generation parameters. The current backend will be affected immediately.

ALTER SEQUENCE does not affect the currval status for the sequence. (Before PostgreSQL 8.3, it sometimes did.)

For historical reasons, ALTER TABLE can be used with sequences too; but the only variants of ALTER TABLE that are allowed with sequences are equivalent to the forms shown above.

Examples

Restart a sequence called serial, at 105:

```
ALTER SEQUENCE serial RESTART WITH 105;
```

Compatibility

ALTER SEQUENCE conforms to the SQL standard, except for the START WITH, OWNED BY, OWNER TO, RENAME TO, and SET SCHEMA clauses, which are PostgreSQL extensions.

See Also

CREATE SEQUENCE, DROP SEQUENCE

ALTER SERVER

Name

ALTER SERVER — change the definition of a foreign server

Synopsis

```
ALTER SERVER name [ VERSION 'new_version' ]
    [ OPTIONS ( [ ADD | SET | DROP ] option ['value'] [, ... ] ) ]
ALTER SERVER name OWNER TO new_owner
ALTER SERVER name RENAME TO new_name
```

Description

ALTER SERVER changes the definition of a foreign server. The first form changes the server version string or the generic options of the server (at least one clause is required). The second form changes the owner of the server.

To alter the server you must be the owner of the server. Additionally to alter the owner, you must own the server and also be a direct or indirect member of the new owning role, and you must have USAGE privilege on the server's foreign-data wrapper. (Note that superusers satisfy all these criteria automatically.)

Parameters

name

> The name of an existing server.

new_version

> New server version.

OPTIONS ([ADD | SET | DROP] option ['value'] [, ...])

> Change options for the server. ADD, SET, and DROP specify the action to be performed. ADD is assumed if no operation is explicitly specified. Option names must be unique; names and values are also validated using the server's foreign-data wrapper library.

new_owner

> The user name of the new owner of the foreign server.

new_name

> The new name for the foreign server.

Examples

Alter server `foo`, add connection options:

```
ALTER SERVER foo OPTIONS (host 'foo', dbname 'foodb');
```

Alter server `foo`, change version, change `host` option:

```
ALTER SERVER foo VERSION '8.4' OPTIONS (SET host 'baz');
```

Compatibility

`ALTER SERVER` conforms to ISO/IEC 9075-9 (SQL/MED). The `OWNER TO` and `RENAME` forms are Post-greSQL extensions.

See Also

CREATE SERVER, DROP SERVER

ALTER SYSTEM

Name

ALTER SYSTEM — change a server configuration parameter

Synopsis

```
ALTER SYSTEM SET configuration_parameter { TO | = } { value | 'value' | DEFAULT }

ALTER SYSTEM RESET configuration_parameter
ALTER SYSTEM RESET ALL
```

Description

ALTER SYSTEM is used for changing server configuration parameters across the entire database cluster. It can be more convenient than the traditional method of manually editing the postgresql.conf file. ALTER SYSTEM writes the given parameter setting to the postgresql.auto.conf file, which is read in addition to postgresql.conf. Setting a parameter to DEFAULT, or using the RESET variant, removes that configuration entry from the postgresql.auto.conf file. Use RESET ALL to remove all such configuration entries.

Values set with ALTER SYSTEM will be effective after the next server configuration reload (SIGHUP or pg_ctl reload), or after the next server restart in the case of parameters that can only be changed at server start.

Only superusers can use ALTER SYSTEM. Also, since this command acts directly on the file system and cannot be rolled back, it is not allowed inside a transaction block or function.

Parameters

configuration_parameter

> Name of a settable configuration parameter. Available parameters are documented in Chapter 18.

value

> New value of the parameter. Values can be specified as string constants, identifiers, numbers, or comma-separated lists of these, as appropriate for the particular parameter. DEFAULT can be written to specify removing the parameter and its value from postgresql.auto.conf.

Notes

This command can't be used to set data_directory, nor parameters that are not allowed in postgresql.conf (e.g., preset options).

See Section 18.1 for other ways to set the parameters.

Examples

Set the `wal_level`:

```
ALTER SYSTEM SET wal_level = hot_standby;
```

Undo that, restoring whatever setting was effective in `postgresql.conf`:

```
ALTER SYSTEM RESET wal_level;
```

Compatibility

The `ALTER SYSTEM` statement is a PostgreSQL extension.

See Also

SET, SHOW

ALTER TABLE

Name

ALTER TABLE — change the definition of a table

Synopsis

```
ALTER TABLE [ IF EXISTS ] [ ONLY ] name [ * ]
    action [, ... ]
ALTER TABLE [ IF EXISTS ] [ ONLY ] name [ * ]
    RENAME [ COLUMN ] column_name TO new_column_name
ALTER TABLE [ IF EXISTS ] [ ONLY ] name [ * ]
    RENAME CONSTRAINT constraint_name TO new_constraint_name
ALTER TABLE [ IF EXISTS ] name
    RENAME TO new_name
ALTER TABLE [ IF EXISTS ] name
    SET SCHEMA new_schema
ALTER TABLE ALL IN TABLESPACE name [ OWNED BY role_name [, ... ] ]
    SET TABLESPACE new_tablespace [ NOWAIT ]

where action is one of:

    ADD [ COLUMN ] column_name data_type [ COLLATE collation ] [ column_constraint
    DROP [ COLUMN ] [ IF EXISTS ] column_name [ RESTRICT | CASCADE ]
    ALTER [ COLUMN ] column_name [ SET DATA ] TYPE data_type [ COLLATE collation ]
    ALTER [ COLUMN ] column_name SET DEFAULT expression
    ALTER [ COLUMN ] column_name DROP DEFAULT
    ALTER [ COLUMN ] column_name { SET | DROP } NOT NULL
    ALTER [ COLUMN ] column_name SET STATISTICS integer
    ALTER [ COLUMN ] column_name SET ( attribute_option = value [, ... ] )
    ALTER [ COLUMN ] column_name RESET ( attribute_option [, ... ] )
    ALTER [ COLUMN ] column_name SET STORAGE { PLAIN | EXTERNAL | EXTENDED | MAI
    ADD table_constraint [ NOT VALID ]
    ADD table_constraint_using_index
    ALTER CONSTRAINT constraint_name [ DEFERRABLE | NOT DEFERRABLE ] [ INITIALLY
    VALIDATE CONSTRAINT constraint_name
    DROP CONSTRAINT [ IF EXISTS ]  constraint_name [ RESTRICT | CASCADE ]
    DISABLE TRIGGER [ trigger_name | ALL | USER ]
    ENABLE TRIGGER [ trigger_name | ALL | USER ]
    ENABLE REPLICA TRIGGER trigger_name
    ENABLE ALWAYS TRIGGER trigger_name
    DISABLE RULE rewrite_rule_name
    ENABLE RULE rewrite_rule_name
    ENABLE REPLICA RULE rewrite_rule_name
    ENABLE ALWAYS RULE rewrite_rule_name
    CLUSTER ON index_name
    SET WITHOUT CLUSTER
    SET WITH OIDS
    SET WITHOUT OIDS
    SET ( storage_parameter = value [, ... ] )
```

```
RESET ( storage_parameter [, ... ] )
INHERIT parent_table
NO INHERIT parent_table
OF type_name
NOT OF
OWNER TO new_owner
SET TABLESPACE new_tablespace
REPLICA IDENTITY {DEFAULT | USING INDEX index_name | FULL | NOTHING}
```

and *table_constraint_using_index* is:

```
[ CONSTRAINT constraint_name ]
{ UNIQUE | PRIMARY KEY } USING INDEX index_name
[ DEFERRABLE | NOT DEFERRABLE ] [ INITIALLY DEFERRED | INITIALLY IMMEDIATE
```

Description

ALTER TABLE changes the definition of an existing table. There are several subforms described below. Note that the lock level required may differ for each subform. An ACCESS EXCLUSIVE lock is held unless explicitly noted. When multiple subcommands are listed, the lock held will be the strictest one required from any subcommand.

ADD COLUMN

> This form adds a new column to the table, using the same syntax as CREATE TABLE.

DROP COLUMN [IF EXISTS]

> This form drops a column from a table. Indexes and table constraints involving the column will be automatically dropped as well. You will need to say CASCADE if anything outside the table depends on the column, for example, foreign key references or views. If IF EXISTS is specified and the column does not exist, no error is thrown. In this case a notice is issued instead.

IF EXISTS

> Do not throw an error if the table does not exist. A notice is issued in this case.

SET DATA TYPE

> This form changes the type of a column of a table. Indexes and simple table constraints involving the column will be automatically converted to use the new column type by reparsing the originally supplied expression. The optional COLLATE clause specifies a collation for the new column; if omitted, the collation is the default for the new column type. The optional USING clause specifies how to compute the new column value from the old; if omitted, the default conversion is the same as an assignment cast from old data type to new. A USING clause must be provided if there is no implicit or assignment cast from old to new type.

SET/DROP DEFAULT

> These forms set or remove the default value for a column. Default values only apply in subsequent INSERT or UPDATE commands; they do not cause rows already in the table to change.

SET/DROP NOT NULL

These forms change whether a column is marked to allow null values or to reject null values. You can only use SET NOT NULL when the column contains no null values.

SET STATISTICS

This form sets the per-column statistics-gathering target for subsequent ANALYZE operations. The target can be set in the range 0 to 10000; alternatively, set it to -1 to revert to using the system default statistics target (default_statistics_target). For more information on the use of statistics by the PostgreSQL query planner, refer to Section 14.2.

SET STATISTICS acquires a SHARE UPDATE EXCLUSIVE lock.

SET (*attribute_option* = *value* [, ...])
RESET (*attribute_option* [, ...])

This form sets or resets per-attribute options. Currently, the only defined per-attribute options are n_distinct and n_distinct_inherited, which override the number-of-distinct-values estimates made by subsequent ANALYZE operations. n_distinct affects the statistics for the table itself, while n_distinct_inherited affects the statistics gathered for the table plus its inheritance children. When set to a positive value, ANALYZE will assume that the column contains exactly the specified number of distinct nonnull values. When set to a negative value, which must be greater than or equal to -1, ANALYZE will assume that the number of distinct nonnull values in the column is linear in the size of the table; the exact count is to be computed by multiplying the estimated table size by the absolute value of the given number. For example, a value of -1 implies that all values in the column are distinct, while a value of -0.5 implies that each value appears twice on the average. This can be useful when the size of the table changes over time, since the multiplication by the number of rows in the table is not performed until query planning time. Specify a value of 0 to revert to estimating the number of distinct values normally. For more information on the use of statistics by the PostgreSQL query planner, refer to Section 14.2.

Changing per-attribute options acquires a SHARE UPDATE EXCLUSIVE lock.

SET STORAGE

This form sets the storage mode for a column. This controls whether this column is held inline or in a secondary TOAST table, and whether the data should be compressed or not. PLAIN must be used for fixed-length values such as integer and is inline, uncompressed. MAIN is for inline, compressible data. EXTERNAL is for external, uncompressed data, and EXTENDED is for external, compressed data. EXTENDED is the default for most data types that support non-PLAIN storage. Use of EXTERNAL will make substring operations on very large text and bytea values run faster, at the penalty of increased storage space. Note that SET STORAGE doesn't itself change anything in the table, it just sets the strategy to be pursued during future table updates. See Section 59.2 for more information.

ADD *table_constraint* [NOT VALID]

This form adds a new constraint to a table using the same syntax as CREATE TABLE, plus the option NOT VALID, which is currently only allowed for foreign key and CHECK constraints. If the constraint is marked NOT VALID, the potentially-lengthy initial check to verify that all rows in the table satisfy the constraint is skipped. The constraint will still be enforced against subsequent inserts or updates (that is, they'll fail unless there is a matching row in the referenced table, in the case of foreign keys; and they'll fail unless the new row matches the specified check constraints). But the database will not assume that the constraint holds for all rows in the table, until it is validated by using the VALIDATE CONSTRAINT option.

ADD `table_constraint_using_index`

This form adds a new `PRIMARY KEY` or `UNIQUE` constraint to a table based on an existing unique index. All the columns of the index will be included in the constraint.

The index cannot have expression columns nor be a partial index. Also, it must be a b-tree index with default sort ordering. These restrictions ensure that the index is equivalent to one that would be built by a regular `ADD PRIMARY KEY` or `ADD UNIQUE` command.

If `PRIMARY KEY` is specified, and the index's columns are not already marked `NOT NULL`, then this command will attempt to do `ALTER COLUMN SET NOT NULL` against each such column. That requires a full table scan to verify the column(s) contain no nulls. In all other cases, this is a fast operation.

If a constraint name is provided then the index will be renamed to match the constraint name. Otherwise the constraint will be named the same as the index.

After this command is executed, the index is "owned" by the constraint, in the same way as if the index had been built by a regular `ADD PRIMARY KEY` or `ADD UNIQUE` command. In particular, dropping the constraint will make the index disappear too.

> **Note:** Adding a constraint using an existing index can be helpful in situations where a new constraint needs to be added without blocking table updates for a long time. To do that, create the index using `CREATE INDEX CONCURRENTLY`, and then install it as an official constraint using this syntax. See the example below.

ALTER CONSTRAINT

This form alters the attributes of a constraint that was previously created. Currently only foreign key constraints may be altered.

VALIDATE CONSTRAINT

This form validates a foreign key or check constraint that was previously created as `NOT VALID`, by scanning the table to ensure there are no rows for which the constraint is not satisfied. Nothing happens if the constraint is already marked valid.

Validation can be a long process on larger tables. The value of separating validation from initial creation is that you can defer validation to less busy times, or can be used to give additional time to correct pre-existing errors while preventing new errors. Note also that validation on its own does not prevent normal write commands against the table while it runs.

Validation acquires only a `SHARE UPDATE EXCLUSIVE` lock on the table being altered. If the constraint is a foreign key then a `ROW SHARE` lock is also required on the table referenced by the constraint.

DROP CONSTRAINT [IF EXISTS]

This form drops the specified constraint on a table. If `IF EXISTS` is specified and the constraint does not exist, no error is thrown. In this case a notice is issued instead.

DISABLE/ENABLE [REPLICA | ALWAYS] TRIGGER

These forms configure the firing of trigger(s) belonging to the table. A disabled trigger is still known to the system, but is not executed when its triggering event occurs. For a deferred trigger, the enable status is checked when the event occurs, not when the trigger function is actually executed. One can disable or enable a single trigger specified by name, or all triggers on the table, or only user triggers (this option excludes internally generated constraint triggers such as those that are used to implement foreign key constraints or deferrable uniqueness and exclusion constraints). Disabling or enabling internally generated constraint triggers requires superuser privileges; it should be done with caution since of course the integrity of the constraint cannot be guaranteed if the triggers are not executed. The trigger firing mechanism is also affected by the configuration variable session_replication_role. Simply enabled triggers will fire when the replication role is "origin" (the default) or "local". Triggers configured as ENABLE REPLICA will only fire if the session is in "replica" mode, and triggers configured as ENABLE ALWAYS will fire regardless of the current replication mode.

DISABLE/ENABLE [REPLICA | ALWAYS] RULE

These forms configure the firing of rewrite rules belonging to the table. A disabled rule is still known to the system, but is not applied during query rewriting. The semantics are as for disabled/enabled triggers. This configuration is ignored for ON SELECT rules, which are always applied in order to keep views working even if the current session is in a non-default replication role.

CLUSTER ON

This form selects the default index for future CLUSTER operations. It does not actually re-cluster the table.

Changing cluster options acquires a SHARE UPDATE EXCLUSIVE lock.

SET WITHOUT CLUSTER

This form removes the most recently used CLUSTER index specification from the table. This affects future cluster operations that don't specify an index.

Changing cluster options acquires a SHARE UPDATE EXCLUSIVE lock.

SET WITH OIDS

This form adds an oid system column to the table (see Section 5.4). It does nothing if the table already has OIDs.

Note that this is not equivalent to ADD COLUMN oid oid; that would add a normal column that happened to be named oid, not a system column.

SET WITHOUT OIDS

This form removes the oid system column from the table. This is exactly equivalent to DROP COLUMN oid RESTRICT, except that it will not complain if there is already no oid column.

SET (*storage_parameter* = *value* [, ...])

This form changes one or more storage parameters for the table. See *Storage Parameters* for details on the available parameters. Note that the table contents will not be modified immediately by this command; depending on the parameter you might need to rewrite the table to get the desired effects. That can be done with VACUUM FULL, CLUSTER or one of the forms of ALTER TABLE that forces a table rewrite.

> **Note:** While CREATE TABLE allows OIDS to be specified in the WITH (*storage_parameter*) syntax, ALTER TABLE does not treat OIDS as a storage parameter. Instead use the SET WITH OIDS and SET WITHOUT OIDS forms to change OID status.

RESET (*storage_parameter* [, ...])

This form resets one or more storage parameters to their defaults. As with SET, a table rewrite might be needed to update the table entirely.

INHERIT *parent_table*

This form adds the target table as a new child of the specified parent table. Subsequently, queries against the parent will include records of the target table. To be added as a child, the target table must already contain all the same columns as the parent (it could have additional columns, too). The columns must have matching data types, and if they have NOT NULL constraints in the parent then they must also have NOT NULL constraints in the child.

There must also be matching child-table constraints for all CHECK constraints of the parent, except those marked non-inheritable (that is, created with ALTER TABLE ... ADD CONSTRAINT ... NO INHERIT) in the parent, which are ignored; all child-table constraints matched must not be marked non-inheritable. Currently UNIQUE, PRIMARY KEY, and FOREIGN KEY constraints are not considered, but this might change in the future.

NO INHERIT *parent_table*

This form removes the target table from the list of children of the specified parent table. Queries against the parent table will no longer include records drawn from the target table.

OF *type_name*

This form links the table to a composite type as though CREATE TABLE OF had formed it. The table's list of column names and types must precisely match that of the composite type; the presence of an oid system column is permitted to differ. The table must not inherit from any other table. These restrictions ensure that CREATE TABLE OF would permit an equivalent table definition.

NOT OF

This form dissociates a typed table from its type.

OWNER

This form changes the owner of the table, sequence, view, materialized view, or foreign table to the specified user.

SET TABLESPACE

This form changes the table's tablespace to the specified tablespace and moves the data file(s) associated with the table to the new tablespace. Indexes on the table, if any, are not moved; but they can be moved separately with additional SET TABLESPACE commands. All tables in the current database in a tablespace can be moved by using the ALL IN TABLESPACE form, which will lock all tables to be moved first and then move each one. This form also supports OWNED BY, which will only move tables owned by the roles specified. If the NOWAIT option is specified then the command will fail if it is unable to acquire all of the locks required immediately. Note that system catalogs are not moved by this command, use ALTER DATABASE or explicit ALTER TABLE invocations instead if desired. The information_schema relations are not considered part of the system catalogs and will be moved. See also CREATE TABLESPACE.

REPLICA IDENTITY

This form changes the information which is written to the write-ahead log to identify rows which are updated or deleted. This option has no effect except when logical replication is in use. DEFAULT (the default for non-system tables) records the old values of the columns of the primary key, if any.

USING INDEX records the old values of the columns covered by the named index, which must be unique, not partial, not deferrable, and include only columns marked NOT NULL. FULL records the old values of all columns in the row. NOTHING records no information about the old row. (This is the default for system tables.) In all cases, no old values are logged unless at least one of the columns that would be logged differs between the old and new versions of the row.

RENAME

>The RENAME forms change the name of a table (or an index, sequence, view, materialized view, or foreign table), the name of an individual column in a table, or the name of a constraint of the table. There is no effect on the stored data.

SET SCHEMA

>This form moves the table into another schema. Associated indexes, constraints, and sequences owned by table columns are moved as well.

All the actions except RENAME, SET TABLESPACE and SET SCHEMA can be combined into a list of multiple alterations to apply in parallel. For example, it is possible to add several columns and/or alter the type of several columns in a single command. This is particularly useful with large tables, since only one pass over the table need be made.

You must own the table to use ALTER TABLE. To change the schema or tablespace of a table, you must also have CREATE privilege on the new schema or tablespace. To add the table as a new child of a parent table, you must own the parent table as well. To alter the owner, you must also be a direct or indirect member of the new owning role, and that role must have CREATE privilege on the table's schema. (These restrictions enforce that altering the owner doesn't do anything you couldn't do by dropping and recreating the table. However, a superuser can alter ownership of any table anyway.) To add a column or alter a column type or use the OF clause, you must also have USAGE privilege on the data type.

Parameters

name

>The name (optionally schema-qualified) of an existing table to alter. If ONLY is specified before the table name, only that table is altered. If ONLY is not specified, the table and all its descendant tables (if any) are altered. Optionally, * can be specified after the table name to explicitly indicate that descendant tables are included.

column_name

>Name of a new or existing column.

new_column_name

>New name for an existing column.

new_name

>New name for the table.

data_type

>Data type of the new column, or new data type for an existing column.

table_constraint

> New table constraint for the table.

constraint_name

> Name of a new or existing constraint.

CASCADE

> Automatically drop objects that depend on the dropped column or constraint (for example, views referencing the column).

RESTRICT

> Refuse to drop the column or constraint if there are any dependent objects. This is the default behavior.

trigger_name

> Name of a single trigger to disable or enable.

ALL

> Disable or enable all triggers belonging to the table. (This requires superuser privilege if any of the triggers are internally generated constraint triggers such as those that are used to implement foreign key constraints or deferrable uniqueness and exclusion constraints.)

USER

> Disable or enable all triggers belonging to the table except for internally generated constraint triggers such as those that are used to implement foreign key constraints or deferrable uniqueness and exclusion constraints.

index_name

> The name of an existing index.

storage_parameter

> The name of a table storage parameter.

value

> The new value for a table storage parameter. This might be a number or a word depending on the parameter.

parent_table

> A parent table to associate or de-associate with this table.

new_owner

> The user name of the new owner of the table.

new_tablespace

> The name of the tablespace to which the table will be moved.

new_schema

> The name of the schema to which the table will be moved.

Notes

The key word COLUMN is noise and can be omitted.

When a column is added with ADD COLUMN, all existing rows in the table are initialized with the column's default value (NULL if no DEFAULT clause is specified). If there is no DEFAULT clause, this is merely a metadata change and does not require any immediate update of the table's data; the added NULL values are supplied on readout, instead.

Adding a column with a DEFAULT clause or changing the type of an existing column will require the entire table and its indexes to be rewritten. As an exception when changing the type of an existing column, if the USING clause does not change the column contents and the old type is either binary coercible to the new type or an unconstrained domain over the new type, a table rewrite is not needed; but any indexes on the affected columns must still be rebuilt. Adding or removing a system oid column also requires rewriting the entire table. Table and/or index rebuilds may take a significant amount of time for a large table; and will temporarily require as much as double the disk space.

Adding a CHECK or NOT NULL constraint requires scanning the table to verify that existing rows meet the constraint.

The main reason for providing the option to specify multiple changes in a single ALTER TABLE is that multiple table scans or rewrites can thereby be combined into a single pass over the table.

The DROP COLUMN form does not physically remove the column, but simply makes it invisible to SQL operations. Subsequent insert and update operations in the table will store a null value for the column. Thus, dropping a column is quick but it will not immediately reduce the on-disk size of your table, as the space occupied by the dropped column is not reclaimed. The space will be reclaimed over time as existing rows are updated. (These statements do not apply when dropping the system oid column; that is done with an immediate rewrite.)

To force an immediate rewrite of the table, you can use VACUUM FULL, CLUSTER or one of the forms of ALTER TABLE that forces a rewrite. This results in no semantically-visible change in the table, but gets rid of no-longer-useful data.

The USING option of SET DATA TYPE can actually specify any expression involving the old values of the row; that is, it can refer to other columns as well as the one being converted. This allows very general conversions to be done with the SET DATA TYPE syntax. Because of this flexibility, the USING expression is not applied to the column's default value (if any); the result might not be a constant expression as required for a default. This means that when there is no implicit or assignment cast from old to new type, SET DATA TYPE might fail to convert the default even though a USING clause is supplied. In such cases, drop the default with DROP DEFAULT, perform the ALTER TYPE, and then use SET DEFAULT to add a suitable new default. Similar considerations apply to indexes and constraints involving the column.

If a table has any descendant tables, it is not permitted to add, rename, or change the type of a column, or rename an inherited constraint in the parent table without doing the same to the descendants. That is, ALTER TABLE ONLY will be rejected. This ensures that the descendants always have columns matching the parent.

A recursive DROP COLUMN operation will remove a descendant table's column only if the descendant does not inherit that column from any other parents and never had an independent definition of the column. A nonrecursive DROP COLUMN (i.e., ALTER TABLE ONLY ... DROP COLUMN) never removes any descendant columns, but instead marks them as independently defined rather than inherited.

The TRIGGER, CLUSTER, OWNER, and TABLESPACE actions never recurse to descendant tables; that is, they always act as though ONLY were specified. Adding a constraint recurses only for CHECK constraints that are not marked NO INHERIT.

Changing any part of a system catalog table is not permitted.

Refer to CREATE TABLE for a further description of valid parameters. Chapter 5 has further information on inheritance.

Examples

To add a column of type varchar to a table:

```
ALTER TABLE distributors ADD COLUMN address varchar(30);
```

To drop a column from a table:

```
ALTER TABLE distributors DROP COLUMN address RESTRICT;
```

To change the types of two existing columns in one operation:

```
ALTER TABLE distributors
    ALTER COLUMN address TYPE varchar(80),
    ALTER COLUMN name TYPE varchar(100);
```

To change an integer column containing UNIX timestamps to timestamp with time zone via a USING clause:

```
ALTER TABLE foo
    ALTER COLUMN foo_timestamp SET DATA TYPE timestamp with time zone
    USING
        timestamp with time zone 'epoch' + foo_timestamp * interval '1 second';
```

The same, when the column has a default expression that won't automatically cast to the new data type:

```
ALTER TABLE foo
    ALTER COLUMN foo_timestamp DROP DEFAULT,
    ALTER COLUMN foo_timestamp TYPE timestamp with time zone
    USING
        timestamp with time zone 'epoch' + foo_timestamp * interval '1 second',
    ALTER COLUMN foo_timestamp SET DEFAULT now();
```

To rename an existing column:

```
ALTER TABLE distributors RENAME COLUMN address TO city;
```

To rename an existing table:

```
ALTER TABLE distributors RENAME TO suppliers;
```

To rename an existing constraint:

```
ALTER TABLE distributors RENAME CONSTRAINT zipchk TO zip_check;
```

To add a not-null constraint to a column:

```
ALTER TABLE distributors ALTER COLUMN street SET NOT NULL;
```

To remove a not-null constraint from a column:

```
ALTER TABLE distributors ALTER COLUMN street DROP NOT NULL;
```

To add a check constraint to a table and all its children:

```
ALTER TABLE distributors ADD CONSTRAINT zipchk CHECK (char_length(zipcode) = 5)
```

To add a check constraint only to a table and not to its children:

```
ALTER TABLE distributors ADD CONSTRAINT zipchk CHECK (char_length(zipcode) = 5)
```

(The check constraint will not be inherited by future children, either.)

To remove a check constraint from a table and all its children:

```
ALTER TABLE distributors DROP CONSTRAINT zipchk;
```

To remove a check constraint from one table only:

```
ALTER TABLE ONLY distributors DROP CONSTRAINT zipchk;
```

(The check constraint remains in place for any child tables.)

To add a foreign key constraint to a table:

```
ALTER TABLE distributors ADD CONSTRAINT distfk FOREIGN KEY (address) REFERENCES
```

To add a foreign key constraint to a table with the least impact on other work:

```
ALTER TABLE distributors ADD CONSTRAINT distfk FOREIGN KEY (address) REFERENCES
ALTER TABLE distributors VALIDATE CONSTRAINT distfk;
```

To add a (multicolumn) unique constraint to a table:

```
ALTER TABLE distributors ADD CONSTRAINT dist_id_zipcode_key UNIQUE (dist_id, zi
```

To add an automatically named primary key constraint to a table, noting that a table can only ever have one primary key:

```
ALTER TABLE distributors ADD PRIMARY KEY (dist_id);
```

To move a table to a different tablespace:

```
ALTER TABLE distributors SET TABLESPACE fasttablespace;
```

To move a table to a different schema:

```
ALTER TABLE myschema.distributors SET SCHEMA yourschema;
```

To recreate a primary key constraint, without blocking updates while the index is rebuilt:

```
CREATE UNIQUE INDEX CONCURRENTLY dist_id_temp_idx ON distributors (dist_id);
ALTER TABLE distributors DROP CONSTRAINT distributors_pkey,
    ADD CONSTRAINT distributors_pkey PRIMARY KEY USING INDEX dist_id_temp_idx;
```

Compatibility

The forms ADD (without USING INDEX), DROP, SET DEFAULT, and SET DATA TYPE (without USING) conform with the SQL standard. The other forms are PostgreSQL extensions of the SQL standard. Also, the ability to specify more than one manipulation in a single ALTER TABLE command is an extension.

ALTER TABLE DROP COLUMN can be used to drop the only column of a table, leaving a zero-column table. This is an extension of SQL, which disallows zero-column tables.

See Also

CREATE TABLE

ALTER TABLESPACE

Name

ALTER TABLESPACE — change the definition of a tablespace

Synopsis

```
ALTER TABLESPACE name RENAME TO new_name
ALTER TABLESPACE name OWNER TO new_owner
ALTER TABLESPACE name SET ( tablespace_option = value [, ... ] )
ALTER TABLESPACE name RESET ( tablespace_option [, ... ] )
```

Description

ALTER TABLESPACE can be used to change the definition of a tablespace.

You must own the tablespace to change the definition of a tablespace. To alter the owner, you must also be a direct or indirect member of the new owning role. (Note that superusers have these privileges automatically.)

Parameters

name

> The name of an existing tablespace.

new_name

> The new name of the tablespace. The new name cannot begin with pg_, as such names are reserved for system tablespaces.

new_owner

> The new owner of the tablespace.

tablespace_option

> A tablespace parameter to be set or reset. Currently, the only available parameters are seq_page_cost and random_page_cost. Setting either value for a particular tablespace will override the planner's usual estimate of the cost of reading pages from tables in that tablespace, as established by the configuration parameters of the same name (see seq_page_cost, random_page_cost). This may be useful if one tablespace is located on a disk which is faster or slower than the remainder of the I/O subsystem.

Examples

Rename tablespace `index_space` to `fast_raid`:

```
ALTER TABLESPACE index_space RENAME TO fast_raid;
```

Change the owner of tablespace `index_space`:

```
ALTER TABLESPACE index_space OWNER TO mary;
```

Compatibility

There is no `ALTER TABLESPACE` statement in the SQL standard.

See Also

CREATE TABLESPACE, DROP TABLESPACE

ALTER TEXT SEARCH CONFIGURATION

Name

ALTER TEXT SEARCH CONFIGURATION — change the definition of a text search configuration

Synopsis

```
ALTER TEXT SEARCH CONFIGURATION name
    ADD MAPPING FOR token_type [, ... ] WITH dictionary_name [, ... ]
ALTER TEXT SEARCH CONFIGURATION name
    ALTER MAPPING FOR token_type [, ... ] WITH dictionary_name [, ... ]
ALTER TEXT SEARCH CONFIGURATION name
    ALTER MAPPING REPLACE old_dictionary WITH new_dictionary
ALTER TEXT SEARCH CONFIGURATION name
    ALTER MAPPING FOR token_type [, ... ] REPLACE old_dictionary WITH new_dictiona
ALTER TEXT SEARCH CONFIGURATION name
    DROP MAPPING [ IF EXISTS ] FOR token_type [, ... ]
ALTER TEXT SEARCH CONFIGURATION name RENAME TO new_name
ALTER TEXT SEARCH CONFIGURATION name OWNER TO new_owner
ALTER TEXT SEARCH CONFIGURATION name SET SCHEMA new_schema
```

Description

ALTER TEXT SEARCH CONFIGURATION changes the definition of a text search configuration. You can modify its mappings from token types to dictionaries, or change the configuration's name or owner.

You must be the owner of the configuration to use ALTER TEXT SEARCH CONFIGURATION.

Parameters

name

The name (optionally schema-qualified) of an existing text search configuration.

token_type

The name of a token type that is emitted by the configuration's parser.

dictionary_name

The name of a text search dictionary to be consulted for the specified token type(s). If multiple dictionaries are listed, they are consulted in the specified order.

old_dictionary

The name of a text search dictionary to be replaced in the mapping.

new_dictionary

The name of a text search dictionary to be substituted for old_dictionary.

`new_name`

> The new name of the text search configuration.

`new_owner`

> The new owner of the text search configuration.

`new_schema`

> The new schema for the text search configuration.

The ADD MAPPING FOR form installs a list of dictionaries to be consulted for the specified token type(s); it is an error if there is already a mapping for any of the token types. The ALTER MAPPING FOR form does the same, but first removing any existing mapping for those token types. The ALTER MAPPING REPLACE forms substitute `new_dictionary` for `old_dictionary` anywhere the latter appears. This is done for only the specified token types when FOR appears, or for all mappings of the configuration when it doesn't. The DROP MAPPING form removes all dictionaries for the specified token type(s), causing tokens of those types to be ignored by the text search configuration. It is an error if there is no mapping for the token types, unless IF EXISTS appears.

Examples

The following example replaces the `english` dictionary with the `swedish` dictionary anywhere that `english` is used within `my_config`.

```
ALTER TEXT SEARCH CONFIGURATION my_config
  ALTER MAPPING REPLACE english WITH swedish;
```

Compatibility

There is no ALTER TEXT SEARCH CONFIGURATION statement in the SQL standard.

See Also

CREATE TEXT SEARCH CONFIGURATION, DROP TEXT SEARCH CONFIGURATION

ALTER TEXT SEARCH DICTIONARY

Name

ALTER TEXT SEARCH DICTIONARY — change the definition of a text search dictionary

Synopsis

```
ALTER TEXT SEARCH DICTIONARY name (
    option [ = value ] [, ... ]
)
ALTER TEXT SEARCH DICTIONARY name RENAME TO new_name
ALTER TEXT SEARCH DICTIONARY name OWNER TO new_owner
ALTER TEXT SEARCH DICTIONARY name SET SCHEMA new_schema
```

Description

ALTER TEXT SEARCH DICTIONARY changes the definition of a text search dictionary. You can change the dictionary's template-specific options, or change the dictionary's name or owner.

You must be the owner of the dictionary to use ALTER TEXT SEARCH DICTIONARY.

Parameters

name

   The name (optionally schema-qualified) of an existing text search dictionary.

option

   The name of a template-specific option to be set for this dictionary.

value

   The new value to use for a template-specific option. If the equal sign and value are omitted, then any previous setting for the option is removed from the dictionary, allowing the default to be used.

new_name

   The new name of the text search dictionary.

new_owner

   The new owner of the text search dictionary.

new_schema

   The new schema for the text search dictionary.

Template-specific options can appear in any order.

Examples

The following example command changes the stopword list for a Snowball-based dictionary. Other parameters remain unchanged.

```
ALTER TEXT SEARCH DICTIONARY my_dict ( StopWords = newrussian );
```

The following example command changes the language option to dutch, and removes the stopword option entirely.

```
ALTER TEXT SEARCH DICTIONARY my_dict ( language = dutch, StopWords );
```

The following example command "updates" the dictionary's definition without actually changing anything.

```
ALTER TEXT SEARCH DICTIONARY my_dict ( dummy );
```

(The reason this works is that the option removal code doesn't complain if there is no such option.) This trick is useful when changing configuration files for the dictionary: the ALTER will force existing database sessions to re-read the configuration files, which otherwise they would never do if they had read them earlier.

Compatibility

There is no ALTER TEXT SEARCH DICTIONARY statement in the SQL standard.

See Also

CREATE TEXT SEARCH DICTIONARY, DROP TEXT SEARCH DICTIONARY

ALTER TEXT SEARCH PARSER

Name

ALTER TEXT SEARCH PARSER — change the definition of a text search parser

Synopsis

```
ALTER TEXT SEARCH PARSER name RENAME TO new_name
ALTER TEXT SEARCH PARSER name SET SCHEMA new_schema
```

Description

ALTER TEXT SEARCH PARSER changes the definition of a text search parser. Currently, the only supported functionality is to change the parser's name.

You must be a superuser to use ALTER TEXT SEARCH PARSER.

Parameters

name

The name (optionally schema-qualified) of an existing text search parser.

new_name

The new name of the text search parser.

new_schema

The new schema for the text search parser.

Compatibility

There is no ALTER TEXT SEARCH PARSER statement in the SQL standard.

See Also

CREATE TEXT SEARCH PARSER, DROP TEXT SEARCH PARSER

ALTER TEXT SEARCH TEMPLATE

Name

`ALTER TEXT SEARCH TEMPLATE` — change the definition of a text search template

Synopsis

```
ALTER TEXT SEARCH TEMPLATE name RENAME TO new_name
ALTER TEXT SEARCH TEMPLATE name SET SCHEMA new_schema
```

Description

`ALTER TEXT SEARCH TEMPLATE` changes the definition of a text search template. Currently, the only supported functionality is to change the template's name.

You must be a superuser to use `ALTER TEXT SEARCH TEMPLATE`.

Parameters

name

The name (optionally schema-qualified) of an existing text search template.

new_name

The new name of the text search template.

new_schema

The new schema for the text search template.

Compatibility

There is no `ALTER TEXT SEARCH TEMPLATE` statement in the SQL standard.

See Also

CREATE TEXT SEARCH TEMPLATE, DROP TEXT SEARCH TEMPLATE

ALTER TRIGGER

Name

ALTER TRIGGER — change the definition of a trigger

Synopsis

```
ALTER TRIGGER name ON table_name RENAME TO new_name
```

Description

ALTER TRIGGER changes properties of an existing trigger. The RENAME clause changes the name of the given trigger without otherwise changing the trigger definition.

You must own the table on which the trigger acts to be allowed to change its properties.

Parameters

name

    The name of an existing trigger to alter.

table_name

    The name of the table on which this trigger acts.

new_name

    The new name for the trigger.

Notes

The ability to temporarily enable or disable a trigger is provided by ALTER TABLE, not by ALTER TRIGGER, because ALTER TRIGGER has no convenient way to express the option of enabling or disabling all of a table's triggers at once.

Examples

To rename an existing trigger:

```
ALTER TRIGGER emp_stamp ON emp RENAME TO emp_track_chgs;
```

Compatibility

ALTER TRIGGER is a PostgreSQL extension of the SQL standard.

See Also

ALTER TABLE

ALTER TYPE

Name

ALTER TYPE — change the definition of a type

Synopsis

```
ALTER TYPE name action [, ... ]
ALTER TYPE name OWNER TO new_owner
ALTER TYPE name RENAME ATTRIBUTE attribute_name TO new_attribute_name [ CASCADE | ]
ALTER TYPE name RENAME TO new_name
ALTER TYPE name SET SCHEMA new_schema
ALTER TYPE name ADD VALUE [ IF NOT EXISTS ] new_enum_value [ { BEFORE | AFTER } ᴇ

where action is one of:

    ADD ATTRIBUTE attribute_name data_type [ COLLATE collation ] [ CASCADE | RESTR
    DROP ATTRIBUTE [ IF EXISTS ] attribute_name [ CASCADE | RESTRICT ]
    ALTER ATTRIBUTE attribute_name [ SET DATA ] TYPE data_type [ COLLATE collation
```

Description

ALTER TYPE changes the definition of an existing type. There are several subforms:

ADD ATTRIBUTE

> This form adds a new attribute to a composite type, using the same syntax as CREATE TYPE.

DROP ATTRIBUTE [IF EXISTS]

> This form drops an attribute from a composite type. If IF EXISTS is specified and the attribute does not exist, no error is thrown. In this case a notice is issued instead.

SET DATA TYPE

> This form changes the type of an attribute of a composite type.

OWNER

> This form changes the owner of the type.

RENAME

> This form changes the name of the type or the name of an individual attribute of a composite type.

SET SCHEMA

> This form moves the type into another schema.

ADD VALUE [IF NOT EXISTS] [BEFORE | AFTER]

> This form adds a new value to an enum type. The new value's place in the enum's ordering can be specified as being BEFORE or AFTER one of the existing values. Otherwise, the new item is added at the end of the list of values.
>
> If IF NOT EXISTS is specified, it is not an error if the type already contains the new value: a notice is issued but no other action is taken. Otherwise, an error will occur if the new value is already present.

CASCADE

> Automatically propagate the operation to typed tables of the type being altered, and their descendants.

RESTRICT

> Refuse the operation if the type being altered is the type of a typed table. This is the default.

The ADD ATTRIBUTE, DROP ATTRIBUTE, and ALTER ATTRIBUTE actions can be combined into a list of multiple alterations to apply in parallel. For example, it is possible to add several attributes and/or alter the type of several attributes in a single command.

You must own the type to use ALTER TYPE. To change the schema of a type, you must also have CREATE privilege on the new schema. To alter the owner, you must also be a direct or indirect member of the new owning role, and that role must have CREATE privilege on the type's schema. (These restrictions enforce that altering the owner doesn't do anything you couldn't do by dropping and recreating the type. However, a superuser can alter ownership of any type anyway.) To add an attribute or alter an attribute type, you must also have USAGE privilege on the data type.

Parameters

name

> The name (possibly schema-qualified) of an existing type to alter.

new_name

> The new name for the type.

new_owner

> The user name of the new owner of the type.

new_schema

> The new schema for the type.

attribute_name

> The name of the attribute to add, alter, or drop.

new_attribute_name

> The new name of the attribute to be renamed.

data_type

The data type of the attribute to add, or the new type of the attribute to alter.

new_enum_value

The new value to be added to an enum type's list of values. Like all enum literals, it needs to be quoted.

existing_enum_value

The existing enum value that the new value should be added immediately before or after in the enum type's sort ordering. Like all enum literals, it needs to be quoted.

Notes

ALTER TYPE ... ADD VALUE (the form that adds a new value to an enum type) cannot be executed inside a transaction block.

Comparisons involving an added enum value will sometimes be slower than comparisons involving only original members of the enum type. This will usually only occur if BEFORE or AFTER is used to set the new value's sort position somewhere other than at the end of the list. However, sometimes it will happen even though the new value is added at the end (this occurs if the OID counter "wrapped around" since the original creation of the enum type). The slowdown is usually insignificant; but if it matters, optimal performance can be regained by dropping and recreating the enum type, or by dumping and reloading the database.

Examples

To rename a data type:

```
ALTER TYPE electronic_mail RENAME TO email;
```

To change the owner of the type email to joe:

```
ALTER TYPE email OWNER TO joe;
```

To change the schema of the type email to customers:

```
ALTER TYPE email SET SCHEMA customers;
```

To add a new attribute to a type:

```
ALTER TYPE compfoo ADD ATTRIBUTE f3 int;
```

To add a new value to an enum type in a particular sort position:

```
ALTER TYPE colors ADD VALUE 'orange' AFTER 'red';
```

Compatibility

The variants to add and drop attributes are part of the SQL standard; the other variants are PostgreSQL extensions.

See Also

CREATE TYPE, DROP TYPE

ALTER USER

Name

ALTER USER — change a database role

Synopsis

```
ALTER USER name [ [ WITH ] option [ ... ] ]

where option can be:

    SUPERUSER | NOSUPERUSER
  | CREATEDB | NOCREATEDB
  | CREATEROLE | NOCREATEROLE
  | CREATEUSER | NOCREATEUSER
  | INHERIT | NOINHERIT
  | LOGIN | NOLOGIN
  | REPLICATION | NOREPLICATION
  | CONNECTION LIMIT connlimit
  | [ ENCRYPTED | UNENCRYPTED ] PASSWORD 'password'
  | VALID UNTIL 'timestamp'

ALTER USER name RENAME TO new_name

ALTER USER name SET configuration_parameter { TO | = } { value | DEFAULT }
ALTER USER name SET configuration_parameter FROM CURRENT
ALTER USER name RESET configuration_parameter
ALTER USER name RESET ALL
```

Description

ALTER USER is now an alias for ALTER ROLE.

Compatibility

The ALTER USER statement is a PostgreSQL extension. The SQL standard leaves the definition of users to the implementation.

See Also

ALTER ROLE

ALTER USER MAPPING

Name

ALTER USER MAPPING — change the definition of a user mapping

Synopsis

```
ALTER USER MAPPING FOR { user_name | USER | CURRENT_USER | PUBLIC }
    SERVER server_name
    OPTIONS ( [ ADD | SET | DROP ] option ['value'] [, ... ] )
```

Description

ALTER USER MAPPING changes the definition of a user mapping.

The owner of a foreign server can alter user mappings for that server for any user. Also, a user can alter a user mapping for his own user name if USAGE privilege on the server has been granted to the user.

Parameters

user_name

> User name of the mapping. CURRENT_USER and USER match the name of the current user. PUBLIC is used to match all present and future user names in the system.

server_name

> Server name of the user mapping.

OPTIONS ([ADD | SET | DROP] option ['value'] [, ...])

> Change options for the user mapping. The new options override any previously specified options. ADD, SET, and DROP specify the action to be performed. ADD is assumed if no operation is explicitly specified. Option names must be unique; options are also validated by the server's foreign-data wrapper.

Examples

Change the password for user mapping bob, server foo:

```
ALTER USER MAPPING FOR bob SERVER foo OPTIONS (user 'bob', password 'public');
```

Compatibility

ALTER USER MAPPING conforms to ISO/IEC 9075-9 (SQL/MED). There is a subtle syntax issue: The standard omits the FOR key word. Since both CREATE USER MAPPING and DROP USER MAPPING use FOR in analogous positions, and IBM DB2 (being the other major SQL/MED implementation) also requires it for ALTER USER MAPPING, PostgreSQL diverges from the standard here in the interest of consistency and interoperability.

See Also

CREATE USER MAPPING, DROP USER MAPPING

ALTER VIEW

Name

ALTER VIEW — change the definition of a view

Synopsis

```
ALTER VIEW [ IF EXISTS ] name ALTER [ COLUMN ] column_name SET DEFAULT expression
ALTER VIEW [ IF EXISTS ] name ALTER [ COLUMN ] column_name DROP DEFAULT
ALTER VIEW [ IF EXISTS ] name OWNER TO new_owner
ALTER VIEW [ IF EXISTS ] name RENAME TO new_name
ALTER VIEW [ IF EXISTS ] name SET SCHEMA new_schema
ALTER VIEW [ IF EXISTS ] name SET ( view_option_name [= view_option_value] [, ...
ALTER VIEW [ IF EXISTS ] name RESET ( view_option_name [, ... ] )
```

Description

ALTER VIEW changes various auxiliary properties of a view. (If you want to modify the view's defining query, use CREATE OR REPLACE VIEW.)

You must own the view to use ALTER VIEW. To change a view's schema, you must also have CREATE privilege on the new schema. To alter the owner, you must also be a direct or indirect member of the new owning role, and that role must have CREATE privilege on the view's schema. (These restrictions enforce that altering the owner doesn't do anything you couldn't do by dropping and recreating the view. However, a superuser can alter ownership of any view anyway.)

Parameters

name

The name (optionally schema-qualified) of an existing view.

IF EXISTS

Do not throw an error if the view does not exist. A notice is issued in this case.

SET/DROP DEFAULT

These forms set or remove the default value for a column. A view column's default value is substituted into any INSERT or UPDATE command whose target is the view, before applying any rules or triggers for the view. The view's default will therefore take precedence over any default values from underlying relations.

new_owner

The user name of the new owner of the view.

new_name

> The new name for the view.

new_schema

> The new schema for the view.

SET (*view_option_name* [= *view_option_value*] [, ...])
RESET (*view_option_name* [, ...])

> Sets or resets a view option. Currently supported options are:
>
> check_option (string)
>
> > Changes the check option of the view. The value must be local or cascaded.
>
> security_barrier (boolean)
>
> > Changes the security-barrier property of the view. The value must be Boolean value, such as true or false.

Notes

For historical reasons, ALTER TABLE can be used with views too; but the only variants of ALTER TABLE that are allowed with views are equivalent to the ones shown above.

Examples

To rename the view foo to bar:

ALTER VIEW foo RENAME TO bar;

To attach a default column value to an updatable view:

```
CREATE TABLE base_table (id int, ts timestamptz);
CREATE VIEW a_view AS SELECT * FROM base_table;
ALTER VIEW a_view ALTER COLUMN ts SET DEFAULT now();
INSERT INTO base_table(id) VALUES(1);  -- ts will receive a NULL
INSERT INTO a_view(id) VALUES(2);  -- ts will receive the current time
```

Compatibility

ALTER VIEW is a PostgreSQL extension of the SQL standard.

See Also

CREATE VIEW, DROP VIEW

ANALYZE

Name

ANALYZE — collect statistics about a database

Synopsis

```
ANALYZE [ VERBOSE ] [ table_name [ ( column_name [, ...] ) ] ]
```

Description

ANALYZE collects statistics about the contents of tables in the database, and stores the results in the pg_statistic system catalog. Subsequently, the query planner uses these statistics to help determine the most efficient execution plans for queries.

With no parameter, ANALYZE examines every table in the current database. With a parameter, ANALYZE examines only that table. It is further possible to give a list of column names, in which case only the statistics for those columns are collected.

Parameters

VERBOSE

    Enables display of progress messages.

table_name

    The name (possibly schema-qualified) of a specific table to analyze. If omitted, all regular tables (but not foreign tables) in the current database are analyzed.

column_name

    The name of a specific column to analyze. Defaults to all columns.

Outputs

When VERBOSE is specified, ANALYZE emits progress messages to indicate which table is currently being processed. Various statistics about the tables are printed as well.

Notes

Foreign tables are analyzed only when explicitly selected. Not all foreign data wrappers support ANALYZE. If the table's wrapper does not support ANALYZE, the command prints a warning and does nothing.

In the default PostgreSQL configuration, the autovacuum daemon (see Section 23.1.6) takes care of automatic analyzing of tables when they are first loaded with data, and as they change throughout regular operation. When autovacuum is disabled, it is a good idea to run ANALYZE periodically, or just after making major changes in the contents of a table. Accurate statistics will help the planner to choose the most appropriate query plan, and thereby improve the speed of query processing. A common strategy for read-mostly databases is to run VACUUM and ANALYZE once a day during a low-usage time of day. (This will not be sufficient if there is heavy update activity.)

ANALYZE requires only a read lock on the target table, so it can run in parallel with other activity on the table.

The statistics collected by ANALYZE usually include a list of some of the most common values in each column and a histogram showing the approximate data distribution in each column. One or both of these can be omitted if ANALYZE deems them uninteresting (for example, in a unique-key column, there are no common values) or if the column data type does not support the appropriate operators. There is more information about the statistics in Chapter 23.

For large tables, ANALYZE takes a random sample of the table contents, rather than examining every row. This allows even very large tables to be analyzed in a small amount of time. Note, however, that the statistics are only approximate, and will change slightly each time ANALYZE is run, even if the actual table contents did not change. This might result in small changes in the planner's estimated costs shown by EXPLAIN. In rare situations, this non-determinism will cause the planner's choices of query plans to change after ANALYZE is run. To avoid this, raise the amount of statistics collected by ANALYZE, as described below.

The extent of analysis can be controlled by adjusting the default_statistics_target configuration variable, or on a column-by-column basis by setting the per-column statistics target with ALTER TABLE ... ALTER COLUMN ... SET STATISTICS (see ALTER TABLE). The target value sets the maximum number of entries in the most-common-value list and the maximum number of bins in the histogram. The default target value is 100, but this can be adjusted up or down to trade off accuracy of planner estimates against the time taken for ANALYZE and the amount of space occupied in pg_statistic. In particular, setting the statistics target to zero disables collection of statistics for that column. It might be useful to do that for columns that are never used as part of the WHERE, GROUP BY, or ORDER BY clauses of queries, since the planner will have no use for statistics on such columns.

The largest statistics target among the columns being analyzed determines the number of table rows sampled to prepare the statistics. Increasing the target causes a proportional increase in the time and space needed to do ANALYZE.

One of the values estimated by ANALYZE is the number of distinct values that appear in each column. Because only a subset of the rows are examined, this estimate can sometimes be quite inaccurate, even with the largest possible statistics target. If this inaccuracy leads to bad query plans, a more accurate value can be determined manually and then installed with ALTER TABLE ... ALTER COLUMN ... SET (n_distinct = ...) (see ALTER TABLE).

If the table being analyzed has one or more children, ANALYZE will gather statistics twice: once on the rows of the parent table only, and a second time on the rows of the parent table with all of its children. This second set of statistics is needed when planning queries that traverse the entire inheritance tree. The autovacuum daemon, however, will only consider inserts or updates on the parent table itself when deciding whether to trigger an automatic analyze for that table. If that table is rarely inserted into or updated, the inheritance statistics will not be up to date unless you run ANALYZE manually.

If the table being analyzed is completely empty, ANALYZE will not record new statistics for that table. Any existing statistics will be retained.

Compatibility

There is no ANALYZE statement in the SQL standard.

See Also

VACUUM, vacuumdb, Section 18.4.4, Section 23.1.6

BEGIN

Name

BEGIN — start a transaction block

Synopsis

```
BEGIN [ WORK | TRANSACTION ] [ transaction_mode [, ...] ]

where transaction_mode is one of:

    ISOLATION LEVEL { SERIALIZABLE | REPEATABLE READ | READ COMMITTED | READ UN
    READ WRITE | READ ONLY
    [ NOT ] DEFERRABLE
```

Description

BEGIN initiates a transaction block, that is, all statements after a BEGIN command will be executed in a single transaction until an explicit COMMIT or ROLLBACK is given. By default (without BEGIN), PostgreSQL executes transactions in "autocommit" mode, that is, each statement is executed in its own transaction and a commit is implicitly performed at the end of the statement (if execution was successful, otherwise a rollback is done).

Statements are executed more quickly in a transaction block, because transaction start/commit requires significant CPU and disk activity. Execution of multiple statements inside a transaction is also useful to ensure consistency when making several related changes: other sessions will be unable to see the intermediate states wherein not all the related updates have been done.

If the isolation level, read/write mode, or deferrable mode is specified, the new transaction has those characteristics, as if SET TRANSACTION was executed.

Parameters

WORK
TRANSACTION

    Optional key words. They have no effect.

Refer to SET TRANSACTION for information on the meaning of the other parameters to this statement.

Notes

START TRANSACTION has the same functionality as BEGIN.

Use COMMIT or ROLLBACK to terminate a transaction block.

Issuing BEGIN when already inside a transaction block will provoke a warning message. The state of the transaction is not affected. To nest transactions within a transaction block, use savepoints (see SAVE-POINT).

For reasons of backwards compatibility, the commas between successive *transaction_modes* can be omitted.

Examples

To begin a transaction block:

BEGIN;

Compatibility

BEGIN is a PostgreSQL language extension. It is equivalent to the SQL-standard command START TRANSACTION, whose reference page contains additional compatibility information.

The DEFERRABLE *transaction_mode* is a PostgreSQL language extension.

Incidentally, the BEGIN key word is used for a different purpose in embedded SQL. You are advised to be careful about the transaction semantics when porting database applications.

See Also

COMMIT, ROLLBACK, START TRANSACTION, SAVEPOINT

CHECKPOINT

Name

CHECKPOINT — force a transaction log checkpoint

Synopsis

```
CHECKPOINT
```

Description

A checkpoint is a point in the transaction log sequence at which all data files have been updated to reflect the information in the log. All data files will be flushed to disk. Refer to Section 29.4 for more details about what happens during a checkpoint.

The CHECKPOINT command forces an immediate checkpoint when the command is issued, without waiting for a regular checkpoint scheduled by the system (controlled by the settings in Section 18.5.2). CHECKPOINT is not intended for use during normal operation.

If executed during recovery, the CHECKPOINT command will force a restartpoint (see Section 29.4) rather than writing a new checkpoint.

Only superusers can call CHECKPOINT.

Compatibility

The CHECKPOINT command is a PostgreSQL language extension.

CLOSE

Name

CLOSE — close a cursor

Synopsis

```
CLOSE { name | ALL }
```

Description

CLOSE frees the resources associated with an open cursor. After the cursor is closed, no subsequent operations are allowed on it. A cursor should be closed when it is no longer needed.

Every non-holdable open cursor is implicitly closed when a transaction is terminated by COMMIT or ROLLBACK. A holdable cursor is implicitly closed if the transaction that created it aborts via ROLLBACK. If the creating transaction successfully commits, the holdable cursor remains open until an explicit CLOSE is executed, or the client disconnects.

Parameters

name

> The name of an open cursor to close.

ALL

> Close all open cursors.

Notes

PostgreSQL does not have an explicit OPEN cursor statement; a cursor is considered open when it is declared. Use the DECLARE statement to declare a cursor.

You can see all available cursors by querying the pg_cursors system view.

If a cursor is closed after a savepoint which is later rolled back, the CLOSE is not rolled back; that is, the cursor remains closed.

Examples

Close the cursor liahona:

```
CLOSE liahona;
```

Compatibility

CLOSE is fully conforming with the SQL standard. CLOSE ALL is a PostgreSQL extension.

See Also

DECLARE, FETCH, MOVE

CLUSTER

Name

CLUSTER — cluster a table according to an index

Synopsis

```
CLUSTER [VERBOSE] table_name [ USING index_name ]
CLUSTER [VERBOSE]
```

Description

CLUSTER instructs PostgreSQL to cluster the table specified by *table_name* based on the index specified by *index_name*. The index must already have been defined on *table_name*.

When a table is clustered, it is physically reordered based on the index information. Clustering is a one-time operation: when the table is subsequently updated, the changes are not clustered. That is, no attempt is made to store new or updated rows according to their index order. (If one wishes, one can periodically recluster by issuing the command again. Also, setting the table's FILLFACTOR storage parameter to less than 100% can aid in preserving cluster ordering during updates, since updated rows are kept on the same page if enough space is available there.)

When a table is clustered, PostgreSQL remembers which index it was clustered by. The form CLUSTER *table_name* reclusters the table using the same index as before. You can also use the CLUSTER or SET WITHOUT CLUSTER forms of ALTER TABLE to set the index to be used for future cluster operations, or to clear any previous setting.

CLUSTER without any parameter reclusters all the previously-clustered tables in the current database that the calling user owns, or all such tables if called by a superuser. This form of CLUSTER cannot be executed inside a transaction block.

When a table is being clustered, an ACCESS EXCLUSIVE lock is acquired on it. This prevents any other database operations (both reads and writes) from operating on the table until the CLUSTER is finished.

Parameters

table_name

The name (possibly schema-qualified) of a table.

index_name

The name of an index.

VERBOSE

Prints a progress report as each table is clustered.

Notes

In cases where you are accessing single rows randomly within a table, the actual order of the data in the table is unimportant. However, if you tend to access some data more than others, and there is an index that groups them together, you will benefit from using CLUSTER. If you are requesting a range of indexed values from a table, or a single indexed value that has multiple rows that match, CLUSTER will help because once the index identifies the table page for the first row that matches, all other rows that match are probably already on the same table page, and so you save disk accesses and speed up the query.

CLUSTER can re-sort the table using either an index scan on the specified index, or (if the index is a b-tree) a sequential scan followed by sorting. It will attempt to choose the method that will be faster, based on planner cost parameters and available statistical information.

When an index scan is used, a temporary copy of the table is created that contains the table data in the index order. Temporary copies of each index on the table are created as well. Therefore, you need free space on disk at least equal to the sum of the table size and the index sizes.

When a sequential scan and sort is used, a temporary sort file is also created, so that the peak temporary space requirement is as much as double the table size, plus the index sizes. This method is often faster than the index scan method, but if the disk space requirement is intolerable, you can disable this choice by temporarily setting enable_sort to off.

It is advisable to set maintenance_work_mem to a reasonably large value (but not more than the amount of RAM you can dedicate to the CLUSTER operation) before clustering.

Because the planner records statistics about the ordering of tables, it is advisable to run ANALYZE on the newly clustered table. Otherwise, the planner might make poor choices of query plans.

Because CLUSTER remembers which indexes are clustered, one can cluster the tables one wants clustered manually the first time, then set up a periodic maintenance script that executes CLUSTER without any parameters, so that the desired tables are periodically reclustered.

Examples

Cluster the table employees on the basis of its index employees_ind:

```
CLUSTER employees USING employees_ind;
```

Cluster the employees table using the same index that was used before:

```
CLUSTER employees;
```

Cluster all tables in the database that have previously been clustered:

```
CLUSTER;
```

Compatibility

There is no CLUSTER statement in the SQL standard.

The syntax

```
CLUSTER index_name ON table_name
```

is also supported for compatibility with pre-8.3 PostgreSQL versions.

See Also

clusterdb

COMMENT

Name

COMMENT — define or change the comment of an object

Synopsis

```
COMMENT ON
{
  AGGREGATE aggregate_name ( aggregate_signature ) |
  CAST (source_type AS target_type) |
  COLLATION object_name |
  COLUMN relation_name.column_name |
  CONSTRAINT constraint_name ON table_name |
  CONVERSION object_name |
  DATABASE object_name |
  DOMAIN object_name |
  EXTENSION object_name |
  EVENT TRIGGER object_name |
  FOREIGN DATA WRAPPER object_name |
  FOREIGN TABLE object_name |
  FUNCTION function_name ( [ [ argmode ] [ argname ] argtype [, ...] ] ) |
  INDEX object_name |
  LARGE OBJECT large_object_oid |
  MATERIALIZED VIEW object_name |
  OPERATOR operator_name (left_type, right_type) |
  OPERATOR CLASS object_name USING index_method |
  OPERATOR FAMILY object_name USING index_method |
  [ PROCEDURAL ] LANGUAGE object_name |
  ROLE object_name |
  RULE rule_name ON table_name |
  SCHEMA object_name |
  SEQUENCE object_name |
  SERVER object_name |
  TABLE object_name |
  TABLESPACE object_name |
  TEXT SEARCH CONFIGURATION object_name |
  TEXT SEARCH DICTIONARY object_name |
  TEXT SEARCH PARSER object_name |
  TEXT SEARCH TEMPLATE object_name |
  TRIGGER trigger_name ON table_name |
  TYPE object_name |
  VIEW object_name
} IS 'text'

where aggregate_signature is:

* |
[ argmode ] [ argname ] argtype [ , ... ] |
[ [ argmode ] [ argname ] argtype [ , ... ] ] ORDER BY [ argmode ] [ argname ] argt
```

Description

COMMENT stores a comment about a database object.

Only one comment string is stored for each object, so to modify a comment, issue a new COMMENT command for the same object. To remove a comment, write NULL in place of the text string. Comments are automatically dropped when their object is dropped.

For most kinds of object, only the object's owner can set the comment. Roles don't have owners, so the rule for COMMENT ON ROLE is that you must be superuser to comment on a superuser role, or have the CREATEROLE privilege to comment on non-superuser roles. Of course, a superuser can comment on anything.

Comments can be viewed using psql's \d family of commands. Other user interfaces to retrieve comments can be built atop the same built-in functions that psql uses, namely obj_description, col_description, and shobj_description (see Table 9-60).

Parameters

object_name
relation_name.column_name
aggregate_name
constraint_name
function_name
operator_name
rule_name
trigger_name

> The name of the object to be commented. Names of tables, aggregates, collations, conversions, domains, foreign tables, functions, indexes, operators, operator classes, operator families, sequences, text search objects, types, and views can be schema-qualified. When commenting on a column, relation_name must refer to a table, view, composite type, or foreign table.

source_type

> The name of the source data type of the cast.

target_type

> The name of the target data type of the cast.

argmode

> The mode of a function or aggregate argument: IN, OUT, INOUT, or VARIADIC. If omitted, the default is IN. Note that COMMENT does not actually pay any attention to OUT arguments, since only the input arguments are needed to determine the function's identity. So it is sufficient to list the IN, INOUT, and VARIADIC arguments.

argname

> The name of a function or aggregate argument. Note that COMMENT does not actually pay any attention to argument names, since only the argument data types are needed to determine the function's identity.

argtype

> The data type of a function or aggregate argument.

large_object_oid

> The OID of the large object.

left_type
right_type

> The data type(s) of the operator's arguments (optionally schema-qualified). Write NONE for the missing argument of a prefix or postfix operator.

PROCEDURAL

> This is a noise word.

text

> The new comment, written as a string literal; or NULL to drop the comment.

Notes

There is presently no security mechanism for viewing comments: any user connected to a database can see all the comments for objects in that database. For shared objects such as databases, roles, and tablespaces, comments are stored globally so any user connected to any database in the cluster can see all the comments for shared objects. Therefore, don't put security-critical information in comments.

Examples

Attach a comment to the table mytable:

```
COMMENT ON TABLE mytable IS 'This is my table.';
```

Remove it again:

```
COMMENT ON TABLE mytable IS NULL;
```

Some more examples:

```
COMMENT ON AGGREGATE my_aggregate (double precision) IS 'Computes sample variar
COMMENT ON CAST (text AS int4) IS 'Allow casts from text to int4';
COMMENT ON COLLATION "fr_CA" IS 'Canadian French';
COMMENT ON COLUMN my_table.my_column IS 'Employee ID number';
COMMENT ON CONVERSION my_conv IS 'Conversion to UTF8';
COMMENT ON CONSTRAINT bar_col_cons ON bar IS 'Constrains column col';
COMMENT ON DATABASE my_database IS 'Development Database';
COMMENT ON DOMAIN my_domain IS 'Email Address Domain';
COMMENT ON EXTENSION hstore IS 'implements the hstore data type';
COMMENT ON FOREIGN DATA WRAPPER mywrapper IS 'my foreign data wrapper';
COMMENT ON FOREIGN TABLE my_foreign_table IS 'Employee Information in other dat
```

```
COMMENT ON FUNCTION my_function (timestamp) IS 'Returns Roman Numeral';
COMMENT ON INDEX my_index IS 'Enforces uniqueness on employee ID';
COMMENT ON LANGUAGE plpython IS 'Python support for stored procedures';
COMMENT ON LARGE OBJECT 346344 IS 'Planning document';
COMMENT ON MATERIALIZED VIEW my_matview IS 'Summary of order history';
COMMENT ON OPERATOR ^ (text, text) IS 'Performs intersection of two texts';
COMMENT ON OPERATOR - (NONE, integer) IS 'Unary minus';
COMMENT ON OPERATOR CLASS int4ops USING btree IS '4 byte integer operators for
COMMENT ON OPERATOR FAMILY integer_ops USING btree IS 'all integer operators fc
COMMENT ON ROLE my_role IS 'Administration group for finance tables';
COMMENT ON RULE my_rule ON my_table IS 'Logs updates of employee records';
COMMENT ON SCHEMA my_schema IS 'Departmental data';
COMMENT ON SEQUENCE my_sequence IS 'Used to generate primary keys';
COMMENT ON SERVER myserver IS 'my foreign server';
COMMENT ON TABLE my_schema.my_table IS 'Employee Information';
COMMENT ON TABLESPACE my_tablespace IS 'Tablespace for indexes';
COMMENT ON TEXT SEARCH CONFIGURATION my_config IS 'Special word filtering';
COMMENT ON TEXT SEARCH DICTIONARY swedish IS 'Snowball stemmer for Swedish lanc
COMMENT ON TEXT SEARCH PARSER my_parser IS 'Splits text into words';
COMMENT ON TEXT SEARCH TEMPLATE snowball IS 'Snowball stemmer';
COMMENT ON TRIGGER my_trigger ON my_table IS 'Used for RI';
COMMENT ON TYPE complex IS 'Complex number data type';
COMMENT ON VIEW my_view IS 'View of departmental costs';
```

Compatibility

There is no COMMENT command in the SQL standard.

COMMIT

Name

COMMIT — commit the current transaction

Synopsis

```
COMMIT [ WORK | TRANSACTION ]
```

Description

COMMIT commits the current transaction. All changes made by the transaction become visible to others and are guaranteed to be durable if a crash occurs.

Parameters

```
WORK
TRANSACTION
```

    Optional key words. They have no effect.

Notes

Use ROLLBACK to abort a transaction.

Issuing COMMIT when not inside a transaction does no harm, but it will provoke a warning message.

Examples

To commit the current transaction and make all changes permanent:

```
COMMIT;
```

Compatibility

The SQL standard only specifies the two forms COMMIT and COMMIT WORK. Otherwise, this command is fully conforming.

See Also

BEGIN, ROLLBACK

COMMIT PREPARED

Name

COMMIT PREPARED — commit a transaction that was earlier prepared for two-phase commit

Synopsis

```
COMMIT PREPARED transaction_id
```

Description

COMMIT PREPARED commits a transaction that is in prepared state.

Parameters

transaction_id

> The transaction identifier of the transaction that is to be committed.

Notes

To commit a prepared transaction, you must be either the same user that executed the transaction originally, or a superuser. But you do not have to be in the same session that executed the transaction.

This command cannot be executed inside a transaction block. The prepared transaction is committed immediately.

All currently available prepared transactions are listed in the pg_prepared_xacts system view.

Examples

Commit the transaction identified by the transaction identifier foobar:

```
COMMIT PREPARED 'foobar';
```

Compatibility

COMMIT PREPARED is a PostgreSQL extension. It is intended for use by external transaction management systems, some of which are covered by standards (such as X/Open XA), but the SQL side of those systems is not standardized.

See Also

PREPARE TRANSACTION, ROLLBACK PREPARED

COPY

Name

COPY — copy data between a file and a table

Synopsis

```
COPY table_name [ ( column_name [, ...] ) ]
    FROM { 'filename' | PROGRAM 'command' | STDIN }
    [ [ WITH ] ( option [, ...] ) ]

COPY { table_name [ ( column_name [, ...] ) ] | ( query ) }
    TO { 'filename' | PROGRAM 'command' | STDOUT }
    [ [ WITH ] ( option [, ...] ) ]

where option can be one of:

    FORMAT format_name
    OIDS [ boolean ]
    FREEZE [ boolean ]
    DELIMITER 'delimiter_character'
    NULL 'null_string'
    HEADER [ boolean ]
    QUOTE 'quote_character'
    ESCAPE 'escape_character'
    FORCE_QUOTE { ( column_name [, ...] ) | * }
    FORCE_NOT_NULL ( column_name [, ...] )
    FORCE_NULL ( column_name [, ...] )
    ENCODING 'encoding_name'
```

Description

COPY moves data between PostgreSQL tables and standard file-system files. COPY TO copies the contents of a table *to* a file, while COPY FROM copies data *from* a file to a table (appending the data to whatever is in the table already). COPY TO can also copy the results of a SELECT query.

If a list of columns is specified, COPY will only copy the data in the specified columns to or from the file. If there are any columns in the table that are not in the column list, COPY FROM will insert the default values for those columns.

COPY with a file name instructs the PostgreSQL server to directly read from or write to a file. The file must be accessible by the PostgreSQL user (the user ID the server runs as) and the name must be specified from the viewpoint of the server. When PROGRAM is specified, the server executes the given command and reads from the standard output of the program, or writes to the standard input of the program. The command must be specified from the viewpoint of the server, and be executable by the PostgreSQL user. When STDIN or STDOUT is specified, data is transmitted via the connection between the client and the server.

Parameters

table_name

> The name (optionally schema-qualified) of an existing table.

column_name

> An optional list of columns to be copied. If no column list is specified, all columns of the table will be copied.

query

> A SELECT or VALUES command whose results are to be copied. Note that parentheses are required around the query.

filename

> The path name of the input or output file. An input file name can be an absolute or relative path, but an output file name must be an absolute path. Windows users might need to use an E" string and double any backslashes used in the path name.

PROGRAM

> A command to execute. In COPY FROM, the input is read from standard output of the command, and in COPY TO, the output is written to the standard input of the command.

> Note that the command is invoked by the shell, so if you need to pass any arguments to shell command that come from an untrusted source, you must be careful to strip or escape any special characters that might have a special meaning for the shell. For security reasons, it is best to use a fixed command string, or at least avoid passing any user input in it.

STDIN

> Specifies that input comes from the client application.

STDOUT

> Specifies that output goes to the client application.

boolean

> Specifies whether the selected option should be turned on or off. You can write TRUE, ON, or 1 to enable the option, and FALSE, OFF, or 0 to disable it. The *boolean* value can also be omitted, in which case TRUE is assumed.

FORMAT

> Selects the data format to be read or written: text, csv (Comma Separated Values), or binary. The default is text.

OIDS

> Specifies copying the OID for each row. (An error is raised if OIDS is specified for a table that does not have OIDs, or in the case of copying a *query*.)

FREEZE

> Requests copying the data with rows already frozen, just as they would be after running the VACUUM FREEZE command. This is intended as a performance option for initial data loading. Rows will be

frozen only if the table being loaded has been created or truncated in the current subtransaction, there are no cursors open and there are no older snapshots held by this transaction.

Note that all other sessions will immediately be able to see the data once it has been successfully loaded. This violates the normal rules of MVCC visibility and users specifying should be aware of the potential problems this might cause.

DELIMITER

Specifies the character that separates columns within each row (line) of the file. The default is a tab character in text format, a comma in CSV format. This must be a single one-byte character. This option is not allowed when using binary format.

NULL

Specifies the string that represents a null value. The default is \N (backslash-N) in text format, and an unquoted empty string in CSV format. You might prefer an empty string even in text format for cases where you don't want to distinguish nulls from empty strings. This option is not allowed when using binary format.

> **Note:** When using COPY FROM, any data item that matches this string will be stored as a null value, so you should make sure that you use the same string as you used with COPY TO.

HEADER

Specifies that the file contains a header line with the names of each column in the file. On output, the first line contains the column names from the table, and on input, the first line is ignored. This option is allowed only when using CSV format.

QUOTE

Specifies the quoting character to be used when a data value is quoted. The default is double-quote. This must be a single one-byte character. This option is allowed only when using CSV format.

ESCAPE

Specifies the character that should appear before a data character that matches the QUOTE value. The default is the same as the QUOTE value (so that the quoting character is doubled if it appears in the data). This must be a single one-byte character. This option is allowed only when using CSV format.

FORCE_QUOTE

Forces quoting to be used for all non-NULL values in each specified column. NULL output is never quoted. If * is specified, non-NULL values will be quoted in all columns. This option is allowed only in COPY TO, and only when using CSV format.

FORCE_NOT_NULL

Do not match the specified columns' values against the null string. In the default case where the null string is empty, this means that empty values will be read as zero-length strings rather than nulls, even when they are not quoted. This option is allowed only in COPY FROM, and only when using CSV format.

FORCE_NULL

> Match the specified columns' values against the null string, even if it has been quoted, and if a match is found set the value to NULL. In the default case where the null string is empty, this converts a quoted empty string into NULL. This option is allowed only in COPY FROM, and only when using CSV format.

ENCODING

> Specifies that the file is encoded in the *encoding_name*. If this option is omitted, the current client encoding is used. See the Notes below for more details.

Outputs

On successful completion, a COPY command returns a command tag of the form

COPY *count*

The *count* is the number of rows copied.

> **Note:** psql will print this command tag only if the command was not COPY ... TO STDOUT, or the equivalent psql meta-command \copy ... to stdout. This is to prevent confusing the command tag with the data that was just printed.

Notes

COPY can only be used with plain tables, not with views. However, you can write COPY (SELECT * FROM *viewname*) TO ....

COPY only deals with the specific table named; it does not copy data to or from child tables. Thus for example COPY *table* TO shows the same data as SELECT * FROM ONLY *table*. But COPY (SELECT * FROM *table*) TO ... can be used to dump all of the data in an inheritance hierarchy.

You must have select privilege on the table whose values are read by COPY TO, and insert privilege on the table into which values are inserted by COPY FROM. It is sufficient to have column privileges on the column(s) listed in the command.

Files named in a COPY command are read or written directly by the server, not by the client application. Therefore, they must reside on or be accessible to the database server machine, not the client. They must be accessible to and readable or writable by the PostgreSQL user (the user ID the server runs as), not the client. Similarly, the command specified with PROGRAM is executed directly by the server, not by the client application, must be executable by the PostgreSQL user. COPY naming a file or command is only allowed to database superusers, since it allows reading or writing any file that the server has privileges to access.

Do not confuse COPY with the psql instruction \copy. \copy invokes COPY FROM STDIN or COPY TO STDOUT, and then fetches/stores the data in a file accessible to the psql client. Thus, file accessibility and access rights depend on the client rather than the server when \copy is used.

It is recommended that the file name used in COPY always be specified as an absolute path. This is enforced by the server in the case of COPY TO, but for COPY FROM you do have the option of reading from a file specified by a relative path. The path will be interpreted relative to the working directory of the server process (normally the cluster's data directory), not the client's working directory.

Executing a command with PROGRAM might be restricted by the operating system's access control mechanisms, such as SELinux.

COPY FROM will invoke any triggers and check constraints on the destination table. However, it will not invoke rules.

COPY input and output is affected by DateStyle. To ensure portability to other PostgreSQL installations that might use non-default DateStyle settings, DateStyle should be set to ISO before using COPY TO. It is also a good idea to avoid dumping data with IntervalStyle set to sql_standard, because negative interval values might be misinterpreted by a server that has a different setting for IntervalStyle.

Input data is interpreted according to ENCODING option or the current client encoding, and output data is encoded in ENCODING or the current client encoding, even if the data does not pass through the client but is read from or written to a file directly by the server.

COPY stops operation at the first error. This should not lead to problems in the event of a COPY TO, but the target table will already have received earlier rows in a COPY FROM. These rows will not be visible or accessible, but they still occupy disk space. This might amount to a considerable amount of wasted disk space if the failure happened well into a large copy operation. You might wish to invoke VACUUM to recover the wasted space.

FORCE_NULL and FORCE_NOT_NULL can be used simultaneously on the same column. This results in converting quoted null strings to null values and unquoted null strings to empty strings.

File Formats

Text Format

When the text format is used, the data read or written is a text file with one line per table row. Columns in a row are separated by the delimiter character. The column values themselves are strings generated by the output function, or acceptable to the input function, of each attribute's data type. The specified null string is used in place of columns that are null. COPY FROM will raise an error if any line of the input file contains more or fewer columns than are expected. If OIDS is specified, the OID is read or written as the first column, preceding the user data columns.

End of data can be represented by a single line containing just backslash-period (\.). An end-of-data marker is not necessary when reading from a file, since the end of file serves perfectly well; it is needed only when copying data to or from client applications using pre-3.0 client protocol.

Backslash characters (\) can be used in the COPY data to quote data characters that might otherwise be taken as row or column delimiters. In particular, the following characters *must* be preceded by a backslash if they appear as part of a column value: backslash itself, newline, carriage return, and the current delimiter character.

The specified null string is sent by COPY TO without adding any backslashes; conversely, COPY FROM matches the input against the null string before removing backslashes. Therefore, a null string such as \N cannot be confused with the actual data value \N (which would be represented as \\N).

The following special backslash sequences are recognized by COPY FROM:

Sequence	Represents
\b	Backspace (ASCII 8)
\f	Form feed (ASCII 12)
\n	Newline (ASCII 10)
\r	Carriage return (ASCII 13)
\t	Tab (ASCII 9)
\v	Vertical tab (ASCII 11)
digits	Backslash followed by one to three octal digits specifies the character with that numeric code
\x*digits*	Backslash x followed by one or two hex digits specifies the character with that numeric code

Presently, COPY TO will never emit an octal or hex-digits backslash sequence, but it does use the other sequences listed above for those control characters.

Any other backslashed character that is not mentioned in the above table will be taken to represent itself. However, beware of adding backslashes unnecessarily, since that might accidentally produce a string matching the end-of-data marker (\.) or the null string (\N by default). These strings will be recognized before any other backslash processing is done.

It is strongly recommended that applications generating COPY data convert data newlines and carriage returns to the \n and \r sequences respectively. At present it is possible to represent a data carriage return by a backslash and carriage return, and to represent a data newline by a backslash and newline. However, these representations might not be accepted in future releases. They are also highly vulnerable to corruption if the COPY file is transferred across different machines (for example, from Unix to Windows or vice versa).

COPY TO will terminate each row with a Unix-style newline ("\n"). Servers running on Microsoft Windows instead output carriage return/newline ("\r\n"), but only for COPY to a server file; for consistency across platforms, COPY TO STDOUT always sends "\n" regardless of server platform. COPY FROM can handle lines ending with newlines, carriage returns, or carriage return/newlines. To reduce the risk of error due to un-backslashed newlines or carriage returns that were meant as data, COPY FROM will complain if the line endings in the input are not all alike.

CSV Format

This format option is used for importing and exporting the Comma Separated Value (CSV) file format used by many other programs, such as spreadsheets. Instead of the escaping rules used by PostgreSQL's standard text format, it produces and recognizes the common CSV escaping mechanism.

The values in each record are separated by the DELIMITER character. If the value contains the delimiter character, the QUOTE character, the NULL string, a carriage return, or line feed character, then the whole value is prefixed and suffixed by the QUOTE character, and any occurrence within the value of a QUOTE character or the ESCAPE character is preceded by the escape character. You can also use FORCE_QUOTE to force quotes when outputting non-NULL values in specific columns.

The CSV format has no standard way to distinguish a NULL value from an empty string. PostgreSQL's COPY handles this by quoting. A NULL is output as the NULL parameter string and is not quoted, while a non-NULL value matching the NULL parameter string is quoted. For example, with the default settings, a NULL is written as an unquoted empty string, while an empty string data value is written with double quotes (""). Reading values follows similar rules. You can use FORCE_NOT_NULL to prevent NULL input comparisons for specific columns. You can also use FORCE_NULL to convert quoted null string data values to NULL.

Because backslash is not a special character in the CSV format, \., the end-of-data marker, could also appear as a data value. To avoid any misinterpretation, a \. data value appearing as a lone entry on a line is automatically quoted on output, and on input, if quoted, is not interpreted as the end-of-data marker. If you are loading a file created by another application that has a single unquoted column and might have a value of \., you might need to quote that value in the input file.

> **Note:** In CSV format, all characters are significant. A quoted value surrounded by white space, or any characters other than DELIMITER, will include those characters. This can cause errors if you import data from a system that pads CSV lines with white space out to some fixed width. If such a situation arises you might need to preprocess the CSV file to remove the trailing white space, before importing the data into PostgreSQL.

> **Note:** CSV format will both recognize and produce CSV files with quoted values containing embedded carriage returns and line feeds. Thus the files are not strictly one line per table row like text-format files.

> **Note:** Many programs produce strange and occasionally perverse CSV files, so the file format is more a convention than a standard. Thus you might encounter some files that cannot be imported using this mechanism, and COPY might produce files that other programs cannot process.

Binary Format

The binary format option causes all data to be stored/read as binary format rather than as text. It is somewhat faster than the text and CSV formats, but a binary-format file is less portable across machine architectures and PostgreSQL versions. Also, the binary format is very data type specific; for example it will not work to output binary data from a smallint column and read it into an integer column, even though that would work fine in text format.

The binary file format consists of a file header, zero or more tuples containing the row data, and a file trailer. Headers and data are in network byte order.

> **Note:** PostgreSQL releases before 7.4 used a different binary file format.

File Header

The file header consists of 15 bytes of fixed fields, followed by a variable-length header extension area. The fixed fields are:

Signature

11-byte sequence PGCOPY\n\377\r\n\0 — note that the zero byte is a required part of the signature. (The signature is designed to allow easy identification of files that have been munged by a non-8-bit-clean transfer. This signature will be changed by end-of-line-translation filters, dropped zero bytes, dropped high bits, or parity changes.)

Flags field

32-bit integer bit mask to denote important aspects of the file format. Bits are numbered from 0 (LSB) to 31 (MSB). Note that this field is stored in network byte order (most significant byte first), as are all the integer fields used in the file format. Bits 16-31 are reserved to denote critical file format issues; a reader should abort if it finds an unexpected bit set in this range. Bits 0-15 are reserved to signal backwards-compatible format issues; a reader should simply ignore any unexpected bits set in this range. Currently only one flag bit is defined, and the rest must be zero:

Bit 16

if 1, OIDs are included in the data; if 0, not

Header extension area length

32-bit integer, length in bytes of remainder of header, not including self. Currently, this is zero, and the first tuple follows immediately. Future changes to the format might allow additional data to be present in the header. A reader should silently skip over any header extension data it does not know what to do with.

The header extension area is envisioned to contain a sequence of self-identifying chunks. The flags field is not intended to tell readers what is in the extension area. Specific design of header extension contents is left for a later release.

This design allows for both backwards-compatible header additions (add header extension chunks, or set low-order flag bits) and non-backwards-compatible changes (set high-order flag bits to signal such changes, and add supporting data to the extension area if needed).

Tuples

Each tuple begins with a 16-bit integer count of the number of fields in the tuple. (Presently, all tuples in a table will have the same count, but that might not always be true.) Then, repeated for each field in the tuple, there is a 32-bit length word followed by that many bytes of field data. (The length word does not include itself, and can be zero.) As a special case, -1 indicates a NULL field value. No value bytes follow in the NULL case.

There is no alignment padding or any other extra data between fields.

Presently, all data values in a binary-format file are assumed to be in binary format (format code one). It is anticipated that a future extension might add a header field that allows per-column format codes to be specified.

To determine the appropriate binary format for the actual tuple data you should consult the PostgreSQL source, in particular the `*send` and `*recv` functions for each column's data type (typically these functions are found in the `src/backend/utils/adt/` directory of the source distribution).

If OIDs are included in the file, the OID field immediately follows the field-count word. It is a normal field except that it's not included in the field-count. In particular it has a length word — this will allow handling of 4-byte vs. 8-byte OIDs without too much pain, and will allow OIDs to be shown as null if that ever proves desirable.

File Trailer

The file trailer consists of a 16-bit integer word containing -1. This is easily distinguished from a tuple's field-count word.

A reader should report an error if a field-count word is neither -1 nor the expected number of columns. This provides an extra check against somehow getting out of sync with the data.

Examples

The following example copies a table to the client using the vertical bar (|) as the field delimiter:

```
COPY country TO STDOUT (DELIMITER '|');
```

To copy data from a file into the `country` table:

```
COPY country FROM '/usr1/proj/bray/sql/country_data';
```

To copy into a file just the countries whose names start with 'A':

```
COPY (SELECT * FROM country WHERE country_name LIKE 'A%') TO '/usr1/proj/bray/s
```

To copy into a compressed file, you can pipe the output through an external compression program:

```
COPY country TO PROGRAM 'gzip > /usr1/proj/bray/sql/country_data.gz';
```

Here is a sample of data suitable for copying into a table from `STDIN`:

```
AF      AFGHANISTAN
AL      ALBANIA
DZ      ALGERIA
```

```
ZM      ZAMBIA
ZW      ZIMBABWE
```

Note that the white space on each line is actually a tab character.

The following is the same data, output in binary format. The data is shown after filtering through the Unix utility `od -c`. The table has three columns; the first has type `char(2)`, the second has type `text`, and the third has type `integer`. All the rows have a null value in the third column.

```
0000000    P   G   C   O   P   Y  \n 377  \r  \n  \0  \0  \0  \0  \0  \0
0000020   \0  \0  \0  \0 003  \0  \0  \0 002   A   F  \0  \0  \0 013   A
0000040    F   G   H   A   N   I   S   T   A   N 377 377 377 377  \0 003
0000060   \0  \0  \0 002   A   L  \0  \0  \0 007   A   L   B   A   N   I
0000100    A 377 377 377 377  \0 003  \0  \0  \0 002   D   Z  \0  \0  \0
0000120  007   A   L   G   E   R   I   A 377 377 377 377  \0 003  \0  \0
0000140   \0 002   Z   M  \0  \0  \0 006   Z   A   M   B   I   A 377 377
0000160  377 377  \0 003  \0  \0  \0 002   Z   W  \0  \0  \0  \b   Z   I
0000200    M   B   A   B   W   E 377 377 377 377 377 377
```

Compatibility

There is no `COPY` statement in the SQL standard.

The following syntax was used before PostgreSQL version 9.0 and is still supported:

```
COPY table_name [ ( column_name [, ...] ) ]
    FROM { 'filename' | STDIN }
    [ [ WITH ]
          [ BINARY ]
          [ OIDS ]
          [ DELIMITER [ AS ] 'delimiter' ]
          [ NULL [ AS ] 'null string' ]
          [ CSV [ HEADER ]
                [ QUOTE [ AS ] 'quote' ]
                [ ESCAPE [ AS ] 'escape' ]
                [ FORCE NOT NULL column_name [, ...] ] ] ]

COPY { table_name [ ( column_name [, ...] ) ] | ( query ) }
    TO { 'filename' | STDOUT }
    [ [ WITH ]
          [ BINARY ]
          [ OIDS ]
          [ DELIMITER [ AS ] 'delimiter' ]
          [ NULL [ AS ] 'null string' ]
          [ CSV [ HEADER ]
                [ QUOTE [ AS ] 'quote' ]
                [ ESCAPE [ AS ] 'escape' ]
                [ FORCE QUOTE { column_name [, ...] | * } ] ] ]
```

Note that in this syntax, BINARY and CSV are treated as independent keywords, not as arguments of a FORMAT option.

The following syntax was used before PostgreSQL version 7.3 and is still supported:

```
COPY [ BINARY ] table_name [ WITH OIDS ]
    FROM { 'filename' | STDIN }
    [ [USING] DELIMITERS 'delimiter' ]
    [ WITH NULL AS 'null string' ]

COPY [ BINARY ] table_name [ WITH OIDS ]
    TO { 'filename' | STDOUT }
    [ [USING] DELIMITERS 'delimiter' ]
    [ WITH NULL AS 'null string' ]
```

CREATE AGGREGATE

Name

CREATE AGGREGATE — define a new aggregate function

Synopsis

```
CREATE AGGREGATE name ( [ argmode ] [ argname ] arg_data_type [ , ... ] ) (
    SFUNC = sfunc,
    STYPE = state_data_type
    [ , SSPACE = state_data_size ]
    [ , FINALFUNC = ffunc ]
    [ , FINALFUNC_EXTRA ]
    [ , INITCOND = initial_condition ]
    [ , MSFUNC = msfunc ]
    [ , MINVFUNC = minvfunc ]
    [ , MSTYPE = mstate_data_type ]
    [ , MSSPACE = mstate_data_size ]
    [ , MFINALFUNC = mffunc ]
    [ , MFINALFUNC_EXTRA ]
    [ , MINITCOND = minitial_condition ]
    [ , SORTOP = sort_operator ]
)

CREATE AGGREGATE name ( [ [ argmode ] [ argname ] arg_data_type [ , ... ] ]
                        ORDER BY [ argmode ] [ argname ] arg_data_type [ , ... ] )
    SFUNC = sfunc,
    STYPE = state_data_type
    [ , SSPACE = state_data_size ]
    [ , FINALFUNC = ffunc ]
    [ , FINALFUNC_EXTRA ]
    [ , INITCOND = initial_condition ]
    [ , HYPOTHETICAL ]
)

or the old syntax

CREATE AGGREGATE name (
    BASETYPE = base_type,
    SFUNC = sfunc,
    STYPE = state_data_type
    [ , SSPACE = state_data_size ]
    [ , FINALFUNC = ffunc ]
    [ , FINALFUNC_EXTRA ]
    [ , INITCOND = initial_condition ]
    [ , MSFUNC = msfunc ]
    [ , MINVFUNC = minvfunc ]
    [ , MSTYPE = mstate_data_type ]
    [ , MSSPACE = mstate_data_size ]
    [ , MFINALFUNC = mffunc ]
```

```
    [ , MFINALFUNC_EXTRA ]
    [ , MINITCOND = minitial_condition ]
    [ , SORTOP = sort_operator ]
)
```

Description

CREATE AGGREGATE defines a new aggregate function. Some basic and commonly-used aggregate functions are included with the distribution; they are documented in Section 9.20. If one defines new types or needs an aggregate function not already provided, then CREATE AGGREGATE can be used to provide the desired features.

If a schema name is given (for example, CREATE AGGREGATE myschema.myagg ...) then the aggregate function is created in the specified schema. Otherwise it is created in the current schema.

An aggregate function is identified by its name and input data type(s). Two aggregates in the same schema can have the same name if they operate on different input types. The name and input data type(s) of an aggregate must also be distinct from the name and input data type(s) of every ordinary function in the same schema. This behavior is identical to overloading of ordinary function names (see CREATE FUNCTION).

A simple aggregate function is made from one or two ordinary functions: a state transition function *sfunc*, and an optional final calculation function *ffunc*. These are used as follows:

```
sfunc( internal-state, next-data-values ) ---> next-internal-state
ffunc( internal-state ) ---> aggregate-value
```

PostgreSQL creates a temporary variable of data type *stype* to hold the current internal state of the aggregate. At each input row, the aggregate argument value(s) are calculated and the state transition function is invoked with the current state value and the new argument value(s) to calculate a new internal state value. After all the rows have been processed, the final function is invoked once to calculate the aggregate's return value. If there is no final function then the ending state value is returned as-is.

An aggregate function can provide an initial condition, that is, an initial value for the internal state value. This is specified and stored in the database as a value of type text, but it must be a valid external representation of a constant of the state value data type. If it is not supplied then the state value starts out null.

If the state transition function is declared "strict", then it cannot be called with null inputs. With such a transition function, aggregate execution behaves as follows. Rows with any null input values are ignored (the function is not called and the previous state value is retained). If the initial state value is null, then at the first row with all-nonnull input values, the first argument value replaces the state value, and the transition function is invoked at each subsequent row with all-nonnull input values. This is handy for implementing aggregates like max. Note that this behavior is only available when *state_data_type* is the same as the first *arg_data_type*. When these types are different, you must supply a nonnull initial condition or use a nonstrict transition function.

If the state transition function is not strict, then it will be called unconditionally at each input row, and must deal with null inputs and null state values for itself. This allows the aggregate author to have full control over the aggregate's handling of null values.

If the final function is declared "strict", then it will not be called when the ending state value is null; instead a null result will be returned automatically. (Of course this is just the normal behavior of strict functions.) In any case the final function has the option of returning a null value. For example, the final function for `avg` returns null when it sees there were zero input rows.

Sometimes it is useful to declare the final function as taking not just the state value, but extra parameters corresponding to the aggregate's input values. The main reason for doing this is if the final function is polymorphic and the state value's data type would be inadequate to pin down the result type. These extra parameters are always passed as NULL (and so the final function must not be strict when the `FINALFUNC_EXTRA` option is used), but nonetheless they are valid parameters. The final function could for example make use of `get_fn_expr_argtype` to identify the actual argument type in the current call.

An aggregate can optionally support *moving-aggregate mode*, as described in Section 35.10.1. This requires specifying the `MSFUNC`, `MINVFUNC`, and `MSTYPE` parameters, and optionally the `MSPACE`, `MFINALFUNC`, `MFINALFUNC_EXTRA`, and `MINITCOND` parameters. Except for `MINVFUNC`, these parameters work like the corresponding simple-aggregate parameters without `M`; they define a separate implementation of the aggregate that includes an inverse transition function.

The syntax with `ORDER BY` in the parameter list creates a special type of aggregate called an *ordered-set aggregate*; or if `HYPOTHETICAL` is specified, then a *hypothetical-set aggregate* is created. These aggregates operate over groups of sorted values in order-dependent ways, so that specification of an input sort order is an essential part of a call. Also, they can have *direct* arguments, which are arguments that are evaluated only once per aggregation rather than once per input row. Hypothetical-set aggregates are a subclass of ordered-set aggregates in which some of the direct arguments are required to match, in number and data types, the aggregated argument columns. This allows the values of those direct arguments to be added to the collection of aggregate-input rows as an additional "hypothetical" row.

Aggregates that behave like `MIN` or `MAX` can sometimes be optimized by looking into an index instead of scanning every input row. If this aggregate can be so optimized, indicate it by specifying a *sort operator*. The basic requirement is that the aggregate must yield the first element in the sort ordering induced by the operator; in other words:

```
SELECT agg(col) FROM tab;
```

must be equivalent to:

```
SELECT col FROM tab ORDER BY col USING sortop LIMIT 1;
```

Further assumptions are that the aggregate ignores null inputs, and that it delivers a null result if and only if there were no non-null inputs. Ordinarily, a data type's < operator is the proper sort operator for `MIN`, and > is the proper sort operator for `MAX`. Note that the optimization will never actually take effect unless the specified operator is the "less than" or "greater than" strategy member of a B-tree index operator class.

To be able to create an aggregate function, you must have `USAGE` privilege on the argument types, the state type(s), and the return type, as well as `EXECUTE` privilege on the transition and final functions.

Parameters

name

    The name (optionally schema-qualified) of the aggregate function to create.

argmode

> The mode of an argument: IN or VARIADIC. (Aggregate functions do not support OUT arguments.) If omitted, the default is IN. Only the last argument can be marked VARIADIC.

argname

> The name of an argument. This is currently only useful for documentation purposes. If omitted, the argument has no name.

arg_data_type

> An input data type on which this aggregate function operates. To create a zero-argument aggregate function, write * in place of the list of argument specifications. (An example of such an aggregate is count(*).)

base_type

> In the old syntax for CREATE AGGREGATE, the input data type is specified by a basetype parameter rather than being written next to the aggregate name. Note that this syntax allows only one input parameter. To define a zero-argument aggregate function with this syntax, specify the basetype as "ANY" (not *). Ordered-set aggregates cannot be defined with the old syntax.

sfunc

> The name of the state transition function to be called for each input row. For a normal *N*-argument aggregate function, the *sfunc* must take *N*+1 arguments, the first being of type *state_data_type* and the rest matching the declared input data type(s) of the aggregate. The function must return a value of type *state_data_type*. This function takes the current state value and the current input data value(s), and returns the next state value.

> For ordered-set (including hypothetical-set) aggregates, the state transition function receives only the current state value and the aggregated arguments, not the direct arguments. Otherwise it is the same.

state_data_type

> The data type for the aggregate's state value.

state_data_size

> The approximate average size (in bytes) of the aggregate's state value. If this parameter is omitted or is zero, a default estimate is used based on the *state_data_type*. The planner uses this value to estimate the memory required for a grouped aggregate query. The planner will consider using hash aggregation for such a query only if the hash table is estimated to fit in work_mem; therefore, large values of this parameter discourage use of hash aggregation.

ffunc

> The name of the final function called to compute the aggregate's result after all input rows have been traversed. For a normal aggregate, this function must take a single argument of type *state_data_type*. The return data type of the aggregate is defined as the return type of this function. If *ffunc* is not specified, then the ending state value is used as the aggregate's result, and the return type is *state_data_type*.

> For ordered-set (including hypothetical-set) aggregates, the final function receives not only the final state value, but also the values of all the direct arguments.

> If FINALFUNC_EXTRA is specified, then in addition to the final state value and any direct arguments, the final function receives extra NULL values corresponding to the aggregate's regular (aggregated)

arguments. This is mainly useful to allow correct resolution of the aggregate result type when a polymorphic aggregate is being defined.

initial_condition

The initial setting for the state value. This must be a string constant in the form accepted for the data type *state_data_type*. If not specified, the state value starts out null.

msfunc

The name of the forward state transition function to be called for each input row in moving-aggregate mode. This is exactly like the regular transition function, except that its first argument and result are of type *mstate_data_type*, which might be different from *state_data_type*.

minvfunc

The name of the inverse state transition function to be used in moving-aggregate mode. This function has the same argument and result types as *msfunc*, but it is used to remove a value from the current aggregate state, rather than add a value to it. The inverse transition function must have the same strictness attribute as the forward state transition function.

mstate_data_type

The data type for the aggregate's state value, when using moving-aggregate mode.

mstate_data_size

The approximate average size (in bytes) of the aggregate's state value, when using moving-aggregate mode. This works the same as *state_data_size*.

mffunc

The name of the final function called to compute the aggregate's result after all input rows have been traversed, when using moving-aggregate mode. This works the same as *ffunc*, except that its first argument's type is *mstate_data_type* and extra dummy arguments are specified by writing MFINALFUNC_EXTRA. The aggregate result type determined by *mffunc* or *mstate_data_type* must match that determined by the aggregate's regular implementation.

minitial_condition

The initial setting for the state value, when using moving-aggregate mode. This works the same as *initial_condition*.

sort_operator

The associated sort operator for a MIN- or MAX-like aggregate. This is just an operator name (possibly schema-qualified). The operator is assumed to have the same input data types as the aggregate (which must be a single-argument normal aggregate).

HYPOTHETICAL

For ordered-set aggregates only, this flag specifies that the aggregate arguments are to be processed according to the requirements for hypothetical-set aggregates: that is, the last few direct arguments must match the data types of the aggregated (WITHIN GROUP) arguments. The HYPOTHETICAL flag has no effect on run-time behavior, only on parse-time resolution of the data types and collations of the aggregate's arguments.

The parameters of CREATE AGGREGATE can be written in any order, not just the order illustrated above.

Notes

In parameters that specify support function names, you can write a schema name if needed, for example SFUNC = public.sum. Do not write argument types there, however — the argument types of the support functions are determined from other parameters.

If an aggregate supports moving-aggregate mode, it will improve calculation efficiency when the aggregate is used as a window function for a window with moving frame start (that is, a frame start mode other than UNBOUNDED PRECEDING). Conceptually, the forward transition function adds input values to the aggregate's state when they enter the window frame from the bottom, and the inverse transition function removes them again when they leave the frame at the top. So, when values are removed, they are always removed in the same order they were added. Whenever the inverse transition function is invoked, it will thus receive the earliest added but not yet removed argument value(s). The inverse transition function can assume that at least one row will remain in the current state after it removes the oldest row. (When this would not be the case, the window function mechanism simply starts a fresh aggregation, rather than using the inverse transition function.)

The forward transition function for moving-aggregate mode is not allowed to return NULL as the new state value. If the inverse transition function returns NULL, this is taken as an indication that the inverse function cannot reverse the state calculation for this particular input, and so the aggregate calculation will be redone from scratch for the current frame starting position. This convention allows moving-aggregate mode to be used in situations where there are some infrequent cases that are impractical to reverse out of the running state value.

If no moving-aggregate implementation is supplied, the aggregate can still be used with moving frames, but PostgreSQL will recompute the whole aggregation whenever the start of the frame moves. Note that whether or not the aggregate supports moving-aggregate mode, PostgreSQL can handle a moving frame end without recalculation; this is done by continuing to add new values to the aggregate's state. It is assumed that the final function does not damage the aggregate's state value, so that the aggregation can be continued even after an aggregate result value has been obtained for one set of frame boundaries.

The syntax for ordered-set aggregates allows VARIADIC to be specified for both the last direct parameter and the last aggregated (WITHIN GROUP) parameter. However, the current implementation restricts use of VARIADIC in two ways. First, ordered-set aggregates can only use VARIADIC "any", not other variadic array types. Second, if the last direct parameter is VARIADIC "any", then there can be only one aggregated parameter and it must also be VARIADIC "any". (In the representation used in the system catalogs, these two parameters are merged into a single VARIADIC "any" item, since pg_proc cannot represent functions with more than one VARIADIC parameter.) If the aggregate is a hypothetical-set aggregate, the direct arguments that match the VARIADIC "any" parameter are the hypothetical ones; any preceding parameters represent additional direct arguments that are not constrained to match the aggregated arguments.

Currently, ordered-set aggregates do not need to support moving-aggregate mode, since they cannot be used as window functions.

Examples

See Section 35.10.

Compatibility

CREATE AGGREGATE is a PostgreSQL language extension. The SQL standard does not provide for user-defined aggregate functions.

See Also

ALTER AGGREGATE, DROP AGGREGATE

CREATE CAST

Name

CREATE CAST — define a new cast

Synopsis

```
CREATE CAST (source_type AS target_type)
    WITH FUNCTION function_name (argument_type [, ...])
    [ AS ASSIGNMENT | AS IMPLICIT ]

CREATE CAST (source_type AS target_type)
    WITHOUT FUNCTION
    [ AS ASSIGNMENT | AS IMPLICIT ]

CREATE CAST (source_type AS target_type)
    WITH INOUT
    [ AS ASSIGNMENT | AS IMPLICIT ]
```

Description

CREATE CAST defines a new cast. A cast specifies how to perform a conversion between two data types. For example,

```
SELECT CAST(42 AS float8);
```

converts the integer constant 42 to type float8 by invoking a previously specified function, in this case float8(int4). (If no suitable cast has been defined, the conversion fails.)

Two types can be *binary coercible*, which means that the conversion can be performed "for free" without invoking any function. This requires that corresponding values use the same internal representation. For instance, the types text and varchar are binary coercible both ways. Binary coercibility is not necessarily a symmetric relationship. For example, the cast from xml to text can be performed for free in the present implementation, but the reverse direction requires a function that performs at least a syntax check. (Two types that are binary coercible both ways are also referred to as binary compatible.)

You can define a cast as an *I/O conversion cast* by using the WITH INOUT syntax. An I/O conversion cast is performed by invoking the output function of the source data type, and passing the resulting string to the input function of the target data type. In many common cases, this feature avoids the need to write a separate cast function for conversion. An I/O conversion cast acts the same as a regular function-based cast; only the implementation is different.

By default, a cast can be invoked only by an explicit cast request, that is an explicit CAST(x AS typename) or x::typename construct.

If the cast is marked AS ASSIGNMENT then it can be invoked implicitly when assigning a value to a column of the target data type. For example, supposing that foo.f1 is a column of type text, then:

```
INSERT INTO foo (f1) VALUES (42);
```

will be allowed if the cast from type `integer` to type `text` is marked `AS ASSIGNMENT`, otherwise not. (We generally use the term *assignment cast* to describe this kind of cast.)

If the cast is marked `AS IMPLICIT` then it can be invoked implicitly in any context, whether assignment or internally in an expression. (We generally use the term *implicit cast* to describe this kind of cast.) For example, consider this query:

```
SELECT 2 + 4.0;
```

The parser initially marks the constants as being of type `integer` and `numeric` respectively. There is no `integer + numeric` operator in the system catalogs, but there is a `numeric + numeric` operator. The query will therefore succeed if a cast from `integer` to `numeric` is available and is marked `AS IMPLICIT` — which in fact it is. The parser will apply the implicit cast and resolve the query as if it had been written

```
SELECT CAST ( 2 AS numeric ) + 4.0;
```

Now, the catalogs also provide a cast from `numeric` to `integer`. If that cast were marked `AS IMPLICIT` — which it is not — then the parser would be faced with choosing between the above interpretation and the alternative of casting the `numeric` constant to `integer` and applying the `integer + integer` operator. Lacking any knowledge of which choice to prefer, it would give up and declare the query ambiguous. The fact that only one of the two casts is implicit is the way in which we teach the parser to prefer resolution of a mixed `numeric`-and-`integer` expression as `numeric`; there is no built-in knowledge about that.

It is wise to be conservative about marking casts as implicit. An overabundance of implicit casting paths can cause PostgreSQL to choose surprising interpretations of commands, or to be unable to resolve commands at all because there are multiple possible interpretations. A good rule of thumb is to make a cast implicitly invokable only for information-preserving transformations between types in the same general type category. For example, the cast from `int2` to `int4` can reasonably be implicit, but the cast from `float8` to `int4` should probably be assignment-only. Cross-type-category casts, such as `text` to `int4`, are best made explicit-only.

> **Note:** Sometimes it is necessary for usability or standards-compliance reasons to provide multiple implicit casts among a set of types, resulting in ambiguity that cannot be avoided as above. The parser has a fallback heuristic based on *type categories* and *preferred types* that can help to provide desired behavior in such cases. See CREATE TYPE for more information.

To be able to create a cast, you must own the source or the target data type and have `USAGE` privilege on the other type. To create a binary-coercible cast, you must be superuser. (This restriction is made because an erroneous binary-coercible cast conversion can easily crash the server.)

Parameters

source_type

The name of the source data type of the cast.

target_type

> The name of the target data type of the cast.

function_name(argument_type [, ...])

> The function used to perform the cast. The function name can be schema-qualified. If it is not, the function will be looked up in the schema search path. The function's result data type must match the target type of the cast. Its arguments are discussed below.

WITHOUT FUNCTION

> Indicates that the source type is binary-coercible to the target type, so no function is required to perform the cast.

WITH INOUT

> Indicates that the cast is an I/O conversion cast, performed by invoking the output function of the source data type, and passing the resulting string to the input function of the target data type.

AS ASSIGNMENT

> Indicates that the cast can be invoked implicitly in assignment contexts.

AS IMPLICIT

> Indicates that the cast can be invoked implicitly in any context.

Cast implementation functions can have one to three arguments. The first argument type must be identical to or binary-coercible from the cast's source type. The second argument, if present, must be type integer; it receives the type modifier associated with the destination type, or -1 if there is none. The third argument, if present, must be type boolean; it receives true if the cast is an explicit cast, false otherwise. (Bizarrely, the SQL standard demands different behaviors for explicit and implicit casts in some cases. This argument is supplied for functions that must implement such casts. It is not recommended that you design your own data types so that this matters.)

The return type of a cast function must be identical to or binary-coercible to the cast's target type.

Ordinarily a cast must have different source and target data types. However, it is allowed to declare a cast with identical source and target types if it has a cast implementation function with more than one argument. This is used to represent type-specific length coercion functions in the system catalogs. The named function is used to coerce a value of the type to the type modifier value given by its second argument.

When a cast has different source and target types and a function that takes more than one argument, it supports converting from one type to another and applying a length coercion in a single step. When no such entry is available, coercion to a type that uses a type modifier involves two cast steps, one to convert between data types and a second to apply the modifier.

A cast to or from a domain type currently has no effect. Casting to or from a domain uses the casts associated with its underlying type.

Notes

Use DROP CAST to remove user-defined casts.

Remember that if you want to be able to convert types both ways you need to declare casts both ways explicitly.

It is normally not necessary to create casts between user-defined types and the standard string types (text, varchar, and char(n), as well as user-defined types that are defined to be in the string category). PostgreSQL provides automatic I/O conversion casts for that. The automatic casts to string types are treated as assignment casts, while the automatic casts from string types are explicit-only. You can override this behavior by declaring your own cast to replace an automatic cast, but usually the only reason to do so is if you want the conversion to be more easily invokable than the standard assignment-only or explicit-only setting. Another possible reason is that you want the conversion to behave differently from the type's I/O function; but that is sufficiently surprising that you should think twice about whether it's a good idea. (A small number of the built-in types do indeed have different behaviors for conversions, mostly because of requirements of the SQL standard.)

While not required, it is recommended that you continue to follow this old convention of naming cast implementation functions after the target data type. Many users are used to being able to cast data types using a function-style notation, that is *typename*(x). This notation is in fact nothing more nor less than a call of the cast implementation function; it is not specially treated as a cast. If your conversion functions are not named to support this convention then you will have surprised users. Since PostgreSQL allows overloading of the same function name with different argument types, there is no difficulty in having multiple conversion functions from different types that all use the target type's name.

> **Note:** Actually the preceding paragraph is an oversimplification: there are two cases in which a function-call construct will be treated as a cast request without having matched it to an actual function. If a function call *name*(x) does not exactly match any existing function, but *name* is the name of a data type and pg_cast provides a binary-coercible cast to this type from the type of x, then the call will be construed as a binary-coercible cast. This exception is made so that binary-coercible casts can be invoked using functional syntax, even though they lack any function. Likewise, if there is no pg_cast entry but the cast would be to or from a string type, the call will be construed as an I/O conversion cast. This exception allows I/O conversion casts to be invoked using functional syntax.

> **Note:** There is also an exception to the exception: I/O conversion casts from composite types to string types cannot be invoked using functional syntax, but must be written in explicit cast syntax (either CAST or :: notation). This exception was added because after the introduction of automatically-provided I/O conversion casts, it was found too easy to accidentally invoke such a cast when a function or column reference was intended.

Examples

To create an assignment cast from type bigint to type int4 using the function int4(bigint):

```
CREATE CAST (bigint AS int4) WITH FUNCTION int4(bigint) AS ASSIGNMENT;
```

(This cast is already predefined in the system.)

Compatibility

The CREATE CAST command conforms to the SQL standard, except that SQL does not make provisions for binary-coercible types or extra arguments to implementation functions. AS IMPLICIT is a PostgreSQL extension, too.

See Also

CREATE FUNCTION, CREATE TYPE, DROP CAST

CREATE COLLATION

Name

CREATE COLLATION — define a new collation

Synopsis

```
CREATE COLLATION name (
    [ LOCALE = locale, ]
    [ LC_COLLATE = lc_collate, ]
    [ LC_CTYPE = lc_ctype ]
)
CREATE COLLATION name FROM existing_collation
```

Description

CREATE COLLATION defines a new collation using the specified operating system locale settings, or by copying an existing collation.

To be able to create a collation, you must have CREATE privilege on the destination schema.

Parameters

name

> The name of the collation. The collation name can be schema-qualified. If it is not, the collation is defined in the current schema. The collation name must be unique within that schema. (The system catalogs can contain collations with the same name for other encodings, but these are ignored if the database encoding does not match.)

locale

> This is a shortcut for setting LC_COLLATE and LC_CTYPE at once. If you specify this, you cannot specify either of those parameters.

lc_collate

> Use the specified operating system locale for the LC_COLLATE locale category. The locale must be applicable to the current database encoding. (See CREATE DATABASE for the precise rules.)

lc_ctype

> Use the specified operating system locale for the LC_CTYPE locale category. The locale must be applicable to the current database encoding. (See CREATE DATABASE for the precise rules.)

existing_collation

> The name of an existing collation to copy. The new collation will have the same properties as the existing one, but it will be an independent object.

Notes

Use DROP COLLATION to remove user-defined collations.

See Section 22.2 for more information about collation support in PostgreSQL.

Examples

To create a collation from the operating system locale fr_FR.utf8 (assuming the current database encoding is UTF8):

```
CREATE COLLATION french (LOCALE = 'fr_FR.utf8');
```

To create a collation from an existing collation:

```
CREATE COLLATION german FROM "de_DE";
```

This can be convenient to be able to use operating-system-independent collation names in applications.

Compatibility

There is a CREATE COLLATION statement in the SQL standard, but it is limited to copying an existing collation. The syntax to create a new collation is a PostgreSQL extension.

See Also

ALTER COLLATION, DROP COLLATION

CREATE CONVERSION

Name

CREATE CONVERSION — define a new encoding conversion

Synopsis

```
CREATE [ DEFAULT ] CONVERSION name
    FOR source_encoding TO dest_encoding FROM function_name
```

Description

CREATE CONVERSION defines a new conversion between character set encodings. Also, conversions that are marked DEFAULT can be used for automatic encoding conversion between client and server. For this purpose, two conversions, from encoding A to B *and* from encoding B to A, must be defined.

To be able to create a conversion, you must have EXECUTE privilege on the function and CREATE privilege on the destination schema.

Parameters

DEFAULT

> The DEFAULT clause indicates that this conversion is the default for this particular source to destination encoding. There should be only one default encoding in a schema for the encoding pair.

name

> The name of the conversion. The conversion name can be schema-qualified. If it is not, the conversion is defined in the current schema. The conversion name must be unique within a schema.

source_encoding

> The source encoding name.

dest_encoding

> The destination encoding name.

function_name

> The function used to perform the conversion. The function name can be schema-qualified. If it is not, the function will be looked up in the path.

> The function must have the following signature:

```
conv_proc(
    integer,  -- source encoding ID
    integer,  -- destination encoding ID
    cstring,  -- source string (null terminated C string)
```

```
    internal, -- destination (fill with a null terminated C string)
    integer   -- source string length
) RETURNS void;
```

Notes

Use DROP CONVERSION to remove user-defined conversions.

The privileges required to create a conversion might be changed in a future release.

Examples

To create a conversion from encoding UTF8 to LATIN1 using myfunc:

```
CREATE CONVERSION myconv FOR 'UTF8' TO 'LATIN1' FROM myfunc;
```

Compatibility

CREATE CONVERSION is a PostgreSQL extension. There is no CREATE CONVERSION statement in the SQL standard, but a CREATE TRANSLATION statement that is very similar in purpose and syntax.

See Also

ALTER CONVERSION, CREATE FUNCTION, DROP CONVERSION

CREATE DATABASE

Name

CREATE DATABASE — create a new database

Synopsis

```
CREATE DATABASE name
    [ [ WITH ] [ OWNER [=] user_name ]
           [ TEMPLATE [=] template ]
           [ ENCODING [=] encoding ]
           [ LC_COLLATE [=] lc_collate ]
           [ LC_CTYPE [=] lc_ctype ]
           [ TABLESPACE [=] tablespace_name ]
           [ CONNECTION LIMIT [=] connlimit ] ]
```

Description

CREATE DATABASE creates a new PostgreSQL database.

To create a database, you must be a superuser or have the special CREATEDB privilege. See CREATE USER.

By default, the new database will be created by cloning the standard system database template1. A different template can be specified by writing TEMPLATE name. In particular, by writing TEMPLATE template0, you can create a virgin database containing only the standard objects predefined by your version of PostgreSQL. This is useful if you wish to avoid copying any installation-local objects that might have been added to template1.

Parameters

name

> The name of a database to create.

user_name

> The role name of the user who will own the new database, or DEFAULT to use the default (namely, the user executing the command). To create a database owned by another role, you must be a direct or indirect member of that role, or be a superuser.

template

> The name of the template from which to create the new database, or DEFAULT to use the default template (template1).

encoding

> Character set encoding to use in the new database. Specify a string constant (e.g., 'SQL_ASCII'), or an integer encoding number, or DEFAULT to use the default encoding (namely, the encoding of the template database). The character sets supported by the PostgreSQL server are described in Section 22.3.1. See below for additional restrictions.

lc_collate

> Collation order (LC_COLLATE) to use in the new database. This affects the sort order applied to strings, e.g. in queries with ORDER BY, as well as the order used in indexes on text columns. The default is to use the collation order of the template database. See below for additional restrictions.

lc_ctype

> Character classification (LC_CTYPE) to use in the new database. This affects the categorization of characters, e.g. lower, upper and digit. The default is to use the character classification of the template database. See below for additional restrictions.

tablespace_name

> The name of the tablespace that will be associated with the new database, or DEFAULT to use the template database's tablespace. This tablespace will be the default tablespace used for objects created in this database. See CREATE TABLESPACE for more information.

connlimit

> How many concurrent connections can be made to this database. -1 (the default) means no limit.

Optional parameters can be written in any order, not only the order illustrated above.

Notes

CREATE DATABASE cannot be executed inside a transaction block.

Errors along the line of "could not initialize database directory" are most likely related to insufficient permissions on the data directory, a full disk, or other file system problems.

Use DROP DATABASE to remove a database.

The program createdb is a wrapper program around this command, provided for convenience.

Database-level configuration parameters (set via ALTER DATABASE) are not copied from the template database.

Although it is possible to copy a database other than template1 by specifying its name as the template, this is not (yet) intended as a general-purpose "COPY DATABASE" facility. The principal limitation is that no other sessions can be connected to the template database while it is being copied. CREATE DATABASE will fail if any other connection exists when it starts; otherwise, new connections to the template database are locked out until CREATE DATABASE completes. See Section 21.3 for more information.

The character set encoding specified for the new database must be compatible with the chosen locale settings (LC_COLLATE and LC_CTYPE). If the locale is C (or equivalently POSIX), then all encodings are allowed, but for other locale settings there is only one encoding that will work properly. (On Windows, however, UTF-8 encoding can be used with any locale.) CREATE DATABASE will allow superusers to specify SQL_ASCII encoding regardless of the locale settings, but this choice is deprecated and may result in misbehavior of character-string functions if data that is not encoding-compatible with the locale is stored in the database.

The encoding and locale settings must match those of the template database, except when `template0` is used as template. This is because other databases might contain data that does not match the specified encoding, or might contain indexes whose sort ordering is affected by `LC_COLLATE` and `LC_CTYPE`. Copying such data would result in a database that is corrupt according to the new settings. `template0`, however, is known to not contain any data or indexes that would be affected.

The `CONNECTION LIMIT` option is only enforced approximately; if two new sessions start at about the same time when just one connection "slot" remains for the database, it is possible that both will fail. Also, the limit is not enforced against superusers.

Examples

To create a new database:

```
CREATE DATABASE lusiadas;
```

To create a database `sales` owned by user `salesapp` with a default tablespace of `salesspace`:

```
CREATE DATABASE sales OWNER salesapp TABLESPACE salesspace;
```

To create a database `music` which supports the ISO-8859-1 character set:

```
CREATE DATABASE music ENCODING 'LATIN1' TEMPLATE template0;
```

In this example, the `TEMPLATE template0` clause would only be required if `template1`'s encoding is not ISO-8859-1. Note that changing encoding might require selecting new `LC_COLLATE` and `LC_CTYPE` settings as well.

Compatibility

There is no `CREATE DATABASE` statement in the SQL standard. Databases are equivalent to catalogs, whose creation is implementation-defined.

See Also

ALTER DATABASE, DROP DATABASE

CREATE DOMAIN

Name

CREATE DOMAIN — define a new domain

Synopsis

```
CREATE DOMAIN name [ AS ] data_type
    [ COLLATE collation ]
    [ DEFAULT expression ]
    [ constraint [ ... ] ]

where constraint is:

[ CONSTRAINT constraint_name ]
{ NOT NULL | NULL | CHECK (expression) }
```

Description

CREATE DOMAIN creates a new domain. A domain is essentially a data type with optional constraints (restrictions on the allowed set of values). The user who defines a domain becomes its owner.

If a schema name is given (for example, CREATE DOMAIN myschema.mydomain ...) then the domain is created in the specified schema. Otherwise it is created in the current schema. The domain name must be unique among the types and domains existing in its schema.

Domains are useful for abstracting common constraints on fields into a single location for maintenance. For example, several tables might contain email address columns, all requiring the same CHECK constraint to verify the address syntax. Define a domain rather than setting up each table's constraint individually.

To be able to create a domain, you must have USAGE privilege on the underlying type.

Parameters

name

   The name (optionally schema-qualified) of a domain to be created.

data_type

   The underlying data type of the domain. This can include array specifiers.

collation

   An optional collation for the domain. If no collation is specified, the underlying data type's default collation is used. The underlying type must be collatable if COLLATE is specified.

DEFAULT *expression*

> The DEFAULT clause specifies a default value for columns of the domain data type. The value is any variable-free expression (but subqueries are not allowed). The data type of the default expression must match the data type of the domain. If no default value is specified, then the default value is the null value.

> The default expression will be used in any insert operation that does not specify a value for the column. If a default value is defined for a particular column, it overrides any default associated with the domain. In turn, the domain default overrides any default value associated with the underlying data type.

CONSTRAINT *constraint_name*

> An optional name for a constraint. If not specified, the system generates a name.

NOT NULL

> Values of this domain are normally prevented from being null. However, it is still possible for a domain with this constraint to take a null value if it is assigned a matching domain type that has become null, e.g. via a LEFT OUTER JOIN, or INSERT INTO tab (domcol) VALUES ((SELECT domcol FROM tab WHERE false)).

NULL

> Values of this domain are allowed to be null. This is the default.

> This clause is only intended for compatibility with nonstandard SQL databases. Its use is discouraged in new applications.

CHECK (*expression*)

> CHECK clauses specify integrity constraints or tests which values of the domain must satisfy. Each constraint must be an expression producing a Boolean result. It should use the key word VALUE to refer to the value being tested.

> Currently, CHECK expressions cannot contain subqueries nor refer to variables other than VALUE.

Examples

This example creates the us_postal_code data type and then uses the type in a table definition. A regular expression test is used to verify that the value looks like a valid US postal code:

```
CREATE DOMAIN us_postal_code AS TEXT
CHECK(
   VALUE ~ '^\d{5}$'
OR VALUE ~ '^\d{5}-\d{4}$'
);

CREATE TABLE us_snail_addy (
  address_id SERIAL PRIMARY KEY,
  street1 TEXT NOT NULL,
  street2 TEXT,
  street3 TEXT,
  city TEXT NOT NULL,
  postal us_postal_code NOT NULL
```

```
);
```

Compatibility

The command CREATE DOMAIN conforms to the SQL standard.

See Also

ALTER DOMAIN, DROP DOMAIN

CREATE EVENT TRIGGER

Name

CREATE EVENT TRIGGER — define a new event trigger

Synopsis

```
CREATE EVENT TRIGGER name
  ON event
  [ WHEN filter_variable IN (filter_value [, ... ]) [ AND ... ] ]
  EXECUTE PROCEDURE function_name()
```

Description

CREATE EVENT TRIGGER creates a new event trigger. Whenever the designated event occurs and the WHEN condition associated with the trigger, if any, is satisfied, the trigger function will be executed. For a general introduction to event triggers, see Chapter 37. The user who creates an event trigger becomes its owner.

Parameters

name

> The name to give the new trigger. This name must be unique within the database.

event

> The name of the event that triggers a call to the given function. See Section 37.1 for more information on event names.

filter_variable

> The name of a variable used to filter events. This makes it possible to restrict the firing of the trigger to a subset of the cases in which it is supported. Currently the only supported filter_variable is TAG.

filter_value

> A list of values for the associated filter_variable for which the trigger should fire. For TAG, this means a list of command tags (e.g. 'DROP FUNCTION').

function_name

> A user-supplied function that is declared as taking no argument and returning type event_trigger.

Notes

Only superusers can create event triggers.

Event triggers are disabled in single-user mode (see postgres). If an erroneous event trigger disables the database so much that you can't even drop the trigger, restart in single-user mode and you'll be able to do that.

Examples

Forbid the execution of any DDL command:

```
CREATE OR REPLACE FUNCTION abort_any_command()
  RETURNS event_trigger
 LANGUAGE plpgsql
  AS $$
BEGIN
  RAISE EXCEPTION 'command % is disabled', tg_tag;
END;
$$;

CREATE EVENT TRIGGER abort_ddl ON ddl_command_start
   EXECUTE PROCEDURE abort_any_command();
```

Compatibility

There is no CREATE EVENT TRIGGER statement in the SQL standard.

See Also

ALTER EVENT TRIGGER, DROP EVENT TRIGGER, CREATE FUNCTION

CREATE EXTENSION

Name

CREATE EXTENSION — install an extension

Synopsis

```
CREATE EXTENSION [ IF NOT EXISTS ] extension_name
    [ WITH ] [ SCHEMA schema_name ]
             [ VERSION version ]
             [ FROM old_version ]
```

Description

CREATE EXTENSION loads a new extension into the current database. There must not be an extension of the same name already loaded.

Loading an extension essentially amounts to running the extension's script file. The script will typically create new SQL objects such as functions, data types, operators and index support methods. CREATE EXTENSION additionally records the identities of all the created objects, so that they can be dropped again if DROP EXTENSION is issued.

Loading an extension requires the same privileges that would be required to create its component objects. For most extensions this means superuser or database owner privileges are needed. The user who runs CREATE EXTENSION becomes the owner of the extension for purposes of later privilege checks, as well as the owner of any objects created by the extension's script.

Parameters

IF NOT EXISTS

> Do not throw an error if an extension with the same name already exists. A notice is issued in this case. Note that there is no guarantee that the existing extension is anything like the one that would have been created from the currently-available script file.

extension_name

> The name of the extension to be installed. PostgreSQL will create the extension using details from the file SHAREDIR/extension/extension_name.control.

schema_name

> The name of the schema in which to install the extension's objects, given that the extension allows its contents to be relocated. The named schema must already exist. If not specified, and the extension's control file does not specify a schema either, the current default object creation schema is used.

Remember that the extension itself is not considered to be within any schema: extensions have unqualified names that must be unique database-wide. But objects belonging to the extension can be within schemas.

version

> The version of the extension to install. This can be written as either an identifier or a string literal. The default version is whatever is specified in the extension's control file.

old_version

> FROM *old_version* must be specified when, and only when, you are attempting to install an extension that replaces an "old style" module that is just a collection of objects not packaged into an extension. This option causes CREATE EXTENSION to run an alternative installation script that absorbs the existing objects into the extension, instead of creating new objects. Be careful that SCHEMA specifies the schema containing these pre-existing objects.

> The value to use for *old_version* is determined by the extension's author, and might vary if there is more than one version of the old-style module that can be upgraded into an extension. For the standard additional modules supplied with pre-9.1 PostgreSQL, use unpackaged for *old_version* when updating a module to extension style.

Notes

Before you can use CREATE EXTENSION to load an extension into a database, the extension's supporting files must be installed. Information about installing the extensions supplied with PostgreSQL can be found in Additional Supplied Modules.

The extensions currently available for loading can be identified from the pg_available_extensions or pg_available_extension_versions system views.

For information about writing new extensions, see Section 35.15.

Examples

Install the hstore extension into the current database:

```
CREATE EXTENSION hstore;
```

Update a pre-9.1 installation of hstore into extension style:

```
CREATE EXTENSION hstore SCHEMA public FROM unpackaged;
```

Be careful to specify the schema in which you installed the existing hstore objects.

Compatibility

CREATE EXTENSION is a PostgreSQL extension.

See Also

ALTER EXTENSION, DROP EXTENSION

CREATE FOREIGN DATA WRAPPER

Name

CREATE FOREIGN DATA WRAPPER — define a new foreign-data wrapper

Synopsis

```
CREATE FOREIGN DATA WRAPPER name
    [ HANDLER handler_function | NO HANDLER ]
    [ VALIDATOR validator_function | NO VALIDATOR ]
    [ OPTIONS ( option 'value' [, ... ] ) ]
```

Description

CREATE FOREIGN DATA WRAPPER creates a new foreign-data wrapper. The user who defines a foreign-data wrapper becomes its owner.

The foreign-data wrapper name must be unique within the database.

Only superusers can create foreign-data wrappers.

Parameters

name

> The name of the foreign-data wrapper to be created.

HANDLER handler_function

> handler_function is the name of a previously registered function that will be called to retrieve the execution functions for foreign tables. The handler function must take no arguments, and its return type must be fdw_handler.

> It is possible to create a foreign-data wrapper with no handler function, but foreign tables using such a wrapper can only be declared, not accessed.

VALIDATOR validator_function

> validator_function is the name of a previously registered function that will be called to check the generic options given to the foreign-data wrapper, as well as options for foreign servers, user mappings and foreign tables using the foreign-data wrapper. If no validator function or NO VALIDATOR is specified, then options will not be checked at creation time. (Foreign-data wrappers will possibly ignore or reject invalid option specifications at run time, depending on the implementation.) The validator function must take two arguments: one of type text[], which will contain the array of options as stored in the system catalogs, and one of type oid, which will be the OID of the system catalog containing the options. The return type is ignored; the function should report invalid options using the ereport(ERROR) function.

```
OPTIONS ( option 'value' [, ... ] )
```

This clause specifies options for the new foreign-data wrapper. The allowed option names and values are specific to each foreign data wrapper and are validated using the foreign-data wrapper's validator function. Option names must be unique.

Notes

PostgreSQL's foreign-data functionality is still under active development. Optimization of queries is primitive (and mostly left to the wrapper, too). Thus, there is considerable room for future performance improvements.

Examples

Create a useless foreign-data wrapper `dummy`:

```
CREATE FOREIGN DATA WRAPPER dummy;
```

Create a foreign-data wrapper `file` with handler function `file_fdw_handler`:

```
CREATE FOREIGN DATA WRAPPER file HANDLER file_fdw_handler;
```

Create a foreign-data wrapper `mywrapper` with some options:

```
CREATE FOREIGN DATA WRAPPER mywrapper
    OPTIONS (debug 'true');
```

Compatibility

`CREATE FOREIGN DATA WRAPPER` conforms to ISO/IEC 9075-9 (SQL/MED), with the exception that the `HANDLER` and `VALIDATOR` clauses are extensions and the standard clauses `LIBRARY` and `LANGUAGE` are not implemented in PostgreSQL.

Note, however, that the SQL/MED functionality as a whole is not yet conforming.

See Also

ALTER FOREIGN DATA WRAPPER, DROP FOREIGN DATA WRAPPER, CREATE SERVER, CREATE USER MAPPING, CREATE FOREIGN TABLE

CREATE FOREIGN TABLE

Name

CREATE FOREIGN TABLE — define a new foreign table

Synopsis

```
CREATE FOREIGN TABLE [ IF NOT EXISTS ] table_name ( [
    column_name data_type [ OPTIONS ( option 'value' [, ... ] ) ] [ COLLATE collat.
    [, ... ]
] )
  SERVER server_name
[ OPTIONS ( option 'value' [, ... ] ) ]

where column_constraint is:

[ CONSTRAINT constraint_name ]
{ NOT NULL |
  NULL |
  DEFAULT default_expr }
```

Description

CREATE FOREIGN TABLE creates a new foreign table in the current database. The table will be owned by the user issuing the command.

If a schema name is given (for example, CREATE FOREIGN TABLE myschema.mytable ...) then the table is created in the specified schema. Otherwise it is created in the current schema. The name of the foreign table must be distinct from the name of any other foreign table, table, sequence, index, view, or materialized view in the same schema.

CREATE FOREIGN TABLE also automatically creates a data type that represents the composite type corresponding to one row of the foreign table. Therefore, foreign tables cannot have the same name as any existing data type in the same schema.

To be able to create a foreign table, you must have USAGE privilege on the foreign server, as well as USAGE privilege on all column types used in the table.

Parameters

IF NOT EXISTS

> Do not throw an error if a relation with the same name already exists. A notice is issued in this case. Note that there is no guarantee that the existing relation is anything like the one that would have been created.

table_name

> The name (optionally schema-qualified) of the table to be created.

column_name

> The name of a column to be created in the new table.

data_type

> The data type of the column. This can include array specifiers. For more information on the data types supported by PostgreSQL, refer to Chapter 8.

NOT NULL

> The column is not allowed to contain null values.

NULL

> The column is allowed to contain null values. This is the default.

> This clause is only provided for compatibility with non-standard SQL databases. Its use is discouraged in new applications.

DEFAULT *default_expr*

> The DEFAULT clause assigns a default data value for the column whose column definition it appears within. The value is any variable-free expression (subqueries and cross-references to other columns in the current table are not allowed). The data type of the default expression must match the data type of the column.

> The default expression will be used in any insert operation that does not specify a value for the column. If there is no default for a column, then the default is null.

server_name

> The name of an existing foreign server to use for the foreign table. For details on defining a server, see CREATE SERVER.

OPTIONS (*option* '*value*' [, ...])

> Options to be associated with the new foreign table or one of its columns. The allowed option names and values are specific to each foreign data wrapper and are validated using the foreign-data wrapper's validator function. Duplicate option names are not allowed (although it's OK for a table option and a column option to have the same name).

Examples

Create foreign table `films`, which will be accessed through the server `film_server`:

```
CREATE FOREIGN TABLE films (
    code        char(5) NOT NULL,
    title       varchar(40) NOT NULL,
    did         integer NOT NULL,
    date_prod   date,
    kind        varchar(10),
    len         interval hour to minute
)
```

```
SERVER film_server;
```

Compatibility

The CREATE FOREIGN TABLE command largely conforms to the SQL standard; however, much as with CREATE TABLE, NULL constraints and zero-column foreign tables are permitted. The ability to specify a default value is also a PostgreSQL extension.

See Also

ALTER FOREIGN TABLE, DROP FOREIGN TABLE, CREATE TABLE, CREATE SERVER

CREATE FUNCTION

Name

CREATE FUNCTION — define a new function

Synopsis

```
CREATE [ OR REPLACE ] FUNCTION
    name ( [ [ argmode ] [ argname ] argtype [ { DEFAULT | = } default_expr ] [, .
    [ RETURNS rettype
      | RETURNS TABLE ( column_name column_type [, ...] ) ]
  { LANGUAGE lang_name
    | WINDOW
    | IMMUTABLE | STABLE | VOLATILE | [ NOT ] LEAKPROOF
    | CALLED ON NULL INPUT | RETURNS NULL ON NULL INPUT | STRICT
    | [ EXTERNAL ] SECURITY INVOKER | [ EXTERNAL ] SECURITY DEFINER
    | COST execution_cost
    | ROWS result_rows
    | SET configuration_parameter { TO value | = value | FROM CURRENT }
    | AS 'definition'
    | AS 'obj_file', 'link_symbol'
  } ...
    [ WITH ( attribute [, ...] ) ]
```

Description

CREATE FUNCTION defines a new function. CREATE OR REPLACE FUNCTION will either create a new function, or replace an existing definition. To be able to define a function, the user must have the USAGE privilege on the language.

If a schema name is included, then the function is created in the specified schema. Otherwise it is created in the current schema. The name of the new function must not match any existing function with the same input argument types in the same schema. However, functions of different argument types can share a name (this is called *overloading*).

To replace the current definition of an existing function, use CREATE OR REPLACE FUNCTION. It is not possible to change the name or argument types of a function this way (if you tried, you would actually be creating a new, distinct function). Also, CREATE OR REPLACE FUNCTION will not let you change the return type of an existing function. To do that, you must drop and recreate the function. (When using OUT parameters, that means you cannot change the types of any OUT parameters except by dropping the function.)

When CREATE OR REPLACE FUNCTION is used to replace an existing function, the ownership and permissions of the function do not change. All other function properties are assigned the values specified or implied in the command. You must own the function to replace it (this includes being a member of the owning role).

If you drop and then recreate a function, the new function is not the same entity as the old; you will have to drop existing rules, views, triggers, etc. that refer to the old function. Use CREATE OR REPLACE FUNCTION to change a function definition without breaking objects that refer to the function. Also, ALTER FUNCTION can be used to change most of the auxiliary properties of an existing function.

The user that creates the function becomes the owner of the function.

To be able to create a function, you must have USAGE privilege on the argument types and the return type.

Parameters

name

> The name (optionally schema-qualified) of the function to create.

argmode

> The mode of an argument: IN, OUT, INOUT, or VARIADIC. If omitted, the default is IN. Only OUT arguments can follow a VARIADIC one. Also, OUT and INOUT arguments cannot be used together with the RETURNS TABLE notation.

argname

> The name of an argument. Some languages (including SQL and PL/pgSQL) let you use the name in the function body. For other languages the name of an input argument is just extra documentation, so far as the function itself is concerned; but you can use input argument names when calling a function to improve readability (see Section 4.3). In any case, the name of an output argument is significant, because it defines the column name in the result row type. (If you omit the name for an output argument, the system will choose a default column name.)

argtype

> The data type(s) of the function's arguments (optionally schema-qualified), if any. The argument types can be base, composite, or domain types, or can reference the type of a table column.

> Depending on the implementation language it might also be allowed to specify "pseudotypes" such as cstring. Pseudotypes indicate that the actual argument type is either incompletely specified, or outside the set of ordinary SQL data types.

> The type of a column is referenced by writing *table_name*.*column_name*%TYPE. Using this feature can sometimes help make a function independent of changes to the definition of a table.

default_expr

> An expression to be used as default value if the parameter is not specified. The expression has to be coercible to the argument type of the parameter. Only input (including INOUT) parameters can have a default value. All input parameters following a parameter with a default value must have default values as well.

rettype

> The return data type (optionally schema-qualified). The return type can be a base, composite, or domain type, or can reference the type of a table column. Depending on the implementation language it might also be allowed to specify "pseudotypes" such as cstring. If the function is not supposed to return a value, specify void as the return type.

When there are OUT or INOUT parameters, the RETURNS clause can be omitted. If present, it must agree with the result type implied by the output parameters: RECORD if there are multiple output parameters, or the same type as the single output parameter.

The SETOF modifier indicates that the function will return a set of items, rather than a single item.

The type of a column is referenced by writing *table_name.column_name%TYPE*.

column_name

The name of an output column in the RETURNS TABLE syntax. This is effectively another way of declaring a named OUT parameter, except that RETURNS TABLE also implies RETURNS SETOF.

column_type

The data type of an output column in the RETURNS TABLE syntax.

lang_name

The name of the language that the function is implemented in. It can be sql, c, internal, or the name of a user-defined procedural language, e.g. plpgsql. Enclosing the name in single quotes is deprecated and requires matching case.

WINDOW

WINDOW indicates that the function is a *window function* rather than a plain function. This is currently only useful for functions written in C. The WINDOW attribute cannot be changed when replacing an existing function definition.

IMMUTABLE
STABLE
VOLATILE

These attributes inform the query optimizer about the behavior of the function. At most one choice can be specified. If none of these appear, VOLATILE is the default assumption.

IMMUTABLE indicates that the function cannot modify the database and always returns the same result when given the same argument values; that is, it does not do database lookups or otherwise use information not directly present in its argument list. If this option is given, any call of the function with all-constant arguments can be immediately replaced with the function value.

STABLE indicates that the function cannot modify the database, and that within a single table scan it will consistently return the same result for the same argument values, but that its result could change across SQL statements. This is the appropriate selection for functions whose results depend on database lookups, parameter variables (such as the current time zone), etc. (It is inappropriate for AFTER triggers that wish to query rows modified by the current command.) Also note that the current_timestamp family of functions qualify as stable, since their values do not change within a transaction.

VOLATILE indicates that the function value can change even within a single table scan, so no optimizations can be made. Relatively few database functions are volatile in this sense; some examples are random(), currval(), timeofday(). But note that any function that has side-effects must be classified volatile, even if its result is quite predictable, to prevent calls from being optimized away; an example is setval().

For additional details see Section 35.6.

LEAKPROOF

> LEAKPROOF indicates that the function has no side effects. It reveals no information about its arguments other than by its return value. For example, a function which throws an error message for some argument values but not others, or which includes the argument values in any error message, is not leakproof. The query planner may push leakproof functions (but not others) into views created with the security_barrier option. See CREATE VIEW and Section 38.5. This option can only be set by the superuser.

CALLED ON NULL INPUT
RETURNS NULL ON NULL INPUT
STRICT

> CALLED ON NULL INPUT (the default) indicates that the function will be called normally when some of its arguments are null. It is then the function author's responsibility to check for null values if necessary and respond appropriately.

> RETURNS NULL ON NULL INPUT or STRICT indicates that the function always returns null whenever any of its arguments are null. If this parameter is specified, the function is not executed when there are null arguments; instead a null result is assumed automatically.

[EXTERNAL] SECURITY INVOKER
[EXTERNAL] SECURITY DEFINER

> SECURITY INVOKER indicates that the function is to be executed with the privileges of the user that calls it. That is the default. SECURITY DEFINER specifies that the function is to be executed with the privileges of the user that created it.

> The key word EXTERNAL is allowed for SQL conformance, but it is optional since, unlike in SQL, this feature applies to all functions not only external ones.

execution_cost

> A positive number giving the estimated execution cost for the function, in units of cpu_operator_cost. If the function returns a set, this is the cost per returned row. If the cost is not specified, 1 unit is assumed for C-language and internal functions, and 100 units for functions in all other languages. Larger values cause the planner to try to avoid evaluating the function more often than necessary.

result_rows

> A positive number giving the estimated number of rows that the planner should expect the function to return. This is only allowed when the function is declared to return a set. The default assumption is 1000 rows.

configuration_parameter
value

> The SET clause causes the specified configuration parameter to be set to the specified value when the function is entered, and then restored to its prior value when the function exits. SET FROM CURRENT saves the session's current value of the parameter as the value to be applied when the function is entered.

> If a SET clause is attached to a function, then the effects of a SET LOCAL command executed inside the function for the same variable are restricted to the function: the configuration parameter's prior value is still restored at function exit. However, an ordinary SET command (without LOCAL) overrides

the SET clause, much as it would do for a previous SET LOCAL command: the effects of such a command will persist after function exit, unless the current transaction is rolled back.

See SET and Chapter 18 for more information about allowed parameter names and values.

definition

> A string constant defining the function; the meaning depends on the language. It can be an internal function name, the path to an object file, an SQL command, or text in a procedural language.

> It is often helpful to use dollar quoting (see Section 4.1.2.4) to write the function definition string, rather than the normal single quote syntax. Without dollar quoting, any single quotes or backslashes in the function definition must be escaped by doubling them.

obj_file, link_symbol

> This form of the AS clause is used for dynamically loadable C language functions when the function name in the C language source code is not the same as the name of the SQL function. The string *obj_file* is the name of the file containing the dynamically loadable object, and *link_symbol* is the function's link symbol, that is, the name of the function in the C language source code. If the link symbol is omitted, it is assumed to be the same as the name of the SQL function being defined.

> When repeated CREATE FUNCTION calls refer to the same object file, the file is only loaded once per session. To unload and reload the file (perhaps during development), start a new session.

attribute

> The historical way to specify optional pieces of information about the function. The following attributes can appear here:

> isStrict

>> Equivalent to STRICT or RETURNS NULL ON NULL INPUT.

> isCachable

>> isCachable is an obsolete equivalent of IMMUTABLE; it's still accepted for backwards-compatibility reasons.

> Attribute names are not case-sensitive.

Refer to Section 35.3 for further information on writing functions.

Overloading

PostgreSQL allows function *overloading*; that is, the same name can be used for several different functions so long as they have distinct input argument types. However, the C names of all functions must be different, so you must give overloaded C functions different C names (for example, use the argument types as part of the C names).

Two functions are considered the same if they have the same names and *input* argument types, ignoring any OUT parameters. Thus for example these declarations conflict:

```
CREATE FUNCTION foo(int) ...
CREATE FUNCTION foo(int, out text) ...
```

Functions that have different argument type lists will not be considered to conflict at creation time, but if defaults are provided they might conflict in use. For example, consider

```
CREATE FUNCTION foo(int) ...
CREATE FUNCTION foo(int, int default 42) ...
```

A call `foo(10)` will fail due to the ambiguity about which function should be called.

Notes

The full SQL type syntax is allowed for declaring a function's arguments and return value. However, parenthesized type modifiers (e.g., the precision field for type `numeric`) are discarded by CREATE FUNCTION. Thus for example `CREATE FUNCTION foo (varchar(10))` ... is exactly the same as `CREATE FUNCTION foo (varchar)` ....

When replacing an existing function with `CREATE OR REPLACE FUNCTION`, there are restrictions on changing parameter names. You cannot change the name already assigned to any input parameter (although you can add names to parameters that had none before). If there is more than one output parameter, you cannot change the names of the output parameters, because that would change the column names of the anonymous composite type that describes the function's result. These restrictions are made to ensure that existing calls of the function do not stop working when it is replaced.

If a function is declared STRICT with a VARIADIC argument, the strictness check tests that the variadic array *as a whole* is non-null. The function will still be called if the array has null elements.

Examples

Here are some trivial examples to help you get started. For more information and examples, see Section 35.3.

```
CREATE FUNCTION add(integer, integer) RETURNS integer
    AS 'select $1 + $2;'
    LANGUAGE SQL
    IMMUTABLE
    RETURNS NULL ON NULL INPUT;
```

Increment an integer, making use of an argument name, in PL/pgSQL:

```
CREATE OR REPLACE FUNCTION increment(i integer) RETURNS integer AS $$
        BEGIN
                RETURN i + 1;
        END;
$$ LANGUAGE plpgsql;
```

Return a record containing multiple output parameters:

```
CREATE FUNCTION dup(in int, out f1 int, out f2 text)
```

```
        AS $$ SELECT $1, CAST($1 AS text) || ' is text' $$
        LANGUAGE SQL;

SELECT * FROM dup(42);
```

You can do the same thing more verbosely with an explicitly named composite type:

```
CREATE TYPE dup_result AS (f1 int, f2 text);

CREATE FUNCTION dup(int) RETURNS dup_result
        AS $$ SELECT $1, CAST($1 AS text) || ' is text' $$
        LANGUAGE SQL;

SELECT * FROM dup(42);
```

Another way to return multiple columns is to use a TABLE function:

```
CREATE FUNCTION dup(int) RETURNS TABLE(f1 int, f2 text)
        AS $$ SELECT $1, CAST($1 AS text) || ' is text' $$
        LANGUAGE SQL;

SELECT * FROM dup(42);
```

However, a TABLE function is different from the preceding examples, because it actually returns a *set* of records, not just one record.

Writing SECURITY DEFINER Functions Safely

Because a SECURITY DEFINER function is executed with the privileges of the user that created it, care is needed to ensure that the function cannot be misused. For security, search_path should be set to exclude any schemas writable by untrusted users. This prevents malicious users from creating objects that mask objects used by the function. Particularly important in this regard is the temporary-table schema, which is searched first by default, and is normally writable by anyone. A secure arrangement can be had by forcing the temporary schema to be searched last. To do this, write pg_temp as the last entry in search_path. This function illustrates safe usage:

```
CREATE FUNCTION check_password(uname TEXT, pass TEXT)
RETURNS BOOLEAN AS $$
DECLARE passed BOOLEAN;
BEGIN
        SELECT  (pwd = $2) INTO passed
        FROM    pwds
        WHERE   username = $1;

        RETURN passed;
END;
$$  LANGUAGE plpgsql
    SECURITY DEFINER
    -- Set a secure search_path: trusted schema(s), then 'pg_temp'.
    SET search_path = admin, pg_temp;
```

Before PostgreSQL version 8.3, the SET option was not available, and so older functions may contain rather complicated logic to save, set, and restore search_path. The SET option is far easier to use for this purpose.

Another point to keep in mind is that by default, execute privilege is granted to PUBLIC for newly created functions (see GRANT for more information). Frequently you will wish to restrict use of a security definer function to only some users. To do that, you must revoke the default PUBLIC privileges and then grant execute privilege selectively. To avoid having a window where the new function is accessible to all, create it and set the privileges within a single transaction. For example:

```
BEGIN;
CREATE FUNCTION check_password(uname TEXT, pass TEXT) ... SECURITY DEFINER;
REVOKE ALL ON FUNCTION check_password(uname TEXT, pass TEXT) FROM PUBLIC;
GRANT EXECUTE ON FUNCTION check_password(uname TEXT, pass TEXT) TO admins;
COMMIT;
```

Compatibility

A CREATE FUNCTION command is defined in SQL:1999 and later. The PostgreSQL version is similar but not fully compatible. The attributes are not portable, neither are the different available languages.

For compatibility with some other database systems, *argmode* can be written either before or after *argname*. But only the first way is standard-compliant.

For parameter defaults, the SQL standard specifies only the syntax with the DEFAULT key word. The syntax with = is used in T-SQL and Firebird.

See Also

ALTER FUNCTION, DROP FUNCTION, GRANT, LOAD, REVOKE, createlang

CREATE GROUP

Name

CREATE GROUP — define a new database role

Synopsis

```
CREATE GROUP name [ [ WITH ] option [ ... ] ]

where option can be:

    SUPERUSER | NOSUPERUSER
  | CREATEDB | NOCREATEDB
  | CREATEROLE | NOCREATEROLE
  | CREATEUSER | NOCREATEUSER
  | INHERIT | NOINHERIT
  | LOGIN | NOLOGIN
  | [ ENCRYPTED | UNENCRYPTED ] PASSWORD 'password'
  | VALID UNTIL 'timestamp'
  | IN ROLE role_name [, ...]
  | IN GROUP role_name [, ...]
  | ROLE role_name [, ...]
  | ADMIN role_name [, ...]
  | USER role_name [, ...]
  | SYSID uid
```

Description

CREATE GROUP is now an alias for CREATE ROLE.

Compatibility

There is no CREATE GROUP statement in the SQL standard.

See Also

CREATE ROLE

CREATE INDEX

Name

CREATE INDEX — define a new index

Synopsis

```
CREATE [ UNIQUE ] INDEX [ CONCURRENTLY ] [ name ] ON table_name [ USING method ]
    ( { column_name | ( expression ) } [ COLLATE collation ] [ opclass ] [ ASC | DE
    [ WITH ( storage_parameter = value [, ... ] ) ]
    [ TABLESPACE tablespace_name ]
    [ WHERE predicate ]
```

Description

CREATE INDEX constructs an index on the specified column(s) of the specified relation, which can be a table or a materialized view. Indexes are primarily used to enhance database performance (though inappropriate use can result in slower performance).

The key field(s) for the index are specified as column names, or alternatively as expressions written in parentheses. Multiple fields can be specified if the index method supports multicolumn indexes.

An index field can be an expression computed from the values of one or more columns of the table row. This feature can be used to obtain fast access to data based on some transformation of the basic data. For example, an index computed on upper(col) would allow the clause WHERE upper(col) = 'JIM' to use an index.

PostgreSQL provides the index methods B-tree, hash, GiST, SP-GiST, and GIN. Users can also define their own index methods, but that is fairly complicated.

When the WHERE clause is present, a *partial index* is created. A partial index is an index that contains entries for only a portion of a table, usually a portion that is more useful for indexing than the rest of the table. For example, if you have a table that contains both billed and unbilled orders where the unbilled orders take up a small fraction of the total table and yet that is an often used section, you can improve performance by creating an index on just that portion. Another possible application is to use WHERE with UNIQUE to enforce uniqueness over a subset of a table. See Section 11.8 for more discussion.

The expression used in the WHERE clause can refer only to columns of the underlying table, but it can use all columns, not just the ones being indexed. Presently, subqueries and aggregate expressions are also forbidden in WHERE. The same restrictions apply to index fields that are expressions.

All functions and operators used in an index definition must be "immutable", that is, their results must depend only on their arguments and never on any outside influence (such as the contents of another table or the current time). This restriction ensures that the behavior of the index is well-defined. To use a user-defined function in an index expression or WHERE clause, remember to mark the function immutable when you create it.

Parameters

UNIQUE

> Causes the system to check for duplicate values in the table when the index is created (if data already exist) and each time data is added. Attempts to insert or update data which would result in duplicate entries will generate an error.

CONCURRENTLY

> When this option is used, PostgreSQL will build the index without taking any locks that prevent concurrent inserts, updates, or deletes on the table; whereas a standard index build locks out writes (but not reads) on the table until it's done. There are several caveats to be aware of when using this option — see *Building Indexes Concurrently*.

name

> The name of the index to be created. No schema name can be included here; the index is always created in the same schema as its parent table. If the name is omitted, PostgreSQL chooses a suitable name based on the parent table's name and the indexed column name(s).

table_name

> The name (possibly schema-qualified) of the table to be indexed.

method

> The name of the index method to be used. Choices are btree, hash, gist, spgist and gin. The default method is btree.

column_name

> The name of a column of the table.

expression

> An expression based on one or more columns of the table. The expression usually must be written with surrounding parentheses, as shown in the syntax. However, the parentheses can be omitted if the expression has the form of a function call.

collation

> The name of the collation to use for the index. By default, the index uses the collation declared for the column to be indexed or the result collation of the expression to be indexed. Indexes with non-default collations can be useful for queries that involve expressions using non-default collations.

opclass

> The name of an operator class. See below for details.

ASC

> Specifies ascending sort order (which is the default).

DESC

> Specifies descending sort order.

NULLS FIRST

> Specifies that nulls sort before non-nulls. This is the default when DESC is specified.

NULLS LAST

> Specifies that nulls sort after non-nulls. This is the default when DESC is not specified.

storage_parameter

> The name of an index-method-specific storage parameter. See *Index Storage Parameters* for details.

tablespace_name

> The tablespace in which to create the index. If not specified, default_tablespace is consulted, or temp_tablespaces for indexes on temporary tables.

predicate

> The constraint expression for a partial index.

Index Storage Parameters

The optional WITH clause specifies *storage parameters* for the index. Each index method has its own set of allowed storage parameters. The B-tree, hash, GiST and SP-GiST index methods all accept this parameter:

FILLFACTOR

> The fillfactor for an index is a percentage that determines how full the index method will try to pack index pages. For B-trees, leaf pages are filled to this percentage during initial index build, and also when extending the index at the right (adding new largest key values). If pages subsequently become completely full, they will be split, leading to gradual degradation in the index's efficiency. B-trees use a default fillfactor of 90, but any integer value from 10 to 100 can be selected. If the table is static then fillfactor 100 is best to minimize the index's physical size, but for heavily updated tables a smaller fillfactor is better to minimize the need for page splits. The other index methods use fillfactor in different but roughly analogous ways; the default fillfactor varies between methods.

GiST indexes additionally accept this parameter:

BUFFERING

> Determines whether the buffering build technique described in Section 56.4.1 is used to build the index. With OFF it is disabled, with ON it is enabled, and with AUTO it is initially disabled, but turned on on-the-fly once the index size reaches effective_cache_size. The default is AUTO.

GIN indexes accept a different parameter:

FASTUPDATE

> This setting controls usage of the fast update technique described in Section 58.4.1. It is a Boolean parameter: ON enables fast update, OFF disables it. (Alternative spellings of ON and OFF are allowed as described in Section 18.1.) The default is ON.

> **Note:** Turning FASTUPDATE off via ALTER INDEX prevents future insertions from going into the list of pending index entries, but does not in itself flush previous entries. You might want to VACUUM the table afterward to ensure the pending list is emptied.

Building Indexes Concurrently

Creating an index can interfere with regular operation of a database. Normally PostgreSQL locks the table to be indexed against writes and performs the entire index build with a single scan of the table. Other transactions can still read the table, but if they try to insert, update, or delete rows in the table they will block until the index build is finished. This could have a severe effect if the system is a live production database. Very large tables can take many hours to be indexed, and even for smaller tables, an index build can lock out writers for periods that are unacceptably long for a production system.

PostgreSQL supports building indexes without locking out writes. This method is invoked by specifying the CONCURRENTLY option of CREATE INDEX. When this option is used, PostgreSQL must perform two scans of the table, and in addition it must wait for all existing transactions that could potentially use the index to terminate. Thus this method requires more total work than a standard index build and takes significantly longer to complete. However, since it allows normal operations to continue while the index is built, this method is useful for adding new indexes in a production environment. Of course, the extra CPU and I/O load imposed by the index creation might slow other operations.

In a concurrent index build, the index is actually entered into the system catalogs in one transaction, then two table scans occur in two more transactions. Any transaction active when the second table scan starts can block concurrent index creation until it completes, even transactions that only reference the table after the second table scan starts. Concurrent index creation serially waits for each old transaction to complete using the method outlined in section Section 48.60.

If a problem arises while scanning the table, such as a deadlock or a uniqueness violation in a unique index, the CREATE INDEX command will fail but leave behind an "invalid" index. This index will be ignored for querying purposes because it might be incomplete; however it will still consume update overhead. The psql \d command will report such an index as INVALID:

```
postgres=# \d tab
        Table "public.tab"
 Column |  Type   | Modifiers
--------+---------+-----------
 col    | integer |
Indexes:
    "idx" btree (col) INVALID
```

The recommended recovery method in such cases is to drop the index and try again to perform CREATE INDEX CONCURRENTLY. (Another possibility is to rebuild the index with REINDEX. However, since REINDEX does not support concurrent builds, this option is unlikely to seem attractive.)

Another caveat when building a unique index concurrently is that the uniqueness constraint is already being enforced against other transactions when the second table scan begins. This means that constraint violations could be reported in other queries prior to the index becoming available for use, or even in cases where the index build eventually fails. Also, if a failure does occur in the second scan, the "invalid" index continues to enforce its uniqueness constraint afterwards.

Concurrent builds of expression indexes and partial indexes are supported. Errors occurring in the evaluation of these expressions could cause behavior similar to that described above for unique constraint violations.

Regular index builds permit other regular index builds on the same table to occur in parallel, but only one concurrent index build can occur on a table at a time. In both cases, no other types of schema modification on the table are allowed meanwhile. Another difference is that a regular `CREATE INDEX` command can be performed within a transaction block, but `CREATE INDEX CONCURRENTLY` cannot.

Notes

See Chapter 11 for information about when indexes can be used, when they are not used, and in which particular situations they can be useful.

> ### Caution
>
> Hash index operations are not presently WAL-logged, so hash indexes might need to be rebuilt with `REINDEX` after a database crash if there were unwritten changes. Also, changes to hash indexes are not replicated over streaming or file-based replication after the initial base backup, so they give wrong answers to queries that subsequently use them. For these reasons, hash index use is presently discouraged.

Currently, only the B-tree, GiST and GIN index methods support multicolumn indexes. Up to 32 fields can be specified by default. (This limit can be altered when building PostgreSQL.) Only B-tree currently supports unique indexes.

An *operator class* can be specified for each column of an index. The operator class identifies the operators to be used by the index for that column. For example, a B-tree index on four-byte integers would use the `int4_ops` class; this operator class includes comparison functions for four-byte integers. In practice the default operator class for the column's data type is usually sufficient. The main point of having operator classes is that for some data types, there could be more than one meaningful ordering. For example, we might want to sort a complex-number data type either by absolute value or by real part. We could do this by defining two operator classes for the data type and then selecting the proper class when making an index. More information about operator classes is in Section 11.9 and in Section 35.14.

For index methods that support ordered scans (currently, only B-tree), the optional clauses `ASC`, `DESC`, `NULLS FIRST`, and/or `NULLS LAST` can be specified to modify the sort ordering of the index. Since an ordered index can be scanned either forward or backward, it is not normally useful to create a single-column `DESC` index — that sort ordering is already available with a regular index. The value of these options is that multicolumn indexes can be created that match the sort ordering requested by a mixed-ordering query, such as `SELECT ... ORDER BY x ASC, y DESC`. The `NULLS` options are useful if you need to support "nulls sort low" behavior, rather than the default "nulls sort high", in queries that depend on indexes to avoid sorting steps.

For most index methods, the speed of creating an index is dependent on the setting of maintenance_work_mem. Larger values will reduce the time needed for index creation, so long as you don't make it larger than the amount of memory really available, which would drive the machine into swapping. For hash indexes, the value of effective_cache_size is also relevant to index creation time: PostgreSQL will use one of two different hash index creation methods depending on whether the estimated index size is more or less than `effective_cache_size`. For best results, make sure that this parameter is also set to something reflective of available memory, and be careful that the sum of `maintenance_work_mem` and `effective_cache_size` is less than the machine's RAM less whatever space is needed by other programs.

Use DROP INDEX to remove an index.

Prior releases of PostgreSQL also had an R-tree index method. This method has been removed because it had no significant advantages over the GiST method. If USING rtree is specified, CREATE INDEX will interpret it as USING gist, to simplify conversion of old databases to GiST.

Examples

To create a B-tree index on the column title in the table films:

```
CREATE UNIQUE INDEX title_idx ON films (title);
```

To create an index on the expression lower(title), allowing efficient case-insensitive searches:

```
CREATE INDEX ON films ((lower(title)));
```

(In this example we have chosen to omit the index name, so the system will choose a name, typically films_lower_idx.)

To create an index with non-default collation:

```
CREATE INDEX title_idx_german ON films (title COLLATE "de_DE");
```

To create an index with non-default sort ordering of nulls:

```
CREATE INDEX title_idx_nulls_low ON films (title NULLS FIRST);
```

To create an index with non-default fill factor:

```
CREATE UNIQUE INDEX title_idx ON films (title) WITH (fillfactor = 70);
```

To create a GIN index with fast updates disabled:

```
CREATE INDEX gin_idx ON documents_table USING gin (locations) WITH (fastupdate
```

To create an index on the column code in the table films and have the index reside in the tablespace indexspace:

```
CREATE INDEX code_idx ON films (code) TABLESPACE indexspace;
```

To create a GiST index on a point attribute so that we can efficiently use box operators on the result of the conversion function:

```
CREATE INDEX pointloc
```

```
        ON points USING gist (box(location,location));
SELECT * FROM points
    WHERE box(location,location) && '(0,0),(1,1)'::box;
```

To create an index without locking out writes to the table:

```
CREATE INDEX CONCURRENTLY sales_quantity_index ON sales_table (quantity);
```

Compatibility

CREATE INDEX is a PostgreSQL language extension. There are no provisions for indexes in the SQL standard.

See Also

ALTER INDEX, DROP INDEX

CREATE LANGUAGE

Name

CREATE LANGUAGE — define a new procedural language

Synopsis

```
CREATE [ OR REPLACE ] [ PROCEDURAL ] LANGUAGE name
CREATE [ OR REPLACE ] [ TRUSTED ] [ PROCEDURAL ] LANGUAGE name
    HANDLER call_handler [ INLINE inline_handler ] [ VALIDATOR valfunction ]
```

Description

CREATE LANGUAGE registers a new procedural language with a PostgreSQL database. Subsequently, functions and trigger procedures can be defined in this new language.

> **Note:** As of PostgreSQL 9.1, most procedural languages have been made into "extensions", and should therefore be installed with CREATE EXTENSION not CREATE LANGUAGE. Direct use of CREATE LANGUAGE should now be confined to extension installation scripts. If you have a "bare" language in your database, perhaps as a result of an upgrade, you can convert it to an extension using CREATE EXTENSION langname FROM unpackaged.

CREATE LANGUAGE effectively associates the language name with handler function(s) that are responsible for executing functions written in the language. Refer to Chapter 52 for more information about language handlers.

There are two forms of the CREATE LANGUAGE command. In the first form, the user supplies just the name of the desired language, and the PostgreSQL server consults the pg_pltemplate system catalog to determine the correct parameters. In the second form, the user supplies the language parameters along with the language name. The second form can be used to create a language that is not defined in pg_pltemplate, but this approach is considered obsolescent.

When the server finds an entry in the pg_pltemplate catalog for the given language name, it will use the catalog data even if the command includes language parameters. This behavior simplifies loading of old dump files, which are likely to contain out-of-date information about language support functions.

Ordinarily, the user must have the PostgreSQL superuser privilege to register a new language. However, the owner of a database can register a new language within that database if the language is listed in the pg_pltemplate catalog and is marked as allowed to be created by database owners (tmpldbacreate is true). The default is that trusted languages can be created by database owners, but this can be adjusted by superusers by modifying the contents of pg_pltemplate. The creator of a language becomes its owner and can later drop it, rename it, or assign it to a new owner.

CREATE OR REPLACE LANGUAGE will either create a new language, or replace an existing definition. If the language already exists, its parameters are updated according to the values specified or taken from pg_pltemplate, but the language's ownership and permissions settings do not change, and any existing functions written in the language are assumed to still be valid. In addition to the normal privilege requirements for creating a language, the user must be superuser or owner of the existing language. The REPLACE case is mainly meant to be used to ensure that the language exists. If the language has a pg_pltemplate entry then REPLACE will not actually change anything about an existing definition, except in the unusual case where the pg_pltemplate entry has been modified since the language was created.

Parameters

TRUSTED

> TRUSTED specifies that the language does not grant access to data that the user would not otherwise have. If this key word is omitted when registering the language, only users with the PostgreSQL superuser privilege can use this language to create new functions.

PROCEDURAL

> This is a noise word.

name

> The name of the new procedural language. The name must be unique among the languages in the database.

> For backward compatibility, the name can be enclosed by single quotes.

HANDLER *call_handler*

> *call_handler* is the name of a previously registered function that will be called to execute the procedural language's functions. The call handler for a procedural language must be written in a compiled language such as C with version 1 call convention and registered with PostgreSQL as a function taking no arguments and returning the language_handler type, a placeholder type that is simply used to identify the function as a call handler.

INLINE *inline_handler*

> *inline_handler* is the name of a previously registered function that will be called to execute an anonymous code block (DO command) in this language. If no *inline_handler* function is specified, the language does not support anonymous code blocks. The handler function must take one argument of type internal, which will be the DO command's internal representation, and it will typically return void. The return value of the handler is ignored.

VALIDATOR *valfunction*

> *valfunction* is the name of a previously registered function that will be called when a new function in the language is created, to validate the new function. If no validator function is specified, then a new function will not be checked when it is created. The validator function must take one argument of type oid, which will be the OID of the to-be-created function, and will typically return void.

> A validator function would typically inspect the function body for syntactical correctness, but it can also look at other properties of the function, for example if the language cannot handle certain argument types. To signal an error, the validator function should use the ereport() function. The return value of the function is ignored.

The TRUSTED option and the support function name(s) are ignored if the server has an entry for the specified language name in pg_pltemplate.

Notes

The createlang program is a simple wrapper around the CREATE LANGUAGE command. It eases installation of procedural languages from the shell command line.

Use DROP LANGUAGE, or better yet the droplang program, to drop procedural languages.

The system catalog pg_language (see Section 48.28) records information about the currently installed languages. Also, createlang has an option to list the installed languages.

To create functions in a procedural language, a user must have the USAGE privilege for the language. By default, USAGE is granted to PUBLIC (i.e., everyone) for trusted languages. This can be revoked if desired.

Procedural languages are local to individual databases. However, a language can be installed into the template1 database, which will cause it to be available automatically in all subsequently-created databases.

The call handler function, the inline handler function (if any), and the validator function (if any) must already exist if the server does not have an entry for the language in pg_pltemplate. But when there is an entry, the functions need not already exist; they will be automatically defined if not present in the database. (This might result in CREATE LANGUAGE failing, if the shared library that implements the language is not available in the installation.)

In PostgreSQL versions before 7.3, it was necessary to declare handler functions as returning the place-holder type opaque, rather than language_handler. To support loading of old dump files, CREATE LANGUAGE will accept a function declared as returning opaque, but it will issue a notice and change the function's declared return type to language_handler.

Examples

The preferred way of creating any of the standard procedural languages is just:

```
CREATE LANGUAGE plperl;
```

For a language not known in the pg_pltemplate catalog, a sequence such as this is needed:

```
CREATE FUNCTION plsample_call_handler() RETURNS language_handler
    AS '$libdir/plsample'
    LANGUAGE C;
CREATE LANGUAGE plsample
    HANDLER plsample_call_handler;
```

Compatibility

CREATE LANGUAGE is a PostgreSQL extension.

See Also

ALTER LANGUAGE, CREATE FUNCTION, DROP LANGUAGE, GRANT, REVOKE, createlang, droplang

CREATE MATERIALIZED VIEW

Name

CREATE MATERIALIZED VIEW — define a new materialized view

Synopsis

```
CREATE MATERIALIZED VIEW table_name
    [ (column_name [, ...] ) ]
    [ WITH ( storage_parameter [= value] [, ... ] ) ]
    [ TABLESPACE tablespace_name ]
    AS query
    [ WITH [ NO ] DATA ]
```

Description

CREATE MATERIALIZED VIEW defines a materialized view of a query. The query is executed and used to populate the view at the time the command is issued (unless WITH NO DATA is used) and may be refreshed later using REFRESH MATERIALIZED VIEW.

CREATE MATERIALIZED VIEW is similar to CREATE TABLE AS, except that it also remembers the query used to initialize the view, so that it can be refreshed later upon demand. A materialized view has many of the same properties as a table, but there is no support for temporary materialized views or automatic generation of OIDs.

Parameters

table_name

   The name (optionally schema-qualified) of the materialized view to be created.

column_name

   The name of a column in the new materialized view. If column names are not provided, they are taken from the output column names of the query.

WITH (storage_parameter [= value] [, ...])

   This clause specifies optional storage parameters for the new materialized view; see *Storage Parameters* for more information. All parameters supported for CREATE TABLE are also supported for CREATE MATERIALIZED VIEW with the exception of OIDS. See CREATE TABLE for more information.

TABLESPACE tablespace_name

   The tablespace_name is the name of the tablespace in which the new materialized view is to be created. If not specified, default_tablespace is consulted.

`query`

A SELECT, TABLE, or VALUES command. This query will run within a security-restricted operation; in particular, calls to functions that themselves create temporary tables will fail.

`WITH [ NO ] DATA`

This clause specifies whether or not the materialized view should be populated at creation time. If not, the materialized view will be flagged as unscannable and cannot be queried until `REFRESH MATERIALIZED VIEW` is used.

Compatibility

`CREATE MATERIALIZED VIEW` is a PostgreSQL extension.

See Also

ALTER MATERIALIZED VIEW, CREATE TABLE AS, CREATE VIEW, DROP MATERIALIZED VIEW, REFRESH MATERIALIZED VIEW

CREATE OPERATOR

Name

CREATE OPERATOR — define a new operator

Synopsis

```
CREATE OPERATOR name (
    PROCEDURE = function_name
    [, LEFTARG = left_type ] [, RIGHTARG = right_type ]
    [, COMMUTATOR = com_op ] [, NEGATOR = neg_op ]
    [, RESTRICT = res_proc ] [, JOIN = join_proc ]
    [, HASHES ] [, MERGES ]
)
```

Description

CREATE OPERATOR defines a new operator, name. The user who defines an operator becomes its owner. If a schema name is given then the operator is created in the specified schema. Otherwise it is created in the current schema.

The operator name is a sequence of up to NAMEDATALEN-1 (63 by default) characters from the following list:

+ - * / < > = ~ ! @ # % ^ & | ` ?

There are a few restrictions on your choice of name:

- `--` and `/*` cannot appear anywhere in an operator name, since they will be taken as the start of a comment.

- A multicharacter operator name cannot end in + or -, unless the name also contains at least one of these characters:

  ~ ! @ # % ^ & | ` ?

  For example, @- is an allowed operator name, but *- is not. This restriction allows PostgreSQL to parse SQL-compliant commands without requiring spaces between tokens.

- The use of => as an operator name is deprecated. It may be disallowed altogether in a future release.

The operator != is mapped to <> on input, so these two names are always equivalent.

At least one of LEFTARG and RIGHTARG must be defined. For binary operators, both must be defined. For right unary operators, only LEFTARG should be defined, while for left unary operators only RIGHTARG should be defined.

The *function_name* procedure must have been previously defined using CREATE FUNCTION and must be defined to accept the correct number of arguments (either one or two) of the indicated types.

The other clauses specify optional operator optimization clauses. Their meaning is detailed in Section 35.13.

To be able to create an operator, you must have USAGE privilege on the argument types and the return type, as well as EXECUTE privilege on the underlying function. If a commutator or negator operator is specified, you must own these operators.

Parameters

name

The name of the operator to be defined. See above for allowable characters. The name can be schema-qualified, for example CREATE OPERATOR myschema.+ (...). If not, then the operator is created in the current schema. Two operators in the same schema can have the same name if they operate on different data types. This is called *overloading*.

function_name

The function used to implement this operator.

left_type

The data type of the operator's left operand, if any. This option would be omitted for a left-unary operator.

right_type

The data type of the operator's right operand, if any. This option would be omitted for a right-unary operator.

com_op

The commutator of this operator.

neg_op

The negator of this operator.

res_proc

The restriction selectivity estimator function for this operator.

join_proc

The join selectivity estimator function for this operator.

HASHES

Indicates this operator can support a hash join.

MERGES

Indicates this operator can support a merge join.

To give a schema-qualified operator name in *com_op* or the other optional arguments, use the OPERATOR() syntax, for example:

```
COMMUTATOR = OPERATOR(myschema.===) ,
```

Notes

Refer to Section 35.12 for further information.

It is not possible to specify an operator's lexical precedence in CREATE OPERATOR, because the parser's precedence behavior is hard-wired. See Section 4.1.6 for precedence details.

The obsolete options SORT1, SORT2, LTCMP, and GTCMP were formerly used to specify the names of sort operators associated with a merge-joinable operator. This is no longer necessary, since information about associated operators is found by looking at B-tree operator families instead. If one of these options is given, it is ignored except for implicitly setting MERGES true.

Use DROP OPERATOR to delete user-defined operators from a database. Use ALTER OPERATOR to modify operators in a database.

Examples

The following command defines a new operator, area-equality, for the data type box:

```
CREATE OPERATOR === (
    LEFTARG = box,
    RIGHTARG = box,
    PROCEDURE = area_equal_procedure,
    COMMUTATOR = ===,
    NEGATOR = !==,
    RESTRICT = area_restriction_procedure,
    JOIN = area_join_procedure,
    HASHES, MERGES
);
```

Compatibility

CREATE OPERATOR is a PostgreSQL extension. There are no provisions for user-defined operators in the SQL standard.

See Also

ALTER OPERATOR, CREATE OPERATOR CLASS, DROP OPERATOR

CREATE OPERATOR CLASS

Name

CREATE OPERATOR CLASS — define a new operator class

Synopsis

```
CREATE OPERATOR CLASS name [ DEFAULT ] FOR TYPE data_type
  USING index_method [ FAMILY family_name ] AS
  { OPERATOR strategy_number operator_name [ ( op_type, op_type ) ] [ FOR SEARCH |
  | FUNCTION support_number [ ( op_type [ , op_type ] ) ] function_name ( argument_
  | STORAGE storage_type
  } [, ... ]
```

Description

CREATE OPERATOR CLASS creates a new operator class. An operator class defines how a particular data type can be used with an index. The operator class specifies that certain operators will fill particular roles or "strategies" for this data type and this index method. The operator class also specifies the support procedures to be used by the index method when the operator class is selected for an index column. All the operators and functions used by an operator class must be defined before the operator class can be created.

If a schema name is given then the operator class is created in the specified schema. Otherwise it is created in the current schema. Two operator classes in the same schema can have the same name only if they are for different index methods.

The user who defines an operator class becomes its owner. Presently, the creating user must be a superuser. (This restriction is made because an erroneous operator class definition could confuse or even crash the server.)

CREATE OPERATOR CLASS does not presently check whether the operator class definition includes all the operators and functions required by the index method, nor whether the operators and functions form a self-consistent set. It is the user's responsibility to define a valid operator class.

Related operator classes can be grouped into *operator families*. To add a new operator class to an existing family, specify the FAMILY option in CREATE OPERATOR CLASS. Without this option, the new class is placed into a family named the same as the new class (creating that family if it doesn't already exist).

Refer to Section 35.14 for further information.

Parameters

name

The name of the operator class to be created. The name can be schema-qualified.

DEFAULT

> If present, the operator class will become the default operator class for its data type. At most one operator class can be the default for a specific data type and index method.

data_type

> The column data type that this operator class is for.

index_method

> The name of the index method this operator class is for.

family_name

> The name of the existing operator family to add this operator class to. If not specified, a family named the same as the operator class is used (creating it, if it doesn't already exist).

strategy_number

> The index method's strategy number for an operator associated with the operator class.

operator_name

> The name (optionally schema-qualified) of an operator associated with the operator class.

op_type

> In an OPERATOR clause, the operand data type(s) of the operator, or NONE to signify a left-unary or right-unary operator. The operand data types can be omitted in the normal case where they are the same as the operator class's data type.

> In a FUNCTION clause, the operand data type(s) the function is intended to support, if different from the input data type(s) of the function (for B-tree comparison functions and hash functions) or the class's data type (for B-tree sort support functions and all functions in GiST, SP-GiST and GIN operator classes). These defaults are correct, and so *op_type* need not be specified in FUNCTION clauses, except for the case of a B-tree sort support function that is meant to support cross-data-type comparisons.

sort_family_name

> The name (optionally schema-qualified) of an existing btree operator family that describes the sort ordering associated with an ordering operator.

> If neither FOR SEARCH nor FOR ORDER BY is specified, FOR SEARCH is the default.

support_number

> The index method's support procedure number for a function associated with the operator class.

function_name

> The name (optionally schema-qualified) of a function that is an index method support procedure for the operator class.

argument_type

> The parameter data type(s) of the function.

`storage_type`

> The data type actually stored in the index. Normally this is the same as the column data type, but some index methods (currently GiST and GIN) allow it to be different. The STORAGE clause must be omitted unless the index method allows a different type to be used.

The OPERATOR, FUNCTION, and STORAGE clauses can appear in any order.

Notes

Because the index machinery does not check access permissions on functions before using them, including a function or operator in an operator class is tantamount to granting public execute permission on it. This is usually not an issue for the sorts of functions that are useful in an operator class.

The operators should not be defined by SQL functions. A SQL function is likely to be inlined into the calling query, which will prevent the optimizer from recognizing that the query matches an index.

Before PostgreSQL 8.4, the OPERATOR clause could include a RECHECK option. This is no longer supported because whether an index operator is "lossy" is now determined on-the-fly at run time. This allows efficient handling of cases where an operator might or might not be lossy.

Examples

The following example command defines a GiST index operator class for the data type _int4 (array of int4). See the intarray module for the complete example.

```
CREATE OPERATOR CLASS gist__int_ops
    DEFAULT FOR TYPE _int4 USING gist AS
        OPERATOR        3       &&,
        OPERATOR        6       = (anyarray, anyarray),
        OPERATOR        7       @>,
        OPERATOR        8       <@,
        OPERATOR        20      @@ (_int4, query_int),
        FUNCTION        1       g_int_consistent (internal, _int4, int, oid, ir
        FUNCTION        2       g_int_union (internal, internal),
        FUNCTION        3       g_int_compress (internal),
        FUNCTION        4       g_int_decompress (internal),
        FUNCTION        5       g_int_penalty (internal, internal, internal),
        FUNCTION        6       g_int_picksplit (internal, internal),
        FUNCTION        7       g_int_same (_int4, _int4, internal);
```

Compatibility

CREATE OPERATOR CLASS is a PostgreSQL extension. There is no CREATE OPERATOR CLASS statement in the SQL standard.

See Also

ALTER OPERATOR CLASS, DROP OPERATOR CLASS, CREATE OPERATOR FAMILY, ALTER OPERATOR FAMILY

CREATE OPERATOR FAMILY

Name

CREATE OPERATOR FAMILY — define a new operator family

Synopsis

```
CREATE OPERATOR FAMILY name USING index_method
```

Description

CREATE OPERATOR FAMILY creates a new operator family. An operator family defines a collection of related operator classes, and perhaps some additional operators and support functions that are compatible with these operator classes but not essential for the functioning of any individual index. (Operators and functions that are essential to indexes should be grouped within the relevant operator class, rather than being "loose" in the operator family. Typically, single-data-type operators are bound to operator classes, while cross-data-type operators can be loose in an operator family containing operator classes for both data types.)

The new operator family is initially empty. It should be populated by issuing subsequent CREATE OPERATOR CLASS commands to add contained operator classes, and optionally ALTER OPERATOR FAMILY commands to add "loose" operators and their corresponding support functions.

If a schema name is given then the operator family is created in the specified schema. Otherwise it is created in the current schema. Two operator families in the same schema can have the same name only if they are for different index methods.

The user who defines an operator family becomes its owner. Presently, the creating user must be a superuser. (This restriction is made because an erroneous operator family definition could confuse or even crash the server.)

Refer to Section 35.14 for further information.

Parameters

name

The name of the operator family to be created. The name can be schema-qualified.

index_method

The name of the index method this operator family is for.

Compatibility

CREATE OPERATOR FAMILY is a PostgreSQL extension. There is no CREATE OPERATOR FAMILY statement in the SQL standard.

See Also

ALTER OPERATOR FAMILY, DROP OPERATOR FAMILY, CREATE OPERATOR CLASS, ALTER OPERATOR CLASS, DROP OPERATOR CLASS

CREATE ROLE

Name

CREATE ROLE — define a new database role

Synopsis

```
CREATE ROLE name [ [ WITH ] option [ ... ] ]

where option can be:

    SUPERUSER | NOSUPERUSER
  | CREATEDB | NOCREATEDB
  | CREATEROLE | NOCREATEROLE
  | CREATEUSER | NOCREATEUSER
  | INHERIT | NOINHERIT
  | LOGIN | NOLOGIN
  | REPLICATION | NOREPLICATION
  | CONNECTION LIMIT connlimit
  | [ ENCRYPTED | UNENCRYPTED ] PASSWORD 'password'
  | VALID UNTIL 'timestamp'
  | IN ROLE role_name [, ...]
  | IN GROUP role_name [, ...]
  | ROLE role_name [, ...]
  | ADMIN role_name [, ...]
  | USER role_name [, ...]
  | SYSID uid
```

Description

CREATE ROLE adds a new role to a PostgreSQL database cluster. A role is an entity that can own database objects and have database privileges; a role can be considered a "user", a "group", or both depending on how it is used. Refer to Chapter 20 and Chapter 19 for information about managing users and authentication. You must have CREATEROLE privilege or be a database superuser to use this command.

Note that roles are defined at the database cluster level, and so are valid in all databases in the cluster.

Parameters

name

    The name of the new role.

SUPERUSER
NOSUPERUSER

These clauses determine whether the new role is a "superuser", who can override all access restrictions within the database. Superuser status is dangerous and should be used only when really needed. You must yourself be a superuser to create a new superuser. If not specified, NOSUPERUSER is the default.

CREATEDB
NOCREATEDB

These clauses define a role's ability to create databases. If CREATEDB is specified, the role being defined will be allowed to create new databases. Specifying NOCREATEDB will deny a role the ability to create databases. If not specified, NOCREATEDB is the default.

CREATEROLE
NOCREATEROLE

These clauses determine whether a role will be permitted to create new roles (that is, execute CREATE ROLE). A role with CREATEROLE privilege can also alter and drop other roles. If not specified, NOCREATEROLE is the default.

CREATEUSER
NOCREATEUSER

These clauses are an obsolete, but still accepted, spelling of SUPERUSER and NOSUPERUSER. Note that they are *not* equivalent to CREATEROLE as one might naively expect!

INHERIT
NOINHERIT

These clauses determine whether a role "inherits" the privileges of roles it is a member of. A role with the INHERIT attribute can automatically use whatever database privileges have been granted to all roles it is directly or indirectly a member of. Without INHERIT, membership in another role only grants the ability to SET ROLE to that other role; the privileges of the other role are only available after having done so. If not specified, INHERIT is the default.

LOGIN
NOLOGIN

These clauses determine whether a role is allowed to log in; that is, whether the role can be given as the initial session authorization name during client connection. A role having the LOGIN attribute can be thought of as a user. Roles without this attribute are useful for managing database privileges, but are not users in the usual sense of the word. If not specified, NOLOGIN is the default, except when CREATE ROLE is invoked through its alternative spelling CREATE USER.

REPLICATION
NOREPLICATION

These clauses determine whether a role is allowed to initiate streaming replication or put the system in and out of backup mode. A role having the REPLICATION attribute is a very highly privileged role, and should only be used on roles actually used for replication. If not specified, NOREPLICATION is the default.

CONNECTION LIMIT *connlimit*

> If role can log in, this specifies how many concurrent connections the role can make. -1 (the default) means no limit.

PASSWORD *password*

> Sets the role's password. (A password is only of use for roles having the LOGIN attribute, but you can nonetheless define one for roles without it.) If you do not plan to use password authentication you can omit this option. If no password is specified, the password will be set to null and password authentication will always fail for that user. A null password can optionally be written explicitly as PASSWORD NULL.

ENCRYPTED
UNENCRYPTED

> These key words control whether the password is stored encrypted in the system catalogs. (If neither is specified, the default behavior is determined by the configuration parameter password_encryption.) If the presented password string is already in MD5-encrypted format, then it is stored encrypted as-is, regardless of whether ENCRYPTED or UNENCRYPTED is specified (since the system cannot decrypt the specified encrypted password string). This allows reloading of encrypted passwords during dump/restore.

> Note that older clients might lack support for the MD5 authentication mechanism that is needed to work with passwords that are stored encrypted.

VALID UNTIL '*timestamp*'

> The VALID UNTIL clause sets a date and time after which the role's password is no longer valid. If this clause is omitted the password will be valid for all time.

IN ROLE *role_name*

> The IN ROLE clause lists one or more existing roles to which the new role will be immediately added as a new member. (Note that there is no option to add the new role as an administrator; use a separate GRANT command to do that.)

IN GROUP *role_name*

> IN GROUP is an obsolete spelling of IN ROLE.

ROLE *role_name*

> The ROLE clause lists one or more existing roles which are automatically added as members of the new role. (This in effect makes the new role a "group".)

ADMIN *role_name*

> The ADMIN clause is like ROLE, but the named roles are added to the new role WITH ADMIN OPTION, giving them the right to grant membership in this role to others.

USER *role_name*

> The USER clause is an obsolete spelling of the ROLE clause.

SYSID *uid*

> The SYSID clause is ignored, but is accepted for backwards compatibility.

Notes

Use ALTER ROLE to change the attributes of a role, and DROP ROLE to remove a role. All the attributes specified by CREATE ROLE can be modified by later ALTER ROLE commands.

The preferred way to add and remove members of roles that are being used as groups is to use GRANT and REVOKE.

The VALID UNTIL clause defines an expiration time for a password only, not for the role *per se*. In particular, the expiration time is not enforced when logging in using a non-password-based authentication method.

The INHERIT attribute governs inheritance of grantable privileges (that is, access privileges for database objects and role memberships). It does not apply to the special role attributes set by CREATE ROLE and ALTER ROLE. For example, being a member of a role with CREATEDB privilege does not immediately grant the ability to create databases, even if INHERIT is set; it would be necessary to become that role via SET ROLE before creating a database.

The INHERIT attribute is the default for reasons of backwards compatibility: in prior releases of PostgreSQL, users always had access to all privileges of groups they were members of. However, NOINHERIT provides a closer match to the semantics specified in the SQL standard.

Be careful with the CREATEROLE privilege. There is no concept of inheritance for the privileges of a CREATEROLE-role. That means that even if a role does not have a certain privilege but is allowed to create other roles, it can easily create another role with different privileges than its own (except for creating roles with superuser privileges). For example, if the role "user" has the CREATEROLE privilege but not the CREATEDB privilege, nonetheless it can create a new role with the CREATEDB privilege. Therefore, regard roles that have the CREATEROLE privilege as almost-superuser-roles.

PostgreSQL includes a program createuser that has the same functionality as CREATE ROLE (in fact, it calls this command) but can be run from the command shell.

The CONNECTION LIMIT option is only enforced approximately; if two new sessions start at about the same time when just one connection "slot" remains for the role, it is possible that both will fail. Also, the limit is never enforced for superusers.

Caution must be exercised when specifying an unencrypted password with this command. The password will be transmitted to the server in cleartext, and it might also be logged in the client's command history or the server log. The command createuser, however, transmits the password encrypted. Also, psql contains a command \password that can be used to safely change the password later.

Examples

Create a role that can log in, but don't give it a password:

```
CREATE ROLE jonathan LOGIN;
```

Create a role with a password:

```
CREATE USER davide WITH PASSWORD 'jw8s0F4';
```

(CREATE USER is the same as CREATE ROLE except that it implies LOGIN.)

Create a role with a password that is valid until the end of 2004. After one second has ticked in 2005, the password is no longer valid.

```
CREATE ROLE miriam WITH LOGIN PASSWORD 'jw8s0F4' VALID UNTIL '2005-01-01';
```

Create a role that can create databases and manage roles:

```
CREATE ROLE admin WITH CREATEDB CREATEROLE;
```

Compatibility

The CREATE ROLE statement is in the SQL standard, but the standard only requires the syntax

```
CREATE ROLE name [ WITH ADMIN role_name ]
```

Multiple initial administrators, and all the other options of CREATE ROLE, are PostgreSQL extensions.

The SQL standard defines the concepts of users and roles, but it regards them as distinct concepts and leaves all commands defining users to be specified by each database implementation. In PostgreSQL we have chosen to unify users and roles into a single kind of entity. Roles therefore have many more optional attributes than they do in the standard.

The behavior specified by the SQL standard is most closely approximated by giving users the NOINHERIT attribute, while roles are given the INHERIT attribute.

See Also

SET ROLE, ALTER ROLE, DROP ROLE, GRANT, REVOKE, createuser

CREATE RULE

Name

CREATE RULE — define a new rewrite rule

Synopsis

```
CREATE [ OR REPLACE ] RULE name AS ON event
    TO table_name [ WHERE condition ]
    DO [ ALSO | INSTEAD ] { NOTHING | command | ( command ; command ... ) }

where event can be one of:

    SELECT | INSERT | UPDATE | DELETE
```

Description

CREATE RULE defines a new rule applying to a specified table or view. CREATE OR REPLACE RULE will either create a new rule, or replace an existing rule of the same name for the same table.

The PostgreSQL rule system allows one to define an alternative action to be performed on insertions, updates, or deletions in database tables. Roughly speaking, a rule causes additional commands to be executed when a given command on a given table is executed. Alternatively, an INSTEAD rule can replace a given command by another, or cause a command not to be executed at all. Rules are used to implement SQL views as well. It is important to realize that a rule is really a command transformation mechanism, or command macro. The transformation happens before the execution of the command starts. If you actually want an operation that fires independently for each physical row, you probably want to use a trigger, not a rule. More information about the rules system is in Chapter 38.

Presently, ON SELECT rules must be unconditional INSTEAD rules and must have actions that consist of a single SELECT command. Thus, an ON SELECT rule effectively turns the table into a view, whose visible contents are the rows returned by the rule's SELECT command rather than whatever had been stored in the table (if anything). It is considered better style to write a CREATE VIEW command than to create a real table and define an ON SELECT rule for it.

You can create the illusion of an updatable view by defining ON INSERT, ON UPDATE, and ON DELETE rules (or any subset of those that's sufficient for your purposes) to replace update actions on the view with appropriate updates on other tables. If you want to support INSERT RETURNING and so on, then be sure to put a suitable RETURNING clause into each of these rules.

There is a catch if you try to use conditional rules for complex view updates: there *must* be an unconditional INSTEAD rule for each action you wish to allow on the view. If the rule is conditional, or is not INSTEAD, then the system will still reject attempts to perform the update action, because it thinks it might end up trying to perform the action on the dummy table of the view in some cases. If you want to handle all the useful cases in conditional rules, add an unconditional DO INSTEAD NOTHING rule to ensure that the system understands it will never be called on to update the dummy table. Then make the conditional rules non-INSTEAD; in the cases where they are applied, they add to the default INSTEAD NOTHING action. (This method does not currently work to support RETURNING queries, however.)

> **Note:** A view that is simple enough to be automatically updatable (see CREATE VIEW) does not require a user-created rule in order to be updatable. While you can create an explicit rule anyway, the automatic update transformation will generally outperform an explicit rule.
>
> Another alternative worth considering is to use INSTEAD OF triggers (see CREATE TRIGGER) in place of rules.

Parameters

name

> The name of a rule to create. This must be distinct from the name of any other rule for the same table. Multiple rules on the same table and same event type are applied in alphabetical name order.

event

> The event is one of SELECT, INSERT, UPDATE, or DELETE.

table_name

> The name (optionally schema-qualified) of the table or view the rule applies to.

condition

> Any SQL conditional expression (returning boolean). The condition expression cannot refer to any tables except NEW and OLD, and cannot contain aggregate functions.

INSTEAD

> INSTEAD indicates that the commands should be executed *instead of* the original command.

ALSO

> ALSO indicates that the commands should be executed *in addition to* the original command.
>
> If neither ALSO nor INSTEAD is specified, ALSO is the default.

command

> The command or commands that make up the rule action. Valid commands are SELECT, INSERT, UPDATE, DELETE, or NOTIFY.

Within *condition* and *command*, the special table names NEW and OLD can be used to refer to values in the referenced table. NEW is valid in ON INSERT and ON UPDATE rules to refer to the new row being inserted or updated. OLD is valid in ON UPDATE and ON DELETE rules to refer to the existing row being updated or deleted.

Notes

You must be the owner of a table to create or change rules for it.

In a rule for INSERT, UPDATE, or DELETE on a view, you can add a RETURNING clause that emits the view's columns. This clause will be used to compute the outputs if the rule is triggered by an INSERT RETURNING, UPDATE RETURNING, or DELETE RETURNING command respectively. When the rule is triggered by a command without RETURNING, the rule's RETURNING clause will be ignored. The current implementation allows only unconditional INSTEAD rules to contain RETURNING; furthermore there can be at most one RETURNING clause among all the rules for the same event. (This ensures that there is only one candidate RETURNING clause to be used to compute the results.) RETURNING queries on the view will be rejected if there is no RETURNING clause in any available rule.

It is very important to take care to avoid circular rules. For example, though each of the following two rule definitions are accepted by PostgreSQL, the SELECT command would cause PostgreSQL to report an error because of recursive expansion of a rule:

```
CREATE RULE "_RETURN" AS
    ON SELECT TO t1
    DO INSTEAD
        SELECT * FROM t2;

CREATE RULE "_RETURN" AS
    ON SELECT TO t2
    DO INSTEAD
        SELECT * FROM t1;

SELECT * FROM t1;
```

Presently, if a rule action contains a NOTIFY command, the NOTIFY command will be executed unconditionally, that is, the NOTIFY will be issued even if there are not any rows that the rule should apply to. For example, in:

```
CREATE RULE notify_me AS ON UPDATE TO mytable DO ALSO NOTIFY mytable;

UPDATE mytable SET name = 'foo' WHERE id = 42;
```

one NOTIFY event will be sent during the UPDATE, whether or not there are any rows that match the condition id = 42. This is an implementation restriction that might be fixed in future releases.

Compatibility

CREATE RULE is a PostgreSQL language extension, as is the entire query rewrite system.

See Also

ALTER RULE, DROP RULE

CREATE SCHEMA

Name

CREATE SCHEMA — define a new schema

Synopsis

```
CREATE SCHEMA schema_name [ AUTHORIZATION user_name ] [ schema_element [ ... ] ]
CREATE SCHEMA AUTHORIZATION user_name [ schema_element [ ... ] ]
CREATE SCHEMA IF NOT EXISTS schema_name [ AUTHORIZATION user_name ]
CREATE SCHEMA IF NOT EXISTS AUTHORIZATION user_name
```

Description

CREATE SCHEMA enters a new schema into the current database. The schema name must be distinct from the name of any existing schema in the current database.

A schema is essentially a namespace: it contains named objects (tables, data types, functions, and operators) whose names can duplicate those of other objects existing in other schemas. Named objects are accessed either by "qualifying" their names with the schema name as a prefix, or by setting a search path that includes the desired schema(s). A CREATE command specifying an unqualified object name creates the object in the current schema (the one at the front of the search path, which can be determined with the function current_schema).

Optionally, CREATE SCHEMA can include subcommands to create objects within the new schema. The subcommands are treated essentially the same as separate commands issued after creating the schema, except that if the AUTHORIZATION clause is used, all the created objects will be owned by that user.

Parameters

schema_name

> The name of a schema to be created. If this is omitted, the user_name is used as the schema name. The name cannot begin with pg_, as such names are reserved for system schemas.

user_name

> The role name of the user who will own the new schema. If omitted, defaults to the user executing the command. To create a schema owned by another role, you must be a direct or indirect member of that role, or be a superuser.

schema_element

> An SQL statement defining an object to be created within the schema. Currently, only CREATE TABLE, CREATE VIEW, CREATE INDEX, CREATE SEQUENCE, CREATE TRIGGER and GRANT are accepted as clauses within CREATE SCHEMA. Other kinds of objects may be created in separate commands after the schema is created.

```
IF NOT EXISTS
```

Do nothing (except issuing a notice) if a schema with the same name already exists. `schema_element` subcommands cannot be included when this option is used.

Notes

To create a schema, the invoking user must have the CREATE privilege for the current database. (Of course, superusers bypass this check.)

Examples

Create a schema:

```
CREATE SCHEMA myschema;
```

Create a schema for user joe; the schema will also be named joe:

```
CREATE SCHEMA AUTHORIZATION joe;
```

Create a schema named test that will be owned by user joe, unless there already is a schema named test. (It does not matter whether joe owns the pre-existing schema.)

```
CREATE SCHEMA IF NOT EXISTS test AUTHORIZATION joe;
```

Create a schema and create a table and view within it:

```
CREATE SCHEMA hollywood
    CREATE TABLE films (title text, release date, awards text[])
    CREATE VIEW winners AS
        SELECT title, release FROM films WHERE awards IS NOT NULL;
```

Notice that the individual subcommands do not end with semicolons.

The following is an equivalent way of accomplishing the same result:

```
CREATE SCHEMA hollywood;
CREATE TABLE hollywood.films (title text, release date, awards text[]);
CREATE VIEW hollywood.winners AS
    SELECT title, release FROM hollywood.films WHERE awards IS NOT NULL;
```

Compatibility

The SQL standard allows a DEFAULT CHARACTER SET clause in CREATE SCHEMA, as well as more sub-command types than are presently accepted by PostgreSQL.

The SQL standard specifies that the subcommands in CREATE SCHEMA can appear in any order. The present PostgreSQL implementation does not handle all cases of forward references in subcommands; it might sometimes be necessary to reorder the subcommands in order to avoid forward references.

According to the SQL standard, the owner of a schema always owns all objects within it. PostgreSQL allows schemas to contain objects owned by users other than the schema owner. This can happen only if the schema owner grants the CREATE privilege on his schema to someone else, or a superuser chooses to create objects in it.

The IF NOT EXISTS option is a PostgreSQL extension.

See Also

ALTER SCHEMA, DROP SCHEMA

CREATE SEQUENCE

Name

CREATE SEQUENCE — define a new sequence generator

Synopsis

```
CREATE [ TEMPORARY | TEMP ] SEQUENCE name [ INCREMENT [ BY ] increment ]
    [ MINVALUE minvalue | NO MINVALUE ] [ MAXVALUE maxvalue | NO MAXVALUE ]
    [ START [ WITH ] start ] [ CACHE cache ] [ [ NO ] CYCLE ]
    [ OWNED BY { table_name.column_name | NONE } ]
```

Description

CREATE SEQUENCE creates a new sequence number generator. This involves creating and initializing a new special single-row table with the name name. The generator will be owned by the user issuing the command.

If a schema name is given then the sequence is created in the specified schema. Otherwise it is created in the current schema. Temporary sequences exist in a special schema, so a schema name cannot be given when creating a temporary sequence. The sequence name must be distinct from the name of any other sequence, table, index, view, or foreign table in the same schema.

After a sequence is created, you use the functions nextval, currval, and setval to operate on the sequence. These functions are documented in Section 9.16.

Although you cannot update a sequence directly, you can use a query like:

```
SELECT * FROM name;
```

to examine the parameters and current state of a sequence. In particular, the last_value field of the sequence shows the last value allocated by any session. (Of course, this value might be obsolete by the time it's printed, if other sessions are actively doing nextval calls.)

Parameters

TEMPORARY or TEMP

> If specified, the sequence object is created only for this session, and is automatically dropped on session exit. Existing permanent sequences with the same name are not visible (in this session) while the temporary sequence exists, unless they are referenced with schema-qualified names.

name

> The name (optionally schema-qualified) of the sequence to be created.

increment

The optional clause `INCREMENT BY` *increment* specifies which value is added to the current sequence value to create a new value. A positive value will make an ascending sequence, a negative one a descending sequence. The default value is 1.

minvalue
`NO MINVALUE`

The optional clause `MINVALUE` *minvalue* determines the minimum value a sequence can generate. If this clause is not supplied or `NO MINVALUE` is specified, then defaults will be used. The defaults are 1 and $-2^{63}-1$ for ascending and descending sequences, respectively.

maxvalue
`NO MAXVALUE`

The optional clause `MAXVALUE` *maxvalue* determines the maximum value for the sequence. If this clause is not supplied or `NO MAXVALUE` is specified, then default values will be used. The defaults are $2^{63}-1$ and -1 for ascending and descending sequences, respectively.

start

The optional clause `START WITH` *start* allows the sequence to begin anywhere. The default starting value is *minvalue* for ascending sequences and *maxvalue* for descending ones.

cache

The optional clause `CACHE` *cache* specifies how many sequence numbers are to be preallocated and stored in memory for faster access. The minimum value is 1 (only one value can be generated at a time, i.e., no cache), and this is also the default.

`CYCLE`
`NO CYCLE`

The `CYCLE` option allows the sequence to wrap around when the *maxvalue* or *minvalue* has been reached by an ascending or descending sequence respectively. If the limit is reached, the next number generated will be the *minvalue* or *maxvalue*, respectively.

If `NO CYCLE` is specified, any calls to `nextval` after the sequence has reached its maximum value will return an error. If neither `CYCLE` or `NO CYCLE` are specified, `NO CYCLE` is the default.

`OWNED BY` *table_name.column_name*
`OWNED BY NONE`

The `OWNED BY` option causes the sequence to be associated with a specific table column, such that if that column (or its whole table) is dropped, the sequence will be automatically dropped as well. The specified table must have the same owner and be in the same schema as the sequence. `OWNED BY NONE`, the default, specifies that there is no such association.

Notes

Use `DROP SEQUENCE` to remove a sequence.

Sequences are based on `bigint` arithmetic, so the range cannot exceed the range of an eight-byte integer (-9223372036854775808 to 9223372036854775807).

Unexpected results might be obtained if a *cache* setting greater than one is used for a sequence object that will be used concurrently by multiple sessions. Each session will allocate and cache successive sequence values during one access to the sequence object and increase the sequence object's last_value accordingly. Then, the next *cache*-1 uses of nextval within that session simply return the preallocated values without touching the sequence object. So, any numbers allocated but not used within a session will be lost when that session ends, resulting in "holes" in the sequence.

Furthermore, although multiple sessions are guaranteed to allocate distinct sequence values, the values might be generated out of sequence when all the sessions are considered. For example, with a *cache* setting of 10, session A might reserve values 1..10 and return nextval=1, then session B might reserve values 11..20 and return nextval=11 before session A has generated nextval=2. Thus, with a *cache* setting of one it is safe to assume that nextval values are generated sequentially; with a *cache* setting greater than one you should only assume that the nextval values are all distinct, not that they are generated purely sequentially. Also, last_value will reflect the latest value reserved by any session, whether or not it has yet been returned by nextval.

Another consideration is that a setval executed on such a sequence will not be noticed by other sessions until they have used up any preallocated values they have cached.

Examples

Create an ascending sequence called serial, starting at 101:

```
CREATE SEQUENCE serial START 101;
```

Select the next number from this sequence:

```
SELECT nextval('serial');

 nextval
---------
     101
```

Select the next number from this sequence:

```
SELECT nextval('serial');

 nextval
---------
     102
```

Use this sequence in an INSERT command:

```
INSERT INTO distributors VALUES (nextval('serial'), 'nothing');
```

Update the sequence value after a COPY FROM:

```
BEGIN;
COPY distributors FROM 'input_file';
SELECT setval('serial', max(id)) FROM distributors;
END;
```

Compatibility

CREATE SEQUENCE conforms to the SQL standard, with the following exceptions:

- The standard's AS <data type> expression is not supported.
- Obtaining the next value is done using the nextval() function instead of the standard's NEXT VALUE FOR expression.
- The OWNED BY clause is a PostgreSQL extension.

See Also

ALTER SEQUENCE, DROP SEQUENCE

CREATE SERVER

Name

CREATE SERVER — define a new foreign server

Synopsis

```
CREATE SERVER server_name [ TYPE 'server_type' ] [ VERSION 'server_version' ]
    FOREIGN DATA WRAPPER fdw_name
    [ OPTIONS ( option 'value' [, ... ] ) ]
```

Description

CREATE SERVER defines a new foreign server. The user who defines the server becomes its owner.

A foreign server typically encapsulates connection information that a foreign-data wrapper uses to access an external data resource. Additional user-specific connection information may be specified by means of user mappings.

The server name must be unique within the database.

Creating a server requires USAGE privilege on the foreign-data wrapper being used.

Parameters

server_name

   The name of the foreign server to be created.

server_type

   Optional server type, potentially useful to foreign-data wrappers.

server_version

   Optional server version, potentially useful to foreign-data wrappers.

fdw_name

   The name of the foreign-data wrapper that manages the server.

OPTIONS (option 'value' [, ...])

   This clause specifies the options for the server. The options typically define the connection details of the server, but the actual names and values are dependent on the server's foreign-data wrapper.

Notes

When using the dblink module, a foreign server's name can be used as an argument of the dblink_connect function to indicate the connection parameters. It is necessary to have the USAGE privilege on the foreign server to be able to use it in this way.

Examples

Create a server `myserver` that uses the foreign-data wrapper `postgres_fdw`:

```
CREATE SERVER myserver FOREIGN DATA WRAPPER postgres_fdw OPTIONS (host 'foo', c
```

See postgres_fdw for more details.

Compatibility

CREATE SERVER conforms to ISO/IEC 9075-9 (SQL/MED).

See Also

ALTER SERVER, DROP SERVER, CREATE FOREIGN DATA WRAPPER, CREATE FOREIGN TABLE, CREATE USER MAPPING

CREATE TABLE

Name

CREATE TABLE — define a new table

Synopsis

```
CREATE [ [ GLOBAL | LOCAL ] { TEMPORARY | TEMP } | UNLOGGED ] TABLE [ IF NOT EX
  { column_name data_type [ COLLATE collation ] [ column_constraint [ ... ] ]
    | table_constraint
    | LIKE source_table [ like_option ... ] }
    [, ... ]
] )
[ INHERITS ( parent_table [, ... ] ) ]
[ WITH ( storage_parameter [= value] [, ... ] ) | WITH OIDS | WITHOUT OIDS ]
[ ON COMMIT { PRESERVE ROWS | DELETE ROWS | DROP } ]
[ TABLESPACE tablespace_name ]

CREATE [ [ GLOBAL | LOCAL ] { TEMPORARY | TEMP } | UNLOGGED ] TABLE [ IF NOT EX
    OF type_name [ (
  { column_name WITH OPTIONS [ column_constraint [ ... ] ]
    | table_constraint }
    [, ... ]
) ]
[ WITH ( storage_parameter [= value] [, ... ] ) | WITH OIDS | WITHOUT OIDS ]
[ ON COMMIT { PRESERVE ROWS | DELETE ROWS | DROP } ]
[ TABLESPACE tablespace_name ]

where column_constraint is:

[ CONSTRAINT constraint_name ]
{ NOT NULL |
  NULL |
  CHECK ( expression ) [ NO INHERIT ] |
  DEFAULT default_expr |
  UNIQUE index_parameters |
  PRIMARY KEY index_parameters |
  REFERENCES reftable [ ( refcolumn ) ] [ MATCH FULL | MATCH PARTIAL | MATCH SIM
    [ ON DELETE action ] [ ON UPDATE action ] }
[ DEFERRABLE | NOT DEFERRABLE ] [ INITIALLY DEFERRED | INITIALLY IMMEDIATE ]

and table_constraint is:

[ CONSTRAINT constraint_name ]
{ CHECK ( expression ) [ NO INHERIT ] |
  UNIQUE ( column_name [, ... ] ) index_parameters |
  PRIMARY KEY ( column_name [, ... ] ) index_parameters |
  EXCLUDE [ USING index_method ] ( exclude_element WITH operator [, ... ] ) index_p
  FOREIGN KEY ( column_name [, ... ] ) REFERENCES reftable [ ( refcolumn [, ... ]
    [ MATCH FULL | MATCH PARTIAL | MATCH SIMPLE ] [ ON DELETE action ] [ ON UPD
```

```
[ DEFERRABLE | NOT DEFERRABLE ] [ INITIALLY DEFERRED | INITIALLY IMMEDIATE ]
```

and *like_option* is:

```
{ INCLUDING | EXCLUDING } { DEFAULTS | CONSTRAINTS | INDEXES | STORAGE | COMMEN
```

index_parameters in UNIQUE, PRIMARY KEY, and EXCLUDE constraints are:

```
[ WITH ( storage_parameter [= value] [, ... ] ) ]
[ USING INDEX TABLESPACE tablespace_name ]
```

exclude_element in an EXCLUDE constraint is:

```
{ column_name | ( expression ) } [ opclass ] [ ASC | DESC ] [ NULLS { FIRST | LAS1
```

Description

CREATE TABLE will create a new, initially empty table in the current database. The table will be owned by the user issuing the command.

If a schema name is given (for example, CREATE TABLE myschema.mytable ...) then the table is created in the specified schema. Otherwise it is created in the current schema. Temporary tables exist in a special schema, so a schema name cannot be given when creating a temporary table. The name of the table must be distinct from the name of any other table, sequence, index, view, or foreign table in the same schema.

CREATE TABLE also automatically creates a data type that represents the composite type corresponding to one row of the table. Therefore, tables cannot have the same name as any existing data type in the same schema.

The optional constraint clauses specify constraints (tests) that new or updated rows must satisfy for an insert or update operation to succeed. A constraint is an SQL object that helps define the set of valid values in the table in various ways.

There are two ways to define constraints: table constraints and column constraints. A column constraint is defined as part of a column definition. A table constraint definition is not tied to a particular column, and it can encompass more than one column. Every column constraint can also be written as a table constraint; a column constraint is only a notational convenience for use when the constraint only affects one column.

To be able to create a table, you must have USAGE privilege on all column types or the type in the OF clause, respectively.

Parameters

TEMPORARY or TEMP

> If specified, the table is created as a temporary table. Temporary tables are automatically dropped at the end of a session, or optionally at the end of the current transaction (see ON COMMIT below). Existing permanent tables with the same name are not visible to the current session while the tempo-

rary table exists, unless they are referenced with schema-qualified names. Any indexes created on a temporary table are automatically temporary as well.

The autovacuum daemon cannot access and therefore cannot vacuum or analyze temporary tables. For this reason, appropriate vacuum and analyze operations should be performed via session SQL commands. For example, if a temporary table is going to be used in complex queries, it is wise to run ANALYZE on the temporary table after it is populated.

Optionally, GLOBAL or LOCAL can be written before TEMPORARY or TEMP. This presently makes no difference in PostgreSQL and is deprecated; see *Compatibility*.

UNLOGGED

If specified, the table is created as an unlogged table. Data written to unlogged tables is not written to the write-ahead log (see Chapter 29), which makes them considerably faster than ordinary tables. However, they are not crash-safe: an unlogged table is automatically truncated after a crash or unclean shutdown. The contents of an unlogged table are also not replicated to standby servers. Any indexes created on an unlogged table are automatically unlogged as well.

IF NOT EXISTS

Do not throw an error if a relation with the same name already exists. A notice is issued in this case. Note that there is no guarantee that the existing relation is anything like the one that would have been created.

table_name

The name (optionally schema-qualified) of the table to be created.

OF *type_name*

Creates a *typed table*, which takes its structure from the specified composite type (name optionally schema-qualified). A typed table is tied to its type; for example the table will be dropped if the type is dropped (with DROP TYPE ... CASCADE).

When a typed table is created, then the data types of the columns are determined by the underlying composite type and are not specified by the CREATE TABLE command. But the CREATE TABLE command can add defaults and constraints to the table and can specify storage parameters.

column_name

The name of a column to be created in the new table.

data_type

The data type of the column. This can include array specifiers. For more information on the data types supported by PostgreSQL, refer to Chapter 8.

COLLATE *collation*

The COLLATE clause assigns a collation to the column (which must be of a collatable data type). If not specified, the column data type's default collation is used.

INHERITS (*parent_table* [, ...])

The optional INHERITS clause specifies a list of tables from which the new table automatically inherits all columns.

Use of INHERITS creates a persistent relationship between the new child table and its parent table(s). Schema modifications to the parent(s) normally propagate to children as well, and by default the data of the child table is included in scans of the parent(s).

If the same column name exists in more than one parent table, an error is reported unless the data types of the columns match in each of the parent tables. If there is no conflict, then the duplicate columns are merged to form a single column in the new table. If the column name list of the new table contains a column name that is also inherited, the data type must likewise match the inherited column(s), and the column definitions are merged into one. If the new table explicitly specifies a default value for the column, this default overrides any defaults from inherited declarations of the column. Otherwise, any parents that specify default values for the column must all specify the same default, or an error will be reported.

CHECK constraints are merged in essentially the same way as columns: if multiple parent tables and/or the new table definition contain identically-named CHECK constraints, these constraints must all have the same check expression, or an error will be reported. Constraints having the same name and expression will be merged into one copy. A constraint marked NO INHERIT in a parent will not be considered. Notice that an unnamed CHECK constraint in the new table will never be merged, since a unique name will always be chosen for it.

Column STORAGE settings are also copied from parent tables.

LIKE *source_table* [*like_option* ...]

> The LIKE clause specifies a table from which the new table automatically copies all column names, their data types, and their not-null constraints.
>
> Unlike INHERITS, the new table and original table are completely decoupled after creation is complete. Changes to the original table will not be applied to the new table, and it is not possible to include data of the new table in scans of the original table.
>
> Default expressions for the copied column definitions will only be copied if INCLUDING DEFAULTS is specified. Defaults that call database-modification functions, like nextval, create a linkage between the original and new tables. The default behavior is to exclude default expressions, resulting in the copied columns in the new table having null defaults.
>
> Not-null constraints are always copied to the new table. CHECK constraints will be copied only if INCLUDING CONSTRAINTS is specified. Indexes, PRIMARY KEY, and UNIQUE constraints on the original table will be created on the new table only if the INCLUDING INDEXES clause is specified. No distinction is made between column constraints and table constraints.
>
> STORAGE settings for the copied column definitions will only be copied if INCLUDING STORAGE is specified. The default behavior is to exclude STORAGE settings, resulting in the copied columns in the new table having type-specific default settings. For more on STORAGE settings, see Section 59.2.
>
> Comments for the copied columns, constraints, and indexes will only be copied if INCLUDING COMMENTS is specified. The default behavior is to exclude comments, resulting in the copied columns and constraints in the new table having no comments.
>
> INCLUDING ALL is an abbreviated form of INCLUDING DEFAULTS INCLUDING CONSTRAINTS INCLUDING INDEXES INCLUDING STORAGE INCLUDING COMMENTS.
>
> Note also that unlike INHERITS, columns and constraints copied by LIKE are not merged with similarly named columns and constraints. If the same name is specified explicitly or in another LIKE clause, an error is signaled.

The `LIKE` clause can also be used to copy columns from views, foreign tables, or composite types. Inapplicable options (e.g., `INCLUDING INDEXES` from a view) are ignored.

`CONSTRAINT` *constraint_name*

An optional name for a column or table constraint. If the constraint is violated, the constraint name is present in error messages, so constraint names like `col must be positive` can be used to communicate helpful constraint information to client applications. (Double-quotes are needed to specify constraint names that contain spaces.) If a constraint name is not specified, the system generates a name.

`NOT NULL`

The column is not allowed to contain null values.

`NULL`

The column is allowed to contain null values. This is the default.

This clause is only provided for compatibility with non-standard SQL databases. Its use is discouraged in new applications.

`CHECK ( `*expression*` ) [ NO INHERIT ]`

The `CHECK` clause specifies an expression producing a Boolean result which new or updated rows must satisfy for an insert or update operation to succeed. Expressions evaluating to TRUE or UNKNOWN succeed. Should any row of an insert or update operation produce a FALSE result an error exception is raised and the insert or update does not alter the database. A check constraint specified as a column constraint should reference that column's value only, while an expression appearing in a table constraint can reference multiple columns.

Currently, `CHECK` expressions cannot contain subqueries nor refer to variables other than columns of the current row. The system column `tableoid` may be referenced, but not any other system column.

A constraint marked with `NO INHERIT` will not propagate to child tables.

`DEFAULT` *default_expr*

The `DEFAULT` clause assigns a default data value for the column whose column definition it appears within. The value is any variable-free expression (subqueries and cross-references to other columns in the current table are not allowed). The data type of the default expression must match the data type of the column.

The default expression will be used in any insert operation that does not specify a value for the column. If there is no default for a column, then the default is null.

`UNIQUE` (column constraint)
`UNIQUE ( `*column_name*` [, ... ] )` (table constraint)

The `UNIQUE` constraint specifies that a group of one or more columns of a table can contain only unique values. The behavior of the unique table constraint is the same as that for column constraints, with the additional capability to span multiple columns.

For the purpose of a unique constraint, null values are not considered equal.

Each unique table constraint must name a set of columns that is different from the set of columns named by any other unique or primary key constraint defined for the table. (Otherwise it would just be the same constraint listed twice.)

`PRIMARY KEY` (column constraint)
`PRIMARY KEY ( column_name [, ... ] )` (table constraint)

The primary key constraint specifies that a column or columns of a table can contain only unique (non-duplicate), nonnull values. Technically, `PRIMARY KEY` is merely a combination of `UNIQUE` and `NOT NULL`, but identifying a set of columns as primary key also provides metadata about the design of the schema, as a primary key implies that other tables can rely on this set of columns as a unique identifier for rows.

Only one primary key can be specified for a table, whether as a column constraint or a table constraint.

The primary key constraint should name a set of columns that is different from other sets of columns named by any unique constraint defined for the same table.

`EXCLUDE [ USING index_method ] ( exclude_element WITH operator [, ... ] )`
`index_parameters [ WHERE ( predicate ) ]`

The `EXCLUDE` clause defines an exclusion constraint, which guarantees that if any two rows are compared on the specified column(s) or expression(s) using the specified operator(s), not all of these comparisons will return `TRUE`. If all of the specified operators test for equality, this is equivalent to a `UNIQUE` constraint, although an ordinary unique constraint will be faster. However, exclusion constraints can specify constraints that are more general than simple equality. For example, you can specify a constraint that no two rows in the table contain overlapping circles (see Section 8.8) by using the `&&` operator.

Exclusion constraints are implemented using an index, so each specified operator must be associated with an appropriate operator class (see Section 11.9) for the index access method `index_method`. The operators are required to be commutative. Each `exclude_element` can optionally specify an operator class and/or ordering options; these are described fully under CREATE INDEX.

The access method must support `amgettuple` (see Chapter 55); at present this means GIN cannot be used. Although it's allowed, there is little point in using B-tree or hash indexes with an exclusion constraint, because this does nothing that an ordinary unique constraint doesn't do better. So in practice the access method will always be GiST or SP-GiST.

The `predicate` allows you to specify an exclusion constraint on a subset of the table; internally this creates a partial index. Note that parentheses are required around the predicate.

`REFERENCES reftable [ ( refcolumn ) ] [ MATCH matchtype ] [ ON DELETE action ] [`
`ON UPDATE action ]` (column constraint)
`FOREIGN KEY ( column_name [, ... ] ) REFERENCES reftable [ ( refcolumn [, ... ]`
`) ] [ MATCH matchtype ] [ ON DELETE action ] [ ON UPDATE action ]` (table constraint)

These clauses specify a foreign key constraint, which requires that a group of one or more columns of the new table must only contain values that match values in the referenced column(s) of some row of the referenced table. If the `refcolumn` list is omitted, the primary key of the `reftable` is used. The referenced columns must be the columns of a non-deferrable unique or primary key constraint in the referenced table. Note that foreign key constraints cannot be defined between temporary tables and permanent tables.

A value inserted into the referencing column(s) is matched against the values of the referenced table and referenced columns using the given match type. There are three match types: `MATCH FULL`, `MATCH PARTIAL`, and `MATCH SIMPLE` (which is the default). `MATCH FULL` will not allow one column of a multicolumn foreign key to be null unless all foreign key columns are null; if they are all null, the row is not required to have a match in the referenced table. `MATCH SIMPLE` allows any of the foreign key columns to be null; if any of them are null, the row is not required to have a match in the referenced table. MATCH PARTIAL is not yet implemented. (Of course, NOT NULL constraints can be applied to the referencing column(s) to prevent these cases from arising.)

In addition, when the data in the referenced columns is changed, certain actions are performed on the data in this table's columns. The ON DELETE clause specifies the action to perform when a referenced row in the referenced table is being deleted. Likewise, the ON UPDATE clause specifies the action to perform when a referenced column in the referenced table is being updated to a new value. If the row is updated, but the referenced column is not actually changed, no action is done. Referential actions other than the NO ACTION check cannot be deferred, even if the constraint is declared deferrable. There are the following possible actions for each clause:

NO ACTION

> Produce an error indicating that the deletion or update would create a foreign key constraint violation. If the constraint is deferred, this error will be produced at constraint check time if there still exist any referencing rows. This is the default action.

RESTRICT

> Produce an error indicating that the deletion or update would create a foreign key constraint violation. This is the same as NO ACTION except that the check is not deferrable.

CASCADE

> Delete any rows referencing the deleted row, or update the values of the referencing column(s) to the new values of the referenced columns, respectively.

SET NULL

> Set the referencing column(s) to null.

SET DEFAULT

> Set the referencing column(s) to their default values. (There must be a row in the referenced table matching the default values, if they are not null, or the operation will fail.)

> If the referenced column(s) are changed frequently, it might be wise to add an index to the referencing column(s) so that referential actions associated with the foreign key constraint can be performed more efficiently.

DEFERRABLE
NOT DEFERRABLE

> This controls whether the constraint can be deferred. A constraint that is not deferrable will be checked immediately after every command. Checking of constraints that are deferrable can be postponed until the end of the transaction (using the SET CONSTRAINTS command). NOT DEFERRABLE is the default. Currently, only UNIQUE, PRIMARY KEY, EXCLUDE, and REFERENCES (foreign key) constraints accept this clause. NOT NULL and CHECK constraints are not deferrable.

INITIALLY IMMEDIATE
INITIALLY DEFERRED

> If a constraint is deferrable, this clause specifies the default time to check the constraint. If the constraint is INITIALLY IMMEDIATE, it is checked after each statement. This is the default. If the

constraint is `INITIALLY DEFERRED`, it is checked only at the end of the transaction. The constraint check time can be altered with the SET CONSTRAINTS command.

`WITH ( storage_parameter [= value] [, ... ] )`

This clause specifies optional storage parameters for a table or index; see *Storage Parameters* for more information. The `WITH` clause for a table can also include `OIDS=TRUE` (or just `OIDS`) to specify that rows of the new table should have OIDs (object identifiers) assigned to them, or `OIDS=FALSE` to specify that the rows should not have OIDs. If `OIDS` is not specified, the default setting depends upon the default_with_oids configuration parameter. (If the new table inherits from any tables that have OIDs, then `OIDS=TRUE` is forced even if the command says `OIDS=FALSE`.)

If `OIDS=FALSE` is specified or implied, the new table does not store OIDs and no OID will be assigned for a row inserted into it. This is generally considered worthwhile, since it will reduce OID consumption and thereby postpone the wraparound of the 32-bit OID counter. Once the counter wraps around, OIDs can no longer be assumed to be unique, which makes them considerably less useful. In addition, excluding OIDs from a table reduces the space required to store the table on disk by 4 bytes per row (on most machines), slightly improving performance.

To remove OIDs from a table after it has been created, use ALTER TABLE.

`WITH OIDS`
`WITHOUT OIDS`

These are obsolescent syntaxes equivalent to `WITH (OIDS)` and `WITH (OIDS=FALSE)`, respectively. If you wish to give both an `OIDS` setting and storage parameters, you must use the `WITH ( ... )` syntax; see above.

`ON COMMIT`

The behavior of temporary tables at the end of a transaction block can be controlled using `ON COMMIT`. The three options are:

`PRESERVE ROWS`

No special action is taken at the ends of transactions. This is the default behavior.

`DELETE ROWS`

All rows in the temporary table will be deleted at the end of each transaction block. Essentially, an automatic TRUNCATE is done at each commit.

`DROP`

The temporary table will be dropped at the end of the current transaction block.

`TABLESPACE tablespace_name`

The `tablespace_name` is the name of the tablespace in which the new table is to be created. If not specified, default_tablespace is consulted, or temp_tablespaces if the table is temporary.

`USING INDEX TABLESPACE tablespace_name`

This clause allows selection of the tablespace in which the index associated with a `UNIQUE`, `PRIMARY KEY`, or `EXCLUDE` constraint will be created. If not specified, default_tablespace is consulted, or temp_tablespaces if the table is temporary.

Storage Parameters

The WITH clause can specify *storage parameters* for tables, and for indexes associated with a UNIQUE, PRIMARY KEY, or EXCLUDE constraint. Storage parameters for indexes are documented in CREATE IN-DEX. The storage parameters currently available for tables are listed below. For each parameter, unless noted, there is an additional parameter with the same name prefixed with toast., which can be used to control the behavior of the table's secondary TOAST table, if any (see Section 59.2 for more information about TOAST). Note that the TOAST table inherits the autovacuum_* values from its parent table, if there are no toast.autovacuum_* settings set.

fillfactor (integer)

> The fillfactor for a table is a percentage between 10 and 100. 100 (complete packing) is the default. When a smaller fillfactor is specified, INSERT operations pack table pages only to the indicated percentage; the remaining space on each page is reserved for updating rows on that page. This gives UPDATE a chance to place the updated copy of a row on the same page as the original, which is more efficient than placing it on a different page. For a table whose entries are never updated, complete packing is the best choice, but in heavily updated tables smaller fillfactors are appropriate. This parameter cannot be set for TOAST tables.

autovacuum_enabled, toast.autovacuum_enabled (boolean)

> Enables or disables the autovacuum daemon on a particular table. If true, the autovacuum daemon will initiate a VACUUM operation on a particular table when the number of updated or deleted tuples exceeds autovacuum_vacuum_threshold plus autovacuum_vacuum_scale_factor times the number of live tuples currently estimated to be in the relation. Similarly, it will initiate an ANALYZE operation when the number of inserted, updated or deleted tuples exceeds autovacuum_analyze_threshold plus autovacuum_analyze_scale_factor times the number of live tuples currently estimated to be in the relation. If false, this table will not be autovacuumed, except to prevent transaction Id wraparound. See Section 23.1.5 for more about wraparound prevention. Observe that this variable inherits its value from the autovacuum setting.

autovacuum_vacuum_threshold, toast.autovacuum_vacuum_threshold (integer)

> Minimum number of updated or deleted tuples before initiate a VACUUM operation on a particular table.

autovacuum_vacuum_scale_factor, toast.autovacuum_vacuum_scale_factor (float4)

> Multiplier for reltuples to add to autovacuum_vacuum_threshold.

autovacuum_analyze_threshold (integer)

> Minimum number of inserted, updated, or deleted tuples before initiate an ANALYZE operation on a particular table.

autovacuum_analyze_scale_factor (float4)

> Multiplier for reltuples to add to autovacuum_analyze_threshold.

autovacuum_vacuum_cost_delay, toast.autovacuum_vacuum_cost_delay (integer)

> Custom autovacuum_vacuum_cost_delay parameter.

autovacuum_vacuum_cost_limit, toast.autovacuum_vacuum_cost_limit (integer)

> Custom autovacuum_vacuum_cost_limit parameter.

`autovacuum_freeze_min_age`, `toast.autovacuum_freeze_min_age` (`integer`)

> Custom vacuum_freeze_min_age parameter. Note that autovacuum will ignore attempts to set a per-table `autovacuum_freeze_min_age` larger than half the system-wide autovacuum_freeze_max_age setting.

`autovacuum_freeze_max_age`, `toast.autovacuum_freeze_max_age` (`integer`)

> Custom autovacuum_freeze_max_age parameter. Note that autovacuum will ignore attempts to set a per-table `autovacuum_freeze_max_age` larger than the system-wide setting (it can only be set smaller). Note that while you can set `autovacuum_freeze_max_age` very small, or even zero, this is usually unwise since it will force frequent vacuuming.

`autovacuum_freeze_table_age`, `toast.autovacuum_freeze_table_age` (`integer`)

> Custom vacuum_freeze_table_age parameter.

`autovacuum_multixact_freeze_min_age`, `toast.autovacuum_multixact_freeze_min_age` (`integer`)

> Custom vacuum_multixact_freeze_min_age parameter. Note that autovacuum will ignore attempts to set a per-table `autovacuum_multixact_freeze_min_age` larger than half the system-wide autovacuum_multixact_freeze_max_age setting.

`autovacuum_multixact_freeze_max_age`, `toast.autovacuum_multixact_freeze_max_age` (`integer`)

> Custom autovacuum_multixact_freeze_max_age parameter. Note that autovacuum will ignore attempts to set a per-table `autovacuum_multixact_freeze_max_age` larger than the system-wide setting (it can only be set smaller). Note that while you can set `autovacuum_multixact_freeze_max_age` very small, or even zero, this is usually unwise since it will force frequent vacuuming.

`autovacuum_multixact_freeze_table_age`, `toast.autovacuum_multixact_freeze_table_a` (`integer`)

> Custom vacuum_multixact_freeze_table_age parameter.

`user_catalog_table` (`boolean`)

> Declare a table as an additional catalog table, e.g. for the purpose of logical replication. See Section 46.6.2 for details.

Notes

Using OIDs in new applications is not recommended: where possible, using a SERIAL or other sequence generator as the table's primary key is preferred. However, if your application does make use of OIDs to identify specific rows of a table, it is recommended to create a unique constraint on the oid column of that table, to ensure that OIDs in the table will indeed uniquely identify rows even after counter wraparound. Avoid assuming that OIDs are unique across tables; if you need a database-wide unique identifier, use the combination of tableoid and row OID for the purpose.

> **Tip:** The use of OIDS=FALSE is not recommended for tables with no primary key, since without either an OID or a unique data key, it is difficult to identify specific rows.

PostgreSQL automatically creates an index for each unique constraint and primary key constraint to enforce uniqueness. Thus, it is not necessary to create an index explicitly for primary key columns. (See CREATE INDEX for more information.)

Unique constraints and primary keys are not inherited in the current implementation. This makes the combination of inheritance and unique constraints rather dysfunctional.

A table cannot have more than 1600 columns. (In practice, the effective limit is usually lower because of tuple-length constraints.)

Examples

Create table `films` and table `distributors`:

```
CREATE TABLE films (
    code        char(5) CONSTRAINT firstkey PRIMARY KEY,
    title       varchar(40) NOT NULL,
    did         integer NOT NULL,
    date_prod   date,
    kind        varchar(10),
    len         interval hour to minute
);

CREATE TABLE distributors (
    did    integer PRIMARY KEY DEFAULT nextval('serial'),
    name   varchar(40) NOT NULL CHECK (name <> ")
);
```

Create a table with a 2-dimensional array:

```
CREATE TABLE array_int (
    vector   int[][]
);
```

Define a unique table constraint for the table `films`. Unique table constraints can be defined on one or more columns of the table:

```
CREATE TABLE films (
    code        char(5),
    title       varchar(40),
    did         integer,
    date_prod   date,
    kind        varchar(10),
    len         interval hour to minute,
    CONSTRAINT production UNIQUE(date_prod)
);
```

Define a check column constraint:

```
CREATE TABLE distributors (
    did     integer CHECK (did > 100),
    name    varchar(40)
);
```

Define a check table constraint:

```
CREATE TABLE distributors (
    did     integer,
    name    varchar(40)
    CONSTRAINT con1 CHECK (did > 100 AND name <> ")
);
```

Define a primary key table constraint for the table `films`:

```
CREATE TABLE films (
    code        char(5),
    title       varchar(40),
    did         integer,
    date_prod   date,
    kind        varchar(10),
    len         interval hour to minute,
    CONSTRAINT code_title PRIMARY KEY(code,title)
);
```

Define a primary key constraint for table `distributors`. The following two examples are equivalent, the first using the table constraint syntax, the second the column constraint syntax:

```
CREATE TABLE distributors (
    did     integer,
    name    varchar(40),
    PRIMARY KEY(did)
);
```

```
CREATE TABLE distributors (
    did     integer PRIMARY KEY,
    name    varchar(40)
);
```

Assign a literal constant default value for the column `name`, arrange for the default value of column `did` to be generated by selecting the next value of a sequence object, and make the default value of `modtime` be the time at which the row is inserted:

```
CREATE TABLE distributors (
```

```
    name      varchar(40) DEFAULT 'Luso Films',
    did       integer DEFAULT nextval('distributors_serial'),
    modtime   timestamp DEFAULT current_timestamp
);
```

Define two NOT NULL column constraints on the table distributors, one of which is explicitly given a name:

```
CREATE TABLE distributors (
    did     integer CONSTRAINT no_null NOT NULL,
    name    varchar(40) NOT NULL
);
```

Define a unique constraint for the name column:

```
CREATE TABLE distributors (
    did     integer,
    name    varchar(40) UNIQUE
);
```

The same, specified as a table constraint:

```
CREATE TABLE distributors (
    did     integer,
    name    varchar(40),
    UNIQUE(name)
);
```

Create the same table, specifying 70% fill factor for both the table and its unique index:

```
CREATE TABLE distributors (
    did     integer,
    name    varchar(40),
    UNIQUE(name) WITH (fillfactor=70)
)
WITH (fillfactor=70);
```

Create table circles with an exclusion constraint that prevents any two circles from overlapping:

```
CREATE TABLE circles (
    c circle,
    EXCLUDE USING gist (c WITH &&)
);
```

Create table cinemas in tablespace diskvol1:

```
CREATE TABLE cinemas (
        id serial,
        name text,
        location text
) TABLESPACE diskvol1;
```

Create a composite type and a typed table:

```
CREATE TYPE employee_type AS (name text, salary numeric);

CREATE TABLE employees OF employee_type (
    PRIMARY KEY (name),
    salary WITH OPTIONS DEFAULT 1000
);
```

Compatibility

The CREATE TABLE command conforms to the SQL standard, with exceptions listed below.

Temporary Tables

Although the syntax of CREATE TEMPORARY TABLE resembles that of the SQL standard, the effect is not the same. In the standard, temporary tables are defined just once and automatically exist (starting with empty contents) in every session that needs them. PostgreSQL instead requires each session to issue its own CREATE TEMPORARY TABLE command for each temporary table to be used. This allows different sessions to use the same temporary table name for different purposes, whereas the standard's approach constrains all instances of a given temporary table name to have the same table structure.

The standard's definition of the behavior of temporary tables is widely ignored. PostgreSQL's behavior on this point is similar to that of several other SQL databases.

The SQL standard also distinguishes between global and local temporary tables, where a local temporary table has a separate set of contents for each SQL module within each session, though its definition is still shared across sessions. Since PostgreSQL does not support SQL modules, this distinction is not relevant in PostgreSQL.

For compatibility's sake, PostgreSQL will accept the GLOBAL and LOCAL keywords in a temporary table declaration, but they currently have no effect. Use of these keywords is discouraged, since future versions of PostgreSQL might adopt a more standard-compliant interpretation of their meaning.

The ON COMMIT clause for temporary tables also resembles the SQL standard, but has some differences. If the ON COMMIT clause is omitted, SQL specifies that the default behavior is ON COMMIT DELETE ROWS. However, the default behavior in PostgreSQL is ON COMMIT PRESERVE ROWS. The ON COMMIT DROP option does not exist in SQL.

Non-deferred Uniqueness Constraints

When a UNIQUE or PRIMARY KEY constraint is not deferrable, PostgreSQL checks for uniqueness immediately whenever a row is inserted or modified. The SQL standard says that uniqueness should be enforced only at the end of the statement; this makes a difference when, for example, a single command updates multiple key values. To obtain standard-compliant behavior, declare the constraint as DEFERRABLE but not deferred (i.e., INITIALLY IMMEDIATE). Be aware that this can be significantly slower than immediate uniqueness checking.

Column Check Constraints

The SQL standard says that CHECK column constraints can only refer to the column they apply to; only CHECK table constraints can refer to multiple columns. PostgreSQL does not enforce this restriction; it treats column and table check constraints alike.

EXCLUDE Constraint

The EXCLUDE constraint type is a PostgreSQL extension.

NULL "Constraint"

The NULL "constraint" (actually a non-constraint) is a PostgreSQL extension to the SQL standard that is included for compatibility with some other database systems (and for symmetry with the NOT NULL constraint). Since it is the default for any column, its presence is simply noise.

Inheritance

Multiple inheritance via the INHERITS clause is a PostgreSQL language extension. SQL:1999 and later define single inheritance using a different syntax and different semantics. SQL:1999-style inheritance is not yet supported by PostgreSQL.

Zero-column Tables

PostgreSQL allows a table of no columns to be created (for example, CREATE TABLE foo();). This is an extension from the SQL standard, which does not allow zero-column tables. Zero-column tables are not in themselves very useful, but disallowing them creates odd special cases for ALTER TABLE DROP COLUMN, so it seems cleaner to ignore this spec restriction.

WITH Clause

The WITH clause is a PostgreSQL extension; neither storage parameters nor OIDs are in the standard.

Tablespaces

The PostgreSQL concept of tablespaces is not part of the standard. Hence, the clauses `TABLESPACE` and `USING INDEX TABLESPACE` are extensions.

Typed Tables

Typed tables implement a subset of the SQL standard. According to the standard, a typed table has columns corresponding to the underlying composite type as well as one other column that is the "self-referencing column". PostgreSQL does not support these self-referencing columns explicitly, but the same effect can be had using the OID feature.

See Also

ALTER TABLE, DROP TABLE, CREATE TABLE AS, CREATE TABLESPACE, CREATE TYPE

CREATE TABLE AS

Name

CREATE TABLE AS — define a new table from the results of a query

Synopsis

```
CREATE [ [ GLOBAL | LOCAL ] { TEMPORARY | TEMP } | UNLOGGED ] TABLE table_name
    [ (column_name [, ...] ) ]
    [ WITH ( storage_parameter [= value] [, ... ] ) | WITH OIDS | WITHOUT OIDS ]
    [ ON COMMIT { PRESERVE ROWS | DELETE ROWS | DROP } ]
    [ TABLESPACE tablespace_name ]
    AS query
    [ WITH [ NO ] DATA ]
```

Description

CREATE TABLE AS creates a table and fills it with data computed by a SELECT command. The table columns have the names and data types associated with the output columns of the SELECT (except that you can override the column names by giving an explicit list of new column names).

CREATE TABLE AS bears some resemblance to creating a view, but it is really quite different: it creates a new table and evaluates the query just once to fill the new table initially. The new table will not track subsequent changes to the source tables of the query. In contrast, a view re-evaluates its defining SELECT statement whenever it is queried.

Parameters

GLOBAL or LOCAL

Ignored for compatibility. Use of these keywords is deprecated; refer to CREATE TABLE for details.

TEMPORARY or TEMP

If specified, the table is created as a temporary table. Refer to CREATE TABLE for details.

UNLOGGED

If specified, the table is created as an unlogged table. Refer to CREATE TABLE for details.

table_name

The name (optionally schema-qualified) of the table to be created.

column_name

The name of a column in the new table. If column names are not provided, they are taken from the output column names of the query.

```
WITH ( storage_parameter [= value] [, ... ] )
```

This clause specifies optional storage parameters for the new table; see *Storage Parameters* for more information. The WITH clause can also include OIDS=TRUE (or just OIDS) to specify that rows of the new table should have OIDs (object identifiers) assigned to them, or OIDS=FALSE to specify that the rows should not have OIDs. See CREATE TABLE for more information.

```
WITH OIDS
WITHOUT OIDS
```

These are obsolescent syntaxes equivalent to WITH (OIDS) and WITH (OIDS=FALSE), respectively. If you wish to give both an OIDS setting and storage parameters, you must use the WITH (...) syntax; see above.

```
ON COMMIT
```

The behavior of temporary tables at the end of a transaction block can be controlled using ON COMMIT. The three options are:

```
PRESERVE ROWS
```

No special action is taken at the ends of transactions. This is the default behavior.

```
DELETE ROWS
```

All rows in the temporary table will be deleted at the end of each transaction block. Essentially, an automatic TRUNCATE is done at each commit.

```
DROP
```

The temporary table will be dropped at the end of the current transaction block.

```
TABLESPACE tablespace_name
```

The tablespace_name is the name of the tablespace in which the new table is to be created. If not specified, default_tablespace is consulted, or temp_tablespaces if the table is temporary.

```
query
```

A SELECT, TABLE, or VALUES command, or an EXECUTE command that runs a prepared SELECT, TABLE, or VALUES query.

```
WITH [ NO ] DATA
```

This clause specifies whether or not the data produced by the query should be copied into the new table. If not, only the table structure is copied. The default is to copy the data.

Notes

This command is functionally similar to SELECT INTO, but it is preferred since it is less likely to be confused with other uses of the SELECT INTO syntax. Furthermore, CREATE TABLE AS offers a superset of the functionality offered by SELECT INTO.

The CREATE TABLE AS command allows the user to explicitly specify whether OIDs should be included. If the presence of OIDs is not explicitly specified, the default_with_oids configuration variable is used.

Examples

Create a new table `films_recent` consisting of only recent entries from the table `films`:

```
CREATE TABLE films_recent AS
  SELECT * FROM films WHERE date_prod >= '2002-01-01';
```

To copy a table completely, the short form using the `TABLE` command can also be used:

```
CREATE TABLE films2 AS
  TABLE films;
```

Create a new temporary table `films_recent`, consisting of only recent entries from the table `films`, using a prepared statement. The new table has OIDs and will be dropped at commit:

```
PREPARE recentfilms(date) AS
  SELECT * FROM films WHERE date_prod > $1;
CREATE TEMP TABLE films_recent WITH (OIDS) ON COMMIT DROP AS
  EXECUTE recentfilms('2002-01-01');
```

Compatibility

`CREATE TABLE AS` conforms to the SQL standard. The following are nonstandard extensions:

- The standard requires parentheses around the subquery clause; in PostgreSQL, these parentheses are optional.
- In the standard, the `WITH [ NO ] DATA` clause is required; in PostgreSQL it is optional.
- PostgreSQL handles temporary tables in a way rather different from the standard; see **CREATE TABLE** for details.
- The `WITH` clause is a PostgreSQL extension; neither storage parameters nor OIDs are in the standard.
- The PostgreSQL concept of tablespaces is not part of the standard. Hence, the clause `TABLESPACE` is an extension.

See Also

CREATE MATERIALIZED VIEW, CREATE TABLE, EXECUTE, SELECT, SELECT INTO, VALUES

CREATE TABLESPACE

Name

CREATE TABLESPACE — define a new tablespace

Synopsis

```
CREATE TABLESPACE tablespace_name
    [ OWNER user_name ]
    LOCATION 'directory'
    [ WITH ( tablespace_option = value [, ... ] ) ]
```

Description

CREATE TABLESPACE registers a new cluster-wide tablespace. The tablespace name must be distinct from the name of any existing tablespace in the database cluster.

A tablespace allows superusers to define an alternative location on the file system where the data files containing database objects (such as tables and indexes) can reside.

A user with appropriate privileges can pass tablespace_name to CREATE DATABASE, CREATE TABLE, CREATE INDEX or ADD CONSTRAINT to have the data files for these objects stored within the specified tablespace.

Warning

A tablespace cannot be used independently of the cluster in which it is defined; see Section 21.6.

Parameters

tablespace_name

> The name of a tablespace to be created. The name cannot begin with pg_, as such names are reserved for system tablespaces.

user_name

> The name of the user who will own the tablespace. If omitted, defaults to the user executing the command. Only superusers can create tablespaces, but they can assign ownership of tablespaces to non-superusers.

directory

> The directory that will be used for the tablespace. The directory should be empty and must be owned by the PostgreSQL system user. The directory must be specified by an absolute path name.

`tablespace_option`

> A tablespace parameter to be set or reset. Currently, the only available parameters are `seq_page_cost` and `random_page_cost`. Setting either value for a particular tablespace will override the planner's usual estimate of the cost of reading pages from tables in that tablespace, as established by the configuration parameters of the same name (see seq_page_cost, random_page_cost). This may be useful if one tablespace is located on a disk which is faster or slower than the remainder of the I/O subsystem.

Notes

Tablespaces are only supported on systems that support symbolic links.

`CREATE TABLESPACE` cannot be executed inside a transaction block.

Examples

Create a tablespace `dbspace` at `/data/dbs`:

```
CREATE TABLESPACE dbspace LOCATION '/data/dbs';
```

Create a tablespace `indexspace` at `/data/indexes` owned by user `genevieve`:

```
CREATE TABLESPACE indexspace OWNER genevieve LOCATION '/data/indexes';
```

Compatibility

`CREATE TABLESPACE` is a PostgreSQL extension.

See Also

CREATE DATABASE, CREATE TABLE, CREATE INDEX, DROP TABLESPACE, ALTER TABLESPACE

CREATE TEXT SEARCH CONFIGURATION

Name

CREATE TEXT SEARCH CONFIGURATION — define a new text search configuration

Synopsis

```
CREATE TEXT SEARCH CONFIGURATION name (
    PARSER = parser_name |
    COPY = source_config
)
```

Description

CREATE TEXT SEARCH CONFIGURATION creates a new text search configuration. A text search configuration specifies a text search parser that can divide a string into tokens, plus dictionaries that can be used to determine which tokens are of interest for searching.

If only the parser is specified, then the new text search configuration initially has no mappings from token types to dictionaries, and therefore will ignore all words. Subsequent ALTER TEXT SEARCH CONFIGURATION commands must be used to create mappings to make the configuration useful. Alternatively, an existing text search configuration can be copied.

If a schema name is given then the text search configuration is created in the specified schema. Otherwise it is created in the current schema.

The user who defines a text search configuration becomes its owner.

Refer to Chapter 12 for further information.

Parameters

name

The name of the text search configuration to be created. The name can be schema-qualified.

parser_name

The name of the text search parser to use for this configuration.

source_config

The name of an existing text search configuration to copy.

Notes

The PARSER and COPY options are mutually exclusive, because when an existing configuration is copied, its parser selection is copied too.

Compatibility

There is no CREATE TEXT SEARCH CONFIGURATION statement in the SQL standard.

See Also

ALTER TEXT SEARCH CONFIGURATION, DROP TEXT SEARCH CONFIGURATION

CREATE TEXT SEARCH DICTIONARY

Name

CREATE TEXT SEARCH DICTIONARY — define a new text search dictionary

Synopsis

```
CREATE TEXT SEARCH DICTIONARY name (
    TEMPLATE = template
    [, option = value [, ... ]]
)
```

Description

CREATE TEXT SEARCH DICTIONARY creates a new text search dictionary. A text search dictionary specifies a way of recognizing interesting or uninteresting words for searching. A dictionary depends on a text search template, which specifies the functions that actually perform the work. Typically the dictionary provides some options that control the detailed behavior of the template's functions.

If a schema name is given then the text search dictionary is created in the specified schema. Otherwise it is created in the current schema.

The user who defines a text search dictionary becomes its owner.

Refer to Chapter 12 for further information.

Parameters

name

> The name of the text search dictionary to be created. The name can be schema-qualified.

template

> The name of the text search template that will define the basic behavior of this dictionary.

option

> The name of a template-specific option to be set for this dictionary.

value

> The value to use for a template-specific option. If the value is not a simple identifier or number, it must be quoted (but you can always quote it, if you wish).

The options can appear in any order.

Examples

The following example command creates a Snowball-based dictionary with a nonstandard list of stop words.

```
CREATE TEXT SEARCH DICTIONARY my_russian (
    template = snowball,
    language = russian,
    stopwords = myrussian
);
```

Compatibility

There is no CREATE TEXT SEARCH DICTIONARY statement in the SQL standard.

See Also

ALTER TEXT SEARCH DICTIONARY, DROP TEXT SEARCH DICTIONARY

CREATE TEXT SEARCH PARSER

Name

CREATE TEXT SEARCH PARSER — define a new text search parser

Synopsis

```
CREATE TEXT SEARCH PARSER name (
    START = start_function ,
    GETTOKEN = gettoken_function ,
    END = end_function ,
    LEXTYPES = lextypes_function
    [, HEADLINE = headline_function ]
)
```

Description

CREATE TEXT SEARCH PARSER creates a new text search parser. A text search parser defines a method for splitting a text string into tokens and assigning types (categories) to the tokens. A parser is not particularly useful by itself, but must be bound into a text search configuration along with some text search dictionaries to be used for searching.

If a schema name is given then the text search parser is created in the specified schema. Otherwise it is created in the current schema.

You must be a superuser to use CREATE TEXT SEARCH PARSER. (This restriction is made because an erroneous text search parser definition could confuse or even crash the server.)

Refer to Chapter 12 for further information.

Parameters

name

The name of the text search parser to be created. The name can be schema-qualified.

start_function

The name of the start function for the parser.

gettoken_function

The name of the get-next-token function for the parser.

end_function

The name of the end function for the parser.

lextypes_function

The name of the lextypes function for the parser (a function that returns information about the set of token types it produces).

headline_function

The name of the headline function for the parser (a function that summarizes a set of tokens).

The function names can be schema-qualified if necessary. Argument types are not given, since the argument list for each type of function is predetermined. All except the headline function are required.

The arguments can appear in any order, not only the one shown above.

Compatibility

There is no CREATE TEXT SEARCH PARSER statement in the SQL standard.

See Also

ALTER TEXT SEARCH PARSER, DROP TEXT SEARCH PARSER

CREATE TEXT SEARCH TEMPLATE

Name

CREATE TEXT SEARCH TEMPLATE — define a new text search template

Synopsis

```
CREATE TEXT SEARCH TEMPLATE name (
    [ INIT = init_function , ]
    LEXIZE = lexize_function
)
```

Description

CREATE TEXT SEARCH TEMPLATE creates a new text search template. Text search templates define the functions that implement text search dictionaries. A template is not useful by itself, but must be instantiated as a dictionary to be used. The dictionary typically specifies parameters to be given to the template functions.

If a schema name is given then the text search template is created in the specified schema. Otherwise it is created in the current schema.

You must be a superuser to use CREATE TEXT SEARCH TEMPLATE. This restriction is made because an erroneous text search template definition could confuse or even crash the server. The reason for separating templates from dictionaries is that a template encapsulates the "unsafe" aspects of defining a dictionary. The parameters that can be set when defining a dictionary are safe for unprivileged users to set, and so creating a dictionary need not be a privileged operation.

Refer to Chapter 12 for further information.

Parameters

name

> The name of the text search template to be created. The name can be schema-qualified.

init_function

> The name of the init function for the template.

lexize_function

> The name of the lexize function for the template.

The function names can be schema-qualified if necessary. Argument types are not given, since the argument list for each type of function is predetermined. The lexize function is required, but the init function is optional.

The arguments can appear in any order, not only the one shown above.

Compatibility

There is no CREATE TEXT SEARCH TEMPLATE statement in the SQL standard.

See Also

ALTER TEXT SEARCH TEMPLATE, DROP TEXT SEARCH TEMPLATE

CREATE TRIGGER

Name

CREATE TRIGGER — define a new trigger

Synopsis

```
CREATE [ CONSTRAINT ] TRIGGER name { BEFORE | AFTER | INSTEAD OF } { event [ OR
    ON table_name
    [ FROM referenced_table_name ]
    [ NOT DEFERRABLE | [ DEFERRABLE ] { INITIALLY IMMEDIATE | INITIALLY DEFERRE
    [ FOR [ EACH ] { ROW | STATEMENT } ]
    [ WHEN ( condition ) ]
    EXECUTE PROCEDURE function_name ( arguments )

where event can be one of:

    INSERT
    UPDATE [ OF column_name [, ... ] ]
    DELETE
    TRUNCATE
```

Description

CREATE TRIGGER creates a new trigger. The trigger will be associated with the specified table, view, or foreign table and will execute the specified function function_name when certain events occur.

The trigger can be specified to fire before the operation is attempted on a row (before constraints are checked and the INSERT, UPDATE, or DELETE is attempted); or after the operation has completed (after constraints are checked and the INSERT, UPDATE, or DELETE has completed); or instead of the operation (in the case of inserts, updates or deletes on a view). If the trigger fires before or instead of the event, the trigger can skip the operation for the current row, or change the row being inserted (for INSERT and UPDATE operations only). If the trigger fires after the event, all changes, including the effects of other triggers, are "visible" to the trigger.

A trigger that is marked FOR EACH ROW is called once for every row that the operation modifies. For example, a DELETE that affects 10 rows will cause any ON DELETE triggers on the target relation to be called 10 separate times, once for each deleted row. In contrast, a trigger that is marked FOR EACH STATEMENT only executes once for any given operation, regardless of how many rows it modifies (in particular, an operation that modifies zero rows will still result in the execution of any applicable FOR EACH STATEMENT triggers).

Triggers that are specified to fire INSTEAD OF the trigger event must be marked FOR EACH ROW, and can only be defined on views. BEFORE and AFTER triggers on a view must be marked as FOR EACH STATEMENT.

In addition, triggers may be defined to fire for TRUNCATE, though only FOR EACH STATEMENT.

The following table summarizes which types of triggers may be used on tables, views, and foreign tables:

When	Event	Row-level	Statement-level
BEFORE	INSERT/UPDATE/DELETE	Tables and foreign tables	Tables, views, and foreign tables
	TRUNCATE	—	Tables
AFTER	INSERT/UPDATE/DELETE	Tables and foreign tables	Tables, views, and foreign tables
	TRUNCATE	—	Tables
INSTEAD OF	INSERT/UPDATE/DELETE	Views	—
	TRUNCATE	—	—

Also, a trigger definition can specify a Boolean WHEN condition, which will be tested to see whether the trigger should be fired. In row-level triggers the WHEN condition can examine the old and/or new values of columns of the row. Statement-level triggers can also have WHEN conditions, although the feature is not so useful for them since the condition cannot refer to any values in the table.

If multiple triggers of the same kind are defined for the same event, they will be fired in alphabetical order by name.

When the CONSTRAINT option is specified, this command creates a *constraint trigger*. This is the same as a regular trigger except that the timing of the trigger firing can be adjusted using SET CONSTRAINTS. Constraint triggers must be AFTER ROW triggers on tables. They can be fired either at the end of the statement causing the triggering event, or at the end of the containing transaction; in the latter case they are said to be *deferred*. A pending deferred-trigger firing can also be forced to happen immediately by using SET CONSTRAINTS. Constraint triggers are expected to raise an exception when the constraints they implement are violated.

SELECT does not modify any rows so you cannot create SELECT triggers. Rules and views are more appropriate in such cases.

Refer to Chapter 36 for more information about triggers.

Parameters

name

> The name to give the new trigger. This must be distinct from the name of any other trigger for the same table. The name cannot be schema-qualified — the trigger inherits the schema of its table. For a constraint trigger, this is also the name to use when modifying the trigger's behavior using SET CONSTRAINTS.

BEFORE
AFTER
INSTEAD OF

> Determines whether the function is called before, after, or instead of the event. A constraint trigger can only be specified as AFTER.

event

> One of INSERT, UPDATE, DELETE, or TRUNCATE; this specifies the event that will fire the trigger. Multiple events can be specified using OR.

> For UPDATE events, it is possible to specify a list of columns using this syntax:

> UPDATE OF *column_name1* [, *column_name2* ...]
> The trigger will only fire if at least one of the listed columns is mentioned as a target of the UPDATE command.

> INSTEAD OF UPDATE events do not support lists of columns.

table_name

> The name (optionally schema-qualified) of the table, view, or foreign table the trigger is for.

referenced_table_name

> The (possibly schema-qualified) name of another table referenced by the constraint. This option is used for foreign-key constraints and is not recommended for general use. This can only be specified for constraint triggers.

DEFERRABLE
NOT DEFERRABLE
INITIALLY IMMEDIATE
INITIALLY DEFERRED

> The default timing of the trigger. See the CREATE TABLE documentation for details of these constraint options. This can only be specified for constraint triggers.

FOR EACH ROW
FOR EACH STATEMENT

> This specifies whether the trigger procedure should be fired once for every row affected by the trigger event, or just once per SQL statement. If neither is specified, FOR EACH STATEMENT is the default. Constraint triggers can only be specified FOR EACH ROW.

condition

> A Boolean expression that determines whether the trigger function will actually be executed. If WHEN is specified, the function will only be called if the *condition* returns true. In FOR EACH ROW triggers, the WHEN condition can refer to columns of the old and/or new row values by writing OLD.*column_name* or NEW.*column_name* respectively. Of course, INSERT triggers cannot refer to OLD and DELETE triggers cannot refer to NEW.

> INSTEAD OF triggers do not support WHEN conditions.

> Currently, WHEN expressions cannot contain subqueries.

> Note that for constraint triggers, evaluation of the WHEN condition is not deferred, but occurs immediately after the row update operation is performed. If the condition does not evaluate to true then the trigger is not queued for deferred execution.

function_name

> A user-supplied function that is declared as taking no arguments and returning type `trigger`, which is executed when the trigger fires.

arguments

> An optional comma-separated list of arguments to be provided to the function when the trigger is executed. The arguments are literal string constants. Simple names and numeric constants can be written here, too, but they will all be converted to strings. Please check the description of the implementation language of the trigger function to find out how these arguments can be accessed within the function; it might be different from normal function arguments.

Notes

To create a trigger on a table, the user must have the `TRIGGER` privilege on the table. The user must also have `EXECUTE` privilege on the trigger function.

Use **DROP TRIGGER** to remove a trigger.

A column-specific trigger (one defined using the `UPDATE OF column_name` syntax) will fire when any of its columns are listed as targets in the `UPDATE` command's `SET` list. It is possible for a column's value to change even when the trigger is not fired, because changes made to the row's contents by `BEFORE UPDATE` triggers are not considered. Conversely, a command such as `UPDATE ... SET x = x ...` will fire a trigger on column x, even though the column's value did not change.

In a `BEFORE` trigger, the `WHEN` condition is evaluated just before the function is or would be executed, so using `WHEN` is not materially different from testing the same condition at the beginning of the trigger function. Note in particular that the `NEW` row seen by the condition is the current value, as possibly modified by earlier triggers. Also, a `BEFORE` trigger's `WHEN` condition is not allowed to examine the system columns of the `NEW` row (such as `oid`), because those won't have been set yet.

In an `AFTER` trigger, the `WHEN` condition is evaluated just after the row update occurs, and it determines whether an event is queued to fire the trigger at the end of statement. So when an `AFTER` trigger's `WHEN` condition does not return true, it is not necessary to queue an event nor to re-fetch the row at end of statement. This can result in significant speedups in statements that modify many rows, if the trigger only needs to be fired for a few of the rows.

In PostgreSQL versions before 7.3, it was necessary to declare trigger functions as returning the place-holder type `opaque`, rather than `trigger`. To support loading of old dump files, `CREATE TRIGGER` will accept a function declared as returning `opaque`, but it will issue a notice and change the function's declared return type to `trigger`.

Examples

Execute the function `check_account_update` whenever a row of the table `accounts` is about to be updated:

```
CREATE TRIGGER check_update
    BEFORE UPDATE ON accounts
    FOR EACH ROW
```

```
    EXECUTE PROCEDURE check_account_update();
```

The same, but only execute the function if column `balance` is specified as a target in the `UPDATE` command:

```
CREATE TRIGGER check_update
    BEFORE UPDATE OF balance ON accounts
    FOR EACH ROW
    EXECUTE PROCEDURE check_account_update();
```

This form only executes the function if column `balance` has in fact changed value:

```
CREATE TRIGGER check_update
    BEFORE UPDATE ON accounts
    FOR EACH ROW
    WHEN (OLD.balance IS DISTINCT FROM NEW.balance)
    EXECUTE PROCEDURE check_account_update();
```

Call a function to log updates of `accounts`, but only if something changed:

```
CREATE TRIGGER log_update
    AFTER UPDATE ON accounts
    FOR EACH ROW
    WHEN (OLD.* IS DISTINCT FROM NEW.*)
    EXECUTE PROCEDURE log_account_update();
```

Execute the function `view_insert_row` for each row to insert rows into the tables underlying a view:

```
CREATE TRIGGER view_insert
    INSTEAD OF INSERT ON my_view
    FOR EACH ROW
    EXECUTE PROCEDURE view_insert_row();
```

Section 36.4 contains a complete example of a trigger function written in C.

Compatibility

The `CREATE TRIGGER` statement in PostgreSQL implements a subset of the SQL standard. The following functionalities are currently missing:

- SQL allows you to define aliases for the "old" and "new" rows or tables for use in the definition of the triggered action (e.g., `CREATE TRIGGER ... ON tablename REFERENCING OLD ROW AS somename NEW ROW AS othername ...`). Since PostgreSQL allows trigger procedures to be written in any number of user-defined languages, access to the data is handled in a language-specific way.

- PostgreSQL does not allow the old and new tables to be referenced in statement-level triggers, i.e., the tables that contain all the old and/or new rows, which are referred to by the `OLD TABLE` and `NEW TABLE` clauses in the SQL standard.

- PostgreSQL only allows the execution of a user-defined function for the triggered action. The standard allows the execution of a number of other SQL commands, such as CREATE TABLE, as the triggered action. This limitation is not hard to work around by creating a user-defined function that executes the desired commands.

SQL specifies that multiple triggers should be fired in time-of-creation order. PostgreSQL uses name order, which was judged to be more convenient.

SQL specifies that BEFORE DELETE triggers on cascaded deletes fire *after* the cascaded DELETE completes. The PostgreSQL behavior is for BEFORE DELETE to always fire before the delete action, even a cascading one. This is considered more consistent. There is also nonstandard behavior if BEFORE triggers modify rows or prevent updates during an update that is caused by a referential action. This can lead to constraint violations or stored data that does not honor the referential constraint.

The ability to specify multiple actions for a single trigger using OR is a PostgreSQL extension of the SQL standard.

The ability to fire triggers for TRUNCATE is a PostgreSQL extension of the SQL standard, as is the ability to define statement-level triggers on views.

CREATE CONSTRAINT TRIGGER is a PostgreSQL extension of the SQL standard.

See Also

ALTER TRIGGER, DROP TRIGGER, CREATE FUNCTION, SET CONSTRAINTS

CREATE TYPE

Name

CREATE TYPE — define a new data type

Synopsis

```
CREATE TYPE name AS
    ( [ attribute_name data_type [ COLLATE collation ] [, ... ] ] )

CREATE TYPE name AS ENUM
    ( [ 'label' [, ... ] ] )

CREATE TYPE name AS RANGE (
    SUBTYPE = subtype
    [ , SUBTYPE_OPCLASS = subtype_operator_class ]
    [ , COLLATION = collation ]
    [ , CANONICAL = canonical_function ]
    [ , SUBTYPE_DIFF = subtype_diff_function ]
)

CREATE TYPE name (
    INPUT = input_function,
    OUTPUT = output_function
    [ , RECEIVE = receive_function ]
    [ , SEND = send_function ]
    [ , TYPMOD_IN = type_modifier_input_function ]
    [ , TYPMOD_OUT = type_modifier_output_function ]
    [ , ANALYZE = analyze_function ]
    [ , INTERNALLENGTH = { internallength | VARIABLE } ]
    [ , PASSEDBYVALUE ]
    [ , ALIGNMENT = alignment ]
    [ , STORAGE = storage ]
    [ , LIKE = like_type ]
    [ , CATEGORY = category ]
    [ , PREFERRED = preferred ]
    [ , DEFAULT = default ]
    [ , ELEMENT = element ]
    [ , DELIMITER = delimiter ]
    [ , COLLATABLE = collatable ]
)

CREATE TYPE name
```

Description

CREATE TYPE registers a new data type for use in the current database. The user who defines a type becomes its owner.

If a schema name is given then the type is created in the specified schema. Otherwise it is created in the current schema. The type name must be distinct from the name of any existing type or domain in the same schema. (Because tables have associated data types, the type name must also be distinct from the name of any existing table in the same schema.)

There are five forms of CREATE TYPE, as shown in the syntax synopsis above. They respectively create a *composite type*, an *enum type*, a *range type*, a *base type*, or a *shell type*. The first four of these are discussed in turn below. A shell type is simply a placeholder for a type to be defined later; it is created by issuing CREATE TYPE with no parameters except for the type name. Shell types are needed as forward references when creating range types and base types, as discussed in those sections.

Composite Types

The first form of CREATE TYPE creates a composite type. The composite type is specified by a list of attribute names and data types. An attribute's collation can be specified too, if its data type is collatable. A composite type is essentially the same as the row type of a table, but using CREATE TYPE avoids the need to create an actual table when all that is wanted is to define a type. A stand-alone composite type is useful, for example, as the argument or return type of a function.

To be able to create a composite type, you must have USAGE privilege on all attribute types.

Enumerated Types

The second form of CREATE TYPE creates an enumerated (enum) type, as described in Section 8.7. Enum types take a list of one or more quoted labels, each of which must be less than NAMEDATALEN bytes long (64 bytes in a standard PostgreSQL build).

Range Types

The third form of CREATE TYPE creates a new range type, as described in Section 8.17.

The range type's *subtype* can be any type with an associated b-tree operator class (to determine the ordering of values for the range type). Normally the subtype's default b-tree operator class is used to determine ordering; to use a non-default operator class, specify its name with *subtype_opclass*. If the subtype is collatable, and you want to use a non-default collation in the range's ordering, specify the desired collation with the *collation* option.

The optional *canonical* function must take one argument of the range type being defined, and return a value of the same type. This is used to convert range values to a canonical form, when applicable. See Section 8.17.8 for more information. Creating a *canonical* function is a bit tricky, since it must be defined before the range type can be declared. To do this, you must first create a shell type, which is a placeholder type that has no properties except a name and an owner. This is done by issuing the command CREATE TYPE *name*, with no additional parameters. Then the function can be declared using the shell type as argument and result, and finally the range type can be declared using the same name. This automatically replaces the shell type entry with a valid range type.

The optional *subtype_diff* function must take two values of the *subtype* type as argument, and return a double precision value representing the difference between the two given values. While this is optional, providing it allows much greater efficiency of GiST indexes on columns of the range type. See Section 8.17.8 for more information.

Base Types

The fourth form of CREATE TYPE creates a new base type (scalar type). To create a new base type, you must be a superuser. (This restriction is made because an erroneous type definition could confuse or even crash the server.)

The parameters can appear in any order, not only that illustrated above, and most are optional. You must register two or more functions (using CREATE FUNCTION) before defining the type. The support functions *input_function* and *output_function* are required, while the functions *receive_function*, *send_function*, *type_modifier_input_function*, *type_modifier_output_function* and *analyze_function* are optional. Generally these functions have to be coded in C or another low-level language.

The *input_function* converts the type's external textual representation to the internal representation used by the operators and functions defined for the type. *output_function* performs the reverse transformation. The input function can be declared as taking one argument of type cstring, or as taking three arguments of types cstring, oid, integer. The first argument is the input text as a C string, the second argument is the type's own OID (except for array types, which instead receive their element type's OID), and the third is the typmod of the destination column, if known (-1 will be passed if not). The input function must return a value of the data type itself. Usually, an input function should be declared STRICT; if it is not, it will be called with a NULL first parameter when reading a NULL input value. The function must still return NULL in this case, unless it raises an error. (This case is mainly meant to support domain input functions, which might need to reject NULL inputs.) The output function must be declared as taking one argument of the new data type. The output function must return type cstring. Output functions are not invoked for NULL values.

The optional *receive_function* converts the type's external binary representation to the internal representation. If this function is not supplied, the type cannot participate in binary input. The binary representation should be chosen to be cheap to convert to internal form, while being reasonably portable. (For example, the standard integer data types use network byte order as the external binary representation, while the internal representation is in the machine's native byte order.) The receive function should perform adequate checking to ensure that the value is valid. The receive function can be declared as taking one argument of type internal, or as taking three arguments of types internal, oid, integer. The first argument is a pointer to a StringInfo buffer holding the received byte string; the optional arguments are the same as for the text input function. The receive function must return a value of the data type itself. Usually, a receive function should be declared STRICT; if it is not, it will be called with a NULL first parameter when reading a NULL input value. The function must still return NULL in this case, unless it raises an error. (This case is mainly meant to support domain receive functions, which might need to reject NULL inputs.) Similarly, the optional *send_function* converts from the internal representation to the external binary representation. If this function is not supplied, the type cannot participate in binary output. The send function must be declared as taking one argument of the new data type. The send function must return type bytea. Send functions are not invoked for NULL values.

You should at this point be wondering how the input and output functions can be declared to have results or arguments of the new type, when they have to be created before the new type can be created. The answer is that the type should first be defined as a *shell type*, which is a placeholder type that has no properties except a name and an owner. This is done by issuing the command CREATE TYPE *name*, with no additional parameters. Then the I/O functions can be defined referencing the shell type. Finally, CREATE TYPE with a full definition replaces the shell entry with a complete, valid type definition, after which the new type can be used normally.

The optional *type_modifier_input_function* and *type_modifier_output_function* are needed if the type supports modifiers, that is optional constraints attached to a type declaration, such as char(5) or numeric(30,2). PostgreSQL allows user-defined types to take one or more simple constants or identifiers as modifiers. However, this information must be capable of being packed into a single non-negative integer value for storage in the system catalogs. The *type_modifier_input_function* is passed the declared modifier(s) in the form of a cstring array. It must check the values for validity (throwing an error if they are wrong), and if they are correct, return a single non-negative integer value that will be stored as the column "typmod". Type modifiers will be rejected if the type does not have a *type_modifier_input_function*. The *type_modifier_output_function* converts the internal integer typmod value back to the correct form for user display. It must return a cstring value that is the exact string to append to the type name; for example numeric's function might return (30,2). It is allowed to omit the *type_modifier_output_function*, in which case the default display format is just the stored typmod integer value enclosed in parentheses.

The optional *analyze_function* performs type-specific statistics collection for columns of the data type. By default, ANALYZE will attempt to gather statistics using the type's "equals" and "less-than" operators, if there is a default b-tree operator class for the type. For non-scalar types this behavior is likely to be unsuitable, so it can be overridden by specifying a custom analysis function. The analysis function must be declared to take a single argument of type internal, and return a boolean result. The detailed API for analysis functions appears in src/include/commands/vacuum.h.

While the details of the new type's internal representation are only known to the I/O functions and other functions you create to work with the type, there are several properties of the internal representation that must be declared to PostgreSQL. Foremost of these is *internallength*. Base data types can be fixed-length, in which case *internallength* is a positive integer, or variable length, indicated by setting *internallength* to VARIABLE. (Internally, this is represented by setting typlen to -1.) The internal representation of all variable-length types must start with a 4-byte integer giving the total length of this value of the type.

The optional flag PASSEDBYVALUE indicates that values of this data type are passed by value, rather than by reference. You cannot pass by value types whose internal representation is larger than the size of the Datum type (4 bytes on most machines, 8 bytes on a few).

The *alignment* parameter specifies the storage alignment required for the data type. The allowed values equate to alignment on 1, 2, 4, or 8 byte boundaries. Note that variable-length types must have an alignment of at least 4, since they necessarily contain an int4 as their first component.

The *storage* parameter allows selection of storage strategies for variable-length data types. (Only plain is allowed for fixed-length types.) plain specifies that data of the type will always be stored in-line and not compressed. extended specifies that the system will first try to compress a long data value, and will move the value out of the main table row if it's still too long. external allows the value to be moved out of the main table, but the system will not try to compress it. main allows compression, but discourages moving the value out of the main table. (Data items with this storage strategy might still be moved out of the main table if there is no other way to make a row fit, but they will be kept in the main table preferentially over `extended` and `external` items.)

The `like_type` parameter provides an alternative method for specifying the basic representation properties of a data type: copy them from some existing type. The values of `internallength`, `passedbyvalue`, `alignment`, and `storage` are copied from the named type. (It is possible, though usually undesirable, to override some of these values by specifying them along with the `LIKE` clause.) Specifying representation this way is especially useful when the low-level implementation of the new type "piggybacks" on an existing type in some fashion.

The `category` and `preferred` parameters can be used to help control which implicit cast will be applied in ambiguous situations. Each data type belongs to a category named by a single ASCII character, and each type is either "preferred" or not within its category. The parser will prefer casting to preferred types (but only from other types within the same category) when this rule is helpful in resolving overloaded functions or operators. For more details see Chapter 10. For types that have no implicit casts to or from any other types, it is sufficient to leave these settings at the defaults. However, for a group of related types that have implicit casts, it is often helpful to mark them all as belonging to a category and select one or two of the "most general" types as being preferred within the category. The `category` parameter is especially useful when adding a user-defined type to an existing built-in category, such as the numeric or string types. However, it is also possible to create new entirely-user-defined type categories. Select any ASCII character other than an upper-case letter to name such a category.

A default value can be specified, in case a user wants columns of the data type to default to something other than the null value. Specify the default with the `DEFAULT` key word. (Such a default can be overridden by an explicit `DEFAULT` clause attached to a particular column.)

To indicate that a type is an array, specify the type of the array elements using the `ELEMENT` key word. For example, to define an array of 4-byte integers (`int4`), specify `ELEMENT = int4`. More details about array types appear below.

To indicate the delimiter to be used between values in the external representation of arrays of this type, `delimiter` can be set to a specific character. The default delimiter is the comma (`,`). Note that the delimiter is associated with the array element type, not the array type itself.

If the optional Boolean parameter `collatable` is true, column definitions and expressions of the type may carry collation information through use of the `COLLATE` clause. It is up to the implementations of the functions operating on the type to actually make use of the collation information; this does not happen automatically merely by marking the type collatable.

Array Types

Whenever a user-defined type is created, PostgreSQL automatically creates an associated array type, whose name consists of the element type's name prepended with an underscore, and truncated if necessary to keep it less than `NAMEDATALEN` bytes long. (If the name so generated collides with an existing type name, the process is repeated until a non-colliding name is found.) This implicitly-created array type is variable length and uses the built-in input and output functions `array_in` and `array_out`. The array type tracks any changes in its element type's owner or schema, and is dropped if the element type is.

You might reasonably ask why there is an `ELEMENT` option, if the system makes the correct array type automatically. The only case where it's useful to use `ELEMENT` is when you are making a fixed-length type that happens to be internally an array of a number of identical things, and you want to allow these things to be accessed directly by subscripting, in addition to whatever operations you plan to provide for the type as a whole. For example, type `point` is represented as just two floating-point numbers, each can be accessed using `point[0]` and `point[1]`. Note that this facility only works for fixed-length types whose internal form is exactly a sequence of identical fixed-length fields. A subscriptable variable-length type must have the generalized internal representation used by `array_in` and `array_out`. For historical reasons (i.e., this is clearly wrong but it's far too late to change it), subscripting of fixed-length array types starts from zero, rather than from one as for variable-length arrays.

Parameters

name

The name (optionally schema-qualified) of a type to be created.

attribute_name

The name of an attribute (column) for the composite type.

data_type

The name of an existing data type to become a column of the composite type.

collation

The name of an existing collation to be associated with a column of a composite type, or with a range type.

label

A string literal representing the textual label associated with one value of an enum type.

subtype

The name of the element type that the range type will represent ranges of.

subtype_operator_class

The name of a b-tree operator class for the subtype.

canonical_function

The name of the canonicalization function for the range type.

subtype_diff_function

The name of a difference function for the subtype.

input_function

The name of a function that converts data from the type's external textual form to its internal form.

output_function

The name of a function that converts data from the type's internal form to its external textual form.

receive_function

The name of a function that converts data from the type's external binary form to its internal form.

send_function

The name of a function that converts data from the type's internal form to its external binary form.

`type_modifier_input_function`

> The name of a function that converts an array of modifier(s) for the type into internal form.

`type_modifier_output_function`

> The name of a function that converts the internal form of the type's modifier(s) to external textual form.

`analyze_function`

> The name of a function that performs statistical analysis for the data type.

`internallength`

> A numeric constant that specifies the length in bytes of the new type's internal representation. The default assumption is that it is variable-length.

`alignment`

> The storage alignment requirement of the data type. If specified, it must be `char`, `int2`, `int4`, or `double`; the default is `int4`.

`storage`

> The storage strategy for the data type. If specified, must be `plain`, `external`, `extended`, or `main`; the default is `plain`.

`like_type`

> The name of an existing data type that the new type will have the same representation as. The values of `internallength`, `passedbyvalue`, `alignment`, and `storage` are copied from that type, unless overridden by explicit specification elsewhere in this CREATE TYPE command.

`category`

> The category code (a single ASCII character) for this type. The default is ′U′ for "user-defined type". Other standard category codes can be found in Table 48-53. You may also choose other ASCII characters in order to create custom categories.

`preferred`

> True if this type is a preferred type within its type category, else false. The default is false. Be very careful about creating a new preferred type within an existing type category, as this could cause surprising changes in behavior.

`default`

> The default value for the data type. If this is omitted, the default is null.

`element`

> The type being created is an array; this specifies the type of the array elements.

`delimiter`

> The delimiter character to be used between values in arrays made of this type.

`collatable`

> True if this type's operations can use collation information. The default is false.

Notes

Because there are no restrictions on use of a data type once it's been created, creating a base type or range type is tantamount to granting public execute permission on the functions mentioned in the type definition. This is usually not an issue for the sorts of functions that are useful in a type definition. But you might want to think twice before designing a type in a way that would require "secret" information to be used while converting it to or from external form.

Before PostgreSQL version 8.3, the name of a generated array type was always exactly the element type's name with one underscore character (_) prepended. (Type names were therefore restricted in length to one less character than other names.) While this is still usually the case, the array type name may vary from this in case of maximum-length names or collisions with user type names that begin with underscore. Writing code that depends on this convention is therefore deprecated. Instead, use `pg_type.typarray` to locate the array type associated with a given type.

It may be advisable to avoid using type and table names that begin with underscore. While the server will change generated array type names to avoid collisions with user-given names, there is still risk of confusion, particularly with old client software that may assume that type names beginning with underscores always represent arrays.

Before PostgreSQL version 8.2, the shell-type creation syntax `CREATE TYPE name` did not exist. The way to create a new base type was to create its input function first. In this approach, PostgreSQL will first see the name of the new data type as the return type of the input function. The shell type is implicitly created in this situation, and then it can be referenced in the definitions of the remaining I/O functions. This approach still works, but is deprecated and might be disallowed in some future release. Also, to avoid accidentally cluttering the catalogs with shell types as a result of simple typos in function definitions, a shell type will only be made this way when the input function is written in C.

In PostgreSQL versions before 7.3, it was customary to avoid creating a shell type at all, by replacing the functions' forward references to the type name with the placeholder pseudotype `opaque`. The `cstring` arguments and results also had to be declared as `opaque` before 7.3. To support loading of old dump files, `CREATE TYPE` will accept I/O functions declared using `opaque`, but it will issue a notice and change the function declarations to use the correct types.

Examples

This example creates a composite type and uses it in a function definition:

```
CREATE TYPE compfoo AS (f1 int, f2 text);

CREATE FUNCTION getfoo() RETURNS SETOF compfoo AS $$
    SELECT fooid, fooname FROM foo
$$ LANGUAGE SQL;
```

This example creates an enumerated type and uses it in a table definition:

```
CREATE TYPE bug_status AS ENUM ('new', 'open', 'closed');

CREATE TABLE bug (
    id serial,
```

```
    description text,
    status bug_status
);
```

This example creates a range type:

```
CREATE TYPE float8_range AS RANGE (subtype = float8, subtype_diff = float8mi);
```

This example creates the base data type `box` and then uses the type in a table definition:

```
CREATE TYPE box;

CREATE FUNCTION my_box_in_function(cstring) RETURNS box AS ... ;
CREATE FUNCTION my_box_out_function(box) RETURNS cstring AS ... ;

CREATE TYPE box (
    INTERNALLENGTH = 16,
    INPUT = my_box_in_function,
    OUTPUT = my_box_out_function
);

CREATE TABLE myboxes (
    id integer,
    description box
);
```

If the internal structure of `box` were an array of four `float4` elements, we might instead use:

```
CREATE TYPE box (
    INTERNALLENGTH = 16,
    INPUT = my_box_in_function,
    OUTPUT = my_box_out_function,
    ELEMENT = float4
);
```

which would allow a box value's component numbers to be accessed by subscripting. Otherwise the type behaves the same as before.

This example creates a large object type and uses it in a table definition:

```
CREATE TYPE bigobj (
    INPUT = lo_filein, OUTPUT = lo_fileout,
    INTERNALLENGTH = VARIABLE
);
CREATE TABLE big_objs (
    id integer,
    obj bigobj
);
```

More examples, including suitable input and output functions, are in Section 35.11.

Compatibility

The first form of the CREATE TYPE command, which creates a composite type, conforms to the SQL standard. The other forms are PostgreSQL extensions. The CREATE TYPE statement in the SQL standard also defines other forms that are not implemented in PostgreSQL.

The ability to create a composite type with zero attributes is a PostgreSQL-specific deviation from the standard (analogous to the same case in CREATE TABLE).

See Also

ALTER TYPE, CREATE DOMAIN, CREATE FUNCTION, DROP TYPE

CREATE USER

Name

CREATE USER — define a new database role

Synopsis

```
CREATE USER name [ [ WITH ] option [ ... ] ]

where option can be:

    SUPERUSER | NOSUPERUSER
  | CREATEDB | NOCREATEDB
  | CREATEROLE | NOCREATEROLE
  | CREATEUSER | NOCREATEUSER
  | INHERIT | NOINHERIT
  | LOGIN | NOLOGIN
  | REPLICATION | NOREPLICATION
  | CONNECTION LIMIT connlimit
  | [ ENCRYPTED | UNENCRYPTED ] PASSWORD 'password'
  | VALID UNTIL 'timestamp'
  | IN ROLE role_name [, ...]
  | IN GROUP role_name [, ...]
  | ROLE role_name [, ...]
  | ADMIN role_name [, ...]
  | USER role_name [, ...]
  | SYSID uid
```

Description

CREATE USER is now an alias for CREATE ROLE. The only difference is that when the command is spelled CREATE USER, LOGIN is assumed by default, whereas NOLOGIN is assumed when the command is spelled CREATE ROLE.

Compatibility

The CREATE USER statement is a PostgreSQL extension. The SQL standard leaves the definition of users to the implementation.

See Also

CREATE ROLE

CREATE USER MAPPING

Name

CREATE USER MAPPING — define a new mapping of a user to a foreign server

Synopsis

```
CREATE USER MAPPING FOR { user_name | USER | CURRENT_USER | PUBLIC }
    SERVER server_name
    [ OPTIONS ( option 'value' [ , ... ] ) ]
```

Description

CREATE USER MAPPING defines a mapping of a user to a foreign server. A user mapping typically encapsulates connection information that a foreign-data wrapper uses together with the information encapsulated by a foreign server to access an external data resource.

The owner of a foreign server can create user mappings for that server for any user. Also, a user can create a user mapping for his own user name if USAGE privilege on the server has been granted to the user.

Parameters

user_name

> The name of an existing user that is mapped to foreign server. CURRENT_USER and USER match the name of the current user. When PUBLIC is specified, a so-called public mapping is created that is used when no user-specific mapping is applicable.

server_name

> The name of an existing server for which the user mapping is to be created.

OPTIONS (option 'value' [, ...])

> This clause specifies the options of the user mapping. The options typically define the actual user name and password of the mapping. Option names must be unique. The allowed option names and values are specific to the server's foreign-data wrapper.

Examples

Create a user mapping for user bob, server foo:

```
CREATE USER MAPPING FOR bob SERVER foo OPTIONS (user 'bob', password 'secret');
```

Compatibility

CREATE USER MAPPING conforms to ISO/IEC 9075-9 (SQL/MED).

See Also

ALTER USER MAPPING, DROP USER MAPPING, CREATE FOREIGN DATA WRAPPER, CREATE SERVER

CREATE VIEW

Name

CREATE VIEW — define a new view

Synopsis

```
CREATE [ OR REPLACE ] [ TEMP | TEMPORARY ] [ RECURSIVE ] VIEW name [ ( column_na
    [ WITH ( view_option_name [= view_option_value] [, ... ] ) ]
    AS query
    [ WITH [ CASCADED | LOCAL ] CHECK OPTION ]
```

Description

CREATE VIEW defines a view of a query. The view is not physically materialized. Instead, the query is run every time the view is referenced in a query.

CREATE OR REPLACE VIEW is similar, but if a view of the same name already exists, it is replaced. The new query must generate the same columns that were generated by the existing view query (that is, the same column names in the same order and with the same data types), but it may add additional columns to the end of the list. The calculations giving rise to the output columns may be completely different.

If a schema name is given (for example, CREATE VIEW myschema.myview ...) then the view is created in the specified schema. Otherwise it is created in the current schema. Temporary views exist in a special schema, so a schema name cannot be given when creating a temporary view. The name of the view must be distinct from the name of any other view, table, sequence, index or foreign table in the same schema.

Parameters

TEMPORARY or TEMP

> If specified, the view is created as a temporary view. Temporary views are automatically dropped at the end of the current session. Existing permanent relations with the same name are not visible to the current session while the temporary view exists, unless they are referenced with schema-qualified names.

> If any of the tables referenced by the view are temporary, the view is created as a temporary view (whether TEMPORARY is specified or not).

RECURSIVE

> Creates a recursive view. The syntax

> ```
> CREATE RECURSIVE VIEW name (columns) AS SELECT ...;
> ```
> is equivalent to

> ```
> CREATE VIEW name AS WITH RECURSIVE name (columns) AS (SELECT ...) SELECT colu.
> ```

A view column list must be specified for a recursive view.

name

The name (optionally schema-qualified) of a view to be created.

column_name

An optional list of names to be used for columns of the view. If not given, the column names are deduced from the query.

WITH (*view_option_name* [= *view_option_value*] [, ...])

This clause specifies optional parameters for a view; the following parameters are supported:

check_option (string)

This parameter may be either local or cascaded, and is equivalent to specifying WITH [CASCADED | LOCAL] CHECK OPTION (see below). This option can be changed on existing views using ALTER VIEW.

security_barrier (string)

This should be used if the view is intended to provide row-level security. See Section 38.5 for full details.

query

A SELECT or VALUES command which will provide the columns and rows of the view.

WITH [CASCADED | LOCAL] CHECK OPTION

This option controls the behavior of automatically updatable views. When this option is specified, INSERT and UPDATE commands on the view will be checked to ensure that new rows satisfy the view-defining condition (that is, the new rows are checked to ensure that they are visible through the view). If they are not, the update will be rejected. If the CHECK OPTION is not specified, INSERT and UPDATE commands on the view are allowed to create rows that are not visible through the view. The following check options are supported:

LOCAL

New rows are only checked against the conditions defined directly in the view itself. Any conditions defined on underlying base views are not checked (unless they also specify the CHECK OPTION).

CASCADED

New rows are checked against the conditions of the view and all underlying base views. If the CHECK OPTION is specified, and neither LOCAL nor CASCADED is specified, then CASCADED is assumed.

The CHECK OPTION may not be used with RECURSIVE views.

Note that the CHECK OPTION is only supported on views that are automatically updatable, and do not have INSTEAD OF triggers or INSTEAD rules. If an automatically updatable view is defined on top of a base view that has INSTEAD OF triggers, then the LOCAL CHECK OPTION may be used to check the conditions on the automatically updatable view, but the conditions on the base view with INSTEAD OF triggers will not be checked (a cascaded check option will not cascade down to a trigger-updatable view, and any check options defined directly on a trigger-updatable view will be ignored). If the view or any of its base relations has an INSTEAD rule that causes the INSERT or UPDATE command to be rewritten, then all check options will be ignored in the rewritten query, including any checks from automatically updatable views defined on top of the relation with the INSTEAD rule.

Notes

Use the DROP VIEW statement to drop views.

Be careful that the names and types of the view's columns will be assigned the way you want. For example:

```
CREATE VIEW vista AS SELECT 'Hello World';
```

is bad form in two ways: the column name defaults to ?column?, and the column data type defaults to unknown. If you want a string literal in a view's result, use something like:

```
CREATE VIEW vista AS SELECT text 'Hello World' AS hello;
```

Access to tables referenced in the view is determined by permissions of the view owner. In some cases, this can be used to provide secure but restricted access to the underlying tables. However, not all views are secure against tampering; see Section 38.5 for details. Functions called in the view are treated the same as if they had been called directly from the query using the view. Therefore the user of a view must have permissions to call all functions used by the view.

When CREATE OR REPLACE VIEW is used on an existing view, only the view's defining SELECT rule is changed. Other view properties, including ownership, permissions, and non-SELECT rules, remain unchanged. You must own the view to replace it (this includes being a member of the owning role).

Updatable Views

Simple views are automatically updatable: the system will allow INSERT, UPDATE and DELETE statements to be used on the view in the same way as on a regular table. A view is automatically updatable if it satisfies all of the following conditions:

- The view must have exactly one entry in its FROM list, which must be a table or another updatable view.
- The view definition must not contain WITH, DISTINCT, GROUP BY, HAVING, LIMIT, or OFFSET clauses at the top level.
- The view definition must not contain set operations (UNION, INTERSECT or EXCEPT) at the top level.
- The view's select list must not contain any aggregates, window functions or set-returning functions.

An automatically updatable view may contain a mix of updatable and non-updatable columns. A column is updatable if it is a simple reference to an updatable column of the underlying base relation; otherwise the column is read-only, and an error will be raised if an INSERT or UPDATE statement attempts to assign a value to it.

If the view is automatically updatable the system will convert any INSERT, UPDATE or DELETE statement on the view into the corresponding statement on the underlying base relation.

If an automatically updatable view contains a WHERE condition, the condition restricts which rows of the base relation are available to be modified by UPDATE and DELETE statements on the view. However, an UPDATE is allowed to change a row so that it no longer satisfies the WHERE condition, and thus is no longer visible through the view. Similarly, an INSERT command can potentially insert base-relation rows that do not satisfy the WHERE condition and thus are not visible through the view. The CHECK OPTION may be used to prevent INSERT and UPDATE commands from creating such rows that are not visible through the view.

If an automatically updatable view is marked with the security_barrier property then all the view's WHERE conditions (and any conditions using operators which are marked as LEAKPROOF) will always be evaluated before any conditions that a user of the view has added. See Section 38.5 for full details. Note that, due to this, rows which are not ultimately returned (because they do not pass the user's WHERE conditions) may still end up being locked. EXPLAIN can be used to see which conditions are applied at the relation level (and therefore do not lock rows) and which are not.

A more complex view that does not satisfy all these conditions is read-only by default: the system will not allow an insert, update, or delete on the view. You can get the effect of an updatable view by creating INSTEAD OF triggers on the view, which must convert attempted inserts, etc. on the view into appropriate actions on other tables. For more information see **CREATE TRIGGER**. Another possibility is to create rules (see **CREATE RULE**), but in practice triggers are easier to understand and use correctly.

Note that the user performing the insert, update or delete on the view must have the corresponding insert, update or delete privilege on the view. In addition the view's owner must have the relevant privileges on the underlying base relations, but the user performing the update does not need any permissions on the underlying base relations (see Section 38.5).

Examples

Create a view consisting of all comedy films:

```
CREATE VIEW comedies AS
    SELECT *
    FROM films
    WHERE kind = 'Comedy';
```

This will create a view containing the columns that are in the film table at the time of view creation. Though * was used to create the view, columns added later to the table will not be part of the view.

Create a view with LOCAL CHECK OPTION:

```
CREATE VIEW universal_comedies AS
    SELECT *
    FROM comedies
    WHERE classification = 'U'
    WITH LOCAL CHECK OPTION;
```

This will create a view based on the `comedies` view, showing only films with `kind = 'Comedy'` and `classification = 'U'`. Any attempt to `INSERT` or `UPDATE` a row in the view will be rejected if the new row doesn't have `classification = 'U'`, but the film `kind` will not be checked.

Create a view with `CASCADED CHECK OPTION`:

```
CREATE VIEW pg_comedies AS
    SELECT *
    FROM comedies
    WHERE classification = 'PG'
    WITH CASCADED CHECK OPTION;
```

This will create a view that checks both the `kind` and `classification` of new rows.

Create a view with a mix of updatable and non-updatable columns:

```
CREATE VIEW comedies AS
    SELECT f.*,
            country_code_to_name(f.country_code) AS country,
            (SELECT avg(r.rating)
             FROM user_ratings r
             WHERE r.film_id = f.id) AS avg_rating
    FROM films f
    WHERE f.kind = 'Comedy';
```

This view will support `INSERT`, `UPDATE` and `DELETE`. All the columns from the `films` table will be updatable, whereas the computed columns `country` and `avg_rating` will be read-only.

Create a recursive view consisting of the numbers from 1 to 100:

```
CREATE RECURSIVE VIEW nums_1_100 (n) AS
    VALUES (1)
UNION ALL
    SELECT n+1 FROM nums_1_100 WHERE n < 100;
```

Compatibility

`CREATE OR REPLACE VIEW` is a PostgreSQL language extension. So is the concept of a temporary view. The `WITH ( ... )` clause is an extension as well.

See Also

ALTER VIEW, DROP VIEW, CREATE MATERIALIZED VIEW

DEALLOCATE

Name

DEALLOCATE — deallocate a prepared statement

Synopsis

```
DEALLOCATE [ PREPARE ] { name | ALL }
```

Description

DEALLOCATE is used to deallocate a previously prepared SQL statement. If you do not explicitly deallocate a prepared statement, it is deallocated when the session ends.

For more information on prepared statements, see PREPARE.

Parameters

PREPARE

This key word is ignored.

name

The name of the prepared statement to deallocate.

ALL

Deallocate all prepared statements.

Compatibility

The SQL standard includes a DEALLOCATE statement, but it is only for use in embedded SQL.

See Also

EXECUTE, PREPARE

DECLARE

Name

DECLARE — define a cursor

Synopsis

```
DECLARE name [ BINARY ] [ INSENSITIVE ] [ [ NO ] SCROLL ]
    CURSOR [ { WITH | WITHOUT } HOLD ] FOR query
```

Description

DECLARE allows a user to create cursors, which can be used to retrieve a small number of rows at a time out of a larger query. After the cursor is created, rows are fetched from it using FETCH.

> **Note:** This page describes usage of cursors at the SQL command level. If you are trying to use cursors inside a PL/pgSQL function, the rules are different — see Section 40.7.

Parameters

name

The name of the cursor to be created.

BINARY

Causes the cursor to return data in binary rather than in text format.

INSENSITIVE

Indicates that data retrieved from the cursor should be unaffected by updates to the table(s) underlying the cursor that occur after the cursor is created. In PostgreSQL, this is the default behavior; so this key word has no effect and is only accepted for compatibility with the SQL standard.

SCROLL
NO SCROLL

SCROLL specifies that the cursor can be used to retrieve rows in a nonsequential fashion (e.g., backward). Depending upon the complexity of the query's execution plan, specifying SCROLL might impose a performance penalty on the query's execution time. NO SCROLL specifies that the cursor cannot be used to retrieve rows in a nonsequential fashion. The default is to allow scrolling in some cases; this is not the same as specifying SCROLL. See *Notes* for details.

```
WITH HOLD
WITHOUT HOLD
```

> WITH HOLD specifies that the cursor can continue to be used after the transaction that created it successfully commits. WITHOUT HOLD specifies that the cursor cannot be used outside of the transaction that created it. If neither WITHOUT HOLD nor WITH HOLD is specified, WITHOUT HOLD is the default.

query

> A SELECT or VALUES command which will provide the rows to be returned by the cursor.

The key words BINARY, INSENSITIVE, and SCROLL can appear in any order.

Notes

Normal cursors return data in text format, the same as a SELECT would produce. The BINARY option specifies that the cursor should return data in binary format. This reduces conversion effort for both the server and client, at the cost of more programmer effort to deal with platform-dependent binary data formats. As an example, if a query returns a value of one from an integer column, you would get a string of 1 with a default cursor, whereas with a binary cursor you would get a 4-byte field containing the internal representation of the value (in big-endian byte order).

Binary cursors should be used carefully. Many applications, including psql, are not prepared to handle binary cursors and expect data to come back in the text format.

> **Note:** When the client application uses the "extended query" protocol to issue a FETCH command, the Bind protocol message specifies whether data is to be retrieved in text or binary format. This choice overrides the way that the cursor is defined. The concept of a binary cursor as such is thus obsolete when using extended query protocol — any cursor can be treated as either text or binary.

Unless WITH HOLD is specified, the cursor created by this command can only be used within the current transaction. Thus, DECLARE without WITH HOLD is useless outside a transaction block: the cursor would survive only to the completion of the statement. Therefore PostgreSQL reports an error if such a command is used outside a transaction block. Use BEGIN and COMMIT (or ROLLBACK) to define a transaction block.

If WITH HOLD is specified and the transaction that created the cursor successfully commits, the cursor can continue to be accessed by subsequent transactions in the same session. (But if the creating transaction is aborted, the cursor is removed.) A cursor created with WITH HOLD is closed when an explicit CLOSE command is issued on it, or the session ends. In the current implementation, the rows represented by a held cursor are copied into a temporary file or memory area so that they remain available for subsequent transactions.

WITH HOLD may not be specified when the query includes FOR UPDATE or FOR SHARE.

The SCROLL option should be specified when defining a cursor that will be used to fetch backwards. This is required by the SQL standard. However, for compatibility with earlier versions, PostgreSQL will allow backward fetches without SCROLL, if the cursor's query plan is simple enough that no extra overhead is needed to support it. However, application developers are advised not to rely on using backward fetches from a cursor that has not been created with SCROLL. If NO SCROLL is specified, then backward fetches are disallowed in any case.

Backward fetches are also disallowed when the query includes FOR UPDATE or FOR SHARE; therefore SCROLL may not be specified in this case.

Caution

Scrollable and WITH HOLD cursors may give unexpected results if they invoke any volatile functions (see Section 35.6). When a previously fetched row is re-fetched, the functions might be re-executed, perhaps leading to results different from the first time. One workaround for such cases is to declare the cursor WITH HOLD and commit the transaction before reading any rows from it. This will force the entire output of the cursor to be materialized in temporary storage, so that volatile functions are executed exactly once for each row.

If the cursor's query includes FOR UPDATE or FOR SHARE, then returned rows are locked at the time they are first fetched, in the same way as for a regular SELECT command with these options. In addition, the returned rows will be the most up-to-date versions; therefore these options provide the equivalent of what the SQL standard calls a "sensitive cursor". (Specifying INSENSITIVE together with FOR UPDATE or FOR SHARE is an error.)

Caution

It is generally recommended to use FOR UPDATE if the cursor is intended to be used with UPDATE ... WHERE CURRENT OF or DELETE ... WHERE CURRENT OF. Using FOR UPDATE prevents other sessions from changing the rows between the time they are fetched and the time they are updated. Without FOR UPDATE, a subsequent WHERE CURRENT OF command will have no effect if the row was changed since the cursor was created.

Another reason to use FOR UPDATE is that without it, a subsequent WHERE CURRENT OF might fail if the cursor query does not meet the SQL standard's rules for being "simply updatable" (in particular, the cursor must reference just one table and not use grouping or ORDER BY). Cursors that are not simply updatable might work, or might not, depending on plan choice details; so in the worst case, an application might work in testing and then fail in production.

The main reason not to use FOR UPDATE with WHERE CURRENT OF is if you need the cursor to be scrollable, or to be insensitive to the subsequent updates (that is, continue to show the old data). If this is a requirement, pay close heed to the caveats shown above.

The SQL standard only makes provisions for cursors in embedded SQL. The PostgreSQL server does not implement an OPEN statement for cursors; a cursor is considered to be open when it is declared. However, ECPG, the embedded SQL preprocessor for PostgreSQL, supports the standard SQL cursor conventions, including those involving DECLARE and OPEN statements.

You can see all available cursors by querying the pg_cursors system view.

Examples

To declare a cursor:

```
DECLARE liahona CURSOR FOR SELECT * FROM films;
```

See FETCH for more examples of cursor usage.

Compatibility

The SQL standard says that it is implementation-dependent whether cursors are sensitive to concurrent updates of the underlying data by default. In PostgreSQL, cursors are insensitive by default, and can be made sensitive by specifying FOR UPDATE. Other products may work differently.

The SQL standard allows cursors only in embedded SQL and in modules. PostgreSQL permits cursors to be used interactively.

Binary cursors are a PostgreSQL extension.

See Also

CLOSE, FETCH, MOVE

DELETE

Name

DELETE — delete rows of a table

Synopsis

```
[ WITH [ RECURSIVE ] with_query [, ...] ]
DELETE FROM [ ONLY ] table_name [ * ] [ [ AS ] alias ]
    [ USING using_list ]
    [ WHERE condition | WHERE CURRENT OF cursor_name ]
    [ RETURNING * | output_expression [ [ AS ] output_name ] [, ...] ]
```

Description

DELETE deletes rows that satisfy the WHERE clause from the specified table. If the WHERE clause is absent, the effect is to delete all rows in the table. The result is a valid, but empty table.

> **Tip:** TRUNCATE is a PostgreSQL extension that provides a faster mechanism to remove all rows from a table.

There are two ways to delete rows in a table using information contained in other tables in the database: using sub-selects, or specifying additional tables in the USING clause. Which technique is more appropriate depends on the specific circumstances.

The optional RETURNING clause causes DELETE to compute and return value(s) based on each row actually deleted. Any expression using the table's columns, and/or columns of other tables mentioned in USING, can be computed. The syntax of the RETURNING list is identical to that of the output list of SELECT.

You must have the DELETE privilege on the table to delete from it, as well as the SELECT privilege for any table in the USING clause or whose values are read in the condition.

Parameters

with_query

> The WITH clause allows you to specify one or more subqueries that can be referenced by name in the DELETE query. See Section 7.8 and SELECT for details.

table_name

> The name (optionally schema-qualified) of the table to delete rows from. If ONLY is specified before the table name, matching rows are deleted from the named table only. If ONLY is not specified, matching rows are also deleted from any tables inheriting from the named table. Optionally, * can be specified after the table name to explicitly indicate that descendant tables are included.

alias

> A substitute name for the target table. When an alias is provided, it completely hides the actual name of the table. For example, given DELETE FROM foo AS f, the remainder of the DELETE statement must refer to this table as f not foo.

using_list

> A list of table expressions, allowing columns from other tables to appear in the WHERE condition. This is similar to the list of tables that can be specified in the *FROM Clause* of a SELECT statement; for example, an alias for the table name can be specified. Do not repeat the target table in the *using_list*, unless you wish to set up a self-join.

condition

> An expression that returns a value of type boolean. Only rows for which this expression returns true will be deleted.

cursor_name

> The name of the cursor to use in a WHERE CURRENT OF condition. The row to be deleted is the one most recently fetched from this cursor. The cursor must be a non-grouping query on the DELETE's target table. Note that WHERE CURRENT OF cannot be specified together with a Boolean condition. See DECLARE for more information about using cursors with WHERE CURRENT OF.

output_expression

> An expression to be computed and returned by the DELETE command after each row is deleted. The expression can use any column names of the table named by *table_name* or table(s) listed in USING. Write * to return all columns.

output_name

> A name to use for a returned column.

Outputs

On successful completion, a DELETE command returns a command tag of the form

DELETE *count*

The *count* is the number of rows deleted. Note that the number may be less than the number of rows that matched the *condition* when deletes were suppressed by a BEFORE DELETE trigger. If *count* is 0, no rows were deleted by the query (this is not considered an error).

If the DELETE command contains a RETURNING clause, the result will be similar to that of a SELECT statement containing the columns and values defined in the RETURNING list, computed over the row(s) deleted by the command.

Notes

PostgreSQL lets you reference columns of other tables in the WHERE condition by specifying the other tables in the USING clause. For example, to delete all films produced by a given producer, one can do:

```
DELETE FROM films USING producers
  WHERE producer_id = producers.id AND producers.name = 'foo';
```

What is essentially happening here is a join between films and producers, with all successfully joined films rows being marked for deletion. This syntax is not standard. A more standard way to do it is:

```
DELETE FROM films
  WHERE producer_id IN (SELECT id FROM producers WHERE name = 'foo');
```

In some cases the join style is easier to write or faster to execute than the sub-select style.

Examples

Delete all films but musicals:

```
DELETE FROM films WHERE kind <> 'Musical';
```

Clear the table films:

```
DELETE FROM films;
```

Delete completed tasks, returning full details of the deleted rows:

```
DELETE FROM tasks WHERE status = 'DONE' RETURNING *;
```

Delete the row of tasks on which the cursor c_tasks is currently positioned:

```
DELETE FROM tasks WHERE CURRENT OF c_tasks;
```

Compatibility

This command conforms to the SQL standard, except that the USING and RETURNING clauses are PostgreSQL extensions, as is the ability to use WITH with DELETE.

DISCARD

Name

DISCARD — discard session state

Synopsis

```
DISCARD { ALL | PLANS | SEQUENCES | TEMPORARY | TEMP }
```

Description

DISCARD releases internal resources associated with a database session. This command is useful for partially or fully resetting the session's state. There are several subcommands to release different types of resources; the DISCARD ALL variant subsumes all the others, and also resets additional state.

Parameters

PLANS

Releases all cached query plans, forcing re-planning to occur the next time the associated prepared statement is used.

SEQUENCES

Discards all cached sequence-related state, including currval()/lastval() information and any preallocated sequence values that have not yet been returned by nextval(). (See CREATE SEQUENCE for a description of preallocated sequence values.)

TEMPORARY or TEMP

Drops all temporary tables created in the current session.

ALL

Releases all temporary resources associated with the current session and resets the session to its initial state. Currently, this has the same effect as executing the following sequence of statements:

```
SET SESSION AUTHORIZATION DEFAULT;
RESET ALL;
DEALLOCATE ALL;
CLOSE ALL;
UNLISTEN *;
SELECT pg_advisory_unlock_all();
DISCARD PLANS;
DISCARD SEQUENCES;
DISCARD TEMP;
```

Notes

`DISCARD ALL` cannot be executed inside a transaction block.

Compatibility

`DISCARD` is a PostgreSQL extension.

DO

Name

DO — execute an anonymous code block

Synopsis

```
DO [ LANGUAGE lang_name ] code
```

Description

DO executes an anonymous code block, or in other words a transient anonymous function in a procedural language.

The code block is treated as though it were the body of a function with no parameters, returning void. It is parsed and executed a single time.

The optional LANGUAGE clause can be written either before or after the code block.

Parameters

code

   The procedural language code to be executed. This must be specified as a string literal, just as in CREATE FUNCTION. Use of a dollar-quoted literal is recommended.

lang_name

   The name of the procedural language the code is written in. If omitted, the default is plpgsql.

Notes

The procedural language to be used must already have been installed into the current database by means of CREATE LANGUAGE. plpgsql is installed by default, but other languages are not.

The user must have USAGE privilege for the procedural language, or must be a superuser if the language is untrusted. This is the same privilege requirement as for creating a function in the language.

Examples

Grant all privileges on all views in schema public to role webuser:

```
DO $$DECLARE r record;
BEGIN
    FOR r IN SELECT table_schema, table_name FROM information_schema.tables
```

```
             WHERE table_type = 'VIEW' AND table_schema = 'public'
    LOOP
         EXECUTE 'GRANT ALL ON ' || quote_ident(r.table_schema) || '.' || quote_
    END LOOP;
END$$;
```

Compatibility

There is no DO statement in the SQL standard.

See Also

CREATE LANGUAGE

DROP AGGREGATE

Name

DROP AGGREGATE — remove an aggregate function

Synopsis

```
DROP AGGREGATE [ IF EXISTS ] name ( aggregate_signature ) [ CASCADE | RESTRICT ]

where aggregate_signature is:

* |
[ argmode ] [ argname ] argtype [ , ... ] |
[ [ argmode ] [ argname ] argtype [ , ... ] ] ORDER BY [ argmode ] [ argname ] argt
```

Description

DROP AGGREGATE removes an existing aggregate function. To execute this command the current user must be the owner of the aggregate function.

Parameters

IF EXISTS

> Do not throw an error if the aggregate does not exist. A notice is issued in this case.

name

> The name (optionally schema-qualified) of an existing aggregate function.

argmode

> The mode of an argument: IN or VARIADIC. If omitted, the default is IN.

argname

> The name of an argument. Note that DROP AGGREGATE does not actually pay any attention to argument names, since only the argument data types are needed to determine the aggregate function's identity.

argtype

> An input data type on which the aggregate function operates. To reference a zero-argument aggregate function, write * in place of the list of argument specifications. To reference an ordered-set aggregate function, write ORDER BY between the direct and aggregated argument specifications.

CASCADE

> Automatically drop objects that depend on the aggregate function.

```
RESTRICT
```

Refuse to drop the aggregate function if any objects depend on it. This is the default.

Notes

Alternative syntaxes for referencing ordered-set aggregates are described under ALTER AGGREGATE.

Examples

To remove the aggregate function `myavg` for type `integer`:

```
DROP AGGREGATE myavg(integer);
```

To remove the hypothetical-set aggregate function `myrank`, which takes an arbitrary list of ordering columns and a matching list of direct arguments:

```
DROP AGGREGATE myrank(VARIADIC "any" ORDER BY VARIADIC "any");
```

Compatibility

There is no `DROP AGGREGATE` statement in the SQL standard.

See Also

ALTER AGGREGATE, CREATE AGGREGATE

DROP CAST

Name

DROP CAST — remove a cast

Synopsis

```
DROP CAST [ IF EXISTS ] (source_type AS target_type) [ CASCADE | RESTRICT ]
```

Description

DROP CAST removes a previously defined cast.

To be able to drop a cast, you must own the source or the target data type. These are the same privileges that are required to create a cast.

Parameters

IF EXISTS

    Do not throw an error if the cast does not exist. A notice is issued in this case.

source_type

    The name of the source data type of the cast.

target_type

    The name of the target data type of the cast.

CASCADE
RESTRICT

    These key words do not have any effect, since there are no dependencies on casts.

Examples

To drop the cast from type text to type int:

```
DROP CAST (text AS int);
```

Compatibility

The DROP CAST command conforms to the SQL standard.

See Also

CREATE CAST

DROP COLLATION

Name

DROP COLLATION — remove a collation

Synopsis

```
DROP COLLATION [ IF EXISTS ] name [ CASCADE | RESTRICT ]
```

Description

DROP COLLATION removes a previously defined collation. To be able to drop a collation, you must own the collation.

Parameters

IF EXISTS

Do not throw an error if the collation does not exist. A notice is issued in this case.

name

The name of the collation. The collation name can be schema-qualified.

CASCADE

Automatically drop objects that depend on the collation.

RESTRICT

Refuse to drop the collation if any objects depend on it. This is the default.

Examples

To drop the collation named german:

```
DROP COLLATION german;
```

Compatibility

The DROP COLLATION command conforms to the SQL standard, apart from the IF EXISTS option, which is a PostgreSQL extension.

See Also

ALTER COLLATION, CREATE COLLATION

DROP CONVERSION

Name

DROP CONVERSION — remove a conversion

Synopsis

```
DROP CONVERSION [ IF EXISTS ] name [ CASCADE | RESTRICT ]
```

Description

DROP CONVERSION removes a previously defined conversion. To be able to drop a conversion, you must own the conversion.

Parameters

IF EXISTS

Do not throw an error if the conversion does not exist. A notice is issued in this case.

name

The name of the conversion. The conversion name can be schema-qualified.

CASCADE
RESTRICT

These key words do not have any effect, since there are no dependencies on conversions.

Examples

To drop the conversion named myname:

```
DROP CONVERSION myname;
```

Compatibility

There is no DROP CONVERSION statement in the SQL standard, but a DROP TRANSLATION statement that goes along with the CREATE TRANSLATION statement that is similar to the CREATE CONVERSION statement in PostgreSQL.

See Also

ALTER CONVERSION, CREATE CONVERSION

DROP DATABASE

Name

DROP DATABASE — remove a database

Synopsis

```
DROP DATABASE [ IF EXISTS ] name
```

Description

DROP DATABASE drops a database. It removes the catalog entries for the database and deletes the directory containing the data. It can only be executed by the database owner. Also, it cannot be executed while you or anyone else are connected to the target database. (Connect to postgres or any other database to issue this command.)

DROP DATABASE cannot be undone. Use it with care!

Parameters

IF EXISTS

> Do not throw an error if the database does not exist. A notice is issued in this case.

name

> The name of the database to remove.

Notes

DROP DATABASE cannot be executed inside a transaction block.

This command cannot be executed while connected to the target database. Thus, it might be more convenient to use the program dropdb instead, which is a wrapper around this command.

Compatibility

There is no DROP DATABASE statement in the SQL standard.

See Also

CREATE DATABASE

DROP DOMAIN

Name

DROP DOMAIN — remove a domain

Synopsis

```
DROP DOMAIN [ IF EXISTS ] name [, ...] [ CASCADE | RESTRICT ]
```

Description

DROP DOMAIN removes a domain. Only the owner of a domain can remove it.

Parameters

IF EXISTS

> Do not throw an error if the domain does not exist. A notice is issued in this case.

name

> The name (optionally schema-qualified) of an existing domain.

CASCADE

> Automatically drop objects that depend on the domain (such as table columns).

RESTRICT

> Refuse to drop the domain if any objects depend on it. This is the default.

Examples

To remove the domain box:

```
DROP DOMAIN box;
```

Compatibility

This command conforms to the SQL standard, except for the IF EXISTS option, which is a PostgreSQL extension.

See Also

CREATE DOMAIN, ALTER DOMAIN

DROP EVENT TRIGGER

Name

DROP EVENT TRIGGER — remove an event trigger

Synopsis

```
DROP EVENT TRIGGER [ IF EXISTS ] name [ CASCADE | RESTRICT ]
```

Description

DROP EVENT TRIGGER removes an existing event trigger. To execute this command, the current user must be the owner of the event trigger.

Parameters

IF EXISTS

> Do not throw an error if the event trigger does not exist. A notice is issued in this case.

name

> The name of the event trigger to remove.

CASCADE

> Automatically drop objects that depend on the trigger.

RESTRICT

> Refuse to drop the trigger if any objects depend on it. This is the default.

Examples

Destroy the trigger snitch:

```
DROP EVENT TRIGGER snitch;
```

Compatibility

There is no DROP EVENT TRIGGER statement in the SQL standard.

See Also

CREATE EVENT TRIGGER, ALTER EVENT TRIGGER

DROP EXTENSION

Name

DROP EXTENSION — remove an extension

Synopsis

```
DROP EXTENSION [ IF EXISTS ] name [, ...] [ CASCADE | RESTRICT ]
```

Description

DROP EXTENSION removes extensions from the database. Dropping an extension causes its component objects to be dropped as well.

You must own the extension to use DROP EXTENSION.

Parameters

IF EXISTS

Do not throw an error if the extension does not exist. A notice is issued in this case.

name

The name of an installed extension.

CASCADE

Automatically drop objects that depend on the extension.

RESTRICT

Refuse to drop the extension if any objects depend on it (other than its own member objects and other extensions listed in the same DROP command). This is the default.

Examples

To remove the extension hstore from the current database:

```
DROP EXTENSION hstore;
```

This command will fail if any of hstore's objects are in use in the database, for example if any tables have columns of the hstore type. Add the CASCADE option to forcibly remove those dependent objects as well.

Compatibility

DROP EXTENSION is a PostgreSQL extension.

See Also

CREATE EXTENSION, ALTER EXTENSION

DROP FOREIGN DATA WRAPPER

Name

DROP FOREIGN DATA WRAPPER — remove a foreign-data wrapper

Synopsis

```
DROP FOREIGN DATA WRAPPER [ IF EXISTS ] name [ CASCADE | RESTRICT ]
```

Description

DROP FOREIGN DATA WRAPPER removes an existing foreign-data wrapper. To execute this command, the current user must be the owner of the foreign-data wrapper.

Parameters

IF EXISTS

> Do not throw an error if the foreign-data wrapper does not exist. A notice is issued in this case.

name

> The name of an existing foreign-data wrapper.

CASCADE

> Automatically drop objects that depend on the foreign-data wrapper (such as servers).

RESTRICT

> Refuse to drop the foreign-data wrappers if any objects depend on it. This is the default.

Examples

Drop the foreign-data wrapper dbi:

```
DROP FOREIGN DATA WRAPPER dbi;
```

Compatibility

DROP FOREIGN DATA WRAPPER conforms to ISO/IEC 9075-9 (SQL/MED). The IF EXISTS clause is a PostgreSQL extension.

See Also

CREATE FOREIGN DATA WRAPPER, ALTER FOREIGN DATA WRAPPER

DROP FOREIGN TABLE

Name

DROP FOREIGN TABLE — remove a foreign table

Synopsis

```
DROP FOREIGN TABLE [ IF EXISTS ] name [, ...] [ CASCADE | RESTRICT ]
```

Description

DROP FOREIGN TABLE removes a foreign table. Only the owner of a foreign table can remove it.

Parameters

IF EXISTS

> Do not throw an error if the foreign table does not exist. A notice is issued in this case.

name

> The name (optionally schema-qualified) of the foreign table to drop.

CASCADE

> Automatically drop objects that depend on the foreign table (such as views).

RESTRICT

> Refuse to drop the foreign table if any objects depend on it. This is the default.

Examples

To destroy two foreign tables, films and distributors:

```
DROP FOREIGN TABLE films, distributors;
```

Compatibility

This command conforms to the ISO/IEC 9075-9 (SQL/MED), except that the standard only allows one foreign table to be dropped per command, and apart from the IF EXISTS option, which is a PostgreSQL extension.

See Also

ALTER FOREIGN TABLE, CREATE FOREIGN TABLE

DROP FUNCTION

Name

DROP FUNCTION — remove a function

Synopsis

```
DROP FUNCTION [ IF EXISTS ] name ( [ [ argmode ] [ argname ] argtype [, ...] ] )
    [ CASCADE | RESTRICT ]
```

Description

DROP FUNCTION removes the definition of an existing function. To execute this command the user must be the owner of the function. The argument types to the function must be specified, since several different functions can exist with the same name and different argument lists.

Parameters

IF EXISTS

Do not throw an error if the function does not exist. A notice is issued in this case.

name

The name (optionally schema-qualified) of an existing function.

argmode

The mode of an argument: IN, OUT, INOUT, or VARIADIC. If omitted, the default is IN. Note that DROP FUNCTION does not actually pay any attention to OUT arguments, since only the input arguments are needed to determine the function's identity. So it is sufficient to list the IN, INOUT, and VARIADIC arguments.

argname

The name of an argument. Note that DROP FUNCTION does not actually pay any attention to argument names, since only the argument data types are needed to determine the function's identity.

argtype

The data type(s) of the function's arguments (optionally schema-qualified), if any.

CASCADE

Automatically drop objects that depend on the function (such as operators or triggers).

RESTRICT

Refuse to drop the function if any objects depend on it. This is the default.

Examples

This command removes the square root function:

```
DROP FUNCTION sqrt(integer);
```

Compatibility

A `DROP FUNCTION` statement is defined in the SQL standard, but it is not compatible with this command.

See Also

CREATE FUNCTION, ALTER FUNCTION

DROP GROUP

Name

DROP GROUP — remove a database role

Synopsis

```
DROP GROUP [ IF EXISTS ] name [, ...]
```

Description

DROP GROUP is now an alias for DROP ROLE.

Compatibility

There is no DROP GROUP statement in the SQL standard.

See Also

DROP ROLE

DROP INDEX

Name

DROP INDEX — remove an index

Synopsis

```
DROP INDEX [ CONCURRENTLY ] [ IF EXISTS ] name [, ...] [ CASCADE | RESTRICT ]
```

Description

DROP INDEX drops an existing index from the database system. To execute this command you must be the owner of the index.

Parameters

CONCURRENTLY

   Drop the index without locking out concurrent selects, inserts, updates, and deletes on the index's table. A normal DROP INDEX acquires exclusive lock on the table, blocking other accesses until the index drop can be completed. With this option, the command instead waits until conflicting transactions have completed.

   There are several caveats to be aware of when using this option. Only one index name can be specified, and the CASCADE option is not supported. (Thus, an index that supports a UNIQUE or PRIMARY KEY constraint cannot be dropped this way.) Also, regular DROP INDEX commands can be performed within a transaction block, but DROP INDEX CONCURRENTLY cannot.

IF EXISTS

   Do not throw an error if the index does not exist. A notice is issued in this case.

name

   The name (optionally schema-qualified) of an index to remove.

CASCADE

   Automatically drop objects that depend on the index.

RESTRICT

   Refuse to drop the index if any objects depend on it. This is the default.

Examples

This command will remove the index `title_idx`:

```
DROP INDEX title_idx;
```

Compatibility

`DROP INDEX` is a PostgreSQL language extension. There are no provisions for indexes in the SQL standard.

See Also

CREATE INDEX

DROP LANGUAGE

Name

DROP LANGUAGE — remove a procedural language

Synopsis

```
DROP [ PROCEDURAL ] LANGUAGE [ IF EXISTS ] name [ CASCADE | RESTRICT ]
```

Description

DROP LANGUAGE removes the definition of a previously registered procedural language. You must be a superuser or the owner of the language to use DROP LANGUAGE.

> **Note:** As of PostgreSQL 9.1, most procedural languages have been made into "extensions", and should therefore be removed with DROP EXTENSION not DROP LANGUAGE.

Parameters

IF EXISTS

Do not throw an error if the language does not exist. A notice is issued in this case.

name

The name of an existing procedural language. For backward compatibility, the name can be enclosed by single quotes.

CASCADE

Automatically drop objects that depend on the language (such as functions in the language).

RESTRICT

Refuse to drop the language if any objects depend on it. This is the default.

Examples

This command removes the procedural language plsample:

```
DROP LANGUAGE plsample;
```

Compatibility

There is no DROP LANGUAGE statement in the SQL standard.

See Also

ALTER LANGUAGE, CREATE LANGUAGE, droplang

DROP MATERIALIZED VIEW

Name

DROP MATERIALIZED VIEW — remove a materialized view

Synopsis

```
DROP MATERIALIZED VIEW [ IF EXISTS ] name [, ...] [ CASCADE | RESTRICT ]
```

Description

DROP MATERIALIZED VIEW drops an existing materialized view. To execute this command you must be the owner of the materialized view.

Parameters

IF EXISTS

    Do not throw an error if the materialized view does not exist. A notice is issued in this case.

name

    The name (optionally schema-qualified) of the materialized view to remove.

CASCADE

    Automatically drop objects that depend on the materialized view (such as other materialized views, or regular views).

RESTRICT

    Refuse to drop the materialized view if any objects depend on it. This is the default.

Examples

This command will remove the materialized view called order_summary:

```
DROP MATERIALIZED VIEW order_summary;
```

Compatibility

DROP MATERIALIZED VIEW is a PostgreSQL extension.

See Also

CREATE MATERIALIZED VIEW, ALTER MATERIALIZED VIEW, REFRESH MATERIALIZED VIEW

DROP OPERATOR

Name

DROP OPERATOR — remove an operator

Synopsis

```
DROP OPERATOR [ IF EXISTS ] name ( { left_type | NONE } , { right_type | NONE } )
```

Description

DROP OPERATOR drops an existing operator from the database system. To execute this command you must be the owner of the operator.

Parameters

IF EXISTS

Do not throw an error if the operator does not exist. A notice is issued in this case.

name

The name (optionally schema-qualified) of an existing operator.

left_type

The data type of the operator's left operand; write NONE if the operator has no left operand.

right_type

The data type of the operator's right operand; write NONE if the operator has no right operand.

CASCADE

Automatically drop objects that depend on the operator.

RESTRICT

Refuse to drop the operator if any objects depend on it. This is the default.

Examples

Remove the power operator a^b for type integer:

```
DROP OPERATOR ^ (integer, integer);
```

Remove the left unary bitwise complement operator ~b for type bit:

```
DROP OPERATOR ~ (none, bit);
```

Remove the right unary factorial operator x! for type `bigint`:

```
DROP OPERATOR ! (bigint, none);
```

Compatibility

There is no DROP OPERATOR statement in the SQL standard.

See Also

CREATE OPERATOR, ALTER OPERATOR

DROP OPERATOR CLASS

Name

DROP OPERATOR CLASS — remove an operator class

Synopsis

```
DROP OPERATOR CLASS [ IF EXISTS ] name USING index_method [ CASCADE | RESTRICT ]
```

Description

DROP OPERATOR CLASS drops an existing operator class. To execute this command you must be the owner of the operator class.

DROP OPERATOR CLASS does not drop any of the operators or functions referenced by the class. If there are any indexes depending on the operator class, you will need to specify CASCADE for the drop to complete.

Parameters

IF EXISTS

    Do not throw an error if the operator class does not exist. A notice is issued in this case.

name

    The name (optionally schema-qualified) of an existing operator class.

index_method

    The name of the index access method the operator class is for.

CASCADE

    Automatically drop objects that depend on the operator class.

RESTRICT

    Refuse to drop the operator class if any objects depend on it. This is the default.

Notes

DROP OPERATOR CLASS will not drop the operator family containing the class, even if there is nothing else left in the family (in particular, in the case where the family was implicitly created by CREATE OPERATOR CLASS). An empty operator family is harmless, but for the sake of tidiness you might wish to remove the family with DROP OPERATOR FAMILY; or perhaps better, use DROP OPERATOR FAMILY in the first place.

Examples

Remove the B-tree operator class `widget_ops`:

```
DROP OPERATOR CLASS widget_ops USING btree;
```

This command will not succeed if there are any existing indexes that use the operator class. Add CASCADE to drop such indexes along with the operator class.

Compatibility

There is no DROP OPERATOR CLASS statement in the SQL standard.

See Also

ALTER OPERATOR CLASS, CREATE OPERATOR CLASS, DROP OPERATOR FAMILY

DROP OPERATOR FAMILY

Name

DROP OPERATOR FAMILY — remove an operator family

Synopsis

```
DROP OPERATOR FAMILY [ IF EXISTS ] name USING index_method [ CASCADE | RESTRICT
```

Description

DROP OPERATOR FAMILY drops an existing operator family. To execute this command you must be the owner of the operator family.

DROP OPERATOR FAMILY includes dropping any operator classes contained in the family, but it does not drop any of the operators or functions referenced by the family. If there are any indexes depending on operator classes within the family, you will need to specify CASCADE for the drop to complete.

Parameters

IF EXISTS

Do not throw an error if the operator family does not exist. A notice is issued in this case.

name

The name (optionally schema-qualified) of an existing operator family.

index_method

The name of the index access method the operator family is for.

CASCADE

Automatically drop objects that depend on the operator family.

RESTRICT

Refuse to drop the operator family if any objects depend on it. This is the default.

Examples

Remove the B-tree operator family float_ops:

```
DROP OPERATOR FAMILY float_ops USING btree;
```

This command will not succeed if there are any existing indexes that use operator classes within the family. Add CASCADE to drop such indexes along with the operator family.

Compatibility

There is no `DROP OPERATOR FAMILY` statement in the SQL standard.

See Also

ALTER OPERATOR FAMILY, CREATE OPERATOR FAMILY, ALTER OPERATOR CLASS, CREATE OPERATOR CLASS, DROP OPERATOR CLASS

DROP OWNED

Name

DROP OWNED — remove database objects owned by a database role

Synopsis

```
DROP OWNED BY name [, ...] [ CASCADE | RESTRICT ]
```

Description

DROP OWNED drops all the objects within the current database that are owned by one of the specified roles. Any privileges granted to the given roles on objects in the current database and on shared objects (databases, tablespaces) will also be revoked.

Parameters

name

The name of a role whose objects will be dropped, and whose privileges will be revoked.

CASCADE

Automatically drop objects that depend on the affected objects.

RESTRICT

Refuse to drop the objects owned by a role if any other database objects depend on one of the affected objects. This is the default.

Notes

DROP OWNED is often used to prepare for the removal of one or more roles. Because DROP OWNED only affects the objects in the current database, it is usually necessary to execute this command in each database that contains objects owned by a role that is to be removed.

Using the CASCADE option might make the command recurse to objects owned by other users.

The REASSIGN OWNED command is an alternative that reassigns the ownership of all the database objects owned by one or more roles.

Databases and tablespaces owned by the role(s) will not be removed.

Compatibility

The DROP OWNED statement is a PostgreSQL extension.

See Also

REASSIGN OWNED, DROP ROLE

DROP ROLE

Name

DROP ROLE — remove a database role

Synopsis

```
DROP ROLE [ IF EXISTS ] name [, ...]
```

Description

DROP ROLE removes the specified role(s). To drop a superuser role, you must be a superuser yourself; to drop non-superuser roles, you must have CREATEROLE privilege.

A role cannot be removed if it is still referenced in any database of the cluster; an error will be raised if so. Before dropping the role, you must drop all the objects it owns (or reassign their ownership) and revoke any privileges the role has been granted. The REASSIGN OWNED and DROP OWNED commands can be useful for this purpose.

However, it is not necessary to remove role memberships involving the role; DROP ROLE automatically revokes any memberships of the target role in other roles, and of other roles in the target role. The other roles are not dropped nor otherwise affected.

Parameters

IF EXISTS

Do not throw an error if the role does not exist. A notice is issued in this case.

name

The name of the role to remove.

Notes

PostgreSQL includes a program dropuser that has the same functionality as this command (in fact, it calls this command) but can be run from the command shell.

Examples

To drop a role:

```
DROP ROLE jonathan;
```

Compatibility

The SQL standard defines DROP ROLE, but it allows only one role to be dropped at a time, and it specifies different privilege requirements than PostgreSQL uses.

See Also

CREATE ROLE, ALTER ROLE, SET ROLE

DROP RULE

Name

DROP RULE — remove a rewrite rule

Synopsis

```
DROP RULE [ IF EXISTS ] name ON table_name [ CASCADE | RESTRICT ]
```

Description

DROP RULE drops a rewrite rule.

Parameters

IF EXISTS

> Do not throw an error if the rule does not exist. A notice is issued in this case.

name

> The name of the rule to drop.

table_name

> The name (optionally schema-qualified) of the table or view that the rule applies to.

CASCADE

> Automatically drop objects that depend on the rule.

RESTRICT

> Refuse to drop the rule if any objects depend on it. This is the default.

Examples

To drop the rewrite rule newrule:

```
DROP RULE newrule ON mytable;
```

Compatibility

DROP RULE is a PostgreSQL language extension, as is the entire query rewrite system.

See Also

CREATE RULE, ALTER RULE

DROP SCHEMA

Name

DROP SCHEMA — remove a schema

Synopsis

```
DROP SCHEMA [ IF EXISTS ] name [, ...] [ CASCADE | RESTRICT ]
```

Description

DROP SCHEMA removes schemas from the database.

A schema can only be dropped by its owner or a superuser. Note that the owner can drop the schema (and thereby all contained objects) even if he does not own some of the objects within the schema.

Parameters

IF EXISTS

> Do not throw an error if the schema does not exist. A notice is issued in this case.

name

> The name of a schema.

CASCADE

> Automatically drop objects (tables, functions, etc.) that are contained in the schema.

RESTRICT

> Refuse to drop the schema if it contains any objects. This is the default.

Examples

To remove schema mystuff from the database, along with everything it contains:

```
DROP SCHEMA mystuff CASCADE;
```

Compatibility

DROP SCHEMA is fully conforming with the SQL standard, except that the standard only allows one schema to be dropped per command, and apart from the IF EXISTS option, which is a PostgreSQL extension.

See Also

ALTER SCHEMA, CREATE SCHEMA

DROP SEQUENCE

Name

DROP SEQUENCE — remove a sequence

Synopsis

```
DROP SEQUENCE [ IF EXISTS ] name [, ...] [ CASCADE | RESTRICT ]
```

Description

DROP SEQUENCE removes sequence number generators. A sequence can only be dropped by its owner or a superuser.

Parameters

IF EXISTS

Do not throw an error if the sequence does not exist. A notice is issued in this case.

name

The name (optionally schema-qualified) of a sequence.

CASCADE

Automatically drop objects that depend on the sequence.

RESTRICT

Refuse to drop the sequence if any objects depend on it. This is the default.

Examples

To remove the sequence serial:

```
DROP SEQUENCE serial;
```

Compatibility

DROP SEQUENCE conforms to the SQL standard, except that the standard only allows one sequence to be dropped per command, and apart from the IF EXISTS option, which is a PostgreSQL extension.

See Also

CREATE SEQUENCE, ALTER SEQUENCE

DROP SERVER

Name

DROP SERVER — remove a foreign server descriptor

Synopsis

```
DROP SERVER [ IF EXISTS ] name [ CASCADE | RESTRICT ]
```

Description

DROP SERVER removes an existing foreign server descriptor. To execute this command, the current user must be the owner of the server.

Parameters

IF EXISTS

> Do not throw an error if the server does not exist. A notice is issued in this case.

name

> The name of an existing server.

CASCADE

> Automatically drop objects that depend on the server (such as user mappings).

RESTRICT

> Refuse to drop the server if any objects depend on it. This is the default.

Examples

Drop a server foo if it exists:

```
DROP SERVER IF EXISTS foo;
```

Compatibility

DROP SERVER conforms to ISO/IEC 9075-9 (SQL/MED). The IF EXISTS clause is a PostgreSQL extension.

See Also

CREATE SERVER, ALTER SERVER

DROP TABLE

Name

DROP TABLE — remove a table

Synopsis

```
DROP TABLE [ IF EXISTS ] name [, ...] [ CASCADE | RESTRICT ]
```

Description

DROP TABLE removes tables from the database. Only the table owner, the schema owner, and superuser can drop a table. To empty a table of rows without destroying the table, use DELETE or TRUNCATE.

DROP TABLE always removes any indexes, rules, triggers, and constraints that exist for the target table. However, to drop a table that is referenced by a view or a foreign-key constraint of another table, CASCADE must be specified. (CASCADE will remove a dependent view entirely, but in the foreign-key case it will only remove the foreign-key constraint, not the other table entirely.)

Parameters

IF EXISTS

Do not throw an error if the table does not exist. A notice is issued in this case.

name

The name (optionally schema-qualified) of the table to drop.

CASCADE

Automatically drop objects that depend on the table (such as views).

RESTRICT

Refuse to drop the table if any objects depend on it. This is the default.

Examples

To destroy two tables, films and distributors:

```
DROP TABLE films, distributors;
```

Compatibility

This command conforms to the SQL standard, except that the standard only allows one table to be dropped per command, and apart from the IF EXISTS option, which is a PostgreSQL extension.

See Also

ALTER TABLE, CREATE TABLE

DROP TABLESPACE

Name

DROP TABLESPACE — remove a tablespace

Synopsis

```
DROP TABLESPACE [ IF EXISTS ] name
```

Description

DROP TABLESPACE removes a tablespace from the system.

A tablespace can only be dropped by its owner or a superuser. The tablespace must be empty of all database objects before it can be dropped. It is possible that objects in other databases might still reside in the tablespace even if no objects in the current database are using the tablespace. Also, if the tablespace is listed in the temp_tablespaces setting of any active session, the DROP might fail due to temporary files residing in the tablespace.

Parameters

IF EXISTS

> Do not throw an error if the tablespace does not exist. A notice is issued in this case.

name

> The name of a tablespace.

Notes

DROP TABLESPACE cannot be executed inside a transaction block.

Examples

To remove tablespace mystuff from the system:

```
DROP TABLESPACE mystuff;
```

Compatibility

`DROP TABLESPACE` is a PostgreSQL extension.

See Also

CREATE TABLESPACE, ALTER TABLESPACE

DROP TEXT SEARCH CONFIGURATION

Name

DROP TEXT SEARCH CONFIGURATION — remove a text search configuration

Synopsis

```
DROP TEXT SEARCH CONFIGURATION [ IF EXISTS ] name [ CASCADE | RESTRICT ]
```

Description

DROP TEXT SEARCH CONFIGURATION drops an existing text search configuration. To execute this command you must be the owner of the configuration.

Parameters

IF EXISTS

> Do not throw an error if the text search configuration does not exist. A notice is issued in this case.

name

> The name (optionally schema-qualified) of an existing text search configuration.

CASCADE

> Automatically drop objects that depend on the text search configuration.

RESTRICT

> Refuse to drop the text search configuration if any objects depend on it. This is the default.

Examples

Remove the text search configuration my_english:

```
DROP TEXT SEARCH CONFIGURATION my_english;
```

This command will not succeed if there are any existing indexes that reference the configuration in to_tsvector calls. Add CASCADE to drop such indexes along with the text search configuration.

Compatibility

There is no DROP TEXT SEARCH CONFIGURATION statement in the SQL standard.

See Also

ALTER TEXT SEARCH CONFIGURATION, CREATE TEXT SEARCH CONFIGURATION

DROP TEXT SEARCH DICTIONARY

Name

DROP TEXT SEARCH DICTIONARY — remove a text search dictionary

Synopsis

```
DROP TEXT SEARCH DICTIONARY [ IF EXISTS ] name [ CASCADE | RESTRICT ]
```

Description

DROP TEXT SEARCH DICTIONARY drops an existing text search dictionary. To execute this command you must be the owner of the dictionary.

Parameters

IF EXISTS

Do not throw an error if the text search dictionary does not exist. A notice is issued in this case.

name

The name (optionally schema-qualified) of an existing text search dictionary.

CASCADE

Automatically drop objects that depend on the text search dictionary.

RESTRICT

Refuse to drop the text search dictionary if any objects depend on it. This is the default.

Examples

Remove the text search dictionary english:

```
DROP TEXT SEARCH DICTIONARY english;
```

This command will not succeed if there are any existing text search configurations that use the dictionary. Add CASCADE to drop such configurations along with the dictionary.

Compatibility

There is no DROP TEXT SEARCH DICTIONARY statement in the SQL standard.

See Also

ALTER TEXT SEARCH DICTIONARY, CREATE TEXT SEARCH DICTIONARY

DROP TEXT SEARCH PARSER

Name

DROP TEXT SEARCH PARSER — remove a text search parser

Synopsis

```
DROP TEXT SEARCH PARSER [ IF EXISTS ] name [ CASCADE | RESTRICT ]
```

Description

DROP TEXT SEARCH PARSER drops an existing text search parser. You must be a superuser to use this command.

Parameters

IF EXISTS

> Do not throw an error if the text search parser does not exist. A notice is issued in this case.

name

> The name (optionally schema-qualified) of an existing text search parser.

CASCADE

> Automatically drop objects that depend on the text search parser.

RESTRICT

> Refuse to drop the text search parser if any objects depend on it. This is the default.

Examples

Remove the text search parser my_parser:

```
DROP TEXT SEARCH PARSER my_parser;
```

This command will not succeed if there are any existing text search configurations that use the parser. Add CASCADE to drop such configurations along with the parser.

Compatibility

There is no DROP TEXT SEARCH PARSER statement in the SQL standard.

See Also

ALTER TEXT SEARCH PARSER, CREATE TEXT SEARCH PARSER

DROP TEXT SEARCH TEMPLATE

Name

DROP TEXT SEARCH TEMPLATE — remove a text search template

Synopsis

```
DROP TEXT SEARCH TEMPLATE [ IF EXISTS ] name [ CASCADE | RESTRICT ]
```

Description

DROP TEXT SEARCH TEMPLATE drops an existing text search template. You must be a superuser to use this command.

Parameters

IF EXISTS

    Do not throw an error if the text search template does not exist. A notice is issued in this case.

name

    The name (optionally schema-qualified) of an existing text search template.

CASCADE

    Automatically drop objects that depend on the text search template.

RESTRICT

    Refuse to drop the text search template if any objects depend on it. This is the default.

Examples

Remove the text search template thesaurus:

```
DROP TEXT SEARCH TEMPLATE thesaurus;
```

This command will not succeed if there are any existing text search dictionaries that use the template. Add CASCADE to drop such dictionaries along with the template.

Compatibility

There is no DROP TEXT SEARCH TEMPLATE statement in the SQL standard.

See Also

ALTER TEXT SEARCH TEMPLATE, CREATE TEXT SEARCH TEMPLATE

DROP TRIGGER

Name

DROP TRIGGER — remove a trigger

Synopsis

```
DROP TRIGGER [ IF EXISTS ] name ON table_name [ CASCADE | RESTRICT ]
```

Description

DROP TRIGGER removes an existing trigger definition. To execute this command, the current user must be the owner of the table for which the trigger is defined.

Parameters

IF EXISTS

> Do not throw an error if the trigger does not exist. A notice is issued in this case.

name

> The name of the trigger to remove.

table_name

> The name (optionally schema-qualified) of the table for which the trigger is defined.

CASCADE

> Automatically drop objects that depend on the trigger.

RESTRICT

> Refuse to drop the trigger if any objects depend on it. This is the default.

Examples

Destroy the trigger if_dist_exists on the table films:

```
DROP TRIGGER if_dist_exists ON films;
```

Compatibility

The DROP TRIGGER statement in PostgreSQL is incompatible with the SQL standard. In the SQL standard, trigger names are not local to tables, so the command is simply DROP TRIGGER *name*.

See Also

CREATE TRIGGER

DROP TYPE

Name

DROP TYPE — remove a data type

Synopsis

```
DROP TYPE [ IF EXISTS ] name [, ...] [ CASCADE | RESTRICT ]
```

Description

DROP TYPE removes a user-defined data type. Only the owner of a type can remove it.

Parameters

IF EXISTS

> Do not throw an error if the type does not exist. A notice is issued in this case.

name

> The name (optionally schema-qualified) of the data type to remove.

CASCADE

> Automatically drop objects that depend on the type (such as table columns, functions, operators).

RESTRICT

> Refuse to drop the type if any objects depend on it. This is the default.

Examples

To remove the data type box:

```
DROP TYPE box;
```

Compatibility

This command is similar to the corresponding command in the SQL standard, apart from the IF EXISTS option, which is a PostgreSQL extension. But note that much of the CREATE TYPE command and the data type extension mechanisms in PostgreSQL differ from the SQL standard.

See Also

ALTER TYPE, CREATE TYPE

DROP USER

Name

DROP USER — remove a database role

Synopsis

```
DROP USER [ IF EXISTS ] name [, ...]
```

Description

DROP USER is now an alias for DROP ROLE.

Compatibility

The DROP USER statement is a PostgreSQL extension. The SQL standard leaves the definition of users to the implementation.

See Also

DROP ROLE

DROP USER MAPPING

Name

DROP USER MAPPING — remove a user mapping for a foreign server

Synopsis

```
DROP USER MAPPING [ IF EXISTS ] FOR { user_name | USER | CURRENT_USER | PUBLIC }
```

Description

DROP USER MAPPING removes an existing user mapping from foreign server.

The owner of a foreign server can drop user mappings for that server for any user. Also, a user can drop a user mapping for his own user name if USAGE privilege on the server has been granted to the user.

Parameters

IF EXISTS

    Do not throw an error if the user mapping does not exist. A notice is issued in this case.

user_name

    User name of the mapping. CURRENT_USER and USER match the name of the current user. PUBLIC is used to match all present and future user names in the system.

server_name

    Server name of the user mapping.

Examples

Drop a user mapping bob, server foo if it exists:

```
DROP USER MAPPING IF EXISTS FOR bob SERVER foo;
```

Compatibility

DROP USER MAPPING conforms to ISO/IEC 9075-9 (SQL/MED). The IF EXISTS clause is a Post-greSQL extension.

See Also

CREATE USER MAPPING, ALTER USER MAPPING

DROP VIEW

Name

DROP VIEW — remove a view

Synopsis

```
DROP VIEW [ IF EXISTS ] name [, ...] [ CASCADE | RESTRICT ]
```

Description

DROP VIEW drops an existing view. To execute this command you must be the owner of the view.

Parameters

IF EXISTS

> Do not throw an error if the view does not exist. A notice is issued in this case.

name

> The name (optionally schema-qualified) of the view to remove.

CASCADE

> Automatically drop objects that depend on the view (such as other views).

RESTRICT

> Refuse to drop the view if any objects depend on it. This is the default.

Examples

This command will remove the view called kinds:

```
DROP VIEW kinds;
```

Compatibility

This command conforms to the SQL standard, except that the standard only allows one view to be dropped per command, and apart from the IF EXISTS option, which is a PostgreSQL extension.

See Also

ALTER VIEW, CREATE VIEW

END

Name

END — commit the current transaction

Synopsis

```
END [ WORK | TRANSACTION ]
```

Description

END commits the current transaction. All changes made by the transaction become visible to others and are guaranteed to be durable if a crash occurs. This command is a PostgreSQL extension that is equivalent to COMMIT.

Parameters

WORK
TRANSACTION

    Optional key words. They have no effect.

Notes

Use ROLLBACK to abort a transaction.

Issuing END when not inside a transaction does no harm, but it will provoke a warning message.

Examples

To commit the current transaction and make all changes permanent:

```
END;
```

Compatibility

END is a PostgreSQL extension that provides functionality equivalent to COMMIT, which is specified in the SQL standard.

See Also

BEGIN, COMMIT, ROLLBACK

EXECUTE

Name

EXECUTE — execute a prepared statement

Synopsis

```
EXECUTE name [ ( parameter [, ...] ) ]
```

Description

EXECUTE is used to execute a previously prepared statement. Since prepared statements only exist for the duration of a session, the prepared statement must have been created by a PREPARE statement executed earlier in the current session.

If the PREPARE statement that created the statement specified some parameters, a compatible set of parameters must be passed to the EXECUTE statement, or else an error is raised. Note that (unlike functions) prepared statements are not overloaded based on the type or number of their parameters; the name of a prepared statement must be unique within a database session.

For more information on the creation and usage of prepared statements, see PREPARE.

Parameters

name

> The name of the prepared statement to execute.

parameter

> The actual value of a parameter to the prepared statement. This must be an expression yielding a value that is compatible with the data type of this parameter, as was determined when the prepared statement was created.

Outputs

The command tag returned by EXECUTE is that of the prepared statement, and not EXECUTE.

Examples

Examples are given in the *Examples* section of the PREPARE documentation.

Compatibility

The SQL standard includes an EXECUTE statement, but it is only for use in embedded SQL. This version of the EXECUTE statement also uses a somewhat different syntax.

See Also

DEALLOCATE, PREPARE

EXPLAIN

Name

EXPLAIN — show the execution plan of a statement

Synopsis

```
EXPLAIN [ ( option [, ...] ) ] statement
EXPLAIN [ ANALYZE ] [ VERBOSE ] statement

where option can be one of:

    ANALYZE [ boolean ]
    VERBOSE [ boolean ]
    COSTS [ boolean ]
    BUFFERS [ boolean ]
    TIMING [ boolean ]
    FORMAT { TEXT | XML | JSON | YAML }
```

Description

This command displays the execution plan that the PostgreSQL planner generates for the supplied statement. The execution plan shows how the table(s) referenced by the statement will be scanned — by plain sequential scan, index scan, etc. — and if multiple tables are referenced, what join algorithms will be used to bring together the required rows from each input table.

The most critical part of the display is the estimated statement execution cost, which is the planner's guess at how long it will take to run the statement (measured in cost units that are arbitrary, but conventionally mean disk page fetches). Actually two numbers are shown: the start-up cost before the first row can be returned, and the total cost to return all the rows. For most queries the total cost is what matters, but in contexts such as a subquery in EXISTS, the planner will choose the smallest start-up cost instead of the smallest total cost (since the executor will stop after getting one row, anyway). Also, if you limit the number of rows to return with a LIMIT clause, the planner makes an appropriate interpolation between the endpoint costs to estimate which plan is really the cheapest.

The ANALYZE option causes the statement to be actually executed, not only planned. Then actual run time statistics are added to the display, including the total elapsed time expended within each plan node (in milliseconds) and the total number of rows it actually returned. This is useful for seeing whether the planner's estimates are close to reality.

> **Important:** Keep in mind that the statement is actually executed when the ANALYZE option is used. Although EXPLAIN will discard any output that a SELECT would return, other side effects of the statement will happen as usual. If you wish to use EXPLAIN ANALYZE on an INSERT, UPDATE, DELETE, CREATE TABLE AS, or EXECUTE statement without letting the command affect your data, use this approach:
>
> ```
> BEGIN;
> EXPLAIN ANALYZE ...;
> ```

```
ROLLBACK;
```

Only the ANALYZE and VERBOSE options can be specified, and only in that order, without surrounding the option list in parentheses. Prior to PostgreSQL 9.0, the unparenthesized syntax was the only one supported. It is expected that all new options will be supported only in the parenthesized syntax.

Parameters

ANALYZE

Carry out the command and show actual run times and other statistics. This parameter defaults to FALSE.

VERBOSE

Display additional information regarding the plan. Specifically, include the output column list for each node in the plan tree, schema-qualify table and function names, always label variables in expressions with their range table alias, and always print the name of each trigger for which statistics are displayed. This parameter defaults to FALSE.

COSTS

Include information on the estimated startup and total cost of each plan node, as well as the estimated number of rows and the estimated width of each row. This parameter defaults to TRUE.

BUFFERS

Include information on buffer usage. Specifically, include the number of shared blocks hit, read, dirtied, and written, the number of local blocks hit, read, dirtied, and written, and the number of temp blocks read and written. A *hit* means that a read was avoided because the block was found already in cache when needed. Shared blocks contain data from regular tables and indexes; local blocks contain data from temporary tables and indexes; while temp blocks contain short-term working data used in sorts, hashes, Materialize plan nodes, and similar cases. The number of blocks *dirtied* indicates the number of previously unmodified blocks that were changed by this query; while the number of blocks *written* indicates the number of previously-dirtied blocks evicted from cache by this backend during query processing. The number of blocks shown for an upper-level node includes those used by all its child nodes. In text format, only non-zero values are printed. This parameter may only be used when ANALYZE is also enabled. It defaults to FALSE.

TIMING

Include actual startup time and time spent in each node in the output. The overhead of repeatedly reading the system clock can slow down the query significantly on some systems, so it may be useful to set this parameter to FALSE when only actual row counts, and not exact times, are needed. Run time of the entire statement is always measured, even when node-level timing is turned off with this option. This parameter may only be used when ANALYZE is also enabled. It defaults to TRUE.

FORMAT

Specify the output format, which can be TEXT, XML, JSON, or YAML. Non-text output contains the same information as the text output format, but is easier for programs to parse. This parameter defaults to TEXT.

boolean

Specifies whether the selected option should be turned on or off. You can write TRUE, ON, or 1 to enable the option, and FALSE, OFF, or 0 to disable it. The *boolean* value can also be omitted, in which case TRUE is assumed.

statement

Any SELECT, INSERT, UPDATE, DELETE, VALUES, EXECUTE, DECLARE, CREATE TABLE AS, or CREATE MATERIALIZED VIEW AS statement, whose execution plan you wish to see.

Outputs

The command's result is a textual description of the plan selected for the *statement*, optionally annotated with execution statistics. Section 14.1 describes the information provided.

Notes

In order to allow the PostgreSQL query planner to make reasonably informed decisions when optimizing queries, the pg_statistic data should be up-to-date for all tables used in the query. Normally the autovacuum daemon will take care of that automatically. But if a table has recently had substantial changes in its contents, you might need to do a manual ANALYZE rather than wait for autovacuum to catch up with the changes.

In order to measure the run-time cost of each node in the execution plan, the current implementation of EXPLAIN ANALYZE adds profiling overhead to query execution. As a result, running EXPLAIN ANALYZE on a query can sometimes take significantly longer than executing the query normally. The amount of overhead depends on the nature of the query, as well as the platform being used. The worst case occurs for plan nodes that in themselves require very little time per execution, and on machines that have relatively slow operating system calls for obtaining the time of day.

Examples

To show the plan for a simple query on a table with a single integer column and 10000 rows:

```
EXPLAIN SELECT * FROM foo;

                      QUERY PLAN
---------------------------------------------------------
 Seq Scan on foo  (cost=0.00..155.00 rows=10000 width=4)
(1 row)
```

Here is the same query, with JSON output formatting:

```
EXPLAIN (FORMAT JSON) SELECT * FROM foo;
          QUERY PLAN
--------------------------------
 [                               +
   {                             +
     "Plan": {                   +
       "Node Type": "Seq Scan", +
       "Relation Name": "foo",  +
       "Alias": "foo",          +
       "Startup Cost": 0.00,    +
       "Total Cost": 155.00,    +
       "Plan Rows": 10000,      +
       "Plan Width": 4          +
     }                           +
   }                             +
 ]
(1 row)
```

If there is an index and we use a query with an indexable WHERE condition, EXPLAIN might show a different plan:

```
EXPLAIN SELECT * FROM foo WHERE i = 4;

                        QUERY PLAN
--------------------------------------------------------------
 Index Scan using fi on foo  (cost=0.00..5.98 rows=1 width=4)
   Index Cond: (i = 4)
(2 rows)
```

Here is the same query, but in YAML format:

```
EXPLAIN (FORMAT YAML) SELECT * FROM foo WHERE i='4';
          QUERY PLAN
--------------------------------
 - Plan:                       +
     Node Type: "Index Scan"   +
     Scan Direction: "Forward" +
     Index Name: "fi"          +
     Relation Name: "foo"      +
     Alias: "foo"              +
     Startup Cost: 0.00        +
     Total Cost: 5.98          +
     Plan Rows: 1              +
     Plan Width: 4             +
     Index Cond: "(i = 4)"
(1 row)
```

XML format is left as an exercise for the reader.

Here is the same plan with cost estimates suppressed:

```
EXPLAIN (COSTS FALSE) SELECT * FROM foo WHERE i = 4;

        QUERY PLAN
----------------------------
 Index Scan using fi on foo
   Index Cond: (i = 4)
(2 rows)
```

Here is an example of a query plan for a query using an aggregate function:

```
EXPLAIN SELECT sum(i) FROM foo WHERE i < 10;

                          QUERY PLAN
---------------------------------------------------------------------
 Aggregate  (cost=23.93..23.93 rows=1 width=4)
   ->  Index Scan using fi on foo  (cost=0.00..23.92 rows=6 width=4)
         Index Cond: (i < 10)
(3 rows)
```

Here is an example of using EXPLAIN EXECUTE to display the execution plan for a prepared query:

```
PREPARE query(int, int) AS SELECT sum(bar) FROM test
    WHERE id > $1 AND id < $2
    GROUP BY foo;

EXPLAIN ANALYZE EXECUTE query(100, 200);

                                                           QUERY PLAN
--------------------------------------------------------------------------------
 HashAggregate  (cost=9.54..9.54 rows=1 width=8) (actual time=0.156..0.161 rows
   Group Key: foo
   ->  Index Scan using test_pkey on test  (cost=0.29..9.29 rows=50 width=8) (a
         Index Cond: ((id > $1) AND (id < $2))
 Planning time: 0.197 ms
 Execution time: 0.225 ms
(6 rows)
```

Of course, the specific numbers shown here depend on the actual contents of the tables involved. Also note that the numbers, and even the selected query strategy, might vary between PostgreSQL releases due to planner improvements. In addition, the ANALYZE command uses random sampling to estimate data statistics; therefore, it is possible for cost estimates to change after a fresh run of ANALYZE, even if the actual distribution of data in the table has not changed.

Compatibility

There is no EXPLAIN statement defined in the SQL standard.

See Also

ANALYZE

FETCH

Name

FETCH — retrieve rows from a query using a cursor

Synopsis

```
FETCH [ direction [ FROM | IN ] ] cursor_name

where direction can be empty or one of:

    NEXT
    PRIOR
    FIRST
    LAST
    ABSOLUTE count
    RELATIVE count
    count
    ALL
    FORWARD
    FORWARD count
    FORWARD ALL
    BACKWARD
    BACKWARD count
    BACKWARD ALL
```

Description

FETCH retrieves rows using a previously-created cursor.

A cursor has an associated position, which is used by FETCH. The cursor position can be before the first row of the query result, on any particular row of the result, or after the last row of the result. When created, a cursor is positioned before the first row. After fetching some rows, the cursor is positioned on the row most recently retrieved. If FETCH runs off the end of the available rows then the cursor is left positioned after the last row, or before the first row if fetching backward. FETCH ALL or FETCH BACKWARD ALL will always leave the cursor positioned after the last row or before the first row.

The forms NEXT, PRIOR, FIRST, LAST, ABSOLUTE, RELATIVE fetch a single row after moving the cursor appropriately. If there is no such row, an empty result is returned, and the cursor is left positioned before the first row or after the last row as appropriate.

The forms using FORWARD and BACKWARD retrieve the indicated number of rows moving in the forward or backward direction, leaving the cursor positioned on the last-returned row (or after/before all rows, if the count exceeds the number of rows available).

RELATIVE 0, FORWARD 0, and BACKWARD 0 all request fetching the current row without moving the cursor, that is, re-fetching the most recently fetched row. This will succeed unless the cursor is positioned before the first row or after the last row; in which case, no row is returned.

Note: This page describes usage of cursors at the SQL command level. If you are trying to use cursors inside a PL/pgSQL function, the rules are different — see Section 40.7.

Parameters

direction

> *direction* defines the fetch direction and number of rows to fetch. It can be one of the following:

NEXT

> Fetch the next row. This is the default if *direction* is omitted.

PRIOR

> Fetch the prior row.

FIRST

> Fetch the first row of the query (same as ABSOLUTE 1).

LAST

> Fetch the last row of the query (same as ABSOLUTE -1).

ABSOLUTE *count*

> Fetch the *count*'th row of the query, or the abs(*count*)'th row from the end if *count* is negative. Position before first row or after last row if *count* is out of range; in particular, ABSOLUTE 0 positions before the first row.

RELATIVE *count*

> Fetch the *count*'th succeeding row, or the abs(*count*)'th prior row if *count* is negative. RELATIVE 0 re-fetches the current row, if any.

count

> Fetch the next *count* rows (same as FORWARD *count*).

ALL

> Fetch all remaining rows (same as FORWARD ALL).

FORWARD

> Fetch the next row (same as NEXT).

FORWARD *count*

> Fetch the next *count* rows. FORWARD 0 re-fetches the current row.

FORWARD ALL

> Fetch all remaining rows.

BACKWARD

> Fetch the prior row (same as PRIOR).

BACKWARD *count*

Fetch the prior *count* rows (scanning backwards). BACKWARD 0 re-fetches the current row.

BACKWARD ALL

Fetch all prior rows (scanning backwards).

count

count is a possibly-signed integer constant, determining the location or number of rows to fetch. For FORWARD and BACKWARD cases, specifying a negative *count* is equivalent to changing the sense of FORWARD and BACKWARD.

cursor_name

An open cursor's name.

Outputs

On successful completion, a FETCH command returns a command tag of the form

FETCH *count*

The *count* is the number of rows fetched (possibly zero). Note that in psql, the command tag will not actually be displayed, since psql displays the fetched rows instead.

Notes

The cursor should be declared with the SCROLL option if one intends to use any variants of FETCH other than FETCH NEXT or FETCH FORWARD with a positive count. For simple queries PostgreSQL will allow backwards fetch from cursors not declared with SCROLL, but this behavior is best not relied on. If the cursor is declared with NO SCROLL, no backward fetches are allowed.

ABSOLUTE fetches are not any faster than navigating to the desired row with a relative move: the underlying implementation must traverse all the intermediate rows anyway. Negative absolute fetches are even worse: the query must be read to the end to find the last row, and then traversed backward from there. However, rewinding to the start of the query (as with FETCH ABSOLUTE 0) is fast.

DECLARE is used to define a cursor. Use MOVE to change cursor position without retrieving data.

Examples

The following example traverses a table using a cursor:

```
BEGIN WORK;

-- Set up a cursor:
DECLARE liahona SCROLL CURSOR FOR SELECT * FROM films;
```

```
-- Fetch the first 5 rows in the cursor liahona:
FETCH FORWARD 5 FROM liahona;

 code  |          title          | did | date_prod  |   kind   |  len
-------+-------------------------+-----+------------+----------+-------
 BL101 | The Third Man           | 101 | 1949-12-23 | Drama    | 01:44
 BL102 | The African Queen       | 101 | 1951-08-11 | Romantic | 01:43
 JL201 | Une Femme est une Femme | 102 | 1961-03-12 | Romantic | 01:25
 P_301 | Vertigo                 | 103 | 1958-11-14 | Action   | 02:08
 P_302 | Becket                  | 103 | 1964-02-03 | Drama    | 02:28

-- Fetch the previous row:
FETCH PRIOR FROM liahona;

 code  | title   | did | date_prod  |  kind  |  len
-------+---------+-----+------------+--------+-------
 P_301 | Vertigo | 103 | 1958-11-14 | Action | 02:08

-- Close the cursor and end the transaction:
CLOSE liahona;
COMMIT WORK;
```

Compatibility

The SQL standard defines FETCH for use in embedded SQL only. The variant of FETCH described here returns the data as if it were a SELECT result rather than placing it in host variables. Other than this point, FETCH is fully upward-compatible with the SQL standard.

The FETCH forms involving FORWARD and BACKWARD, as well as the forms FETCH *count* and FETCH ALL, in which FORWARD is implicit, are PostgreSQL extensions.

The SQL standard allows only FROM preceding the cursor name; the option to use IN, or to leave them out altogether, is an extension.

See Also

CLOSE, DECLARE, MOVE

GRANT

Name

GRANT — define access privileges

Synopsis

```
GRANT { { SELECT | INSERT | UPDATE | DELETE | TRUNCATE | REFERENCES | TRIGGER }
    [, ...] | ALL [ PRIVILEGES ] }
    ON { [ TABLE ] table_name [, ...]
         | ALL TABLES IN SCHEMA schema_name [, ...] }
    TO { [ GROUP ] role_name | PUBLIC } [, ...] [ WITH GRANT OPTION ]

GRANT { { SELECT | INSERT | UPDATE | REFERENCES } ( column_name [, ...] )
    [, ...] | ALL [ PRIVILEGES ] ( column_name [, ...] ) }
    ON [ TABLE ] table_name [, ...]
    TO { [ GROUP ] role_name | PUBLIC } [, ...] [ WITH GRANT OPTION ]

GRANT { { USAGE | SELECT | UPDATE }
    [, ...] | ALL [ PRIVILEGES ] }
    ON { SEQUENCE sequence_name [, ...]
         | ALL SEQUENCES IN SCHEMA schema_name [, ...] }
    TO { [ GROUP ] role_name | PUBLIC } [, ...] [ WITH GRANT OPTION ]

GRANT { { CREATE | CONNECT | TEMPORARY | TEMP } [, ...] | ALL [ PRIVILEGES ] }
    ON DATABASE database_name [, ...]
    TO { [ GROUP ] role_name | PUBLIC } [, ...] [ WITH GRANT OPTION ]

GRANT { USAGE | ALL [ PRIVILEGES ] }
    ON DOMAIN domain_name [, ...]
    TO { [ GROUP ] role_name | PUBLIC } [, ...] [ WITH GRANT OPTION ]

GRANT { USAGE | ALL [ PRIVILEGES ] }
    ON FOREIGN DATA WRAPPER fdw_name [, ...]
    TO { [ GROUP ] role_name | PUBLIC } [, ...] [ WITH GRANT OPTION ]

GRANT { USAGE | ALL [ PRIVILEGES ] }
    ON FOREIGN SERVER server_name [, ...]
    TO { [ GROUP ] role_name | PUBLIC } [, ...] [ WITH GRANT OPTION ]

GRANT { EXECUTE | ALL [ PRIVILEGES ] }
    ON { FUNCTION function_name ( [ [ argmode ] [ arg_name ] arg_type [, ...] ] )
         | ALL FUNCTIONS IN SCHEMA schema_name [, ...] }
    TO { [ GROUP ] role_name | PUBLIC } [, ...] [ WITH GRANT OPTION ]

GRANT { USAGE | ALL [ PRIVILEGES ] }
    ON LANGUAGE lang_name [, ...]
    TO { [ GROUP ] role_name | PUBLIC } [, ...] [ WITH GRANT OPTION ]

GRANT { { SELECT | UPDATE } [, ...] | ALL [ PRIVILEGES ] }
```

```
    ON LARGE OBJECT loid [, ...]
    TO { [ GROUP ] role_name | PUBLIC } [, ...] [ WITH GRANT OPTION ]

GRANT { { CREATE | USAGE } [, ...] | ALL [ PRIVILEGES ] }
    ON SCHEMA schema_name [, ...]
    TO { [ GROUP ] role_name | PUBLIC } [, ...] [ WITH GRANT OPTION ]

GRANT { CREATE | ALL [ PRIVILEGES ] }
    ON TABLESPACE tablespace_name [, ...]
    TO { [ GROUP ] role_name | PUBLIC } [, ...] [ WITH GRANT OPTION ]

GRANT { USAGE | ALL [ PRIVILEGES ] }
    ON TYPE type_name [, ...]
    TO { [ GROUP ] role_name | PUBLIC } [, ...] [ WITH GRANT OPTION ]

GRANT role_name [, ...] TO role_name [, ...] [ WITH ADMIN OPTION ]
```

Description

The GRANT command has two basic variants: one that grants privileges on a database object (table, column, view, foreign table, sequence, database, foreign-data wrapper, foreign server, function, procedural language, schema, or tablespace), and one that grants membership in a role. These variants are similar in many ways, but they are different enough to be described separately.

GRANT on Database Objects

This variant of the GRANT command gives specific privileges on a database object to one or more roles. These privileges are added to those already granted, if any.

There is also an option to grant privileges on all objects of the same type within one or more schemas. This functionality is currently supported only for tables, sequences, and functions (but note that ALL TABLES is considered to include views and foreign tables).

The key word PUBLIC indicates that the privileges are to be granted to all roles, including those that might be created later. PUBLIC can be thought of as an implicitly defined group that always includes all roles. Any particular role will have the sum of privileges granted directly to it, privileges granted to any role it is presently a member of, and privileges granted to PUBLIC.

If WITH GRANT OPTION is specified, the recipient of the privilege can in turn grant it to others. Without a grant option, the recipient cannot do that. Grant options cannot be granted to PUBLIC.

There is no need to grant privileges to the owner of an object (usually the user that created it), as the owner has all privileges by default. (The owner could, however, choose to revoke some of his own privileges for safety.)

The right to drop an object, or to alter its definition in any way, is not treated as a grantable privilege; it is inherent in the owner, and cannot be granted or revoked. (However, a similar effect can be obtained by granting or revoking membership in the role that owns the object; see below.) The owner implicitly has all grant options for the object, too.

PostgreSQL grants default privileges on some types of objects to PUBLIC. No privileges are granted to PUBLIC by default on tables, columns, schemas or tablespaces. For other types, the default privileges granted to PUBLIC are as follows: CONNECT and CREATE TEMP TABLE for databases; EXECUTE privilege for functions; and USAGE privilege for languages. The object owner can, of course, REVOKE both default and expressly granted privileges. (For maximum security, issue the REVOKE in the same transaction that creates the object; then there is no window in which another user can use the object.) Also, these initial default privilege settings can be changed using the ALTER DEFAULT PRIVILEGES command.

The possible privileges are:

SELECT

Allows SELECT from any column, or the specific columns listed, of the specified table, view, or sequence. Also allows the use of COPY TO. This privilege is also needed to reference existing column values in UPDATE or DELETE. For sequences, this privilege also allows the use of the currval function. For large objects, this privilege allows the object to be read.

INSERT

Allows INSERT of a new row into the specified table. If specific columns are listed, only those columns may be assigned to in the INSERT command (other columns will therefore receive default values). Also allows COPY FROM.

UPDATE

Allows UPDATE of any column, or the specific columns listed, of the specified table. (In practice, any nontrivial UPDATE command will require SELECT privilege as well, since it must reference table columns to determine which rows to update, and/or to compute new values for columns.) SELECT ... FOR UPDATE and SELECT ... FOR SHARE also require this privilege on at least one column, in addition to the SELECT privilege. For sequences, this privilege allows the use of the nextval and setval functions. For large objects, this privilege allows writing or truncating the object.

DELETE

Allows DELETE of a row from the specified table. (In practice, any nontrivial DELETE command will require SELECT privilege as well, since it must reference table columns to determine which rows to delete.)

TRUNCATE

Allows TRUNCATE on the specified table.

REFERENCES

To create a foreign key constraint, it is necessary to have this privilege on both the referencing and referenced columns. The privilege may be granted for all columns of a table, or just specific columns.

TRIGGER

Allows the creation of a trigger on the specified table. (See the CREATE TRIGGER statement.)

CREATE

For databases, allows new schemas to be created within the database.

For schemas, allows new objects to be created within the schema. To rename an existing object, you must own the object *and* have this privilege for the containing schema.

For tablespaces, allows tables, indexes, and temporary files to be created within the tablespace, and allows databases to be created that have the tablespace as their default tablespace. (Note that revoking this privilege will not alter the placement of existing objects.)

CONNECT

Allows the user to connect to the specified database. This privilege is checked at connection startup (in addition to checking any restrictions imposed by `pg_hba.conf`).

TEMPORARY
TEMP

Allows temporary tables to be created while using the specified database.

EXECUTE

Allows the use of the specified function and the use of any operators that are implemented on top of the function. This is the only type of privilege that is applicable to functions. (This syntax works for aggregate functions, as well.)

USAGE

For procedural languages, allows the use of the specified language for the creation of functions in that language. This is the only type of privilege that is applicable to procedural languages.

For schemas, allows access to objects contained in the specified schema (assuming that the objects' own privilege requirements are also met). Essentially this allows the grantee to "look up" objects within the schema. Without this permission, it is still possible to see the object names, e.g. by querying the system tables. Also, after revoking this permission, existing backends might have statements that have previously performed this lookup, so this is not a completely secure way to prevent object access.

For sequences, this privilege allows the use of the `currval` and `nextval` functions.

For types and domains, this privilege allow the use of the type or domain in the creation of tables, functions, and other schema objects. (Note that it does not control general "usage" of the type, such as values of the type appearing in queries. It only prevents objects from being created that depend on the type. The main purpose of the privilege is controlling which users create dependencies on a type, which could prevent the owner from changing the type later.)

For foreign-data wrappers, this privilege enables the grantee to create new servers using that foreign-data wrapper.

For servers, this privilege enables the grantee to create foreign tables using the server, and also to create, alter, or drop his own user's user mappings associated with that server.

ALL PRIVILEGES

Grant all of the available privileges at once. The `PRIVILEGES` key word is optional in PostgreSQL, though it is required by strict SQL.

The privileges required by other commands are listed on the reference page of the respective command.

GRANT on Roles

This variant of the `GRANT` command grants membership in a role to one or more other roles. Membership in a role is significant because it conveys the privileges granted to a role to each of its members.

If WITH ADMIN OPTION is specified, the member can in turn grant membership in the role to others, and revoke membership in the role as well. Without the admin option, ordinary users cannot do that. A role is not considered to hold WITH ADMIN OPTION on itself, but it may grant or revoke membership in itself from a database session where the session user matches the role. Database superusers can grant or revoke membership in any role to anyone. Roles having CREATEROLE privilege can grant or revoke membership in any role that is not a superuser.

Unlike the case with privileges, membership in a role cannot be granted to PUBLIC. Note also that this form of the command does not allow the noise word GROUP.

Notes

The REVOKE command is used to revoke access privileges.

Since PostgreSQL 8.1, the concepts of users and groups have been unified into a single kind of entity called a role. It is therefore no longer necessary to use the keyword GROUP to identify whether a grantee is a user or a group. GROUP is still allowed in the command, but it is a noise word.

A user may perform SELECT, INSERT, etc. on a column if he holds that privilege for either the specific column or its whole table. Granting the privilege at the table level and then revoking it for one column will not do what you might wish: the table-level grant is unaffected by a column-level operation.

When a non-owner of an object attempts to GRANT privileges on the object, the command will fail outright if the user has no privileges whatsoever on the object. As long as some privilege is available, the command will proceed, but it will grant only those privileges for which the user has grant options. The GRANT ALL PRIVILEGES forms will issue a warning message if no grant options are held, while the other forms will issue a warning if grant options for any of the privileges specifically named in the command are not held. (In principle these statements apply to the object owner as well, but since the owner is always treated as holding all grant options, the cases can never occur.)

It should be noted that database superusers can access all objects regardless of object privilege settings. This is comparable to the rights of root in a Unix system. As with root, it's unwise to operate as a superuser except when absolutely necessary.

If a superuser chooses to issue a GRANT or REVOKE command, the command is performed as though it were issued by the owner of the affected object. In particular, privileges granted via such a command will appear to have been granted by the object owner. (For role membership, the membership appears to have been granted by the containing role itself.)

GRANT and REVOKE can also be done by a role that is not the owner of the affected object, but is a member of the role that owns the object, or is a member of a role that holds privileges WITH GRANT OPTION on the object. In this case the privileges will be recorded as having been granted by the role that actually owns the object or holds the privileges WITH GRANT OPTION. For example, if table t1 is owned by role g1, of which role u1 is a member, then u1 can grant privileges on t1 to u2, but those privileges will appear to have been granted directly by g1. Any other member of role g1 could revoke them later.

If the role executing GRANT holds the required privileges indirectly via more than one role membership path, it is unspecified which containing role will be recorded as having done the grant. In such cases it is best practice to use SET ROLE to become the specific role you want to do the GRANT as.

Granting permission on a table does not automatically extend permissions to any sequences used by the table, including sequences tied to SERIAL columns. Permissions on sequences must be set separately.

Use psql's `\dp` command to obtain information about existing privileges for tables and columns. For example:

```
=> \dp mytable
                              Access privileges
 Schema |  Name   | Type  |     Access privileges     | Column access privileges
--------+---------+-------+---------------------------+--------------------------
 public | mytable | table | miriam=arwdDxt/miriam     | col1:
                          : =r/miriam                 :   miriam_rw=rw/miriam
                          : admin=arw/miriam
(1 row)
```

The entries shown by `\dp` are interpreted thus:

```
rolename=xxxx -- privileges granted to a role
        =xxxx -- privileges granted to PUBLIC

            r -- SELECT ("read")
            w -- UPDATE ("write")
            a -- INSERT ("append")
            d -- DELETE
            D -- TRUNCATE
            x -- REFERENCES
            t -- TRIGGER
            X -- EXECUTE
            U -- USAGE
            C -- CREATE
            c -- CONNECT
            T -- TEMPORARY
       arwdDxt -- ALL PRIVILEGES (for tables, varies for other objects)
            * -- grant option for preceding privilege

        /yyyy -- role that granted this privilege
```

The above example display would be seen by user `miriam` after creating table `mytable` and doing:

```
GRANT SELECT ON mytable TO PUBLIC;
GRANT SELECT, UPDATE, INSERT ON mytable TO admin;
GRANT SELECT (col1), UPDATE (col1) ON mytable TO miriam_rw;
```

For non-table objects there are other `\d` commands that can display their privileges.

If the "Access privileges" column is empty for a given object, it means the object has default privileges (that is, its privileges column is null). Default privileges always include all privileges for the owner, and can include some privileges for PUBLIC depending on the object type, as explained above. The first GRANT or REVOKE on an object will instantiate the default privileges (producing, for example, {miriam=arwdDxt/miriam}) and then modify them per the specified request. Similarly, entries are shown in "Column access privileges" only for columns with nondefault privileges. (Note: for this purpose, "default privileges" always means the built-in default privileges for the object's type. An object whose privileges have been affected by an ALTER DEFAULT PRIVILEGES command will always be shown with an explicit privilege entry that includes the effects of the ALTER.)

Notice that the owner's implicit grant options are not marked in the access privileges display. A * will appear only when grant options have been explicitly granted to someone.

Examples

Grant insert privilege to all users on table `films`:

```
GRANT INSERT ON films TO PUBLIC;
```

Grant all available privileges to user `manuel` on view `kinds`:

```
GRANT ALL PRIVILEGES ON kinds TO manuel;
```

Note that while the above will indeed grant all privileges if executed by a superuser or the owner of `kinds`, when executed by someone else it will only grant those permissions for which the someone else has grant options.

Grant membership in role `admins` to user `joe`:

```
GRANT admins TO joe;
```

Compatibility

According to the SQL standard, the `PRIVILEGES` key word in `ALL PRIVILEGES` is required. The SQL standard does not support setting the privileges on more than one object per command.

PostgreSQL allows an object owner to revoke his own ordinary privileges: for example, a table owner can make the table read-only to himself by revoking his own `INSERT`, `UPDATE`, `DELETE`, and `TRUNCATE` privileges. This is not possible according to the SQL standard. The reason is that PostgreSQL treats the owner's privileges as having been granted by the owner to himself; therefore he can revoke them too. In the SQL standard, the owner's privileges are granted by an assumed entity "_SYSTEM". Not being "_SYSTEM", the owner cannot revoke these rights.

According to the SQL standard, grant options can be granted to `PUBLIC`; PostgreSQL only supports granting grant options to roles.

The SQL standard provides for a `USAGE` privilege on other kinds of objects: character sets, collations, translations.

In the SQL standard, sequences only have a `USAGE` privilege, which controls the use of the `NEXT VALUE FOR` expression, which is equivalent to the function `nextval` in PostgreSQL. The sequence privileges `SELECT` and `UPDATE` are PostgreSQL extensions. The application of the sequence `USAGE` privilege to the `currval` function is also a PostgreSQL extension (as is the function itself).

Privileges on databases, tablespaces, schemas, and languages are PostgreSQL extensions.

See Also

REVOKE, ALTER DEFAULT PRIVILEGES

INSERT

Name

INSERT — create new rows in a table

Synopsis

```
[ WITH [ RECURSIVE ] with_query [, ...] ]
INSERT INTO table_name [ ( column_name [, ...] ) ]
    { DEFAULT VALUES | VALUES ( { expression | DEFAULT } [, ...] ) [, ...] | que
    [ RETURNING * | output_expression [ [ AS ] output_name ] [, ...] ]
```

Description

INSERT inserts new rows into a table. One can insert one or more rows specified by value expressions, or zero or more rows resulting from a query.

The target column names can be listed in any order. If no list of column names is given at all, the default is all the columns of the table in their declared order; or the first N column names, if there are only N columns supplied by the VALUES clause or query. The values supplied by the VALUES clause or query are associated with the explicit or implicit column list left-to-right.

Each column not present in the explicit or implicit column list will be filled with a default value, either its declared default value or null if there is none.

If the expression for any column is not of the correct data type, automatic type conversion will be attempted.

The optional RETURNING clause causes INSERT to compute and return value(s) based on each row actually inserted. This is primarily useful for obtaining values that were supplied by defaults, such as a serial sequence number. However, any expression using the table's columns is allowed. The syntax of the RETURNING list is identical to that of the output list of SELECT.

You must have INSERT privilege on a table in order to insert into it. If a column list is specified, you only need INSERT privilege on the listed columns. Use of the RETURNING clause requires SELECT privilege on all columns mentioned in RETURNING. If you use the query clause to insert rows from a query, you of course need to have SELECT privilege on any table or column used in the query.

Parameters

with_query

>   The WITH clause allows you to specify one or more subqueries that can be referenced by name in the INSERT query. See Section 7.8 and SELECT for details.

It is possible for the `query` (`SELECT` statement) to also contain a `WITH` clause. In such a case both sets of `with_query` can be referenced within the `query`, but the second one takes precedence since it is more closely nested.

`table_name`

The name (optionally schema-qualified) of an existing table.

`column_name`

The name of a column in the table named by `table_name`. The column name can be qualified with a subfield name or array subscript, if needed. (Inserting into only some fields of a composite column leaves the other fields null.)

`DEFAULT VALUES`

All columns will be filled with their default values.

`expression`

An expression or value to assign to the corresponding column.

`DEFAULT`

The corresponding column will be filled with its default value.

`query`

A query (`SELECT` statement) that supplies the rows to be inserted. Refer to the SELECT statement for a description of the syntax.

`output_expression`

An expression to be computed and returned by the `INSERT` command after each row is inserted. The expression can use any column names of the table named by `table_name`. Write * to return all columns of the inserted row(s).

`output_name`

A name to use for a returned column.

Outputs

On successful completion, an `INSERT` command returns a command tag of the form

`INSERT oid count`

The `count` is the number of rows inserted. If `count` is exactly one, and the target table has OIDs, then `oid` is the OID assigned to the inserted row. Otherwise `oid` is zero.

If the `INSERT` command contains a `RETURNING` clause, the result will be similar to that of a `SELECT` statement containing the columns and values defined in the `RETURNING` list, computed over the row(s) inserted by the command.

Examples

Insert a single row into table `films`:

```
INSERT INTO films VALUES
    ('UA502', 'Bananas', 105, '1971-07-13', 'Comedy', '82 minutes');
```

In this example, the `len` column is omitted and therefore it will have the default value:

```
INSERT INTO films (code, title, did, date_prod, kind)
    VALUES ('T_601', 'Yojimbo', 106, '1961-06-16', 'Drama');
```

This example uses the `DEFAULT` clause for the date columns rather than specifying a value:

```
INSERT INTO films VALUES
    ('UA502', 'Bananas', 105, DEFAULT, 'Comedy', '82 minutes');
INSERT INTO films (code, title, did, date_prod, kind)
    VALUES ('T_601', 'Yojimbo', 106, DEFAULT, 'Drama');
```

To insert a row consisting entirely of default values:

```
INSERT INTO films DEFAULT VALUES;
```

To insert multiple rows using the multirow `VALUES` syntax:

```
INSERT INTO films (code, title, did, date_prod, kind) VALUES
    ('B6717', 'Tampopo', 110, '1985-02-10', 'Comedy'),
    ('HG120', 'The Dinner Game', 140, DEFAULT, 'Comedy');
```

This example inserts some rows into table `films` from a table `tmp_films` with the same column layout as `films`:

```
INSERT INTO films SELECT * FROM tmp_films WHERE date_prod < '2004-05-07';
```

This example inserts into array columns:

```
-- Create an empty 3x3 gameboard for noughts-and-crosses
INSERT INTO tictactoe (game, board[1:3][1:3])
    VALUES (1, '{{" "," "," "},{" "," "," "},{" "," "," "}}');
-- The subscripts in the above example aren't really needed
INSERT INTO tictactoe (game, board)
    VALUES (2, '{{X," "," "},{" ",O," "},{" ",X," "}}');
```

Insert a single row into table `distributors`, returning the sequence number generated by the `DEFAULT` clause:

```
INSERT INTO distributors (did, dname) VALUES (DEFAULT, 'XYZ Widgets')
   RETURNING did;
```

Increment the sales count of the salesperson who manages the account for Acme Corporation, and record the whole updated row along with current time in a log table:

```
WITH upd AS (
  UPDATE employees SET sales_count = sales_count + 1 WHERE id =
    (SELECT sales_person FROM accounts WHERE name = 'Acme Corporation')
    RETURNING *
)
INSERT INTO employees_log SELECT *, current_timestamp FROM upd;
```

Compatibility

`INSERT` conforms to the SQL standard, except that the `RETURNING` clause is a PostgreSQL extension, as is the ability to use `WITH` with `INSERT`. Also, the case in which a column name list is omitted, but not all the columns are filled from the `VALUES` clause or `query`, is disallowed by the standard.

Possible limitations of the `query` clause are documented under SELECT.

LISTEN

Name

LISTEN — listen for a notification

Synopsis

```
LISTEN channel
```

Description

LISTEN registers the current session as a listener on the notification channel named *channel*. If the current session is already registered as a listener for this notification channel, nothing is done.

Whenever the command NOTIFY *channel* is invoked, either by this session or another one connected to the same database, all the sessions currently listening on that notification channel are notified, and each will in turn notify its connected client application.

A session can be unregistered for a given notification channel with the UNLISTEN command. A session's listen registrations are automatically cleared when the session ends.

The method a client application must use to detect notification events depends on which PostgreSQL application programming interface it uses. With the libpq library, the application issues LISTEN as an ordinary SQL command, and then must periodically call the function PQnotifies to find out whether any notification events have been received. Other interfaces such as libpgtcl provide higher-level methods for handling notify events; indeed, with libpgtcl the application programmer should not even issue LISTEN or UNLISTEN directly. See the documentation for the interface you are using for more details.

NOTIFY contains a more extensive discussion of the use of LISTEN and NOTIFY.

Parameters

channel

Name of a notification channel (any identifier).

Notes

LISTEN takes effect at transaction commit. If LISTEN or UNLISTEN is executed within a transaction that later rolls back, the set of notification channels being listened to is unchanged.

A transaction that has executed LISTEN cannot be prepared for two-phase commit.

Examples

Configure and execute a listen/notify sequence from psql:

```
LISTEN virtual;
NOTIFY virtual;
Asynchronous notification "virtual" received from server process with PID 8448.
```

Compatibility

There is no LISTEN statement in the SQL standard.

See Also

NOTIFY, UNLISTEN

LOAD

Name

LOAD — load a shared library file

Synopsis

```
LOAD 'filename'
```

Description

This command loads a shared library file into the PostgreSQL server's address space. If the file has been loaded already, the command does nothing. Shared library files that contain C functions are automatically loaded whenever one of their functions is called. Therefore, an explicit LOAD is usually only needed to load a library that modifies the server's behavior through "hooks" rather than providing a set of functions.

The file name is specified in the same way as for shared library names in CREATE FUNCTION; in particular, one can rely on a search path and automatic addition of the system's standard shared library file name extension. See Section 35.9 for more information on this topic.

Non-superusers can only apply LOAD to library files located in $libdir/plugins/ — the specified filename must begin with exactly that string. (It is the database administrator's responsibility to ensure that only "safe" libraries are installed there.)

Compatibility

LOAD is a PostgreSQL extension.

See Also

CREATE FUNCTION

LOCK

Name

LOCK — lock a table

Synopsis

```
LOCK [ TABLE ] [ ONLY ] name [ * ] [, ...] [ IN lockmode MODE ] [ NOWAIT ]

where lockmode is one of:

    ACCESS SHARE | ROW SHARE | ROW EXCLUSIVE | SHARE UPDATE EXCLUSIVE
    | SHARE | SHARE ROW EXCLUSIVE | EXCLUSIVE | ACCESS EXCLUSIVE
```

Description

LOCK TABLE obtains a table-level lock, waiting if necessary for any conflicting locks to be released. If NOWAIT is specified, LOCK TABLE does not wait to acquire the desired lock: if it cannot be acquired immediately, the command is aborted and an error is emitted. Once obtained, the lock is held for the remainder of the current transaction. (There is no UNLOCK TABLE command; locks are always released at transaction end.)

When acquiring locks automatically for commands that reference tables, PostgreSQL always uses the least restrictive lock mode possible. LOCK TABLE provides for cases when you might need more restrictive locking. For example, suppose an application runs a transaction at the Read Committed isolation level and needs to ensure that data in a table remains stable for the duration of the transaction. To achieve this you could obtain SHARE lock mode over the table before querying. This will prevent concurrent data changes and ensure subsequent reads of the table see a stable view of committed data, because SHARE lock mode conflicts with the ROW EXCLUSIVE lock acquired by writers, and your LOCK TABLE name IN SHARE MODE statement will wait until any concurrent holders of ROW EXCLUSIVE mode locks commit or roll back. Thus, once you obtain the lock, there are no uncommitted writes outstanding; furthermore none can begin until you release the lock.

To achieve a similar effect when running a transaction at the REPEATABLE READ or SERIALIZABLE isolation level, you have to execute the LOCK TABLE statement before executing any SELECT or data modification statement. A REPEATABLE READ or SERIALIZABLE transaction's view of data will be frozen when its first SELECT or data modification statement begins. A LOCK TABLE later in the transaction will still prevent concurrent writes — but it won't ensure that what the transaction reads corresponds to the latest committed values.

If a transaction of this sort is going to change the data in the table, then it should use SHARE ROW EXCLUSIVE lock mode instead of SHARE mode. This ensures that only one transaction of this type runs at a time. Without this, a deadlock is possible: two transactions might both acquire SHARE mode, and then be unable to also acquire ROW EXCLUSIVE mode to actually perform their updates. (Note that a transaction's own locks never conflict, so a transaction can acquire ROW EXCLUSIVE mode when it holds SHARE mode — but not if anyone else holds SHARE mode.) To avoid deadlocks, make sure all transactions acquire locks on the same objects in the same order, and if multiple lock modes are involved for a single object, then transactions should always acquire the most restrictive mode first.

More information about the lock modes and locking strategies can be found in Section 13.3.

Parameters

name

> The name (optionally schema-qualified) of an existing table to lock. If ONLY is specified before the table name, only that table is locked. If ONLY is not specified, the table and all its descendant tables (if any) are locked. Optionally, * can be specified after the table name to explicitly indicate that descendant tables are included.
>
> The command LOCK TABLE a, b; is equivalent to LOCK TABLE a; LOCK TABLE b;. The tables are locked one-by-one in the order specified in the LOCK TABLE command.

lockmode

> The lock mode specifies which locks this lock conflicts with. Lock modes are described in Section 13.3.
>
> If no lock mode is specified, then ACCESS EXCLUSIVE, the most restrictive mode, is used.

NOWAIT

> Specifies that LOCK TABLE should not wait for any conflicting locks to be released: if the specified lock(s) cannot be acquired immediately without waiting, the transaction is aborted.

Notes

LOCK TABLE ... IN ACCESS SHARE MODE requires SELECT privileges on the target table. All other forms of LOCK require table-level UPDATE, DELETE, or TRUNCATE privileges.

LOCK TABLE is useless outside a transaction block: the lock would remain held only to the completion of the statement. Therefore PostgreSQL reports an error if LOCK is used outside a transaction block. Use **BEGIN** and **COMMIT** (or **ROLLBACK**) to define a transaction block.

LOCK TABLE only deals with table-level locks, and so the mode names involving ROW are all misnomers. These mode names should generally be read as indicating the intention of the user to acquire row-level locks within the locked table. Also, ROW EXCLUSIVE mode is a shareable table lock. Keep in mind that all the lock modes have identical semantics so far as LOCK TABLE is concerned, differing only in the rules about which modes conflict with which. For information on how to acquire an actual row-level lock, see Section 13.3.2 and the *The Locking Clause* in the SELECT reference documentation.

Examples

Obtain a SHARE lock on a primary key table when going to perform inserts into a foreign key table:

```
BEGIN WORK;
LOCK TABLE films IN SHARE MODE;
```

```
SELECT id FROM films
    WHERE name = 'Star Wars: Episode I - The Phantom Menace';
-- Do ROLLBACK if record was not returned
INSERT INTO films_user_comments VALUES
    (_id_, 'GREAT! I was waiting for it for so long!');
COMMIT WORK;
```

Take a SHARE ROW EXCLUSIVE lock on a primary key table when going to perform a delete operation:

```
BEGIN WORK;
LOCK TABLE films IN SHARE ROW EXCLUSIVE MODE;
DELETE FROM films_user_comments WHERE id IN
    (SELECT id FROM films WHERE rating < 5);
DELETE FROM films WHERE rating < 5;
COMMIT WORK;
```

Compatibility

There is no LOCK TABLE in the SQL standard, which instead uses SET TRANSACTION to specify concurrency levels on transactions. PostgreSQL supports that too; see SET TRANSACTION for details.

Except for ACCESS SHARE, ACCESS EXCLUSIVE, and SHARE UPDATE EXCLUSIVE lock modes, the PostgreSQL lock modes and the LOCK TABLE syntax are compatible with those present in Oracle.

MOVE

Name

MOVE — position a cursor

Synopsis

```
MOVE [ direction [ FROM | IN ] ] cursor_name
```

where *direction* can be empty or one of:

```
NEXT
PRIOR
FIRST
LAST
ABSOLUTE count
RELATIVE count
count
ALL
FORWARD
FORWARD count
FORWARD ALL
BACKWARD
BACKWARD count
BACKWARD ALL
```

Description

MOVE repositions a cursor without retrieving any data. MOVE works exactly like the FETCH command, except it only positions the cursor and does not return rows.

The parameters for the MOVE command are identical to those of the FETCH command; refer to FETCH for details on syntax and usage.

Outputs

On successful completion, a MOVE command returns a command tag of the form

```
MOVE count
```

The *count* is the number of rows that a FETCH command with the same parameters would have returned (possibly zero).

Examples

```
BEGIN WORK;
DECLARE liahona CURSOR FOR SELECT * FROM films;

-- Skip the first 5 rows:
MOVE FORWARD 5 IN liahona;
MOVE 5

-- Fetch the 6th row from the cursor liahona:
FETCH 1 FROM liahona;
 code  | title  | did | date_prod  |  kind  |  len
-------+--------+-----+------------+--------+-------
 P_303 | 48 Hrs | 103 | 1982-10-22 | Action | 01:37
(1 row)

-- Close the cursor liahona and end the transaction:
CLOSE liahona;
COMMIT WORK;
```

Compatibility

There is no MOVE statement in the SQL standard.

See Also

CLOSE, DECLARE, FETCH

NOTIFY

Name

NOTIFY — generate a notification

Synopsis

```
NOTIFY channel [ , payload ]
```

Description

The NOTIFY command sends a notification event together with an optional "payload" string to each client application that has previously executed LISTEN *channel* for the specified channel name in the current database. Notifications are visible to all users.

NOTIFY provides a simple interprocess communication mechanism for a collection of processes accessing the same PostgreSQL database. A payload string can be sent along with the notification, and higher-level mechanisms for passing structured data can be built by using tables in the database to pass additional data from notifier to listener(s).

The information passed to the client for a notification event includes the notification channel name, the notifying session's server process PID, and the payload string, which is an empty string if it has not been specified.

It is up to the database designer to define the channel names that will be used in a given database and what each one means. Commonly, the channel name is the same as the name of some table in the database, and the notify event essentially means, "I changed this table, take a look at it to see what's new". But no such association is enforced by the NOTIFY and LISTEN commands. For example, a database designer could use several different channel names to signal different sorts of changes to a single table. Alternatively, the payload string could be used to differentiate various cases.

When NOTIFY is used to signal the occurrence of changes to a particular table, a useful programming technique is to put the NOTIFY in a rule that is triggered by table updates. In this way, notification happens automatically when the table is changed, and the application programmer cannot accidentally forget to do it.

NOTIFY interacts with SQL transactions in some important ways. Firstly, if a NOTIFY is executed inside a transaction, the notify events are not delivered until and unless the transaction is committed. This is appropriate, since if the transaction is aborted, all the commands within it have had no effect, including NOTIFY. But it can be disconcerting if one is expecting the notification events to be delivered immediately. Secondly, if a listening session receives a notification signal while it is within a transaction, the notification event will not be delivered to its connected client until just after the transaction is completed (either committed or aborted). Again, the reasoning is that if a notification were delivered within a transaction that was later aborted, one would want the notification to be undone somehow — but the server cannot "take back" a notification once it has sent it to the client. So notification events are only delivered between transactions. The upshot of this is that applications using NOTIFY for real-time signaling should try to keep their transactions short.

If the same channel name is signaled multiple times from the same transaction with identical payload strings, the database server can decide to deliver a single notification only. On the other hand, notifications with distinct payload strings will always be delivered as distinct notifications. Similarly, notifications from different transactions will never get folded into one notification. Except for dropping later instances of duplicate notifications, NOTIFY guarantees that notifications from the same transaction get delivered in the order they were sent. It is also guaranteed that messages from different transactions are delivered in the order in which the transactions committed.

It is common for a client that executes NOTIFY to be listening on the same notification channel itself. In that case it will get back a notification event, just like all the other listening sessions. Depending on the application logic, this could result in useless work, for example, reading a database table to find the same updates that that session just wrote out. It is possible to avoid such extra work by noticing whether the notifying session's server process PID (supplied in the notification event message) is the same as one's own session's PID (available from libpq). When they are the same, the notification event is one's own work bouncing back, and can be ignored.

Parameters

channel

> Name of the notification channel to be signaled (any identifier).

payload

> The "payload" string to be communicated along with the notification. This must be specified as a simple string literal. In the default configuration it must be shorter than 8000 bytes. (If binary data or large amounts of information need to be communicated, it's best to put it in a database table and send the key of the record.)

Notes

There is a queue that holds notifications that have been sent but not yet processed by all listening sessions. If this queue becomes full, transactions calling NOTIFY will fail at commit. The queue is quite large (8GB in a standard installation) and should be sufficiently sized for almost every use case. However, no cleanup can take place if a session executes LISTEN and then enters a transaction for a very long time. Once the queue is half full you will see warnings in the log file pointing you to the session that is preventing cleanup. In this case you should make sure that this session ends its current transaction so that cleanup can proceed.

A transaction that has executed NOTIFY cannot be prepared for two-phase commit.

pg_notify

To send a notification you can also use the function pg_notify(text, text). The function takes the channel name as the first argument and the payload as the second. The function is much easier to use than the NOTIFY command if you need to work with non-constant channel names and payloads.

Examples

Configure and execute a listen/notify sequence from psql:

```
LISTEN virtual;
NOTIFY virtual;
Asynchronous notification "virtual" received from server process with PID 8448.
NOTIFY virtual, 'This is the payload';
Asynchronous notification "virtual" with payload "This is the payload" receivec

LISTEN foo;
SELECT pg_notify('fo' || 'o', 'pay' || 'load');
Asynchronous notification "foo" with payload "payload" received from server prc
```

Compatibility

There is no NOTIFY statement in the SQL standard.

See Also

LISTEN, UNLISTEN

PREPARE

Name

PREPARE — prepare a statement for execution

Synopsis

```
PREPARE name [ ( data_type [, ...] ) ] AS statement
```

Description

PREPARE creates a prepared statement. A prepared statement is a server-side object that can be used to optimize performance. When the PREPARE statement is executed, the specified statement is parsed, analyzed, and rewritten. When an EXECUTE command is subsequently issued, the prepared statement is planned and executed. This division of labor avoids repetitive parse analysis work, while allowing the execution plan to depend on the specific parameter values supplied.

Prepared statements can take parameters: values that are substituted into the statement when it is executed. When creating the prepared statement, refer to parameters by position, using $1, $2, etc. A corresponding list of parameter data types can optionally be specified. When a parameter's data type is not specified or is declared as unknown, the type is inferred from the context in which the parameter is used (if possible). When executing the statement, specify the actual values for these parameters in the EXECUTE statement. Refer to EXECUTE for more information about that.

Prepared statements only last for the duration of the current database session. When the session ends, the prepared statement is forgotten, so it must be recreated before being used again. This also means that a single prepared statement cannot be used by multiple simultaneous database clients; however, each client can create their own prepared statement to use. Prepared statements can be manually cleaned up using the DEALLOCATE command.

Prepared statements have the largest performance advantage when a single session is being used to execute a large number of similar statements. The performance difference will be particularly significant if the statements are complex to plan or rewrite, for example, if the query involves a join of many tables or requires the application of several rules. If the statement is relatively simple to plan and rewrite but relatively expensive to execute, the performance advantage of prepared statements will be less noticeable.

Parameters

name

> An arbitrary name given to this particular prepared statement. It must be unique within a single session and is subsequently used to execute or deallocate a previously prepared statement.

data_type

> The data type of a parameter to the prepared statement. If the data type of a particular parameter is unspecified or is specified as unknown, it will be inferred from the context in which the parameter is used. To refer to the parameters in the prepared statement itself, use $1, $2, etc.

statement

> Any SELECT, INSERT, UPDATE, DELETE, or VALUES statement.

Notes

If a prepared statement is executed enough times, the server may eventually decide to save and re-use a generic plan rather than re-planning each time. This will occur immediately if the prepared statement has no parameters; otherwise it occurs only if the generic plan appears to be not much more expensive than a plan that depends on specific parameter values. Typically, a generic plan will be selected only if the query's performance is estimated to be fairly insensitive to the specific parameter values supplied.

To examine the query plan PostgreSQL is using for a prepared statement, use EXPLAIN. If a generic plan is in use, it will contain parameter symbols $n, while a custom plan will have the current actual parameter values substituted into it.

For more information on query planning and the statistics collected by PostgreSQL for that purpose, see the ANALYZE documentation.

Although the main point of a prepared statement is to avoid repeated parse analysis and planning of the statement, PostgreSQL will force re-analysis and re-planning of the statement before using it whenever database objects used in the statement have undergone definitional (DDL) changes since the previous use of the prepared statement. Also, if the value of search_path changes from one use to the next, the statement will be re-parsed using the new search_path. (This latter behavior is new as of PostgreSQL 9.3.) These rules make use of a prepared statement semantically almost equivalent to re-submitting the same query text over and over, but with a performance benefit if no object definitions are changed, especially if the best plan remains the same across uses. An example of a case where the semantic equivalence is not perfect is that if the statement refers to a table by an unqualified name, and then a new table of the same name is created in a schema appearing earlier in the search_path, no automatic re-parse will occur since no object used in the statement changed. However, if some other change forces a re-parse, the new table will be referenced in subsequent uses.

You can see all prepared statements available in the session by querying the pg_prepared_statements system view.

Examples

Create a prepared statement for an INSERT statement, and then execute it:

```
PREPARE fooplan (int, text, bool, numeric) AS
    INSERT INTO foo VALUES($1, $2, $3, $4);
EXECUTE fooplan(1, 'Hunter Valley', 't', 200.00);
```

Create a prepared statement for a SELECT statement, and then execute it:

```
PREPARE usrrptplan (int) AS
    SELECT * FROM users u, logs l WHERE u.usrid=$1 AND u.usrid=l.usrid
    AND l.date = $2;
EXECUTE usrrptplan(1, current_date);
```

Note that the data type of the second parameter is not specified, so it is inferred from the context in which $2 is used.

Compatibility

The SQL standard includes a PREPARE statement, but it is only for use in embedded SQL. This version of the PREPARE statement also uses a somewhat different syntax.

See Also

DEALLOCATE, EXECUTE

PREPARE TRANSACTION

Name

PREPARE TRANSACTION — prepare the current transaction for two-phase commit

Synopsis

```
PREPARE TRANSACTION transaction_id
```

Description

PREPARE TRANSACTION prepares the current transaction for two-phase commit. After this command, the transaction is no longer associated with the current session; instead, its state is fully stored on disk, and there is a very high probability that it can be committed successfully, even if a database crash occurs before the commit is requested.

Once prepared, a transaction can later be committed or rolled back with COMMIT PREPARED or ROLL-BACK PREPARED, respectively. Those commands can be issued from any session, not only the one that executed the original transaction.

From the point of view of the issuing session, PREPARE TRANSACTION is not unlike a ROLLBACK command: after executing it, there is no active current transaction, and the effects of the prepared transaction are no longer visible. (The effects will become visible again if the transaction is committed.)

If the PREPARE TRANSACTION command fails for any reason, it becomes a ROLLBACK: the current transaction is canceled.

Parameters

transaction_id

An arbitrary identifier that later identifies this transaction for COMMIT PREPARED or ROLLBACK PREPARED. The identifier must be written as a string literal, and must be less than 200 bytes long. It must not be the same as the identifier used for any currently prepared transaction.

Notes

PREPARE TRANSACTION is not intended for use in applications or interactive sessions. Its purpose is to allow an external transaction manager to perform atomic global transactions across multiple databases or other transactional resources. Unless you're writing a transaction manager, you probably shouldn't be using PREPARE TRANSACTION.

This command must be used inside a transaction block. Use BEGIN to start one.

It is not currently allowed to PREPARE a transaction that has executed any operations involving temporary tables, created any cursors WITH HOLD, or executed LISTEN or UNLISTEN. Those features are too tightly tied to the current session to be useful in a transaction to be prepared.

If the transaction modified any run-time parameters with SET (without the LOCAL option), those effects persist after PREPARE TRANSACTION, and will not be affected by any later COMMIT PREPARED or ROLLBACK PREPARED. Thus, in this one respect PREPARE TRANSACTION acts more like COMMIT than ROLLBACK.

All currently available prepared transactions are listed in the pg_prepared_xacts system view.

Caution

It is unwise to leave transactions in the prepared state for a long time. This will interfere with the ability of VACUUM to reclaim storage, and in extreme cases could cause the database to shut down to prevent transaction ID wraparound (see Section 23.1.5). Keep in mind also that the transaction continues to hold whatever locks it held. The intended usage of the feature is that a prepared transaction will normally be committed or rolled back as soon as an external transaction manager has verified that other databases are also prepared to commit.

If you have not set up an external transaction manager to track prepared transactions and ensure they get closed out promptly, it is best to keep the prepared-transaction feature disabled by setting max_prepared_transactions to zero. This will prevent accidental creation of prepared transactions that might then be forgotten and eventually cause problems.

Examples

Prepare the current transaction for two-phase commit, using foobar as the transaction identifier:

```
PREPARE TRANSACTION 'foobar';
```

Compatibility

PREPARE TRANSACTION is a PostgreSQL extension. It is intended for use by external transaction management systems, some of which are covered by standards (such as X/Open XA), but the SQL side of those systems is not standardized.

See Also

COMMIT PREPARED, ROLLBACK PREPARED

REASSIGN OWNED

Name

REASSIGN OWNED — change the ownership of database objects owned by a database role

Synopsis

```
REASSIGN OWNED BY old_role [, ...] TO new_role
```

Description

REASSIGN OWNED instructs the system to change the ownership of database objects owned by one of the old_roles, to new_role.

Parameters

old_role

> The name of a role. The ownership of all the objects within the current database, and of all shared objects (databases, tablespaces), owned by this role will be reassigned to new_role.

new_role

> The name of the role that will be made the new owner of the affected objects.

Notes

REASSIGN OWNED is often used to prepare for the removal of one or more roles. Because REASSIGN OWNED does not affect objects within other databases, it is usually necessary to execute this command in each database that contains objects owned by a role that is to be removed.

REASSIGN OWNED requires privileges on both the source role(s) and the target role.

The DROP OWNED command is an alternative that drops all the database objects owned by one or more roles. Note also that DROP OWNED requires privileges only on the source role(s).

The REASSIGN OWNED command does not affect the privileges granted to the old_roles in objects that are not owned by them. Use DROP OWNED to revoke those privileges.

Compatibility

The REASSIGN OWNED statement is a PostgreSQL extension.

See Also

DROP OWNED, DROP ROLE, ALTER DATABASE

REFRESH MATERIALIZED VIEW

Name

REFRESH MATERIALIZED VIEW — replace the contents of a materialized view

Synopsis

```
REFRESH MATERIALIZED VIEW [ CONCURRENTLY ] name
    [ WITH [ NO ] DATA ]
```

Description

REFRESH MATERIALIZED VIEW completely replaces the contents of a materialized view. The old contents are discarded. If WITH DATA is specified (or defaults) the backing query is executed to provide the new data, and the materialized view is left in a scannable state. If WITH NO DATA is specified no new data is generated and the materialized view is left in an unscannable state.

CONCURRENTLY and WITH NO DATA may not be specified together.

Parameters

CONCURRENTLY

> Refresh the materialized view without locking out concurrent selects on the materialized view. Without this option a refresh which affects a lot of rows will tend to use fewer resources and complete more quickly, but could block other connections which are trying to read from the materialized view. This option may be faster in cases where a small number of rows are affected.

> This option is only allowed if there is at least one UNIQUE index on the materialized view which uses only column names and includes all rows; that is, it must not index on any expressions nor include a WHERE clause.

> This option may not be used when the materialized view is not already populated.

> Even with this option only one REFRESH at a time may run against any one materialized view.

name

> The name (optionally schema-qualified) of the materialized view to refresh.

Notes

While the default index for future CLUSTER operations is retained, REFRESH MATERIALIZED VIEW does not order the generated rows based on this property. If you want the data to be ordered upon generation, you must use an ORDER BY clause in the backing query.

Examples

This command will replace the contents of the materialized view called `order_summary` using the query from the materialized view's definition, and leave it in a scannable state:

```
REFRESH MATERIALIZED VIEW order_summary;
```

This command will free storage associated with the materialized view `annual_statistics_basis` and leave it in an unscannable state:

```
REFRESH MATERIALIZED VIEW annual_statistics_basis WITH NO DATA;
```

Compatibility

`REFRESH MATERIALIZED VIEW` is a PostgreSQL extension.

See Also

CREATE MATERIALIZED VIEW, ALTER MATERIALIZED VIEW, DROP MATERIALIZED VIEW

REINDEX

Name

REINDEX — rebuild indexes

Synopsis

```
REINDEX { INDEX | TABLE | DATABASE | SYSTEM } name [ FORCE ]
```

Description

REINDEX rebuilds an index using the data stored in the index's table, replacing the old copy of the index. There are several scenarios in which to use REINDEX:

- An index has become corrupted, and no longer contains valid data. Although in theory this should never happen, in practice indexes can become corrupted due to software bugs or hardware failures. REINDEX provides a recovery method.

- An index has become "bloated", that is it contains many empty or nearly-empty pages. This can occur with B-tree indexes in PostgreSQL under certain uncommon access patterns. REINDEX provides a way to reduce the space consumption of the index by writing a new version of the index without the dead pages. See Section 23.2 for more information.

- You have altered a storage parameter (such as fillfactor) for an index, and wish to ensure that the change has taken full effect.

- An index build with the CONCURRENTLY option failed, leaving an "invalid" index. Such indexes are useless but it can be convenient to use REINDEX to rebuild them. Note that REINDEX will not perform a concurrent build. To build the index without interfering with production you should drop the index and reissue the CREATE INDEX CONCURRENTLY command.

Parameters

INDEX

Recreate the specified index.

TABLE

Recreate all indexes of the specified table. If the table has a secondary "TOAST" table, that is reindexed as well.

DATABASE

    Recreate all indexes within the current database. Indexes on shared system catalogs are also processed. This form of REINDEX cannot be executed inside a transaction block.

SYSTEM

    Recreate all indexes on system catalogs within the current database. Indexes on shared system catalogs are included. Indexes on user tables are not processed. This form of REINDEX cannot be executed inside a transaction block.

name

    The name of the specific index, table, or database to be reindexed. Index and table names can be schema-qualified. Presently, REINDEX DATABASE and REINDEX SYSTEM can only reindex the current database, so their parameter must match the current database's name.

FORCE

    This is an obsolete option; it is ignored if specified.

Notes

If you suspect corruption of an index on a user table, you can simply rebuild that index, or all indexes on the table, using REINDEX INDEX or REINDEX TABLE.

Things are more difficult if you need to recover from corruption of an index on a system table. In this case it's important for the system to not have used any of the suspect indexes itself. (Indeed, in this sort of scenario you might find that server processes are crashing immediately at start-up, due to reliance on the corrupted indexes.) To recover safely, the server must be started with the -P option, which prevents it from using indexes for system catalog lookups.

One way to do this is to shut down the server and start a single-user PostgreSQL server with the -P option included on its command line. Then, REINDEX DATABASE, REINDEX SYSTEM, REINDEX TABLE, or REINDEX INDEX can be issued, depending on how much you want to reconstruct. If in doubt, use REINDEX SYSTEM to select reconstruction of all system indexes in the database. Then quit the single-user server session and restart the regular server. See the postgres reference page for more information about how to interact with the single-user server interface.

Alternatively, a regular server session can be started with -P included in its command line options. The method for doing this varies across clients, but in all libpq-based clients, it is possible to set the PGOPTIONS environment variable to -P before starting the client. Note that while this method does not require locking out other clients, it might still be wise to prevent other users from connecting to the damaged database until repairs have been completed.

REINDEX is similar to a drop and recreate of the index in that the index contents are rebuilt from scratch. However, the locking considerations are rather different. REINDEX locks out writes but not reads of the index's parent table. It also takes an exclusive lock on the specific index being processed, which will block reads that attempt to use that index. In contrast, DROP INDEX momentarily takes an exclusive lock on the parent table, blocking both writes and reads. The subsequent CREATE INDEX locks out writes but not reads; since the index is not there, no read will attempt to use it, meaning that there will be no blocking but reads might be forced into expensive sequential scans.

Reindexing a single index or table requires being the owner of that index or table. Reindexing a database requires being the owner of the database (note that the owner can therefore rebuild indexes of tables owned by other users). Of course, superusers can always reindex anything.

Examples

Rebuild a single index:

```
REINDEX INDEX my_index;
```

Rebuild all the indexes on the table my_table:

```
REINDEX TABLE my_table;
```

Rebuild all indexes in a particular database, without trusting the system indexes to be valid already:

```
$ export PGOPTIONS="-P"
$ psql broken_db
...
broken_db=> REINDEX DATABASE broken_db;
broken_db=> \q
```

Compatibility

There is no REINDEX command in the SQL standard.

RELEASE SAVEPOINT

Name

RELEASE SAVEPOINT — destroy a previously defined savepoint

Synopsis

```
RELEASE [ SAVEPOINT ] savepoint_name
```

Description

RELEASE SAVEPOINT destroys a savepoint previously defined in the current transaction.

Destroying a savepoint makes it unavailable as a rollback point, but it has no other user visible behavior. It does not undo the effects of commands executed after the savepoint was established. (To do that, see ROLLBACK TO SAVEPOINT.) Destroying a savepoint when it is no longer needed allows the system to reclaim some resources earlier than transaction end.

RELEASE SAVEPOINT also destroys all savepoints that were established after the named savepoint was established.

Parameters

savepoint_name

   The name of the savepoint to destroy.

Notes

Specifying a savepoint name that was not previously defined is an error.

It is not possible to release a savepoint when the transaction is in an aborted state.

If multiple savepoints have the same name, only the one that was most recently defined is released.

Examples

To establish and later destroy a savepoint:

```
BEGIN;
    INSERT INTO table1 VALUES (3);
    SAVEPOINT my_savepoint;
    INSERT INTO table1 VALUES (4);
    RELEASE SAVEPOINT my_savepoint;
```

```
COMMIT;
```

The above transaction will insert both 3 and 4.

Compatibility

This command conforms to the SQL standard. The standard specifies that the key word SAVEPOINT is mandatory, but PostgreSQL allows it to be omitted.

See Also

BEGIN, COMMIT, ROLLBACK, ROLLBACK TO SAVEPOINT, SAVEPOINT

RESET

Name

RESET — restore the value of a run-time parameter to the default value

Synopsis

```
RESET configuration_parameter
RESET ALL
```

Description

RESET restores run-time parameters to their default values. RESET is an alternative spelling for

```
SET configuration_parameter TO DEFAULT
```

Refer to SET for details.

The default value is defined as the value that the parameter would have had, if no SET had ever been issued for it in the current session. The actual source of this value might be a compiled-in default, the configuration file, command-line options, or per-database or per-user default settings. This is subtly different from defining it as "the value that the parameter had at session start", because if the value came from the configuration file, it will be reset to whatever is specified by the configuration file now. See Chapter 18 for details.

The transactional behavior of RESET is the same as SET: its effects will be undone by transaction rollback.

Parameters

configuration_parameter

>   Name of a settable run-time parameter. Available parameters are documented in Chapter 18 and on the SET reference page.

ALL

>   Resets all settable run-time parameters to default values.

Examples

Set the timezone configuration variable to its default value:

```
RESET timezone;
```

Compatibility

RESET is a PostgreSQL extension.

See Also

SET, SHOW

REVOKE

Name

REVOKE — remove access privileges

Synopsis

```
REVOKE [ GRANT OPTION FOR ]
    { { SELECT | INSERT | UPDATE | DELETE | TRUNCATE | REFERENCES | TRIGGER }
    [, ...] | ALL [ PRIVILEGES ] }
    ON { [ TABLE ] table_name [, ...]
        | ALL TABLES IN SCHEMA schema_name [, ...] }
    FROM { [ GROUP ] role_name | PUBLIC } [, ...]
    [ CASCADE | RESTRICT ]

REVOKE [ GRANT OPTION FOR ]
    { { SELECT | INSERT | UPDATE | REFERENCES } ( column_name [, ...] )
    [, ...] | ALL [ PRIVILEGES ] ( column_name [, ...] ) }
    ON [ TABLE ] table_name [, ...]
    FROM { [ GROUP ] role_name | PUBLIC } [, ...]
    [ CASCADE | RESTRICT ]

REVOKE [ GRANT OPTION FOR ]
    { { USAGE | SELECT | UPDATE }
    [, ...] | ALL [ PRIVILEGES ] }
    ON { SEQUENCE sequence_name [, ...]
        | ALL SEQUENCES IN SCHEMA schema_name [, ...] }
    FROM { [ GROUP ] role_name | PUBLIC } [, ...]
    [ CASCADE | RESTRICT ]

REVOKE [ GRANT OPTION FOR ]
    { { CREATE | CONNECT | TEMPORARY | TEMP } [, ...] | ALL [ PRIVILEGES ] }
    ON DATABASE database_name [, ...]
    FROM { [ GROUP ] role_name | PUBLIC } [, ...]
    [ CASCADE | RESTRICT ]

REVOKE [ GRANT OPTION FOR ]
    { USAGE | ALL [ PRIVILEGES ] }
    ON DOMAIN domain_name [, ...]
    FROM { [ GROUP ] role_name | PUBLIC } [, ...]
    [ CASCADE | RESTRICT ]

REVOKE [ GRANT OPTION FOR ]
    { USAGE | ALL [ PRIVILEGES ] }
    ON FOREIGN DATA WRAPPER fdw_name [, ...]
    FROM { [ GROUP ] role_name | PUBLIC } [, ...]
    [ CASCADE | RESTRICT ]

REVOKE [ GRANT OPTION FOR ]
    { USAGE | ALL [ PRIVILEGES ] }
```

```
     ON FOREIGN SERVER server_name [, ...]
     FROM { [ GROUP ] role_name | PUBLIC } [, ...]
     [ CASCADE | RESTRICT ]

REVOKE [ GRANT OPTION FOR ]
     { EXECUTE | ALL [ PRIVILEGES ] }
     ON { FUNCTION function_name ( [ [ argmode ] [ arg_name ] arg_type [, ...] ] )
          | ALL FUNCTIONS IN SCHEMA schema_name [, ...] }
     FROM { [ GROUP ] role_name | PUBLIC } [, ...]
     [ CASCADE | RESTRICT ]

REVOKE [ GRANT OPTION FOR ]
     { USAGE | ALL [ PRIVILEGES ] }
     ON LANGUAGE lang_name [, ...]
     FROM { [ GROUP ] role_name | PUBLIC } [, ...]
     [ CASCADE | RESTRICT ]

REVOKE [ GRANT OPTION FOR ]
     { { SELECT | UPDATE } [, ...] | ALL [ PRIVILEGES ] }
     ON LARGE OBJECT loid [, ...]
     FROM { [ GROUP ] role_name | PUBLIC } [, ...]
     [ CASCADE | RESTRICT ]

REVOKE [ GRANT OPTION FOR ]
     { { CREATE | USAGE } [, ...] | ALL [ PRIVILEGES ] }
     ON SCHEMA schema_name [, ...]
     FROM { [ GROUP ] role_name | PUBLIC } [, ...]
     [ CASCADE | RESTRICT ]

REVOKE [ GRANT OPTION FOR ]
     { CREATE | ALL [ PRIVILEGES ] }
     ON TABLESPACE tablespace_name [, ...]
     FROM { [ GROUP ] role_name | PUBLIC } [, ...]
     [ CASCADE | RESTRICT ]

REVOKE [ GRANT OPTION FOR ]
     { USAGE | ALL [ PRIVILEGES ] }
     ON TYPE type_name [, ...]
     FROM { [ GROUP ] role_name | PUBLIC } [, ...]
     [ CASCADE | RESTRICT ]

REVOKE [ ADMIN OPTION FOR ]
     role_name [, ...] FROM role_name [, ...]
     [ CASCADE | RESTRICT ]
```

Description

The REVOKE command revokes previously granted privileges from one or more roles. The key word PUBLIC refers to the implicitly defined group of all roles.

See the description of the GRANT command for the meaning of the privilege types.

Note that any particular role will have the sum of privileges granted directly to it, privileges granted to any role it is presently a member of, and privileges granted to PUBLIC. Thus, for example, revoking SELECT privilege from PUBLIC does not necessarily mean that all roles have lost SELECT privilege on the object: those who have it granted directly or via another role will still have it. Similarly, revoking SELECT from a user might not prevent that user from using SELECT if PUBLIC or another membership role still has SELECT rights.

If GRANT OPTION FOR is specified, only the grant option for the privilege is revoked, not the privilege itself. Otherwise, both the privilege and the grant option are revoked.

If a user holds a privilege with grant option and has granted it to other users then the privileges held by those other users are called dependent privileges. If the privilege or the grant option held by the first user is being revoked and dependent privileges exist, those dependent privileges are also revoked if CASCADE is specified; if it is not, the revoke action will fail. This recursive revocation only affects privileges that were granted through a chain of users that is traceable to the user that is the subject of this REVOKE command. Thus, the affected users might effectively keep the privilege if it was also granted through other users.

When revoking privileges on a table, the corresponding column privileges (if any) are automatically revoked on each column of the table, as well. On the other hand, if a role has been granted privileges on a table, then revoking the same privileges from individual columns will have no effect.

When revoking membership in a role, GRANT OPTION is instead called ADMIN OPTION, but the behavior is similar. Note also that this form of the command does not allow the noise word GROUP.

Notes

Use psql's \dp command to display the privileges granted on existing tables and columns. See GRANT for information about the format. For non-table objects there are other \d commands that can display their privileges.

A user can only revoke privileges that were granted directly by that user. If, for example, user A has granted a privilege with grant option to user B, and user B has in turned granted it to user C, then user A cannot revoke the privilege directly from C. Instead, user A could revoke the grant option from user B and use the CASCADE option so that the privilege is in turn revoked from user C. For another example, if both A and B have granted the same privilege to C, A can revoke his own grant but not B's grant, so C will still effectively have the privilege.

When a non-owner of an object attempts to REVOKE privileges on the object, the command will fail outright if the user has no privileges whatsoever on the object. As long as some privilege is available, the command will proceed, but it will revoke only those privileges for which the user has grant options. The REVOKE ALL PRIVILEGES forms will issue a warning message if no grant options are held, while the other forms will issue a warning if grant options for any of the privileges specifically named in the command are not held. (In principle these statements apply to the object owner as well, but since the owner is always treated as holding all grant options, the cases can never occur.)

If a superuser chooses to issue a GRANT or REVOKE command, the command is performed as though it were issued by the owner of the affected object. Since all privileges ultimately come from the object owner (possibly indirectly via chains of grant options), it is possible for a superuser to revoke all privileges, but this might require use of CASCADE as stated above.

REVOKE can also be done by a role that is not the owner of the affected object, but is a member of the role that owns the object, or is a member of a role that holds privileges WITH GRANT OPTION on the object.

In this case the command is performed as though it were issued by the containing role that actually owns the object or holds the privileges WITH GRANT OPTION. For example, if table t1 is owned by role g1, of which role u1 is a member, then u1 can revoke privileges on t1 that are recorded as being granted by g1. This would include grants made by u1 as well as by other members of role g1.

If the role executing REVOKE holds privileges indirectly via more than one role membership path, it is unspecified which containing role will be used to perform the command. In such cases it is best practice to use SET ROLE to become the specific role you want to do the REVOKE as. Failure to do so might lead to revoking privileges other than the ones you intended, or not revoking anything at all.

Examples

Revoke insert privilege for the public on table films:

```
REVOKE INSERT ON films FROM PUBLIC;
```

Revoke all privileges from user manuel on view kinds:

```
REVOKE ALL PRIVILEGES ON kinds FROM manuel;
```

Note that this actually means "revoke all privileges that I granted".

Revoke membership in role admins from user joe:

```
REVOKE admins FROM joe;
```

Compatibility

The compatibility notes of the GRANT command apply analogously to REVOKE. The keyword RESTRICT or CASCADE is required according to the standard, but PostgreSQL assumes RESTRICT by default.

See Also

GRANT

ROLLBACK

Name

ROLLBACK — abort the current transaction

Synopsis

```
ROLLBACK [ WORK | TRANSACTION ]
```

Description

ROLLBACK rolls back the current transaction and causes all the updates made by the transaction to be discarded.

Parameters

```
WORK
TRANSACTION
```
> Optional key words. They have no effect.

Notes

Use COMMIT to successfully terminate a transaction.

Issuing ROLLBACK outside of a transaction block emits a warning and otherwise has no effect.

Examples

To abort all changes:

```
ROLLBACK;
```

Compatibility

The SQL standard only specifies the two forms ROLLBACK and ROLLBACK WORK. Otherwise, this command is fully conforming.

See Also

BEGIN, COMMIT, ROLLBACK TO SAVEPOINT

ROLLBACK PREPARED

Name

ROLLBACK PREPARED — cancel a transaction that was earlier prepared for two-phase commit

Synopsis

```
ROLLBACK PREPARED transaction_id
```

Description

ROLLBACK PREPARED rolls back a transaction that is in prepared state.

Parameters

transaction_id

   The transaction identifier of the transaction that is to be rolled back.

Notes

To roll back a prepared transaction, you must be either the same user that executed the transaction originally, or a superuser. But you do not have to be in the same session that executed the transaction.

This command cannot be executed inside a transaction block. The prepared transaction is rolled back immediately.

All currently available prepared transactions are listed in the pg_prepared_xacts system view.

Examples

Roll back the transaction identified by the transaction identifier foobar:

```
ROLLBACK PREPARED 'foobar';
```

Compatibility

ROLLBACK PREPARED is a PostgreSQL extension. It is intended for use by external transaction management systems, some of which are covered by standards (such as X/Open XA), but the SQL side of those systems is not standardized.

See Also

PREPARE TRANSACTION, COMMIT PREPARED

ROLLBACK TO SAVEPOINT

Name

ROLLBACK TO SAVEPOINT — roll back to a savepoint

Synopsis

```
ROLLBACK [ WORK | TRANSACTION ] TO [ SAVEPOINT ] savepoint_name
```

Description

Roll back all commands that were executed after the savepoint was established. The savepoint remains valid and can be rolled back to again later, if needed.

ROLLBACK TO SAVEPOINT implicitly destroys all savepoints that were established after the named savepoint.

Parameters

savepoint_name

> The savepoint to roll back to.

Notes

Use RELEASE SAVEPOINT to destroy a savepoint without discarding the effects of commands executed after it was established.

Specifying a savepoint name that has not been established is an error.

Cursors have somewhat non-transactional behavior with respect to savepoints. Any cursor that is opened inside a savepoint will be closed when the savepoint is rolled back. If a previously opened cursor is affected by a FETCH or MOVE command inside a savepoint that is later rolled back, the cursor remains at the position that FETCH left it pointing to (that is, the cursor motion caused by FETCH is not rolled back). Closing a cursor is not undone by rolling back, either. However, other side-effects caused by the cursor's query (such as side-effects of volatile functions called by the query) *are* rolled back if they occur during a savepoint that is later rolled back. A cursor whose execution causes a transaction to abort is put in a cannot-execute state, so while the transaction can be restored using ROLLBACK TO SAVEPOINT, the cursor can no longer be used.

Examples

To undo the effects of the commands executed after `my_savepoint` was established:

```
ROLLBACK TO SAVEPOINT my_savepoint;
```

Cursor positions are not affected by savepoint rollback:

```
BEGIN;

DECLARE foo CURSOR FOR SELECT 1 UNION SELECT 2;

SAVEPOINT foo;

FETCH 1 FROM foo;
 ?column?
----------
        1

ROLLBACK TO SAVEPOINT foo;

FETCH 1 FROM foo;
 ?column?
----------
        2

COMMIT;
```

Compatibility

The SQL standard specifies that the key word `SAVEPOINT` is mandatory, but PostgreSQL and Oracle allow it to be omitted. SQL allows only `WORK`, not `TRANSACTION`, as a noise word after `ROLLBACK`. Also, SQL has an optional clause `AND [ NO ] CHAIN` which is not currently supported by PostgreSQL. Otherwise, this command conforms to the SQL standard.

See Also

BEGIN, COMMIT, RELEASE SAVEPOINT, ROLLBACK, SAVEPOINT

SAVEPOINT

Name

SAVEPOINT — define a new savepoint within the current transaction

Synopsis

```
SAVEPOINT savepoint_name
```

Description

SAVEPOINT establishes a new savepoint within the current transaction.

A savepoint is a special mark inside a transaction that allows all commands that are executed after it was established to be rolled back, restoring the transaction state to what it was at the time of the savepoint.

Parameters

savepoint_name

    The name to give to the new savepoint.

Notes

Use ROLLBACK TO SAVEPOINT to rollback to a savepoint. Use RELEASE SAVEPOINT to destroy a savepoint, keeping the effects of commands executed after it was established.

Savepoints can only be established when inside a transaction block. There can be multiple savepoints defined within a transaction.

Examples

To establish a savepoint and later undo the effects of all commands executed after it was established:

```
BEGIN;
    INSERT INTO table1 VALUES (1);
    SAVEPOINT my_savepoint;
    INSERT INTO table1 VALUES (2);
    ROLLBACK TO SAVEPOINT my_savepoint;
    INSERT INTO table1 VALUES (3);
COMMIT;
```

The above transaction will insert the values 1 and 3, but not 2.

To establish and later destroy a savepoint:

```
BEGIN;
    INSERT INTO table1 VALUES (3);
    SAVEPOINT my_savepoint;
    INSERT INTO table1 VALUES (4);
    RELEASE SAVEPOINT my_savepoint;
COMMIT;
```

The above transaction will insert both 3 and 4.

Compatibility

SQL requires a savepoint to be destroyed automatically when another savepoint with the same name is established. In PostgreSQL, the old savepoint is kept, though only the more recent one will be used when rolling back or releasing. (Releasing the newer savepoint with RELEASE SAVEPOINT will cause the older one to again become accessible to ROLLBACK TO SAVEPOINT and RELEASE SAVEPOINT.) Otherwise, SAVEPOINT is fully SQL conforming.

See Also

BEGIN, COMMIT, RELEASE SAVEPOINT, ROLLBACK, ROLLBACK TO SAVEPOINT

SECURITY LABEL

Name

SECURITY LABEL — define or change a security label applied to an object

Synopsis

```
SECURITY LABEL [ FOR provider ] ON
{
  TABLE object_name |
  COLUMN table_name.column_name |
  AGGREGATE aggregate_name ( aggregate_signature ) |
  DATABASE object_name |
  DOMAIN object_name |
  EVENT TRIGGER object_name |
  FOREIGN TABLE object_name
  FUNCTION function_name ( [ [ argmode ] [ argname ] argtype [, ...] ] ) |
  LARGE OBJECT large_object_oid |
  MATERIALIZED VIEW object_name |
  [ PROCEDURAL ] LANGUAGE object_name |
  ROLE object_name |
  SCHEMA object_name |
  SEQUENCE object_name |
  TABLESPACE object_name |
  TYPE object_name |
  VIEW object_name
} IS 'label'

where aggregate_signature is:

* |
[ argmode ] [ argname ] argtype [ , ... ] |
[ [ argmode ] [ argname ] argtype [ , ... ] ] ORDER BY [ argmode ] [ argname ] argt
```

Description

SECURITY LABEL applies a security label to a database object. An arbitrary number of security labels, one per label provider, can be associated with a given database object. Label providers are loadable modules which register themselves by using the function register_label_provider.

> **Note:** register_label_provider is not an SQL function; it can only be called from C code loaded into the backend.

The label provider determines whether a given label is valid and whether it is permissible to assign that label to a given object. The meaning of a given label is likewise at the discretion of the label provider.

PostgreSQL places no restrictions on whether or how a label provider must interpret security labels; it merely provides a mechanism for storing them. In practice, this facility is intended to allow integration with label-based mandatory access control (MAC) systems such as SE-Linux. Such systems make all access control decisions based on object labels, rather than traditional discretionary access control (DAC) concepts such as users and groups.

Parameters

`object_name`
`table_name.column_name`
`aggregate_name`
`function_name`

> The name of the object to be labeled. Names of tables, aggregates, domains, foreign tables, functions, sequences, types, and views can be schema-qualified.

`provider`

> The name of the provider with which this label is to be associated. The named provider must be loaded and must consent to the proposed labeling operation. If exactly one provider is loaded, the provider name may be omitted for brevity.

`argmode`

> The mode of a function or aggregate argument: IN, OUT, INOUT, or VARIADIC. If omitted, the default is IN. Note that SECURITY LABEL does not actually pay any attention to OUT arguments, since only the input arguments are needed to determine the function's identity. So it is sufficient to list the IN, INOUT, and VARIADIC arguments.

`argname`

> The name of a function or aggregate argument. Note that SECURITY LABEL does not actually pay any attention to argument names, since only the argument data types are needed to determine the function's identity.

`argtype`

> The data type of a function or aggregate argument.

`large_object_oid`

> The OID of the large object.

PROCEDURAL

> This is a noise word.

`label`

> The new security label, written as a string literal; or NULL to drop the security label.

Examples

The following example shows how the security label of a table might be changed.

```
SECURITY LABEL FOR selinux ON TABLE mytable IS 'system_u:object_r:sepgsql_table
```

Compatibility

There is no SECURITY LABEL command in the SQL standard.

See Also

sepgsql, dummy_seclabel

SELECT

Name

SELECT, TABLE, WITH — retrieve rows from a table or view

Synopsis

```
[ WITH [ RECURSIVE ] with_query [, ...] ]
SELECT [ ALL | DISTINCT [ ON ( expression [, ...] ) ] ]
    [ * | expression [ [ AS ] output_name ] [, ...] ]
    [ FROM from_item [, ...] ]
    [ WHERE condition ]
    [ GROUP BY expression [, ...] ]
    [ HAVING condition [, ...] ]
    [ WINDOW window_name AS ( window_definition ) [, ...] ]
    [ { UNION | INTERSECT | EXCEPT } [ ALL | DISTINCT ] select ]
    [ ORDER BY expression [ ASC | DESC | USING operator ] [ NULLS { FIRST | LAST
    [ LIMIT { count | ALL } ]
    [ OFFSET start [ ROW | ROWS ] ]
    [ FETCH { FIRST | NEXT } [ count ] { ROW | ROWS } ONLY ]
    [ FOR { UPDATE | NO KEY UPDATE | SHARE | KEY SHARE } [ OF table_name [, ...]

where from_item can be one of:

    [ ONLY ] table_name [ * ] [ [ AS ] alias [ ( column_alias [, ...] ) ] ]
    [ LATERAL ] ( select ) [ AS ] alias [ ( column_alias [, ...] ) ]
    with_query_name [ [ AS ] alias [ ( column_alias [, ...] ) ] ]
    [ LATERAL ] function_name ( [ argument [, ...] ] )
              [ WITH ORDINALITY ] [ [ AS ] alias [ ( column_alias [, ...] ) ]
    [ LATERAL ] function_name ( [ argument [, ...] ] ) [ AS ] alias ( column_defini
    [ LATERAL ] function_name ( [ argument [, ...] ] ) AS ( column_definition [, .
    [ LATERAL ] ROWS FROM( function_name ( [ argument [, ...] ] ) [ AS ( column_de
              [ WITH ORDINALITY ] [ [ AS ] alias [ ( column_alias [, ...] ) ]
    from_item [ NATURAL ] join_type from_item [ ON join_condition | USING ( join_co

and with_query is:

    with_query_name [ ( column_name [, ...] ) ] AS ( select | values | insert | upda

TABLE [ ONLY ] table_name [ * ]
```

Description

SELECT retrieves rows from zero or more tables. The general processing of SELECT is as follows:

1. All queries in the WITH list are computed. These effectively serve as temporary tables that can be referenced in the FROM list. A WITH query that is referenced more than once in FROM is computed only once. (See *WITH Clause* below.)

2. All elements in the FROM list are computed. (Each element in the FROM list is a real or virtual table.) If more than one element is specified in the FROM list, they are cross-joined together. (See *FROM Clause* below.)

3. If the WHERE clause is specified, all rows that do not satisfy the condition are eliminated from the output. (See *WHERE Clause* below.)

4. If the GROUP BY clause is specified, or if there are aggregate function calls, the output is combined into groups of rows that match on one or more values, and the results of aggregate functions are computed. If the HAVING clause is present, it eliminates groups that do not satisfy the given condition. (See *GROUP BY Clause* and *HAVING Clause* below.)

5. The actual output rows are computed using the SELECT output expressions for each selected row or row group. (See *SELECT List* below.)

6. SELECT DISTINCT eliminates duplicate rows from the result. SELECT DISTINCT ON eliminates rows that match on all the specified expressions. SELECT ALL (the default) will return all candidate rows, including duplicates. (See *DISTINCT Clause* below.)

7. Using the operators UNION, INTERSECT, and EXCEPT, the output of more than one SELECT statement can be combined to form a single result set. The UNION operator returns all rows that are in one or both of the result sets. The INTERSECT operator returns all rows that are strictly in both result sets. The EXCEPT operator returns the rows that are in the first result set but not in the second. In all three cases, duplicate rows are eliminated unless ALL is specified. The noise word DISTINCT can be added to explicitly specify eliminating duplicate rows. Notice that DISTINCT is the default behavior here, even though ALL is the default for SELECT itself. (See *UNION Clause*, *INTERSECT Clause*, and *EXCEPT Clause* below.)

8. If the ORDER BY clause is specified, the returned rows are sorted in the specified order. If ORDER BY is not given, the rows are returned in whatever order the system finds fastest to produce. (See *ORDER BY Clause* below.)

9. If the LIMIT (or FETCH FIRST) or OFFSET clause is specified, the SELECT statement only returns a subset of the result rows. (See *LIMIT Clause* below.)

10. If FOR UPDATE, FOR NO KEY UPDATE, FOR SHARE or FOR KEY SHARE is specified, the SELECT statement locks the selected rows against concurrent updates. (See *The Locking Clause* below.)

You must have SELECT privilege on each column used in a SELECT command. The use of FOR NO KEY UPDATE, FOR UPDATE, FOR SHARE or FOR KEY SHARE requires UPDATE privilege as well (for at least one column of each table so selected).

Parameters

WITH **Clause**

The WITH clause allows you to specify one or more subqueries that can be referenced by name in the primary query. The subqueries effectively act as temporary tables or views for the duration of the primary query. Each subquery can be a SELECT, TABLE, VALUES, INSERT, UPDATE or DELETE statement. When writing a data-modifying statement (INSERT, UPDATE or DELETE) in WITH, it is usual to include a RETURNING clause. It is the output of RETURNING, *not* the underlying table that the statement modifies, that forms the temporary table that is read by the primary query. If RETURNING is omitted, the statement is still executed, but it produces no output so it cannot be referenced as a table by the primary query.

A name (without schema qualification) must be specified for each WITH query. Optionally, a list of column names can be specified; if this is omitted, the column names are inferred from the subquery.

If RECURSIVE is specified, it allows a SELECT subquery to reference itself by name. Such a subquery must have the form

```
non_recursive_term UNION [ ALL | DISTINCT ] recursive_term
```

where the recursive self-reference must appear on the right-hand side of the UNION. Only one recursive self-reference is permitted per query. Recursive data-modifying statements are not supported, but you can use the results of a recursive SELECT query in a data-modifying statement. See Section 7.8 for an example.

Another effect of RECURSIVE is that WITH queries need not be ordered: a query can reference another one that is later in the list. (However, circular references, or mutual recursion, are not implemented.) Without RECURSIVE, WITH queries can only reference sibling WITH queries that are earlier in the WITH list.

A key property of WITH queries is that they are evaluated only once per execution of the primary query, even if the primary query refers to them more than once. In particular, data-modifying statements are guaranteed to be executed once and only once, regardless of whether the primary query reads all or any of their output.

The primary query and the WITH queries are all (notionally) executed at the same time. This implies that the effects of a data-modifying statement in WITH cannot be seen from other parts of the query, other than by reading its RETURNING output. If two such data-modifying statements attempt to modify the same row, the results are unspecified.

See Section 7.8 for additional information.

FROM **Clause**

The FROM clause specifies one or more source tables for the SELECT. If multiple sources are specified, the result is the Cartesian product (cross join) of all the sources. But usually qualification conditions are added (via WHERE) to restrict the returned rows to a small subset of the Cartesian product.

The FROM clause can contain the following elements:

```
table_name
```

> The name (optionally schema-qualified) of an existing table or view. If ONLY is specified before the table name, only that table is scanned. If ONLY is not specified, the table and all its descendant tables

(if any) are scanned. Optionally, * can be specified after the table name to explicitly indicate that descendant tables are included.

alias

> A substitute name for the FROM item containing the alias. An alias is used for brevity or to eliminate ambiguity for self-joins (where the same table is scanned multiple times). When an alias is provided, it completely hides the actual name of the table or function; for example given FROM foo AS f, the remainder of the SELECT must refer to this FROM item as f not foo. If an alias is written, a column alias list can also be written to provide substitute names for one or more columns of the table.

select

> A sub-SELECT can appear in the FROM clause. This acts as though its output were created as a temporary table for the duration of this single SELECT command. Note that the sub-SELECT must be surrounded by parentheses, and an alias *must* be provided for it. A VALUES command can also be used here.

with_query_name

> A WITH query is referenced by writing its name, just as though the query's name were a table name. (In fact, the WITH query hides any real table of the same name for the purposes of the primary query. If necessary, you can refer to a real table of the same name by schema-qualifying the table's name.) An alias can be provided in the same way as for a table.

function_name

> Function calls can appear in the FROM clause. (This is especially useful for functions that return result sets, but any function can be used.) This acts as though the function's output were created as a temporary table for the duration of this single SELECT command. When the optional WITH ORDINALITY clause is added to the function call, a new column is appended after all the function's output columns with numbering for each row.

> An alias can be provided in the same way as for a table. If an alias is written, a column alias list can also be written to provide substitute names for one or more attributes of the function's composite return type, including the column added by ORDINALITY if present.

> Multiple function calls can be combined into a single FROM-clause item by surrounding them with ROWS FROM(...). The output of such an item is the concatenation of the first row from each function, then the second row from each function, etc. If some of the functions produce fewer rows than others, NULLs are substituted for the missing data, so that the total number of rows returned is always the same as for the function that produced the most rows.

> If the function has been defined as returning the record data type, then an alias or the key word AS must be present, followed by a column definition list in the form (*column_name data_type* [, ...]). The column definition list must match the actual number and types of columns returned by the function.

> When using the ROWS FROM(...) syntax, if one of the functions requires a column definition list, it's preferred to put the column definition list after the function call inside ROWS FROM(...). A column definition list can be placed after the ROWS FROM(...) construct only if there's just a single function and no WITH ORDINALITY clause.

> To use ORDINALITY together with a column definition list, you must use the ROWS FROM(...) syntax and put the column definition list inside ROWS FROM(...).

join_type

One of

- [INNER] JOIN

- LEFT [OUTER] JOIN

- RIGHT [OUTER] JOIN

- FULL [OUTER] JOIN

- CROSS JOIN

For the INNER and OUTER join types, a join condition must be specified, namely exactly one of NATURAL, ON *join_condition*, or USING (*join_column* [, ...]). See below for the meaning. For CROSS JOIN, none of these clauses can appear.

A JOIN clause combines two FROM items, which for convenience we will refer to as "tables", though in reality they can be any type of FROM item. Use parentheses if necessary to determine the order of nesting. In the absence of parentheses, JOINs nest left-to-right. In any case JOIN binds more tightly than the commas separating FROM-list items.

CROSS JOIN and INNER JOIN produce a simple Cartesian product, the same result as you get from listing the two tables at the top level of FROM, but restricted by the join condition (if any). CROSS JOIN is equivalent to INNER JOIN ON (TRUE), that is, no rows are removed by qualification. These join types are just a notational convenience, since they do nothing you couldn't do with plain FROM and WHERE.

LEFT OUTER JOIN returns all rows in the qualified Cartesian product (i.e., all combined rows that pass its join condition), plus one copy of each row in the left-hand table for which there was no right-hand row that passed the join condition. This left-hand row is extended to the full width of the joined table by inserting null values for the right-hand columns. Note that only the JOIN clause's own condition is considered while deciding which rows have matches. Outer conditions are applied afterwards.

Conversely, RIGHT OUTER JOIN returns all the joined rows, plus one row for each unmatched right-hand row (extended with nulls on the left). This is just a notational convenience, since you could convert it to a LEFT OUTER JOIN by switching the left and right tables.

FULL OUTER JOIN returns all the joined rows, plus one row for each unmatched left-hand row (extended with nulls on the right), plus one row for each unmatched right-hand row (extended with nulls on the left).

ON *join_condition*

join_condition is an expression resulting in a value of type boolean (similar to a WHERE clause) that specifies which rows in a join are considered to match.

USING (*join_column* [, ...])

A clause of the form USING (a, b, ...) is shorthand for ON left_table.a = right_table.a AND left_table.b = right_table.b .... Also, USING implies that only one of each pair of equivalent columns will be included in the join output, not both.

NATURAL

NATURAL is shorthand for a USING list that mentions all columns in the two tables that have the same names.

LATERAL

The LATERAL key word can precede a sub-SELECT FROM item. This allows the sub-SELECT to refer to columns of FROM items that appear before it in the FROM list. (Without LATERAL, each sub-SELECT is evaluated independently and so cannot cross-reference any other FROM item.)

LATERAL can also precede a function-call FROM item, but in this case it is a noise word, because the function expression can refer to earlier FROM items in any case.

A LATERAL item can appear at top level in the FROM list, or within a JOIN tree. In the latter case it can also refer to any items that are on the left-hand side of a JOIN that it is on the right-hand side of.

When a FROM item contains LATERAL cross-references, evaluation proceeds as follows: for each row of the FROM item providing the cross-referenced column(s), or set of rows of multiple FROM items providing the columns, the LATERAL item is evaluated using that row or row set's values of the columns. The resulting row(s) are joined as usual with the rows they were computed from. This is repeated for each row or set of rows from the column source table(s).

The column source table(s) must be INNER or LEFT joined to the LATERAL item, else there would not be a well-defined set of rows from which to compute each set of rows for the LATERAL item. Thus, although a construct such as X RIGHT JOIN LATERAL Y is syntactically valid, it is not actually allowed for Y to reference X.

WHERE Clause

The optional WHERE clause has the general form

WHERE *condition*

where *condition* is any expression that evaluates to a result of type boolean. Any row that does not satisfy this condition will be eliminated from the output. A row satisfies the condition if it returns true when the actual row values are substituted for any variable references.

GROUP BY Clause

The optional GROUP BY clause has the general form

GROUP BY *expression* [, ...]

GROUP BY will condense into a single row all selected rows that share the same values for the grouped expressions. *expression* can be an input column name, or the name or ordinal number of an output column (SELECT list item), or an arbitrary expression formed from input-column values. In case of ambiguity, a GROUP BY name will be interpreted as an input-column name rather than an output column name.

Aggregate functions, if any are used, are computed across all rows making up each group, producing a separate value for each group. (If there are aggregate functions but no GROUP BY clause, the query is treated as having a single group comprising all the selected rows.) The set of rows fed to each aggregate function can be further filtered by attaching a FILTER clause to the aggregate function call; see Section

4.2.7 for more information. When a FILTER clause is present, only those rows matching it are included in the input to that aggregate function.

When GROUP BY is present, or any aggregate functions are present, it is not valid for the SELECT list expressions to refer to ungrouped columns except within aggregate functions or when the ungrouped column is functionally dependent on the grouped columns, since there would otherwise be more than one possible value to return for an ungrouped column. A functional dependency exists if the grouped columns (or a subset thereof) are the primary key of the table containing the ungrouped column.

Keep in mind that all aggregate functions are evaluated before evaluating any "scalar" expressions in the HAVING clause or SELECT list. This means that, for example, a CASE expression cannot be used to skip evaluation of an aggregate function; see Section 4.2.14.

Currently, FOR NO KEY UPDATE, FOR UPDATE, FOR SHARE and FOR KEY SHARE cannot be specified with GROUP BY.

HAVING Clause

The optional HAVING clause has the general form

```
HAVING condition
```

where *condition* is the same as specified for the WHERE clause.

HAVING eliminates group rows that do not satisfy the condition. HAVING is different from WHERE: WHERE filters individual rows before the application of GROUP BY, while HAVING filters group rows created by GROUP BY. Each column referenced in *condition* must unambiguously reference a grouping column, unless the reference appears within an aggregate function or the ungrouped column is functionally dependent on the grouping columns.

The presence of HAVING turns a query into a grouped query even if there is no GROUP BY clause. This is the same as what happens when the query contains aggregate functions but no GROUP BY clause. All the selected rows are considered to form a single group, and the SELECT list and HAVING clause can only reference table columns from within aggregate functions. Such a query will emit a single row if the HAVING condition is true, zero rows if it is not true.

Currently, FOR NO KEY UPDATE, FOR UPDATE, FOR SHARE and FOR KEY SHARE cannot be specified with HAVING.

WINDOW Clause

The optional WINDOW clause has the general form

```
WINDOW window_name AS ( window_definition ) [, ...]
```

where *window_name* is a name that can be referenced from OVER clauses or subsequent window definitions, and *window_definition* is

```
[ existing_window_name ]
[ PARTITION BY expression [, ...] ]
[ ORDER BY expression [ ASC | DESC | USING operator ] [ NULLS { FIRST | LAST } ]
[ frame_clause ]
```

If an *existing_window_name* is specified it must refer to an earlier entry in the WINDOW list; the new window copies its partitioning clause from that entry, as well as its ordering clause if any. In this case the new window cannot specify its own PARTITION BY clause, and it can specify ORDER BY only if the copied window does not have one. The new window always uses its own frame clause; the copied window must not specify a frame clause.

The elements of the PARTITION BY list are interpreted in much the same fashion as elements of a *GROUP BY Clause*, except that they are always simple expressions and never the name or number of an output column. Another difference is that these expressions can contain aggregate function calls, which are not allowed in a regular GROUP BY clause. They are allowed here because windowing occurs after grouping and aggregation.

Similarly, the elements of the ORDER BY list are interpreted in much the same fashion as elements of an *ORDER BY Clause*, except that the expressions are always taken as simple expressions and never the name or number of an output column.

The optional *frame_clause* defines the *window frame* for window functions that depend on the frame (not all do). The window frame is a set of related rows for each row of the query (called the *current row*). The *frame_clause* can be one of

```
{ RANGE | ROWS } frame_start
{ RANGE | ROWS } BETWEEN frame_start AND frame_end
```

where *frame_start* and *frame_end* can be one of

```
UNBOUNDED PRECEDING
value PRECEDING
CURRENT ROW
value FOLLOWING
UNBOUNDED FOLLOWING
```

If *frame_end* is omitted it defaults to CURRENT ROW. Restrictions are that *frame_start* cannot be UNBOUNDED FOLLOWING, *frame_end* cannot be UNBOUNDED PRECEDING, and the *frame_end* choice cannot appear earlier in the above list than the *frame_start* choice — for example RANGE BETWEEN CURRENT ROW AND *value* PRECEDING is not allowed.

The default framing option is RANGE UNBOUNDED PRECEDING, which is the same as RANGE BETWEEN UNBOUNDED PRECEDING AND CURRENT ROW; it sets the frame to be all rows from the partition start up through the current row's last peer (a row that ORDER BY considers equivalent to the current row, or all rows if there is no ORDER BY). In general, UNBOUNDED PRECEDING means that the frame starts with the first row of the partition, and similarly UNBOUNDED FOLLOWING means that the frame ends with the last row of the partition (regardless of RANGE or ROWS mode). In ROWS mode, CURRENT ROW means that the frame starts or ends with the current row; but in RANGE mode it means that the frame starts or ends with the current row's first or last peer in the ORDER BY ordering. The *value* PRECEDING and *value* FOLLOWING cases are currently only allowed in ROWS mode. They indicate that the frame starts or ends with the row that many rows before or after the current row. *value* must be an integer expression not containing any variables, aggregate functions, or window functions. The value must not be null or negative; but it can be zero, which selects the current row itself.

Beware that the ROWS options can produce unpredictable results if the ORDER BY ordering does not order the rows uniquely. The RANGE options are designed to ensure that rows that are peers in the ORDER BY ordering are treated alike; all peer rows will be in the same frame.

The purpose of a WINDOW clause is to specify the behavior of *window functions* appearing in the query's *SELECT List* or *ORDER BY Clause*. These functions can reference the WINDOW clause entries by name in their OVER clauses. A WINDOW clause entry does not have to be referenced anywhere, however; if it is not used in the query it is simply ignored. It is possible to use window functions without any WINDOW clause at all, since a window function call can specify its window definition directly in its OVER clause. However, the WINDOW clause saves typing when the same window definition is needed for more than one window function.

Currently, FOR NO KEY UPDATE, FOR UPDATE, FOR SHARE and FOR KEY SHARE cannot be specified with WINDOW.

Window functions are described in detail in Section 3.5, Section 4.2.8, and Section 7.2.4.

SELECT List

The SELECT list (between the key words SELECT and FROM) specifies expressions that form the output rows of the SELECT statement. The expressions can (and usually do) refer to columns computed in the FROM clause.

Just as in a table, every output column of a SELECT has a name. In a simple SELECT this name is just used to label the column for display, but when the SELECT is a sub-query of a larger query, the name is seen by the larger query as the column name of the virtual table produced by the sub-query. To specify the name to use for an output column, write AS output_name after the column's expression. (You can omit AS, but only if the desired output name does not match any PostgreSQL keyword (see Appendix C). For protection against possible future keyword additions, it is recommended that you always either write AS or double-quote the output name.) If you do not specify a column name, a name is chosen automatically by PostgreSQL. If the column's expression is a simple column reference then the chosen name is the same as that column's name. In more complex cases a function or type name may be used, or the system may fall back on a generated name such as ?column?.

An output column's name can be used to refer to the column's value in ORDER BY and GROUP BY clauses, but not in the WHERE or HAVING clauses; there you must write out the expression instead.

Instead of an expression, * can be written in the output list as a shorthand for all the columns of the selected rows. Also, you can write table_name.* as a shorthand for the columns coming from just that table. In these cases it is not possible to specify new names with AS; the output column names will be the same as the table columns' names.

DISTINCT Clause

If SELECT DISTINCT is specified, all duplicate rows are removed from the result set (one row is kept from each group of duplicates). SELECT ALL specifies the opposite: all rows are kept; that is the default.

SELECT DISTINCT ON (expression [, ...]) keeps only the first row of each set of rows where the given expressions evaluate to equal. The DISTINCT ON expressions are interpreted using the same rules as for ORDER BY (see above). Note that the "first row" of each set is unpredictable unless ORDER BY is used to ensure that the desired row appears first. For example:

```
SELECT DISTINCT ON (location) location, time, report
    FROM weather_reports
    ORDER BY location, time DESC;
```

retrieves the most recent weather report for each location. But if we had not used ORDER BY to force descending order of time values for each location, we'd have gotten a report from an unpredictable time for each location.

The DISTINCT ON expression(s) must match the leftmost ORDER BY expression(s). The ORDER BY clause will normally contain additional expression(s) that determine the desired precedence of rows within each DISTINCT ON group.

Currently, FOR NO KEY UPDATE, FOR UPDATE, FOR SHARE and FOR KEY SHARE cannot be specified with DISTINCT.

UNION **Clause**

The UNION clause has this general form:

select_statement UNION [ALL | DISTINCT] *select_statement*

select_statement is any SELECT statement without an ORDER BY, LIMIT, FOR NO KEY UPDATE, FOR UPDATE, FOR SHARE, or FOR KEY SHARE clause. (ORDER BY and LIMIT can be attached to a subexpression if it is enclosed in parentheses. Without parentheses, these clauses will be taken to apply to the result of the UNION, not to its right-hand input expression.)

The UNION operator computes the set union of the rows returned by the involved SELECT statements. A row is in the set union of two result sets if it appears in at least one of the result sets. The two SELECT statements that represent the direct operands of the UNION must produce the same number of columns, and corresponding columns must be of compatible data types.

The result of UNION does not contain any duplicate rows unless the ALL option is specified. ALL prevents elimination of duplicates. (Therefore, UNION ALL is usually significantly quicker than UNION; use ALL when you can.) DISTINCT can be written to explicitly specify the default behavior of eliminating duplicate rows.

Multiple UNION operators in the same SELECT statement are evaluated left to right, unless otherwise indicated by parentheses.

Currently, FOR NO KEY UPDATE, FOR UPDATE, FOR SHARE and FOR KEY SHARE cannot be specified either for a UNION result or for any input of a UNION.

INTERSECT **Clause**

The INTERSECT clause has this general form:

select_statement INTERSECT [ALL | DISTINCT] *select_statement*

select_statement is any SELECT statement without an ORDER BY, LIMIT, FOR NO KEY UPDATE, FOR UPDATE, FOR SHARE, or FOR KEY SHARE clause.

The INTERSECT operator computes the set intersection of the rows returned by the involved SELECT statements. A row is in the intersection of two result sets if it appears in both result sets.

The result of INTERSECT does not contain any duplicate rows unless the ALL option is specified. With ALL, a row that has m duplicates in the left table and n duplicates in the right table will appear $\min(m,n)$ times in the result set. DISTINCT can be written to explicitly specify the default behavior of eliminating duplicate rows.

Multiple INTERSECT operators in the same SELECT statement are evaluated left to right, unless parentheses dictate otherwise. INTERSECT binds more tightly than UNION. That is, A UNION B INTERSECT C will be read as A UNION (B INTERSECT C).

Currently, FOR NO KEY UPDATE, FOR UPDATE, FOR SHARE and FOR KEY SHARE cannot be specified either for an INTERSECT result or for any input of an INTERSECT.

EXCEPT Clause

The EXCEPT clause has this general form:

```
select_statement EXCEPT [ ALL | DISTINCT ] select_statement
```

select_statement is any SELECT statement without an ORDER BY, LIMIT, FOR NO KEY UPDATE, FOR UPDATE, FOR SHARE, or FOR KEY SHARE clause.

The EXCEPT operator computes the set of rows that are in the result of the left SELECT statement but not in the result of the right one.

The result of EXCEPT does not contain any duplicate rows unless the ALL option is specified. With ALL, a row that has m duplicates in the left table and n duplicates in the right table will appear $\max(m-n,0)$ times in the result set. DISTINCT can be written to explicitly specify the default behavior of eliminating duplicate rows.

Multiple EXCEPT operators in the same SELECT statement are evaluated left to right, unless parentheses dictate otherwise. EXCEPT binds at the same level as UNION.

Currently, FOR NO KEY UPDATE, FOR UPDATE, FOR SHARE and FOR KEY SHARE cannot be specified either for an EXCEPT result or for any input of an EXCEPT.

ORDER BY Clause

The optional ORDER BY clause has this general form:

```
ORDER BY expression [ ASC | DESC | USING operator ] [ NULLS { FIRST | LAST } ] [,
```

The ORDER BY clause causes the result rows to be sorted according to the specified expression(s). If two rows are equal according to the leftmost expression, they are compared according to the next expression and so on. If they are equal according to all specified expressions, they are returned in an implementation-dependent order.

Each *expression* can be the name or ordinal number of an output column (SELECT list item), or it can be an arbitrary expression formed from input-column values.

The ordinal number refers to the ordinal (left-to-right) position of the output column. This feature makes it possible to define an ordering on the basis of a column that does not have a unique name. This is never absolutely necessary because it is always possible to assign a name to an output column using the AS clause.

It is also possible to use arbitrary expressions in the ORDER BY clause, including columns that do not appear in the SELECT output list. Thus the following statement is valid:

```
SELECT name FROM distributors ORDER BY code;
```

A limitation of this feature is that an ORDER BY clause applying to the result of a UNION, INTERSECT, or EXCEPT clause can only specify an output column name or number, not an expression.

If an ORDER BY expression is a simple name that matches both an output column name and an input column name, ORDER BY will interpret it as the output column name. This is the opposite of the choice that GROUP BY will make in the same situation. This inconsistency is made to be compatible with the SQL standard.

Optionally one can add the key word ASC (ascending) or DESC (descending) after any expression in the ORDER BY clause. If not specified, ASC is assumed by default. Alternatively, a specific ordering operator name can be specified in the USING clause. An ordering operator must be a less-than or greater-than member of some B-tree operator family. ASC is usually equivalent to USING < and DESC is usually equivalent to USING >. (But the creator of a user-defined data type can define exactly what the default sort ordering is, and it might correspond to operators with other names.)

If NULLS LAST is specified, null values sort after all non-null values; if NULLS FIRST is specified, null values sort before all non-null values. If neither is specified, the default behavior is NULLS LAST when ASC is specified or implied, and NULLS FIRST when DESC is specified (thus, the default is to act as though nulls are larger than non-nulls). When USING is specified, the default nulls ordering depends on whether the operator is a less-than or greater-than operator.

Note that ordering options apply only to the expression they follow; for example ORDER BY x, y DESC does not mean the same thing as ORDER BY x DESC, y DESC.

Character-string data is sorted according to the collation that applies to the column being sorted. That can be overridden at need by including a COLLATE clause in the *expression*, for example ORDER BY mycolumn COLLATE "en_US". For more information see Section 4.2.10 and Section 22.2.

LIMIT Clause

The LIMIT clause consists of two independent sub-clauses:

```
LIMIT { count | ALL }
OFFSET start
```

count specifies the maximum number of rows to return, while *start* specifies the number of rows to skip before starting to return rows. When both are specified, *start* rows are skipped before starting to count the *count* rows to be returned.

If the *count* expression evaluates to NULL, it is treated as LIMIT ALL, i.e., no limit. If *start* evaluates to NULL, it is treated the same as OFFSET 0.

SQL:2008 introduced a different syntax to achieve the same result, which PostgreSQL also supports. It is:

```
OFFSET start { ROW | ROWS }
FETCH { FIRST | NEXT } [ count ] { ROW | ROWS } ONLY
```

In this syntax, to write anything except a simple integer constant for `start` or `count`, you must write parentheses around it. If `count` is omitted in a FETCH clause, it defaults to 1. ROW and ROWS as well as FIRST and NEXT are noise words that don't influence the effects of these clauses. According to the standard, the OFFSET clause must come before the FETCH clause if both are present; but PostgreSQL is laxer and allows either order.

When using LIMIT, it is a good idea to use an ORDER BY clause that constrains the result rows into a unique order. Otherwise you will get an unpredictable subset of the query's rows — you might be asking for the tenth through twentieth rows, but tenth through twentieth in what ordering? You don't know what ordering unless you specify ORDER BY.

The query planner takes LIMIT into account when generating a query plan, so you are very likely to get different plans (yielding different row orders) depending on what you use for LIMIT and OFFSET. Thus, using different LIMIT/OFFSET values to select different subsets of a query result *will give inconsistent results* unless you enforce a predictable result ordering with ORDER BY. This is not a bug; it is an inherent consequence of the fact that SQL does not promise to deliver the results of a query in any particular order unless ORDER BY is used to constrain the order.

It is even possible for repeated executions of the same LIMIT query to return different subsets of the rows of a table, if there is not an ORDER BY to enforce selection of a deterministic subset. Again, this is not a bug; determinism of the results is simply not guaranteed in such a case.

The Locking Clause

FOR UPDATE, FOR NO KEY UPDATE, FOR SHARE and FOR KEY SHARE are *locking clauses*; they affect how SELECT locks rows as they are obtained from the table.

The locking clause has the general form

```
FOR lock_strength [ OF table_name [, ...] ] [ NOWAIT ]
```

where `lock_strength` can be one of

```
UPDATE
NO KEY UPDATE
SHARE
KEY SHARE
```

For more information on each row-level lock mode, refer to Section 13.3.2.

To prevent the operation from waiting for other transactions to commit, use the NOWAIT option. With NOWAIT, the statement reports an error, rather than waiting, if a selected row cannot be locked immediately. Note that NOWAIT applies only to the row-level lock(s) — the required ROW SHARE table-level lock is still taken in the ordinary way (see Chapter 13). You can use LOCK with the NOWAIT option first, if you need to acquire the table-level lock without waiting.

If specific tables are named in a locking clause, then only rows coming from those tables are locked; any other tables used in the SELECT are simply read as usual. A locking clause without a table list affects all tables used in the statement. If a locking clause is applied to a view or sub-query, it affects all tables used in the view or sub-query. However, these clauses do not apply to WITH queries referenced by the primary query. If you want row locking to occur within a WITH query, specify a locking clause within the WITH query.

Multiple locking clauses can be written if it is necessary to specify different locking behavior for different tables. If the same table is mentioned (or implicitly affected) by more than one locking clause, then it is processed as if it was only specified by the strongest one. Similarly, a table is processed as NOWAIT if that is specified in any of the clauses affecting it.

The locking clauses cannot be used in contexts where returned rows cannot be clearly identified with individual table rows; for example they cannot be used with aggregation.

When a locking clause appears at the top level of a SELECT query, the rows that are locked are exactly those that are returned by the query; in the case of a join query, the rows locked are those that contribute to returned join rows. In addition, rows that satisfied the query conditions as of the query snapshot will be locked, although they will not be returned if they were updated after the snapshot and no longer satisfy the query conditions. If a LIMIT is used, locking stops once enough rows have been returned to satisfy the limit (but note that rows skipped over by OFFSET will get locked). Similarly, if a locking clause is used in a cursor's query, only rows actually fetched or stepped past by the cursor will be locked.

When a locking clause appears in a sub-SELECT, the rows locked are those returned to the outer query by the sub-query. This might involve fewer rows than inspection of the sub-query alone would suggest, since conditions from the outer query might be used to optimize execution of the sub-query. For example,

```
SELECT * FROM (SELECT * FROM mytable FOR UPDATE) ss WHERE col1 = 5;
```

will lock only rows having col1 = 5, even though that condition is not textually within the sub-query.

Previous releases failed to preserve a lock which is upgraded by a later savepoint. For example, this code:

```
BEGIN;
SELECT * FROM mytable WHERE key = 1 FOR UPDATE;
SAVEPOINT s;
UPDATE mytable SET ... WHERE key = 1;
ROLLBACK TO s;
```

would fail to preserve the FOR UPDATE lock after the ROLLBACK TO. This has been fixed in release 9.3.

Caution

It is possible for a SELECT command running at the READ COMMITTED transaction isolation level and using ORDER BY and a locking clause to return rows out of order. This is because ORDER BY is applied first. The command sorts the result, but might then block trying to obtain a lock on one or more of the rows. Once the SELECT unblocks, some of the ordering column values might have been modified, leading to those rows appearing to be out of order (though they are in order in terms of the original column values). This can be worked around at need by placing the FOR UPDATE/SHARE clause in a sub-query, for example

```
SELECT * FROM (SELECT * FROM mytable FOR UPDATE) ss ORDER BY co
```

Note that this will result in locking all rows of mytable, whereas FOR UPDATE at the top level would lock only the actually returned rows. This can make for a significant performance difference, particularly if the ORDER BY is combined with LIMIT or other restrictions. So this technique is recommended only if concurrent updates of the ordering columns are expected and a strictly sorted result is required.

At the REPEATABLE READ or SERIALIZABLE transaction isolation level this would cause a serialization failure (with a SQLSTATE of '40001'), so there is no possibility of receiving rows out of order under these isolation levels.

TABLE Command

The command

```
TABLE name
```

is equivalent to

```
SELECT * FROM name
```

It can be used as a top-level command or as a space-saving syntax variant in parts of complex queries. Only the WITH, UNION, INTERSECT, EXCEPT, ORDER BY, LIMIT, OFFSET, FETCH and FOR locking clauses can be used with TABLE; the WHERE clause and any form of aggregation cannot be used.

Examples

To join the table films with the table distributors:

```
SELECT f.title, f.did, d.name, f.date_prod, f.kind
    FROM distributors d, films f
    WHERE f.did = d.did

       title        | did |     name      | date_prod  |  kind
-------------------+-----+---------------+------------+----------
 The Third Man     | 101 | British Lion  | 1949-12-23 | Drama
 The African Queen | 101 | British Lion  | 1951-08-11 | Romantic
 ...
```

To sum the column `len` of all films and group the results by `kind`:

```
SELECT kind, sum(len) AS total FROM films GROUP BY kind;

   kind   | total
----------+-------
 Action   | 07:34
 Comedy   | 02:58
 Drama    | 14:28
 Musical  | 06:42
 Romantic | 04:38
```

To sum the column `len` of all films, group the results by `kind` and show those group totals that are less than 5 hours:

```
SELECT kind, sum(len) AS total
    FROM films
    GROUP BY kind
    HAVING sum(len) < interval '5 hours';

   kind   | total
----------+-------
 Comedy   | 02:58
 Romantic | 04:38
```

The following two examples are identical ways of sorting the individual results according to the contents of the second column (`name`):

```
SELECT * FROM distributors ORDER BY name;
SELECT * FROM distributors ORDER BY 2;

 did |       name
-----+------------------
 109 | 20th Century Fox
 110 | Bavaria Atelier
 101 | British Lion
 107 | Columbia
 102 | Jean Luc Godard
 113 | Luso films
 104 | Mosfilm
 103 | Paramount
 106 | Toho
 105 | United Artists
 111 | Walt Disney
 112 | Warner Bros.
 108 | Westward
```

The next example shows how to obtain the union of the tables distributors and actors, restricting the results to those that begin with the letter W in each table. Only distinct rows are wanted, so the key word ALL is omitted.

```
distributors:                        actors:
 did |      name                      id |       name
-----+--------------                 ----+-----------------
 108 | Westward                        1 | Woody Allen
 111 | Walt Disney                     2 | Warren Beatty
 112 | Warner Bros.                    3 | Walter Matthau
 ...                                  ...

SELECT distributors.name
    FROM distributors
    WHERE distributors.name LIKE 'W%'
UNION
SELECT actors.name
    FROM actors
    WHERE actors.name LIKE 'W%';

      name
----------------
 Walt Disney
 Walter Matthau
 Warner Bros.
 Warren Beatty
 Westward
 Woody Allen
```

This example shows how to use a function in the FROM clause, both with and without a column definition list:

```
CREATE FUNCTION distributors(int) RETURNS SETOF distributors AS $$
    SELECT * FROM distributors WHERE did = $1;
$$ LANGUAGE SQL;

SELECT * FROM distributors(111);
 did |     name
-----+-------------
 111 | Walt Disney

CREATE FUNCTION distributors_2(int) RETURNS SETOF record AS $$
    SELECT * FROM distributors WHERE did = $1;
$$ LANGUAGE SQL;

SELECT * FROM distributors_2(111) AS (f1 int, f2 text);
 f1  |     f2
-----+-------------
 111 | Walt Disney
```

Here is an example of a function with an ordinality column added:

```
SELECT * FROM unnest(ARRAY['a','b','c','d','e','f']) WITH ORDINALITY;
 unnest | ordinality
--------+-----------
 a      |          1
 b      |          2
 c      |          3
 d      |          4
 e      |          5
 f      |          6
(6 rows)
```

This example shows how to use a simple `WITH` clause:

```
WITH t AS (
    SELECT random() as x FROM generate_series(1, 3)
  )
SELECT * FROM t
UNION ALL
SELECT * FROM t

         x
--------------------
  0.534150459803641
  0.520092216785997
 0.0735620250925422
  0.534150459803641
  0.520092216785997
 0.0735620250925422
```

Notice that the `WITH` query was evaluated only once, so that we got two sets of the same three random values.

This example uses `WITH RECURSIVE` to find all subordinates (direct or indirect) of the employee Mary, and their level of indirectness, from a table that shows only direct subordinates:

```
WITH RECURSIVE employee_recursive(distance, employee_name, manager_name) AS (
    SELECT 1, employee_name, manager_name
    FROM employee
    WHERE manager_name = 'Mary'
  UNION ALL
    SELECT er.distance + 1, e.employee_name, e.manager_name
    FROM employee_recursive er, employee e
    WHERE er.employee_name = e.manager_name
  )
SELECT distance, employee_name FROM employee_recursive;
```

Notice the typical form of recursive queries: an initial condition, followed by `UNION`, followed by the recursive part of the query. Be sure that the recursive part of the query will eventually return no tuples, or else the query will loop indefinitely. (See Section 7.8 for more examples.)

This example uses LATERAL to apply a set-returning function get_product_names() for each row of the manufacturers table:

```
SELECT m.name AS mname, pname
FROM manufacturers m, LATERAL get_product_names(m.id) pname;
```

Manufacturers not currently having any products would not appear in the result, since it is an inner join. If we wished to include the names of such manufacturers in the result, we could do:

```
SELECT m.name AS mname, pname
FROM manufacturers m LEFT JOIN LATERAL get_product_names(m.id) pname ON true;
```

Compatibility

Of course, the SELECT statement is compatible with the SQL standard. But there are some extensions and some missing features.

Omitted FROM Clauses

PostgreSQL allows one to omit the FROM clause. It has a straightforward use to compute the results of simple expressions:

```
SELECT 2+2;

 ?column?
----------
        4
```

Some other SQL databases cannot do this except by introducing a dummy one-row table from which to do the SELECT.

Note that if a FROM clause is not specified, the query cannot reference any database tables. For example, the following query is invalid:

```
SELECT distributors.* WHERE distributors.name = 'Westward';
```

PostgreSQL releases prior to 8.1 would accept queries of this form, and add an implicit entry to the query's FROM clause for each table referenced by the query. This is no longer allowed.

Empty SELECT Lists

The list of output expressions after SELECT can be empty, producing a zero-column result table. This is not valid syntax according to the SQL standard. PostgreSQL allows it to be consistent with allowing zero-column tables. However, an empty list is not allowed when DISTINCT is used.

Omitting the AS Key Word

In the SQL standard, the optional key word AS can be omitted before an output column name whenever the new column name is a valid column name (that is, not the same as any reserved keyword). PostgreSQL is slightly more restrictive: AS is required if the new column name matches any keyword at all, reserved or not. Recommended practice is to use AS or double-quote output column names, to prevent any possible conflict against future keyword additions.

In FROM items, both the standard and PostgreSQL allow AS to be omitted before an alias that is an unreserved keyword. But this is impractical for output column names, because of syntactic ambiguities.

ONLY and Inheritance

The SQL standard requires parentheses around the table name when writing ONLY, for example SELECT * FROM ONLY (tab1), ONLY (tab2) WHERE .... PostgreSQL considers these parentheses to be optional.

PostgreSQL allows a trailing * to be written to explicitly specify the non-ONLY behavior of including child tables. The standard does not allow this.

(These points apply equally to all SQL commands supporting the ONLY option.)

Function Calls in FROM

PostgreSQL allows a function call to be written directly as a member of the FROM list. In the SQL standard it would be necessary to wrap such a function call in a sub-SELECT; that is, the syntax FROM *func*(...) *alias* is approximately equivalent to FROM LATERAL (SELECT *func*(...)) *alias*. Note that LATERAL is considered to be implicit; this is because the standard requires LATERAL semantics for an UNNEST() item in FROM. PostgreSQL treats UNNEST() the same as other set-returning functions.

Namespace Available to GROUP BY and ORDER BY

In the SQL-92 standard, an ORDER BY clause can only use output column names or numbers, while a GROUP BY clause can only use expressions based on input column names. PostgreSQL extends each of these clauses to allow the other choice as well (but it uses the standard's interpretation if there is ambiguity). PostgreSQL also allows both clauses to specify arbitrary expressions. Note that names appearing in an expression will always be taken as input-column names, not as output-column names.

SQL:1999 and later use a slightly different definition which is not entirely upward compatible with SQL-92. In most cases, however, PostgreSQL will interpret an ORDER BY or GROUP BY expression the same way SQL:1999 does.

Functional Dependencies

PostgreSQL recognizes functional dependency (allowing columns to be omitted from GROUP BY) only when a table's primary key is included in the GROUP BY list. The SQL standard specifies additional conditions that should be recognized.

WINDOW **Clause Restrictions**

The SQL standard provides additional options for the window *frame_clause*. PostgreSQL currently supports only the options listed above.

LIMIT **and** OFFSET

The clauses LIMIT and OFFSET are PostgreSQL-specific syntax, also used by MySQL. The SQL:2008 standard has introduced the clauses OFFSET ... FETCH {FIRST|NEXT} ... for the same functionality, as shown above in *LIMIT Clause*. This syntax is also used by IBM DB2. (Applications written for Oracle frequently use a workaround involving the automatically generated rownum column, which is not available in PostgreSQL, to implement the effects of these clauses.)

FOR NO KEY UPDATE, FOR UPDATE, FOR SHARE, FOR KEY SHARE

Although FOR UPDATE appears in the SQL standard, the standard allows it only as an option of DECLARE CURSOR. PostgreSQL allows it in any SELECT query as well as in sub-SELECTs, but this is an extension. The FOR NO KEY UPDATE, FOR SHARE and FOR KEY SHARE variants, as well as the NOWAIT option, do not appear in the standard.

Data-Modifying Statements in WITH

PostgreSQL allows INSERT, UPDATE, and DELETE to be used as WITH queries. This is not found in the SQL standard.

Nonstandard Clauses

DISTINCT ON (...) is an extension of the SQL standard.

ROWS FROM(...) is an extension of the SQL standard.

SELECT INTO

Name

SELECT INTO — define a new table from the results of a query

Synopsis

```
[ WITH [ RECURSIVE ] with_query [, ...] ]
SELECT [ ALL | DISTINCT [ ON ( expression [, ...] ) ] ]
    * | expression [ [ AS ] output_name ] [, ...]
    INTO [ TEMPORARY | TEMP | UNLOGGED ] [ TABLE ] new_table
    [ FROM from_item [, ...] ]
    [ WHERE condition ]
    [ GROUP BY expression [, ...] ]
    [ HAVING condition [, ...] ]
    [ WINDOW window_name AS ( window_definition ) [, ...] ]
    [ { UNION | INTERSECT | EXCEPT } [ ALL | DISTINCT ] select ]
    [ ORDER BY expression [ ASC | DESC | USING operator ] [ NULLS { FIRST | LAST
    [ LIMIT { count | ALL } ]
    [ OFFSET start [ ROW | ROWS ] ]
    [ FETCH { FIRST | NEXT } [ count ] { ROW | ROWS } ONLY ]
    [ FOR { UPDATE | SHARE } [ OF table_name [, ...] ] [ NOWAIT ] [...] ]
```

Description

SELECT INTO creates a new table and fills it with data computed by a query. The data is not returned to the client, as it is with a normal SELECT. The new table's columns have the names and data types associated with the output columns of the SELECT.

Parameters

TEMPORARY or TEMP

If specified, the table is created as a temporary table. Refer to CREATE TABLE for details.

UNLOGGED

If specified, the table is created as an unlogged table. Refer to CREATE TABLE for details.

new_table

The name (optionally schema-qualified) of the table to be created.

All other parameters are described in detail under SELECT.

Notes

CREATE TABLE AS is functionally similar to SELECT INTO. CREATE TABLE AS is the recommended syntax, since this form of SELECT INTO is not available in ECPG or PL/pgSQL, because they interpret the INTO clause differently. Furthermore, CREATE TABLE AS offers a superset of the functionality provided by SELECT INTO.

To add OIDs to the table created by SELECT INTO, enable the default_with_oids configuration variable. Alternatively, CREATE TABLE AS can be used with the WITH OIDS clause.

Examples

Create a new table films_recent consisting of only recent entries from the table films:

```
SELECT * INTO films_recent FROM films WHERE date_prod >= '2002-01-01';
```

Compatibility

The SQL standard uses SELECT INTO to represent selecting values into scalar variables of a host program, rather than creating a new table. This indeed is the usage found in ECPG (see Chapter 33) and PL/pgSQL (see Chapter 40). The PostgreSQL usage of SELECT INTO to represent table creation is historical. It is best to use CREATE TABLE AS for this purpose in new code.

See Also

CREATE TABLE AS

SET

Name

SET — change a run-time parameter

Synopsis

```
SET [ SESSION | LOCAL ] configuration_parameter { TO | = } { value | 'value' | DEF
SET [ SESSION | LOCAL ] TIME ZONE { timezone | LOCAL | DEFAULT }
```

Description

The SET command changes run-time configuration parameters. Many of the run-time parameters listed in Chapter 18 can be changed on-the-fly with SET. (But some require superuser privileges to change, and others cannot be changed after server or session start.) SET only affects the value used by the current session.

If SET (or equivalently SET SESSION) is issued within a transaction that is later aborted, the effects of the SET command disappear when the transaction is rolled back. Once the surrounding transaction is committed, the effects will persist until the end of the session, unless overridden by another SET.

The effects of SET LOCAL last only till the end of the current transaction, whether committed or not. A special case is SET followed by SET LOCAL within a single transaction: the SET LOCAL value will be seen until the end of the transaction, but afterwards (if the transaction is committed) the SET value will take effect.

The effects of SET or SET LOCAL are also canceled by rolling back to a savepoint that is earlier than the command.

If SET LOCAL is used within a function that has a SET option for the same variable (see CREATE FUNC-TION), the effects of the SET LOCAL command disappear at function exit; that is, the value in effect when the function was called is restored anyway. This allows SET LOCAL to be used for dynamic or repeated changes of a parameter within a function, while still having the convenience of using the SET option to save and restore the caller's value. However, a regular SET command overrides any surrounding function's SET option; its effects will persist unless rolled back.

> **Note:** In PostgreSQL versions 8.0 through 8.2, the effects of a SET LOCAL would be canceled by releasing an earlier savepoint, or by successful exit from a PL/pgSQL exception block. This behavior has been changed because it was deemed unintuitive.

Parameters

SESSION

Specifies that the command takes effect for the current session. (This is the default if neither SESSION nor LOCAL appears.)

LOCAL

Specifies that the command takes effect for only the current transaction. After COMMIT or ROLLBACK, the session-level setting takes effect again. Issuing this outside of a transaction block emits a warning and otherwise has no effect.

configuration_parameter

Name of a settable run-time parameter. Available parameters are documented in Chapter 18 and below.

value

New value of parameter. Values can be specified as string constants, identifiers, numbers, or comma-separated lists of these, as appropriate for the particular parameter. DEFAULT can be written to specify resetting the parameter to its default value (that is, whatever value it would have had if no SET had been executed in the current session).

Besides the configuration parameters documented in Chapter 18, there are a few that can only be adjusted using the SET command or that have a special syntax:

SCHEMA

SET SCHEMA 'value' is an alias for SET search_path TO value. Only one schema can be specified using this syntax.

NAMES

SET NAMES value is an alias for SET client_encoding TO value.

SEED

Sets the internal seed for the random number generator (the function random). Allowed values are floating-point numbers between -1 and 1, which are then multiplied by 2^{31}-1.

The seed can also be set by invoking the function setseed:

```
SELECT setseed(value);
```

TIME ZONE

SET TIME ZONE value is an alias for SET timezone TO value. The syntax SET TIME ZONE allows special syntax for the time zone specification. Here are examples of valid values:

'PST8PDT'

The time zone for Berkeley, California.

'Europe/Rome'

The time zone for Italy.

-7

The time zone 7 hours west from UTC (equivalent to PDT). Positive values are east from UTC.

```
INTERVAL '-08:00' HOUR TO MINUTE
```

> The time zone 8 hours west from UTC (equivalent to PST).

```
LOCAL
DEFAULT
```

> Set the time zone to your local time zone (that is, the server's default value of `timezone`).

Timezone settings given as numbers or intervals are internally translated to POSIX timezone syntax. For example, after `SET TIME ZONE -7`, `SHOW TIME ZONE` would report `<-07>+07`.

See Section 8.5.3 for more information about time zones.

Notes

The function `set_config` provides equivalent functionality; see Section 9.26. Also, it is possible to UPDATE the `pg_settings` system view to perform the equivalent of `SET`.

Examples

Set the schema search path:

```
SET search_path TO my_schema, public;
```

Set the style of date to traditional POSTGRES with "day before month" input convention:

```
SET datestyle TO postgres, dmy;
```

Set the time zone for Berkeley, California:

```
SET TIME ZONE 'PST8PDT';
```

Set the time zone for Italy:

```
SET TIME ZONE 'Europe/Rome';
```

Compatibility

SET TIME ZONE extends syntax defined in the SQL standard. The standard allows only numeric time zone offsets while PostgreSQL allows more flexible time-zone specifications. All other SET features are PostgreSQL extensions.

See Also

RESET, SHOW

SET CONSTRAINTS

Name

SET CONSTRAINTS — set constraint check timing for the current transaction

Synopsis

```
SET CONSTRAINTS { ALL | name [, ...] } { DEFERRED | IMMEDIATE }
```

Description

SET CONSTRAINTS sets the behavior of constraint checking within the current transaction. IMMEDIATE constraints are checked at the end of each statement. DEFERRED constraints are not checked until transaction commit. Each constraint has its own IMMEDIATE or DEFERRED mode.

Upon creation, a constraint is given one of three characteristics: DEFERRABLE INITIALLY DEFERRED, DEFERRABLE INITIALLY IMMEDIATE, or NOT DEFERRABLE. The third class is always IMMEDIATE and is not affected by the SET CONSTRAINTS command. The first two classes start every transaction in the indicated mode, but their behavior can be changed within a transaction by SET CONSTRAINTS.

SET CONSTRAINTS with a list of constraint names changes the mode of just those constraints (which must all be deferrable). Each constraint name can be schema-qualified. The current schema search path is used to find the first matching name if no schema name is specified. SET CONSTRAINTS ALL changes the mode of all deferrable constraints.

When SET CONSTRAINTS changes the mode of a constraint from DEFERRED to IMMEDIATE, the new mode takes effect retroactively: any outstanding data modifications that would have been checked at the end of the transaction are instead checked during the execution of the SET CONSTRAINTS command. If any such constraint is violated, the SET CONSTRAINTS fails (and does not change the constraint mode). Thus, SET CONSTRAINTS can be used to force checking of constraints to occur at a specific point in a transaction.

Currently, only UNIQUE, PRIMARY KEY, REFERENCES (foreign key), and EXCLUDE constraints are affected by this setting. NOT NULL and CHECK constraints are always checked immediately when a row is inserted or modified (*not* at the end of the statement). Uniqueness and exclusion constraints that have not been declared DEFERRABLE are also checked immediately.

The firing of triggers that are declared as "constraint triggers" is also controlled by this setting — they fire at the same time that the associated constraint should be checked.

Notes

Because PostgreSQL does not require constraint names to be unique within a schema (but only per-table), it is possible that there is more than one match for a specified constraint name. In this case SET CONSTRAINTS will act on all matches. For a non-schema-qualified name, once a match or matches have been found in some schema in the search path, schemas appearing later in the path are not searched.

This command only alters the behavior of constraints within the current transaction. Issuing this outside of a transaction block emits a warning and otherwise has no effect.

Compatibility

This command complies with the behavior defined in the SQL standard, except for the limitation that, in PostgreSQL, it does not apply to NOT NULL and CHECK constraints. Also, PostgreSQL checks non-deferrable uniqueness constraints immediately, not at end of statement as the standard would suggest.

SET ROLE

Name

SET ROLE — set the current user identifier of the current session

Synopsis

```
SET [ SESSION | LOCAL ] ROLE role_name
SET [ SESSION | LOCAL ] ROLE NONE
RESET ROLE
```

Description

This command sets the current user identifier of the current SQL session to be `role_name`. The role name can be written as either an identifier or a string literal. After SET ROLE, permissions checking for SQL commands is carried out as though the named role were the one that had logged in originally.

The specified `role_name` must be a role that the current session user is a member of. (If the session user is a superuser, any role can be selected.)

The SESSION and LOCAL modifiers act the same as for the regular SET command.

The NONE and RESET forms reset the current user identifier to be the current session user identifier. These forms can be executed by any user.

Notes

Using this command, it is possible to either add privileges or restrict one's privileges. If the session user role has the INHERITS attribute, then it automatically has all the privileges of every role that it could SET ROLE to; in this case SET ROLE effectively drops all the privileges assigned directly to the session user and to the other roles it is a member of, leaving only the privileges available to the named role. On the other hand, if the session user role has the NOINHERITS attribute, SET ROLE drops the privileges assigned directly to the session user and instead acquires the privileges available to the named role.

In particular, when a superuser chooses to SET ROLE to a non-superuser role, she loses her superuser privileges.

SET ROLE has effects comparable to SET SESSION AUTHORIZATION, but the privilege checks involved are quite different. Also, SET SESSION AUTHORIZATION determines which roles are allowable for later SET ROLE commands, whereas changing roles with SET ROLE does not change the set of roles allowed to a later SET ROLE.

SET ROLE does not process session variables as specified by the role's ALTER ROLE settings; this only happens during login.

SET ROLE cannot be used within a SECURITY DEFINER function.

Examples

```
SELECT SESSION_USER, CURRENT_USER;

 session_user | current_user
--------------+--------------
 peter        | peter

SET ROLE 'paul';

SELECT SESSION_USER, CURRENT_USER;

 session_user | current_user
--------------+--------------
 peter        | paul
```

Compatibility

PostgreSQL allows identifier syntax (`"rolename"`), while the SQL standard requires the role name to be written as a string literal. SQL does not allow this command during a transaction; PostgreSQL does not make this restriction because there is no reason to. The `SESSION` and `LOCAL` modifiers are a PostgreSQL extension, as is the `RESET` syntax.

See Also

SET SESSION AUTHORIZATION

SET SESSION AUTHORIZATION

Name

SET SESSION AUTHORIZATION — set the session user identifier and the current user identifier of the current session

Synopsis

```
SET [ SESSION | LOCAL ] SESSION AUTHORIZATION user_name
SET [ SESSION | LOCAL ] SESSION AUTHORIZATION DEFAULT
RESET SESSION AUTHORIZATION
```

Description

This command sets the session user identifier and the current user identifier of the current SQL session to be `user_name`. The user name can be written as either an identifier or a string literal. Using this command, it is possible, for example, to temporarily become an unprivileged user and later switch back to being a superuser.

The session user identifier is initially set to be the (possibly authenticated) user name provided by the client. The current user identifier is normally equal to the session user identifier, but might change temporarily in the context of `SECURITY DEFINER` functions and similar mechanisms; it can also be changed by SET ROLE. The current user identifier is relevant for permission checking.

The session user identifier can be changed only if the initial session user (the *authenticated user*) had the superuser privilege. Otherwise, the command is accepted only if it specifies the authenticated user name.

The `SESSION` and `LOCAL` modifiers act the same as for the regular SET command.

The `DEFAULT` and `RESET` forms reset the session and current user identifiers to be the originally authenticated user name. These forms can be executed by any user.

Notes

`SET SESSION AUTHORIZATION` cannot be used within a `SECURITY DEFINER` function.

Examples

```
SELECT SESSION_USER, CURRENT_USER;

 session_user | current_user
--------------+--------------
 peter        | peter

SET SESSION AUTHORIZATION 'paul';
```

```
SELECT SESSION_USER, CURRENT_USER;

 session_user | current_user
--------------+--------------
 paul         | paul
```

Compatibility

The SQL standard allows some other expressions to appear in place of the literal `user_name`, but these options are not important in practice. PostgreSQL allows identifier syntax (`"username"`), which SQL does not. SQL does not allow this command during a transaction; PostgreSQL does not make this restriction because there is no reason to. The `SESSION` and `LOCAL` modifiers are a PostgreSQL extension, as is the `RESET` syntax.

The privileges necessary to execute this command are left implementation-defined by the standard.

See Also

SET ROLE

SET TRANSACTION

Name

SET TRANSACTION — set the characteristics of the current transaction

Synopsis

```
SET TRANSACTION transaction_mode [, ...]
SET TRANSACTION SNAPSHOT snapshot_id
SET SESSION CHARACTERISTICS AS TRANSACTION transaction_mode [, ...]

where transaction_mode is one of:

    ISOLATION LEVEL { SERIALIZABLE | REPEATABLE READ | READ COMMITTED | READ UN
    READ WRITE | READ ONLY
    [ NOT ] DEFERRABLE
```

Description

The SET TRANSACTION command sets the characteristics of the current transaction. It has no effect on any subsequent transactions. SET SESSION CHARACTERISTICS sets the default transaction characteristics for subsequent transactions of a session. These defaults can be overridden by SET TRANSACTION for an individual transaction.

The available transaction characteristics are the transaction isolation level, the transaction access mode (read/write or read-only), and the deferrable mode. In addition, a snapshot can be selected, though only for the current transaction, not as a session default.

The isolation level of a transaction determines what data the transaction can see when other transactions are running concurrently:

READ COMMITTED

A statement can only see rows committed before it began. This is the default.

REPEATABLE READ

All statements of the current transaction can only see rows committed before the first query or data-modification statement was executed in this transaction.

SERIALIZABLE

All statements of the current transaction can only see rows committed before the first query or data-modification statement was executed in this transaction. If a pattern of reads and writes among concurrent serializable transactions would create a situation which could not have occurred for any serial (one-at-a-time) execution of those transactions, one of them will be rolled back with a serialization_failure error.

The SQL standard defines one additional level, READ UNCOMMITTED. In PostgreSQL READ UNCOMMITTED is treated as READ COMMITTED.

The transaction isolation level cannot be changed after the first query or data-modification statement (SELECT, INSERT, DELETE, UPDATE, FETCH, or COPY) of a transaction has been executed. See Chapter 13 for more information about transaction isolation and concurrency control.

The transaction access mode determines whether the transaction is read/write or read-only. Read/write is the default. When a transaction is read-only, the following SQL commands are disallowed: INSERT, UPDATE, DELETE, and COPY FROM if the table they would write to is not a temporary table; all CREATE, ALTER, and DROP commands; COMMENT, GRANT, REVOKE, TRUNCATE; and EXPLAIN ANALYZE and EXECUTE if the command they would execute is among those listed. This is a high-level notion of read-only that does not prevent all writes to disk.

The DEFERRABLE transaction property has no effect unless the transaction is also SERIALIZABLE and READ ONLY. When all three of these properties are selected for a transaction, the transaction may block when first acquiring its snapshot, after which it is able to run without the normal overhead of a SERIALIZABLE transaction and without any risk of contributing to or being canceled by a serialization failure. This mode is well suited for long-running reports or backups.

The SET TRANSACTION SNAPSHOT command allows a new transaction to run with the same *snapshot* as an existing transaction. The pre-existing transaction must have exported its snapshot with the pg_export_snapshot function (see Section 9.26.5). That function returns a snapshot identifier, which must be given to SET TRANSACTION SNAPSHOT to specify which snapshot is to be imported. The identifier must be written as a string literal in this command, for example '000003A1-1'. SET TRANSACTION SNAPSHOT can only be executed at the start of a transaction, before the first query or data-modification statement (SELECT, INSERT, DELETE, UPDATE, FETCH, or COPY) of the transaction. Furthermore, the transaction must already be set to SERIALIZABLE or REPEATABLE READ isolation level (otherwise, the snapshot would be discarded immediately, since READ COMMITTED mode takes a new snapshot for each command). If the importing transaction uses SERIALIZABLE isolation level, then the transaction that exported the snapshot must also use that isolation level. Also, a non-read-only serializable transaction cannot import a snapshot from a read-only transaction.

Notes

If SET TRANSACTION is executed without a prior START TRANSACTION or BEGIN, it emits a warning and otherwise has no effect.

It is possible to dispense with SET TRANSACTION by instead specifying the desired *transaction_modes* in BEGIN or START TRANSACTION. But that option is not available for SET TRANSACTION SNAPSHOT.

The session default transaction modes can also be set by setting the configuration parameters default_transaction_isolation, default_transaction_read_only, and default_transaction_deferrable. (In fact SET SESSION CHARACTERISTICS is just a verbose equivalent for setting these variables with SET.) This means the defaults can be set in the configuration file, via ALTER DATABASE, etc. Consult Chapter 18 for more information.

Examples

To begin a new transaction with the same snapshot as an already existing transaction, first export the snapshot from the existing transaction. That will return the snapshot identifier, for example:

```
BEGIN TRANSACTION ISOLATION LEVEL REPEATABLE READ;
SELECT pg_export_snapshot();
 pg_export_snapshot
--------------------
 000003A1-1
(1 row)
```

Then give the snapshot identifier in a SET TRANSACTION SNAPSHOT command at the beginning of the newly opened transaction:

```
BEGIN TRANSACTION ISOLATION LEVEL REPEATABLE READ;
SET TRANSACTION SNAPSHOT '000003A1-1';
```

Compatibility

These commands are defined in the SQL standard, except for the DEFERRABLE transaction mode and the SET TRANSACTION SNAPSHOT form, which are PostgreSQL extensions.

SERIALIZABLE is the default transaction isolation level in the standard. In PostgreSQL the default is ordinarily READ COMMITTED, but you can change it as mentioned above.

In the SQL standard, there is one other transaction characteristic that can be set with these commands: the size of the diagnostics area. This concept is specific to embedded SQL, and therefore is not implemented in the PostgreSQL server.

The SQL standard requires commas between successive *transaction_modes*, but for historical reasons PostgreSQL allows the commas to be omitted.

SHOW

Name

SHOW — show the value of a run-time parameter

Synopsis

```
SHOW name
SHOW ALL
```

Description

SHOW will display the current setting of run-time parameters. These variables can be set using the SET statement, by editing the postgresql.conf configuration file, through the PGOPTIONS environmental variable (when using libpq or a libpq-based application), or through command-line flags when starting the postgres server. See Chapter 18 for details.

Parameters

name

> The name of a run-time parameter. Available parameters are documented in Chapter 18 and on the SET reference page. In addition, there are a few parameters that can be shown but not set:
>
> SERVER_VERSION
>
>> Shows the server's version number.
>
> SERVER_ENCODING
>
>> Shows the server-side character set encoding. At present, this parameter can be shown but not set, because the encoding is determined at database creation time.
>
> LC_COLLATE
>
>> Shows the database's locale setting for collation (text ordering). At present, this parameter can be shown but not set, because the setting is determined at database creation time.
>
> LC_CTYPE
>
>> Shows the database's locale setting for character classification. At present, this parameter can be shown but not set, because the setting is determined at database creation time.
>
> IS_SUPERUSER
>
>> True if the current role has superuser privileges.

```
ALL
```

Show the values of all configuration parameters, with descriptions.

Notes

The function `current_setting` produces equivalent output; see Section 9.26. Also, the `pg_settings` system view produces the same information.

Examples

Show the current setting of the parameter `DateStyle`:

```
SHOW DateStyle;
 DateStyle
-----------
 ISO, MDY
(1 row)
```

Show the current setting of the parameter `geqo`:

```
SHOW geqo;
 geqo
------
 on
(1 row)
```

Show all settings:

```
SHOW ALL;
           name          | setting |                 description
-------------------------+---------+---------------------------------------------
 allow_system_table_mods | off     | Allows modifications of the structure of .
   .
   .
   .
 xmloption               | content | Sets whether XML data in implicit parsing
 zero_damaged_pages      | off     | Continues processing past damaged page hea
(196 rows)
```

Compatibility

The `SHOW` command is a PostgreSQL extension.

See Also

SET, RESET

START TRANSACTION

Name

START TRANSACTION — start a transaction block

Synopsis

```
START TRANSACTION [ transaction_mode [, ...] ]

where transaction_mode is one of:

    ISOLATION LEVEL { SERIALIZABLE | REPEATABLE READ | READ COMMITTED | READ UN
    READ WRITE | READ ONLY
    [ NOT ] DEFERRABLE
```

Description

This command begins a new transaction block. If the isolation level, read/write mode, or deferrable mode is specified, the new transaction has those characteristics, as if SET TRANSACTION was executed. This is the same as the BEGIN command.

Parameters

Refer to SET TRANSACTION for information on the meaning of the parameters to this statement.

Compatibility

In the standard, it is not necessary to issue START TRANSACTION to start a transaction block: any SQL command implicitly begins a block. PostgreSQL's behavior can be seen as implicitly issuing a COMMIT after each command that does not follow START TRANSACTION (or BEGIN), and it is therefore often called "autocommit". Other relational database systems might offer an autocommit feature as a convenience.

The DEFERRABLE transaction_mode is a PostgreSQL language extension.

The SQL standard requires commas between successive transaction_modes, but for historical reasons PostgreSQL allows the commas to be omitted.

See also the compatibility section of SET TRANSACTION.

See Also

BEGIN, COMMIT, ROLLBACK, SAVEPOINT, SET TRANSACTION

TRUNCATE

Name

TRUNCATE — empty a table or set of tables

Synopsis

```
TRUNCATE [ TABLE ] [ ONLY ] name [ * ] [, ... ]
    [ RESTART IDENTITY | CONTINUE IDENTITY ] [ CASCADE | RESTRICT ]
```

Description

TRUNCATE quickly removes all rows from a set of tables. It has the same effect as an unqualified DELETE on each table, but since it does not actually scan the tables it is faster. Furthermore, it reclaims disk space immediately, rather than requiring a subsequent VACUUM operation. This is most useful on large tables.

Parameters

name

> The name (optionally schema-qualified) of a table to truncate. If ONLY is specified before the table name, only that table is truncated. If ONLY is not specified, the table and all its descendant tables (if any) are truncated. Optionally, * can be specified after the table name to explicitly indicate that descendant tables are included.

RESTART IDENTITY

> Automatically restart sequences owned by columns of the truncated table(s).

CONTINUE IDENTITY

> Do not change the values of sequences. This is the default.

CASCADE

> Automatically truncate all tables that have foreign-key references to any of the named tables, or to any tables added to the group due to CASCADE.

RESTRICT

> Refuse to truncate if any of the tables have foreign-key references from tables that are not listed in the command. This is the default.

Notes

You must have the TRUNCATE privilege on a table to truncate it.

TRUNCATE acquires an ACCESS EXCLUSIVE lock on each table it operates on, which blocks all other concurrent operations on the table. When RESTART IDENTITY is specified, any sequences that are to be restarted are likewise locked exclusively. If concurrent access to a table is required, then the DELETE command should be used instead.

TRUNCATE cannot be used on a table that has foreign-key references from other tables, unless all such tables are also truncated in the same command. Checking validity in such cases would require table scans, and the whole point is not to do one. The CASCADE option can be used to automatically include all dependent tables — but be very careful when using this option, or else you might lose data you did not intend to!

TRUNCATE will not fire any ON DELETE triggers that might exist for the tables. But it will fire ON TRUNCATE triggers. If ON TRUNCATE triggers are defined for any of the tables, then all BEFORE TRUNCATE triggers are fired before any truncation happens, and all AFTER TRUNCATE triggers are fired after the last truncation is performed and any sequences are reset. The triggers will fire in the order that the tables are to be processed (first those listed in the command, and then any that were added due to cascading).

Warning

TRUNCATE is not MVCC-safe (see Chapter 13 for general information about MVCC). After truncation, the table will appear empty to all concurrent transactions, even if they are using a snapshot taken before the truncation occurred. This will only be an issue for a transaction that did not access the truncated table before the truncation happened — any transaction that has done so would hold at least an ACCESS SHARE lock, which would block TRUNCATE until that transaction completes. So truncation will not cause any apparent inconsistency in the table contents for successive queries on the same table, but it could cause visible inconsistency between the contents of the truncated table and other tables in the database.

TRUNCATE is transaction-safe with respect to the data in the tables: the truncation will be safely rolled back if the surrounding transaction does not commit.

When RESTART IDENTITY is specified, the implied ALTER SEQUENCE RESTART operations are also done transactionally; that is, they will be rolled back if the surrounding transaction does not commit. This is unlike the normal behavior of ALTER SEQUENCE RESTART. Be aware that if any additional sequence operations are done on the restarted sequences before the transaction rolls back, the effects of these operations on the sequences will be rolled back, but not their effects on currval(); that is, after the transaction currval() will continue to reflect the last sequence value obtained inside the failed transaction, even though the sequence itself may no longer be consistent with that. This is similar to the usual behavior of currval() after a failed transaction.

Examples

Truncate the tables bigtable and fattable:

```
TRUNCATE bigtable, fattable;
```

The same, and also reset any associated sequence generators:

```
TRUNCATE bigtable, fattable RESTART IDENTITY;
```

Truncate the table `othertable`, and cascade to any tables that reference `othertable` via foreign-key constraints:

```
TRUNCATE othertable CASCADE;
```

Compatibility

The SQL:2008 standard includes a TRUNCATE command with the syntax TRUNCATE TABLE *tablename*. The clauses CONTINUE IDENTITY/RESTART IDENTITY also appear in that standard, but have slightly different though related meanings. Some of the concurrency behavior of this command is left implementation-defined by the standard, so the above notes should be considered and compared with other implementations if necessary.

UNLISTEN

Name

UNLISTEN — stop listening for a notification

Synopsis

```
UNLISTEN { channel | * }
```

Description

UNLISTEN is used to remove an existing registration for NOTIFY events. UNLISTEN cancels any existing registration of the current PostgreSQL session as a listener on the notification channel named channel. The special wildcard * cancels all listener registrations for the current session.

NOTIFY contains a more extensive discussion of the use of LISTEN and NOTIFY.

Parameters

channel

 Name of a notification channel (any identifier).

*

 All current listen registrations for this session are cleared.

Notes

You can unlisten something you were not listening for; no warning or error will appear.

At the end of each session, UNLISTEN * is automatically executed.

A transaction that has executed UNLISTEN cannot be prepared for two-phase commit.

Examples

To make a registration:

```
LISTEN virtual;
NOTIFY virtual;
Asynchronous notification "virtual" received from server process with PID 8448.
```

Once UNLISTEN has been executed, further NOTIFY messages will be ignored:

```
UNLISTEN virtual;
NOTIFY virtual;
-- no NOTIFY event is received
```

Compatibility

There is no UNLISTEN command in the SQL standard.

See Also

LISTEN, NOTIFY

UPDATE

Name

UPDATE — update rows of a table

Synopsis

```
[ WITH [ RECURSIVE ] with_query [, ...] ]
UPDATE [ ONLY ] table_name [ * ] [ [ AS ] alias ]
    SET { column_name = { expression | DEFAULT } |
          ( column_name [, ...] ) = ( { expression | DEFAULT } [, ...] ) } [, ...
    [ FROM from_list ]
    [ WHERE condition | WHERE CURRENT OF cursor_name ]
    [ RETURNING * | output_expression [ [ AS ] output_name ] [, ...] ]
```

Description

UPDATE changes the values of the specified columns in all rows that satisfy the condition. Only the columns to be modified need be mentioned in the SET clause; columns not explicitly modified retain their previous values.

There are two ways to modify a table using information contained in other tables in the database: using sub-selects, or specifying additional tables in the FROM clause. Which technique is more appropriate depends on the specific circumstances.

The optional RETURNING clause causes UPDATE to compute and return value(s) based on each row actually updated. Any expression using the table's columns, and/or columns of other tables mentioned in FROM, can be computed. The new (post-update) values of the table's columns are used. The syntax of the RETURNING list is identical to that of the output list of SELECT.

You must have the UPDATE privilege on the table, or at least on the column(s) that are listed to be updated. You must also have the SELECT privilege on any column whose values are read in the *expressions* or *condition*.

Parameters

with_query

The WITH clause allows you to specify one or more subqueries that can be referenced by name in the UPDATE query. See Section 7.8 and SELECT for details.

table_name

The name (optionally schema-qualified) of the table to update. If ONLY is specified before the table name, matching rows are updated in the named table only. If ONLY is not specified, matching rows are also updated in any tables inheriting from the named table. Optionally, * can be specified after the table name to explicitly indicate that descendant tables are included.

alias

> A substitute name for the target table. When an alias is provided, it completely hides the actual name of the table. For example, given UPDATE foo AS f, the remainder of the UPDATE statement must refer to this table as f not foo.

column_name

> The name of a column in the table named by *table_name*. The column name can be qualified with a subfield name or array subscript, if needed. Do not include the table's name in the specification of a target column — for example, UPDATE tab SET tab.col = 1 is invalid.

expression

> An expression to assign to the column. The expression can use the old values of this and other columns in the table.

DEFAULT

> Set the column to its default value (which will be NULL if no specific default expression has been assigned to it).

from_list

> A list of table expressions, allowing columns from other tables to appear in the WHERE condition and the update expressions. This is similar to the list of tables that can be specified in the *FROM Clause* of a SELECT statement. Note that the target table must not appear in the *from_list*, unless you intend a self-join (in which case it must appear with an alias in the *from_list*).

condition

> An expression that returns a value of type boolean. Only rows for which this expression returns true will be updated.

cursor_name

> The name of the cursor to use in a WHERE CURRENT OF condition. The row to be updated is the one most recently fetched from this cursor. The cursor must be a non-grouping query on the UPDATE's target table. Note that WHERE CURRENT OF cannot be specified together with a Boolean condition. See DECLARE for more information about using cursors with WHERE CURRENT OF.

output_expression

> An expression to be computed and returned by the UPDATE command after each row is updated. The expression can use any column names of the table named by *table_name* or table(s) listed in FROM. Write * to return all columns.

output_name

> A name to use for a returned column.

Outputs

On successful completion, an UPDATE command returns a command tag of the form

UPDATE *count*

The `count` is the number of rows updated, including matched rows whose values did not change. Note that the number may be less than the number of rows that matched the `condition` when updates were suppressed by a `BEFORE UPDATE` trigger. If `count` is 0, no rows were updated by the query (this is not considered an error).

If the `UPDATE` command contains a `RETURNING` clause, the result will be similar to that of a `SELECT` statement containing the columns and values defined in the `RETURNING` list, computed over the row(s) updated by the command.

Notes

When a `FROM` clause is present, what essentially happens is that the target table is joined to the tables mentioned in the `from_list`, and each output row of the join represents an update operation for the target table. When using `FROM` you should ensure that the join produces at most one output row for each row to be modified. In other words, a target row shouldn't join to more than one row from the other table(s). If it does, then only one of the join rows will be used to update the target row, but which one will be used is not readily predictable.

Because of this indeterminacy, referencing other tables only within sub-selects is safer, though often harder to read and slower than using a join.

Examples

Change the word `Drama` to `Dramatic` in the column `kind` of the table `films`:

```
UPDATE films SET kind = 'Dramatic' WHERE kind = 'Drama';
```

Adjust temperature entries and reset precipitation to its default value in one row of the table `weather`:

```
UPDATE weather SET temp_lo = temp_lo+1, temp_hi = temp_lo+15, prcp = DEFAULT
  WHERE city = 'San Francisco' AND date = '2003-07-03';
```

Perform the same operation and return the updated entries:

```
UPDATE weather SET temp_lo = temp_lo+1, temp_hi = temp_lo+15, prcp = DEFAULT
  WHERE city = 'San Francisco' AND date = '2003-07-03'
  RETURNING temp_lo, temp_hi, prcp;
```

Use the alternative column-list syntax to do the same update:

```
UPDATE weather SET (temp_lo, temp_hi, prcp) = (temp_lo+1, temp_lo+15, DEFAULT)
  WHERE city = 'San Francisco' AND date = '2003-07-03';
```

Increment the sales count of the salesperson who manages the account for Acme Corporation, using the FROM clause syntax:

```
UPDATE employees SET sales_count = sales_count + 1 FROM accounts
  WHERE accounts.name = 'Acme Corporation'
  AND employees.id = accounts.sales_person;
```

Perform the same operation, using a sub-select in the WHERE clause:

```
UPDATE employees SET sales_count = sales_count + 1 WHERE id =
  (SELECT sales_person FROM accounts WHERE name = 'Acme Corporation');
```

Attempt to insert a new stock item along with the quantity of stock. If the item already exists, instead update the stock count of the existing item. To do this without failing the entire transaction, use savepoints:

```
BEGIN;
-- other operations
SAVEPOINT sp1;
INSERT INTO wines VALUES('Chateau Lafite 2003', '24');
-- Assume the above fails because of a unique key violation,
-- so now we issue these commands:
ROLLBACK TO sp1;
UPDATE wines SET stock = stock + 24 WHERE winename = 'Chateau Lafite 2003';
-- continue with other operations, and eventually
COMMIT;
```

Change the kind column of the table films in the row on which the cursor c_films is currently positioned:

```
UPDATE films SET kind = 'Dramatic' WHERE CURRENT OF c_films;
```

Compatibility

This command conforms to the SQL standard, except that the FROM and RETURNING clauses are PostgreSQL extensions, as is the ability to use WITH with UPDATE.

According to the standard, the column-list syntax should allow a list of columns to be assigned from a single row-valued expression, such as a sub-select:

```
UPDATE accounts SET (contact_last_name, contact_first_name) =
    (SELECT last_name, first_name FROM salesmen
     WHERE salesmen.id = accounts.sales_id);
```

This is not currently implemented — the source must be a list of independent expressions.

Some other database systems offer a FROM option in which the target table is supposed to be listed again within FROM. That is not how PostgreSQL interprets FROM. Be careful when porting applications that use this extension.

VACUUM

Name

VACUUM — garbage-collect and optionally analyze a database

Synopsis

```
VACUUM [ ( { FULL | FREEZE | VERBOSE | ANALYZE } [, ...] ) ] [ table_name [ (col
VACUUM [ FULL ] [ FREEZE ] [ VERBOSE ] [ table_name ]
VACUUM [ FULL ] [ FREEZE ] [ VERBOSE ] ANALYZE [ table_name [ (column_name [, ...
```

Description

VACUUM reclaims storage occupied by dead tuples. In normal PostgreSQL operation, tuples that are deleted or obsoleted by an update are not physically removed from their table; they remain present until a VACUUM is done. Therefore it's necessary to do VACUUM periodically, especially on frequently-updated tables.

With no parameter, VACUUM processes every table in the current database that the current user has permission to vacuum. With a parameter, VACUUM processes only that table.

VACUUM ANALYZE performs a VACUUM and then an ANALYZE for each selected table. This is a handy combination form for routine maintenance scripts. See ANALYZE for more details about its processing.

Plain VACUUM (without FULL) simply reclaims space and makes it available for re-use. This form of the command can operate in parallel with normal reading and writing of the table, as an exclusive lock is not obtained. However, extra space is not returned to the operating system (in most cases); it's just kept available for re-use within the same table. VACUUM FULL rewrites the entire contents of the table into a new disk file with no extra space, allowing unused space to be returned to the operating system. This form is much slower and requires an exclusive lock on each table while it is being processed.

When the option list is surrounded by parentheses, the options can be written in any order. Without parentheses, options must be specified in exactly the order shown above. The parenthesized syntax was added in PostgreSQL 9.0; the unparenthesized syntax is deprecated.

Parameters

FULL

Selects "full" vacuum, which can reclaim more space, but takes much longer and exclusively locks the table. This method also requires extra disk space, since it writes a new copy of the table and doesn't release the old copy until the operation is complete. Usually this should only be used when a significant amount of space needs to be reclaimed from within the table.

FREEZE

Selects aggressive "freezing" of tuples. Specifying FREEZE is equivalent to performing VACUUM with the vacuum_freeze_min_age and vacuum_freeze_table_age parameters set to zero. Aggressive freezing is always performed when the table is rewritten, so this option is redundant when FULL is specified.

VERBOSE

> Prints a detailed vacuum activity report for each table.

ANALYZE

> Updates statistics used by the planner to determine the most efficient way to execute a query.

table_name

> The name (optionally schema-qualified) of a specific table to vacuum. Defaults to all tables in the current database.

column_name

> The name of a specific column to analyze. Defaults to all columns. If a column list is specified, ANALYZE is implied.

Outputs

When VERBOSE is specified, VACUUM emits progress messages to indicate which table is currently being processed. Various statistics about the tables are printed as well.

Notes

To vacuum a table, one must ordinarily be the table's owner or a superuser. However, database owners are allowed to vacuum all tables in their databases, except shared catalogs. (The restriction for shared catalogs means that a true database-wide VACUUM can only be performed by a superuser.) VACUUM will skip over any tables that the calling user does not have permission to vacuum.

VACUUM cannot be executed inside a transaction block.

For tables with GIN indexes, VACUUM (in any form) also completes any pending index insertions, by moving pending index entries to the appropriate places in the main GIN index structure. See Section 58.4.1 for details.

We recommend that active production databases be vacuumed frequently (at least nightly), in order to remove dead rows. After adding or deleting a large number of rows, it might be a good idea to issue a VACUUM ANALYZE command for the affected table. This will update the system catalogs with the results of all recent changes, and allow the PostgreSQL query planner to make better choices in planning queries.

The FULL option is not recommended for routine use, but might be useful in special cases. An example is when you have deleted or updated most of the rows in a table and would like the table to physically shrink to occupy less disk space and allow faster table scans. VACUUM FULL will usually shrink the table more than a plain VACUUM would.

VACUUM causes a substantial increase in I/O traffic, which might cause poor performance for other active sessions. Therefore, it is sometimes advisable to use the cost-based vacuum delay feature. See Section 18.4.4 for details.

PostgreSQL includes an "autovacuum" facility which can automate routine vacuum maintenance. For more information about automatic and manual vacuuming, see Section 23.1.

Examples

The following is an example from running VACUUM on a table in the regression database:

```
regression=# VACUUM (VERBOSE, ANALYZE) onek;
INFO:  vacuuming "public.onek"
INFO:  index "onek_unique1" now contains 1000 tuples in 14 pages
DETAIL:  3000 index tuples were removed.
0 index pages have been deleted, 0 are currently reusable.
CPU 0.01s/0.08u sec elapsed 0.18 sec.
INFO:  index "onek_unique2" now contains 1000 tuples in 16 pages
DETAIL:  3000 index tuples were removed.
0 index pages have been deleted, 0 are currently reusable.
CPU 0.00s/0.07u sec elapsed 0.23 sec.
INFO:  index "onek_hundred" now contains 1000 tuples in 13 pages
DETAIL:  3000 index tuples were removed.
0 index pages have been deleted, 0 are currently reusable.
CPU 0.01s/0.08u sec elapsed 0.17 sec.
INFO:  index "onek_stringu1" now contains 1000 tuples in 48 pages
DETAIL:  3000 index tuples were removed.
0 index pages have been deleted, 0 are currently reusable.
CPU 0.01s/0.09u sec elapsed 0.59 sec.
INFO:  "onek": removed 3000 tuples in 108 pages
DETAIL:  CPU 0.01s/0.06u sec elapsed 0.07 sec.
INFO:  "onek": found 3000 removable, 1000 nonremovable tuples in 143 pages
DETAIL:  0 dead tuples cannot be removed yet.
There were 0 unused item pointers.
0 pages are entirely empty.
CPU 0.07s/0.39u sec elapsed 1.56 sec.
INFO:  analyzing "public.onek"
INFO:  "onek": 36 pages, 1000 rows sampled, 1000 estimated total rows
VACUUM
```

Compatibility

There is no VACUUM statement in the SQL standard.

See Also

vacuumdb, Section 18.4.4, Section 23.1.6

VALUES

Name

VALUES — compute a set of rows

Synopsis

```
VALUES ( expression [, ...] ) [, ...]
    [ ORDER BY sort_expression [ ASC | DESC | USING operator ] [, ...] ]
    [ LIMIT { count | ALL } ]
    [ OFFSET start [ ROW | ROWS ] ]
    [ FETCH { FIRST | NEXT } [ count ] { ROW | ROWS } ONLY ]
```

Description

VALUES computes a row value or set of row values specified by value expressions. It is most commonly used to generate a "constant table" within a larger command, but it can be used on its own.

When more than one row is specified, all the rows must have the same number of elements. The data types of the resulting table's columns are determined by combining the explicit or inferred types of the expressions appearing in that column, using the same rules as for UNION (see Section 10.5).

Within larger commands, VALUES is syntactically allowed anywhere that SELECT is. Because it is treated like a SELECT by the grammar, it is possible to use the ORDER BY, LIMIT (or equivalently FETCH FIRST), and OFFSET clauses with a VALUES command.

Parameters

expression

A constant or expression to compute and insert at the indicated place in the resulting table (set of rows). In a VALUES list appearing at the top level of an INSERT, an *expression* can be replaced by DEFAULT to indicate that the destination column's default value should be inserted. DEFAULT cannot be used when VALUES appears in other contexts.

sort_expression

An expression or integer constant indicating how to sort the result rows. This expression can refer to the columns of the VALUES result as column1, column2, etc. For more details see *ORDER BY Clause*.

operator

A sorting operator. For details see *ORDER BY Clause*.

count

The maximum number of rows to return. For details see *LIMIT Clause*.

start

The number of rows to skip before starting to return rows. For details see *LIMIT Clause*.

Notes

VALUES lists with very large numbers of rows should be avoided, as you might encounter out-of-memory failures or poor performance. VALUES appearing within INSERT is a special case (because the desired column types are known from the INSERT's target table, and need not be inferred by scanning the VALUES list), so it can handle larger lists than are practical in other contexts.

Examples

A bare VALUES command:

```
VALUES (1, 'one'), (2, 'two'), (3, 'three');
```

This will return a table of two columns and three rows. It's effectively equivalent to:

```
SELECT 1 AS column1, 'one' AS column2
UNION ALL
SELECT 2, 'two'
UNION ALL
SELECT 3, 'three';
```

More usually, VALUES is used within a larger SQL command. The most common use is in INSERT:

```
INSERT INTO films (code, title, did, date_prod, kind)
    VALUES ('T_601', 'Yojimbo', 106, '1961-06-16', 'Drama');
```

In the context of INSERT, entries of a VALUES list can be DEFAULT to indicate that the column default should be used here instead of specifying a value:

```
INSERT INTO films VALUES
    ('UA502', 'Bananas', 105, DEFAULT, 'Comedy', '82 minutes'),
    ('T_601', 'Yojimbo', 106, DEFAULT, 'Drama', DEFAULT);
```

VALUES can also be used where a sub-SELECT might be written, for example in a FROM clause:

```
SELECT f.*
  FROM films f, (VALUES('MGM', 'Horror'), ('UA', 'Sci-Fi')) AS t (studio, kind)
  WHERE f.studio = t.studio AND f.kind = t.kind;

UPDATE employees SET salary = salary * v.increase
  FROM (VALUES(1, 200000, 1.2), (2, 400000, 1.4)) AS v (depno, target, increase
  WHERE employees.depno = v.depno AND employees.sales >= v.target;
```

Note that an AS clause is required when VALUES is used in a FROM clause, just as is true for SELECT. It is not required that the AS clause specify names for all the columns, but it's good practice to do so. (The default column names for VALUES are column1, column2, etc in PostgreSQL, but these names might be different in other database systems.)

When VALUES is used in INSERT, the values are all automatically coerced to the data type of the corresponding destination column. When it's used in other contexts, it might be necessary to specify the correct data type. If the entries are all quoted literal constants, coercing the first is sufficient to determine the assumed type for all:

```
SELECT * FROM machines
WHERE ip_address IN (VALUES('192.168.0.1'::inet), ('192.168.0.10'), ('192.168.1
```

> **Tip:** For simple IN tests, it's better to rely on the list-of-scalars form of IN than to write a VALUES query as shown above. The list of scalars method requires less writing and is often more efficient.

Compatibility

VALUES conforms to the SQL standard. LIMIT and OFFSET are PostgreSQL extensions; see also under SELECT.

See Also

INSERT, SELECT

II. PostgreSQL Client Applications

This part contains reference information for PostgreSQL client applications and utilities. Not all of these commands are of general utility; some might require special privileges. The common feature of these applications is that they can be run on any host, independent of where the database server resides.

When specified on the command line, user and database names have their case preserved — the presence of spaces or special characters might require quoting. Table names and other identifiers do not have their case preserved, except where documented, and might require quoting.

clusterdb

Name

clusterdb — cluster a PostgreSQL database

Synopsis

clusterdb [*connection-option*...] [--verbose | -v] [--table | -t *table*] ... [*dbname*]

clusterdb [*connection-option*...] [--verbose | -v] --all | -a

Description

clusterdb is a utility for reclustering tables in a PostgreSQL database. It finds tables that have previously been clustered, and clusters them again on the same index that was last used. Tables that have never been clustered are not affected.

clusterdb is a wrapper around the SQL command CLUSTER. There is no effective difference between clustering databases via this utility and via other methods for accessing the server.

Options

clusterdb accepts the following command-line arguments:

-a
--all

    Cluster all databases.

[-d] *dbname*
[--dbname=] *dbname*

    Specifies the name of the database to be clustered. If this is not specified and -a (or --all) is not used, the database name is read from the environment variable PGDATABASE. If that is not set, the user name specified for the connection is used.

-e
--echo

    Echo the commands that clusterdb generates and sends to the server.

```
-q
--quiet
```

> Do not display progress messages.

```
-t table
--table=table
```

> Cluster `table` only. Multiple tables can be clustered by writing multiple -t switches.

```
-v
--verbose
```

> Print detailed information during processing.

```
-V
--version
```

> Print the clusterdb version and exit.

```
-?
--help
```

> Show help about clusterdb command line arguments, and exit.

clusterdb also accepts the following command-line arguments for connection parameters:

```
-h host
--host=host
```

> Specifies the host name of the machine on which the server is running. If the value begins with a slash, it is used as the directory for the Unix domain socket.

```
-p port
--port=port
```

> Specifies the TCP port or local Unix domain socket file extension on which the server is listening for connections.

```
-U username
--username=username
```

> User name to connect as.

```
-w
--no-password
```

> Never issue a password prompt. If the server requires password authentication and a password is not available by other means such as a `.pgpass` file, the connection attempt will fail. This option can be useful in batch jobs and scripts where no user is present to enter a password.

```
-W
--password
```

> Force clusterdb to prompt for a password before connecting to a database.
>
> This option is never essential, since clusterdb will automatically prompt for a password if the server demands password authentication. However, clusterdb will waste a connection attempt finding out

that the server wants a password. In some cases it is worth typing -W to avoid the extra connection attempt.

--maintenance-db=*dbname*

> Specifies the name of the database to connect to discover what other databases should be clustered. If not specified, the postgres database will be used, and if that does not exist, template1 will be used.

Environment

PGDATABASE
PGHOST
PGPORT
PGUSER

> Default connection parameters

This utility, like most other PostgreSQL utilities, also uses the environment variables supported by libpq (see Section 31.14).

Diagnostics

In case of difficulty, see CLUSTER and psql for discussions of potential problems and error messages. The database server must be running at the targeted host. Also, any default connection settings and environment variables used by the libpq front-end library will apply.

Examples

To cluster the database test:

```
$ clusterdb test
```

To cluster a single table foo in a database named xyzzy:

```
$ clusterdb --table foo xyzzy
```

See Also

CLUSTER

createdb

Name

createdb — create a new PostgreSQL database

Synopsis

createdb [*connection-option*...] [*option*...] [*dbname* [*description*]]

Description

createdb creates a new PostgreSQL database.

Normally, the database user who executes this command becomes the owner of the new database. However, a different owner can be specified via the -o option, if the executing user has appropriate privileges.

createdb is a wrapper around the SQL command CREATE DATABASE. There is no effective difference between creating databases via this utility and via other methods for accessing the server.

Options

createdb accepts the following command-line arguments:

dbname

> Specifies the name of the database to be created. The name must be unique among all PostgreSQL databases in this cluster. The default is to create a database with the same name as the current system user.

description

> Specifies a comment to be associated with the newly created database.

-D *tablespace*
--tablespace=*tablespace*

> Specifies the default tablespace for the database. (This name is processed as a double-quoted identifier.)

-e
--echo

> Echo the commands that createdb generates and sends to the server.

-E *encoding*
--encoding=*encoding*

> Specifies the character encoding scheme to be used in this database. The character sets supported by the PostgreSQL server are described in Section 22.3.1.

`-l` *locale*

`--locale=`*locale*

> Specifies the locale to be used in this database. This is equivalent to specifying both `--lc-collate` and `--lc-ctype`.

`--lc-collate=`*locale*

> Specifies the LC_COLLATE setting to be used in this database.

`--lc-ctype=`*locale*

> Specifies the LC_CTYPE setting to be used in this database.

`-O` *owner*

`--owner=`*owner*

> Specifies the database user who will own the new database. (This name is processed as a double-quoted identifier.)

`-T` *template*

`--template=`*template*

> Specifies the template database from which to build this database. (This name is processed as a double-quoted identifier.)

`-V`

`--version`

> Print the createdb version and exit.

`-?`

`--help`

> Show help about createdb command line arguments, and exit.

The options `-D`, `-l`, `-E`, `-O`, and `-T` correspond to options of the underlying SQL command CREATE DATABASE; see there for more information about them.

createdb also accepts the following command-line arguments for connection parameters:

`-h` *host*

`--host=`*host*

> Specifies the host name of the machine on which the server is running. If the value begins with a slash, it is used as the directory for the Unix domain socket.

`-p` *port*

`--port=`*port*

> Specifies the TCP port or the local Unix domain socket file extension on which the server is listening for connections.

`-U` *username*

`--username=`*username*

> User name to connect as.

```
-w
--no-password
```

>　Never issue a password prompt. If the server requires password authentication and a password is not available by other means such as a .pgpass file, the connection attempt will fail. This option can be useful in batch jobs and scripts where no user is present to enter a password.

```
-W
--password
```

>　Force createdb to prompt for a password before connecting to a database.

>　This option is never essential, since createdb will automatically prompt for a password if the server demands password authentication. However, createdb will waste a connection attempt finding out that the server wants a password. In some cases it is worth typing -W to avoid the extra connection attempt.

```
--maintenance-db=dbname
```

>　Specifies the name of the database to connect to when creating the new database. If not specified, the postgres database will be used; if that does not exist (or if it is the name of the new database being created), template1 will be used.

Environment

```
PGDATABASE
```

>　If set, the name of the database to create, unless overridden on the command line.

```
PGHOST
PGPORT
PGUSER
```

>　Default connection parameters. PGUSER also determines the name of the database to create, if it is not specified on the command line or by PGDATABASE.

This utility, like most other PostgreSQL utilities, also uses the environment variables supported by libpq (see Section 31.14).

Diagnostics

In case of difficulty, see CREATE DATABASE and psql for discussions of potential problems and error messages. The database server must be running at the targeted host. Also, any default connection settings and environment variables used by the libpq front-end library will apply.

Examples

To create the database `demo` using the default database server:

```
$ createdb demo
```

To create the database `demo` using the server on host `eden`, port 5000, using the `LATIN1` encoding scheme with a look at the underlying command:

```
$ createdb -p 5000 -h eden -E LATIN1 -e demo
CREATE DATABASE demo ENCODING 'LATIN1';
```

See Also

dropdb, CREATE DATABASE

createlang

Name

`createlang` — install a PostgreSQL procedural language

Synopsis

`createlang` [*connection-option*...] *langname* [*dbname*]

`createlang` [*connection-option*...] `--list` | `-l` [*dbname*]

Description

createlang is a utility for adding a procedural language to a PostgreSQL database.

createlang is just a wrapper around the CREATE EXTENSION SQL command.

Caution

createlang is deprecated and may be removed in a future PostgreSQL release. Direct use of the `CREATE EXTENSION` command is recommended instead.

Options

createlang accepts the following command-line arguments:

langname

> Specifies the name of the procedural language to be installed. (This name is lower-cased.)

`[-d]` *dbname*
`[--dbname=]`*dbname*

> Specifies the database to which the language should be added. The default is to use the database with the same name as the current system user.

`-e`
`--echo`

> Display SQL commands as they are executed.

`-l`
`--list`

> Show a list of already installed languages in the target database.

```
-V
--version
```

Print the createlang version and exit.

```
-?
--help
```

Show help about createlang command line arguments, and exit.

createlang also accepts the following command-line arguments for connection parameters:

```
-h host
--host=host
```

Specifies the host name of the machine on which the server is running. If the value begins with a slash, it is used as the directory for the Unix domain socket.

```
-p port
--port=port
```

Specifies the TCP port or local Unix domain socket file extension on which the server is listening for connections.

```
-U username
--username=username
```

User name to connect as.

```
-w
--no-password
```

Never issue a password prompt. If the server requires password authentication and a password is not available by other means such as a .pgpass file, the connection attempt will fail. This option can be useful in batch jobs and scripts where no user is present to enter a password.

```
-W
--password
```

Force createlang to prompt for a password before connecting to a database.

This option is never essential, since createlang will automatically prompt for a password if the server demands password authentication. However, createlang will waste a connection attempt finding out that the server wants a password. In some cases it is worth typing -W to avoid the extra connection attempt.

Environment

```
PGDATABASE
PGHOST
PGPORT
PGUSER
```

Default connection parameters

This utility, like most other PostgreSQL utilities, also uses the environment variables supported by libpq (see Section 31.14).

Diagnostics

Most error messages are self-explanatory. If not, run createlang with the `--echo` option and see the respective SQL command for details. Also, any default connection settings and environment variables used by the libpq front-end library will apply.

Notes

Use droplang to remove a language.

Examples

To install the language `pltcl` into the database `template1`:

```
$ createlang pltcl template1
```

Note that installing the language into `template1` will cause it to be automatically installed into subsequently-created databases as well.

See Also

droplang, CREATE EXTENSION, CREATE LANGUAGE

createuser

Name

`createuser` — define a new PostgreSQL user account

Synopsis

`createuser` [`connection-option`...] [`option`...] [`username`]

Description

createuser creates a new PostgreSQL user (or more precisely, a role). Only superusers and users with `CREATEROLE` privilege can create new users, so createuser must be invoked by someone who can connect as a superuser or a user with `CREATEROLE` privilege.

If you wish to create a new superuser, you must connect as a superuser, not merely with `CREATEROLE` privilege. Being a superuser implies the ability to bypass all access permission checks within the database, so superuserdom should not be granted lightly.

createuser is a wrapper around the SQL command CREATE ROLE. There is no effective difference between creating users via this utility and via other methods for accessing the server.

Options

createuser accepts the following command-line arguments:

`username`

> Specifies the name of the PostgreSQL user to be created. This name must be different from all existing roles in this PostgreSQL installation.

`-c` `number`
`--connection-limit=number`

> Set a maximum number of connections for the new user. The default is to set no limit.

`-d`
`--createdb`

> The new user will be allowed to create databases.

`-D`
`--no-createdb`

> The new user will not be allowed to create databases. This is the default.

`-e`

`--echo`

> Echo the commands that createuser generates and sends to the server.

`-E`

`--encrypted`

> Encrypts the user's password stored in the database. If not specified, the default password behavior is used.

`-g` *role*

`--role=`*role*

> Indicates role to which this role will be added immediately as a new member. Multiple roles to which this role will be added as a member can be specified by writing multiple `-g` switches.

`-i`

`--inherit`

> The new role will automatically inherit privileges of roles it is a member of. This is the default.

`-I`

`--no-inherit`

> The new role will not automatically inherit privileges of roles it is a member of.

`--interactive`

> Prompt for the user name if none is specified on the command line, and also prompt for whichever of the options `-d`/`-D`, `-r`/`-R`, `-s`/`-S` is not specified on the command line. (This was the default behavior up to PostgreSQL 9.1.)

`-l`

`--login`

> The new user will be allowed to log in (that is, the user name can be used as the initial session user identifier). This is the default.

`-L`

`--no-login`

> The new user will not be allowed to log in. (A role without login privilege is still useful as a means of managing database permissions.)

`-N`

`--unencrypted`

> Does not encrypt the user's password stored in the database. If not specified, the default password behavior is used.

`-P`

`--pwprompt`

> If given, createuser will issue a prompt for the password of the new user. This is not necessary if you do not plan on using password authentication.

`-r`

`--createrole`

> The new user will be allowed to create new roles (that is, this user will have CREATEROLE privilege).

```
-R
--no-createrole
```

> The new user will not be allowed to create new roles. This is the default.

```
-s
--superuser
```

> The new user will be a superuser.

```
-S
--no-superuser
```

> The new user will not be a superuser. This is the default.

```
-V
--version
```

> Print the createuser version and exit.

```
--replication
```

> The new user will have the REPLICATION privilege, which is described more fully in the documentation for CREATE ROLE.

```
--no-replication
```

> The new user will not have the REPLICATION privilege, which is described more fully in the documentation for CREATE ROLE.

```
-?
--help
```

> Show help about createuser command line arguments, and exit.

createuser also accepts the following command-line arguments for connection parameters:

```
-h host
--host=host
```

> Specifies the host name of the machine on which the server is running. If the value begins with a slash, it is used as the directory for the Unix domain socket.

```
-p port
--port=port
```

> Specifies the TCP port or local Unix domain socket file extension on which the server is listening for connections.

```
-U username
--username=username
```

> User name to connect as (not the user name to create).

```
-w
--no-password
```

> Never issue a password prompt. If the server requires password authentication and a password is not available by other means such as a .pgpass file, the connection attempt will fail. This option can be useful in batch jobs and scripts where no user is present to enter a password.

```
-W
--password
```

> Force createuser to prompt for a password (for connecting to the server, not for the password of the new user).

> This option is never essential, since createuser will automatically prompt for a password if the server demands password authentication. However, createuser will waste a connection attempt finding out that the server wants a password. In some cases it is worth typing -W to avoid the extra connection attempt.

Environment

```
PGHOST
PGPORT
PGUSER
```

> Default connection parameters

This utility, like most other PostgreSQL utilities, also uses the environment variables supported by libpq (see Section 31.14).

Diagnostics

In case of difficulty, see CREATE ROLE and psql for discussions of potential problems and error messages. The database server must be running at the targeted host. Also, any default connection settings and environment variables used by the libpq front-end library will apply.

Examples

To create a user `joe` on the default database server:

```
$ createuser joe
```

To create a user `joe` on the default database server with prompting for some additional attributes:

```
$ createuser --interactive joe
Shall the new role be a superuser? (y/n) n
Shall the new role be allowed to create databases? (y/n) n
Shall the new role be allowed to create more new roles? (y/n) n
```

To create the same user `joe` using the server on host `eden`, port 5000, with attributes explicitly specified, taking a look at the underlying command:

```
$ createuser -h eden -p 5000 -S -D -R -e joe
CREATE ROLE joe NOSUPERUSER NOCREATEDB NOCREATEROLE INHERIT LOGIN;
```

To create the user `joe` as a superuser, and assign a password immediately:

```
$ createuser -P -s -e joe
Enter password for new role: xyzzy
Enter it again: xyzzy
CREATE ROLE joe PASSWORD 'md5b5f5ba1a423792b526f799ae4eb3d59e' SUPERUSER CREATEDB CREATI
```

In the above example, the new password isn't actually echoed when typed, but we show what was typed for clarity. As you see, the password is encrypted before it is sent to the client. If the option `--unencrypted` is used, the password *will* appear in the echoed command (and possibly also in the server log and elsewhere), so you don't want to use `-e` in that case, if anyone else can see your screen.

See Also

dropuser, CREATE ROLE

dropdb

Name

dropdb — remove a PostgreSQL database

Synopsis

dropdb [*connection-option*...] [*option*...] *dbname*

Description

dropdb destroys an existing PostgreSQL database. The user who executes this command must be a database superuser or the owner of the database.

dropdb is a wrapper around the SQL command DROP DATABASE. There is no effective difference between dropping databases via this utility and via other methods for accessing the server.

Options

dropdb accepts the following command-line arguments:

dbname

> Specifies the name of the database to be removed.

-e
--echo

> Echo the commands that dropdb generates and sends to the server.

-i
--interactive

> Issues a verification prompt before doing anything destructive.

-V
--version

> Print the dropdb version and exit.

--if-exists

> Do not throw an error if the database does not exist. A notice is issued in this case.

-?
--help

> Show help about dropdb command line arguments, and exit.

dropdb also accepts the following command-line arguments for connection parameters:

`-h host`

`--host=host`

> Specifies the host name of the machine on which the server is running. If the value begins with a slash, it is used as the directory for the Unix domain socket.

`-p port`

`--port=port`

> Specifies the TCP port or local Unix domain socket file extension on which the server is listening for connections.

`-U username`

`--username=username`

> User name to connect as.

`-w`

`--no-password`

> Never issue a password prompt. If the server requires password authentication and a password is not available by other means such as a `.pgpass` file, the connection attempt will fail. This option can be useful in batch jobs and scripts where no user is present to enter a password.

`-W`

`--password`

> Force dropdb to prompt for a password before connecting to a database.

> This option is never essential, since dropdb will automatically prompt for a password if the server demands password authentication. However, dropdb will waste a connection attempt finding out that the server wants a password. In some cases it is worth typing `-W` to avoid the extra connection attempt.

`--maintenance-db=dbname`

> Specifies the name of the database to connect to in order to drop the target database. If not specified, the `postgres` database will be used; if that does not exist (or is the database being dropped), `template1` will be used.

Environment

`PGHOST`
`PGPORT`
`PGUSER`

> Default connection parameters

This utility, like most other PostgreSQL utilities, also uses the environment variables supported by libpq (see Section 31.14).

Diagnostics

In case of difficulty, see DROP DATABASE and psql for discussions of potential problems and error messages. The database server must be running at the targeted host. Also, any default connection settings and environment variables used by the libpq front-end library will apply.

Examples

To destroy the database demo on the default database server:

```
$ dropdb demo
```

To destroy the database demo using the server on host eden, port 5000, with verification and a peek at the underlying command:

```
$ dropdb -p 5000 -h eden -i -e demo
Database "demo" will be permanently deleted.
Are you sure? (y/n) y
DROP DATABASE demo;
```

See Also

createdb, DROP DATABASE

droplang

Name

droplang — remove a PostgreSQL procedural language

Synopsis

droplang [*connection-option*...] *langname* [*dbname*]

droplang [*connection-option*...] --list | -l [*dbname*]

Description

droplang is a utility for removing an existing procedural language from a PostgreSQL database.
droplang is just a wrapper around the DROP EXTENSION SQL command.

```
                              Caution
droplang is deprecated and may be removed in a future PostgreSQL release. Direct
use of the DROP EXTENSION command is recommended instead.
```

Options

droplang accepts the following command line arguments:

langname

> Specifies the name of the procedural language to be removed. (This name is lower-cased.)

[-d] *dbname*
[--dbname=]*dbname*

> Specifies from which database the language should be removed. The default is to use the database
> with the same name as the current system user.

-e
--echo

> Display SQL commands as they are executed.

-l
--list

> Show a list of already installed languages in the target database.

```
-V
--version
```

Print the droplang version and exit.

```
-?
--help
```

Show help about droplang command line arguments, and exit.

droplang also accepts the following command line arguments for connection parameters:

```
-h host
--host=host
```

Specifies the host name of the machine on which the server is running. If host begins with a slash, it is used as the directory for the Unix domain socket.

```
-p port
--port=port
```

Specifies the Internet TCP/IP port or local Unix domain socket file extension on which the server is listening for connections.

```
-U username
--username=username
```

User name to connect as.

```
-w
--no-password
```

Never issue a password prompt. If the server requires password authentication and a password is not available by other means such as a .pgpass file, the connection attempt will fail. This option can be useful in batch jobs and scripts where no user is present to enter a password.

```
-W
--password
```

Force droplang to prompt for a password before connecting to a database.

This option is never essential, since droplang will automatically prompt for a password if the server demands password authentication. However, droplang will waste a connection attempt finding out that the server wants a password. In some cases it is worth typing -W to avoid the extra connection attempt.

Environment

```
PGDATABASE
PGHOST
PGPORT
PGUSER
```

> Default connection parameters

This utility, like most other PostgreSQL utilities, also uses the environment variables supported by libpq (see Section 31.14).

Diagnostics

Most error messages are self-explanatory. If not, run droplang with the `--echo` option and see under the respective SQL command for details. Also, any default connection settings and environment variables used by the libpq front-end library will apply.

Notes

Use createlang to add a language.

Examples

To remove the language `pltcl`:

```
$ droplang pltcl dbname
```

See Also

createlang, DROP EXTENSION, DROP LANGUAGE

dropuser

Name

dropuser — remove a PostgreSQL user account

Synopsis

dropuser [*connection-option*...] [*option*...] [*username*]

Description

dropuser removes an existing PostgreSQL user. Only superusers and users with the CREATEROLE privilege can remove PostgreSQL users. (To remove a superuser, you must yourself be a superuser.)

dropuser is a wrapper around the SQL command DROP ROLE. There is no effective difference between dropping users via this utility and via other methods for accessing the server.

Options

dropuser accepts the following command-line arguments:

username

> Specifies the name of the PostgreSQL user to be removed. You will be prompted for a name if none is specified on the command line and the -i/--interactive option is used.

-e
--echo

> Echo the commands that dropuser generates and sends to the server.

-i
--interactive

> Prompt for confirmation before actually removing the user, and prompt for the user name if none is specified on the command line.

-V
--version

> Print the dropuser version and exit.

--if-exists

> Do not throw an error if the user does not exist. A notice is issued in this case.

```
-?
--help
```

Show help about dropuser command line arguments, and exit.

dropuser also accepts the following command-line arguments for connection parameters:

```
-h host
--host=host
```

Specifies the host name of the machine on which the server is running. If the value begins with a slash, it is used as the directory for the Unix domain socket.

```
-p port
--port=port
```

Specifies the TCP port or local Unix domain socket file extension on which the server is listening for connections.

```
-U username
--username=username
```

User name to connect as (not the user name to drop).

```
-w
--no-password
```

Never issue a password prompt. If the server requires password authentication and a password is not available by other means such as a .pgpass file, the connection attempt will fail. This option can be useful in batch jobs and scripts where no user is present to enter a password.

```
-W
--password
```

Force dropuser to prompt for a password before connecting to a database.

This option is never essential, since dropuser will automatically prompt for a password if the server demands password authentication. However, dropuser will waste a connection attempt finding out that the server wants a password. In some cases it is worth typing -W to avoid the extra connection attempt.

Environment

```
PGHOST
PGPORT
PGUSER
```

Default connection parameters

This utility, like most other PostgreSQL utilities, also uses the environment variables supported by libpq (see Section 31.14).

Diagnostics

In case of difficulty, see DROP ROLE and psql for discussions of potential problems and error messages. The database server must be running at the targeted host. Also, any default connection settings and environment variables used by the libpq front-end library will apply.

Examples

To remove user `joe` from the default database server:

```
$ dropuser joe
```

To remove user `joe` using the server on host `eden`, port 5000, with verification and a peek at the underlying command:

```
$ dropuser -p 5000 -h eden -i -e joe
Role "joe" will be permanently removed.
Are you sure? (y/n) y
DROP ROLE joe;
```

See Also

createuser, DROP ROLE

ecpg

Name

ecpg — embedded SQL C preprocessor

Synopsis

ecpg [*option*...] *file*...

Description

ecpg is the embedded SQL preprocessor for C programs. It converts C programs with embedded SQL statements to normal C code by replacing the SQL invocations with special function calls. The output files can then be processed with any C compiler tool chain.

ecpg will convert each input file given on the command line to the corresponding C output file. Input files preferably have the extension .pgc, in which case the extension will be replaced by .c to determine the output file name. If the extension of the input file is not .pgc, then the output file name is computed by appending .c to the full file name. The output file name can also be overridden using the -o option.

This reference page does not describe the embedded SQL language. See Chapter 33 for more information on that topic.

Options

ecpg accepts the following command-line arguments:

-c

Automatically generate certain C code from SQL code. Currently, this works for EXEC SQL TYPE.

-C *mode*

Set a compatibility mode. *mode* can be INFORMIX or INFORMIX_SE.

-D *symbol*

Define a C preprocessor symbol.

-i

Parse system include files as well.

-I *directory*

Specify an additional include path, used to find files included via EXEC SQL INCLUDE. Defaults are . (current directory), /usr/local/include, the PostgreSQL include directory which is defined at compile time (default: /usr/local/pgsql/include), and /usr/include, in that order.

-o *filename*

Specifies that ecpg should write all its output to the given *filename*.

-r *option*

Selects run-time behavior. *Option* can be one of the following:

no_indicator

Do not use indicators but instead use special values to represent null values. Historically there have been databases using this approach.

prepare

Prepare all statements before using them. Libecpg will keep a cache of prepared statements and reuse a statement if it gets executed again. If the cache runs full, libecpg will free the least used statement.

questionmarks

Allow question mark as placeholder for compatibility reasons. This used to be the default long ago.

-t

Turn on autocommit of transactions. In this mode, each SQL command is automatically committed unless it is inside an explicit transaction block. In the default mode, commands are committed only when EXEC SQL COMMIT is issued.

-v

Print additional information including the version and the "include" path.

--version

Print the ecpg version and exit.

-?
--help

Show help about ecpg command line arguments, and exit.

Notes

When compiling the preprocessed C code files, the compiler needs to be able to find the ECPG header files in the PostgreSQL include directory. Therefore, you might have to use the -I option when invoking the compiler (e.g., -I/usr/local/pgsql/include).

Programs using C code with embedded SQL have to be linked against the libecpg library, for example using the linker options -L/usr/local/pgsql/lib -lecpg.

The value of either of these directories that is appropriate for the installation can be found out using pg_config.

Examples

If you have an embedded SQL C source file named `prog1.pgc`, you can create an executable program using the following sequence of commands:

```
ecpg prog1.pgc
cc -I/usr/local/pgsql/include -c prog1.c
cc -o prog1 prog1.o -L/usr/local/pgsql/lib -lecpg
```

pg_basebackup

Name

pg_basebackup — take a base backup of a PostgreSQL cluster

Synopsis

pg_basebackup [option...]

Description

pg_basebackup is used to take base backups of a running PostgreSQL database cluster. These are taken without affecting other clients to the database, and can be used both for point-in-time recovery (see Section 24.3) and as the starting point for a log shipping or streaming replication standby servers (see Section 25.2).

pg_basebackup makes a binary copy of the database cluster files, while making sure the system is put in and out of backup mode automatically. Backups are always taken of the entire database cluster; it is not possible to back up individual databases or database objects. For individual database backups, a tool such as pg_dump must be used.

The backup is made over a regular PostgreSQL connection, and uses the replication protocol. The connection must be made with a superuser or a user having REPLICATION permissions (see Section 20.2), and pg_hba.conf must explicitly permit the replication connection. The server must also be configured with max_wal_senders set high enough to leave at least one session available for the backup.

There can be multiple pg_basebackups running at the same time, but it is better from a performance point of view to take only one backup, and copy the result.

pg_basebackup can make a base backup from not only the master but also the standby. To take a backup from the standby, set up the standby so that it can accept replication connections (that is, set max_wal_senders and hot_standby, and configure host-based authentication). You will also need to enable full_page_writes on the master.

Note that there are some limitations in an online backup from the standby:

- The backup history file is not created in the database cluster backed up.

- There is no guarantee that all WAL files required for the backup are archived at the end of backup. If you are planning to use the backup for an archive recovery and want to ensure that all required files are available at that moment, you need to include them into the backup by using -x option.

- If the standby is promoted to the master during online backup, the backup fails.

- All WAL records required for the backup must contain sufficient full-page writes, which requires you to enable full_page_writes on the master and not to use a tool like pg_compresslog as archive_command to remove full-page writes from WAL files.

Options

The following command-line options control the location and format of the output.

-D *directory*

--pgdata=*directory*

> Directory to write the output to. pg_basebackup will create the directory and any parent directories if necessary. The directory may already exist, but it is an error if the directory already exists and is not empty.
>
> When the backup is in tar mode, and the directory is specified as – (dash), the tar file will be written to stdout.
>
> This option is required.

-F *format*

--format=*format*

> Selects the format for the output. *format* can be one of the following:
>
> p
>
> plain
>
>> Write the output as plain files, with the same layout as the current data directory and tablespaces. When the cluster has no additional tablespaces, the whole database will be placed in the target directory. If the cluster contains additional tablespaces, the main data directory will be placed in the target directory, but all other tablespaces will be placed in the same absolute path as they have on the server.
>>
>> This is the default format.
>
> t
>
> tar
>
>> Write the output as tar files in the target directory. The main data directory will be written to a file named base.tar, and all other tablespaces will be named after the tablespace OID.
>>
>> If the value – (dash) is specified as target directory, the tar contents will be written to standard output, suitable for piping to for example gzip. This is only possible if the cluster has no additional tablespaces.

-r *rate*

--max-rate=*rate*

> The maximum transfer rate of data transferred from the server. Values are in kilobytes per second. Use a suffix of M to indicate megabytes per second. A suffix of k is also accepted, and has no effect. Valid values are between 32 kilobytes per second and 1024 megabytes per second.
>
> The purpose is to limit the impact of pg_basebackup on the running server.
>
> This option always affects transfer of the data directory. Transfer of WAL files is only affected if the collection method is fetch.

```
-R
--write-recovery-conf
```

> Write a minimal `recovery.conf` in the output directory (or into the base archive file when using tar format) to ease setting up a standby server.

```
-T olddir=newdir
--tablespace-mapping=olddir=newdir
```

> Relocate the tablespace in directory `olddir` to `newdir` during the backup. To be effective, `olddir` must exactly match the path specification of the tablespace as it is currently defined. (But it is not an error if there is no tablespace in `olddir` contained in the backup.) Both `olddir` and `newdir` must be absolute paths. If a path happens to contain a = sign, escape it with a backslash. This option can be specified multiple times for multiple tablespaces. See examples below.

> If a tablespace is relocated in this way, the symbolic links inside the main data directory are updated to point to the new location. So the new data directory is ready to be used for a new server instance with all tablespaces in the updated locations.

```
--xlogdir=xlogdir
```

> Specifies the location for the transaction log directory. `xlogdir` must be an absolute path. The transaction log directory can only be specified when the backup is in plain mode.

```
-x
--xlog
```

> Using this option is equivalent of using -X with method `fetch`.

```
-X method
--xlog-method=method
```

> Includes the required transaction log files (WAL files) in the backup. This will include all transaction logs generated during the backup. If this option is specified, it is possible to start a postmaster directly in the extracted directory without the need to consult the log archive, thus making this a completely standalone backup.

> The following methods for collecting the transaction logs are supported:

```
f
fetch
```

> > The transaction log files are collected at the end of the backup. Therefore, it is necessary for the wal_keep_segments parameter to be set high enough that the log is not removed before the end of the backup. If the log has been rotated when it's time to transfer it, the backup will fail and be unusable.

```
s
stream
```

> > Stream the transaction log while the backup is created. This will open a second connection to the server and start streaming the transaction log in parallel while running the backup. Therefore, it will use up two slots configured by the max_wal_senders parameter. As long as the client can keep up with transaction log received, using this mode requires no extra transaction logs to be saved on the master.

-z

--gzip

> Enables gzip compression of tar file output, with the default compression level. Compression is only available when using the tar format.

-Z *level*

--compress=*level*

> Enables gzip compression of tar file output, and specifies the compression level (1 through 9, 9 being best compression). Compression is only available when using the tar format.

The following command-line options control the generation of the backup and the running of the program.

-c *fast|spread*

--checkpoint=*fast|spread*

> Sets checkpoint mode to fast or spread (default) (see Section 24.3.3).

-l *label*

--label=*label*

> Sets the label for the backup. If none is specified, a default value of "pg_basebackup base backup" will be used.

-P

--progress

> Enables progress reporting. Turning this on will deliver an approximate progress report during the backup. Since the database may change during the backup, this is only an approximation and may not end at exactly 100%. In particular, when WAL log is included in the backup, the total amount of data cannot be estimated in advance, and in this case the estimated target size will increase once it passes the total estimate without WAL.

> When this is enabled, the backup will start by enumerating the size of the entire database, and then go back and send the actual contents. This may make the backup take slightly longer, and in particular it will take longer before the first data is sent.

-v

--verbose

> Enables verbose mode. Will output some extra steps during startup and shutdown, as well as show the exact file name that is currently being processed if progress reporting is also enabled.

The following command-line options control the database connection parameters.

-d *connstr*

--dbname=*connstr*

> Specifies parameters used to connect to the server, as a connection string. See Section 31.1.1 for more information.

The option is called `--dbname` for consistency with other client applications, but because pg_basebackup doesn't connect to any particular database in the cluster, database name in the connection string will be ignored.

`-h host`

`--host=host`

Specifies the host name of the machine on which the server is running. If the value begins with a slash, it is used as the directory for the Unix domain socket. The default is taken from the `PGHOST` environment variable, if set, else a Unix domain socket connection is attempted.

`-p port`

`--port=port`

Specifies the TCP port or local Unix domain socket file extension on which the server is listening for connections. Defaults to the `PGPORT` environment variable, if set, or a compiled-in default.

`-s interval`

`--status-interval=interval`

Specifies the number of seconds between status packets sent back to the server. This allows for easier monitoring of the progress from server. A value of zero disables the periodic status updates completely, although an update will still be sent when requested by the server, to avoid timeout disconnect. The default value is 10 seconds.

`-U username`

`--username=username`

User name to connect as.

`-w`

`--no-password`

Never issue a password prompt. If the server requires password authentication and a password is not available by other means such as a `.pgpass` file, the connection attempt will fail. This option can be useful in batch jobs and scripts where no user is present to enter a password.

`-W`

`--password`

Force pg_basebackup to prompt for a password before connecting to a database.

This option is never essential, since pg_basebackup will automatically prompt for a password if the server demands password authentication. However, pg_basebackup will waste a connection attempt finding out that the server wants a password. In some cases it is worth typing `-W` to avoid the extra connection attempt.

Other options are also available:

`-V`

`--version`

Print the pg_basebackup version and exit.

```
-?
--help
```

Show help about pg_basebackup command line arguments, and exit.

Environment

This utility, like most other PostgreSQL utilities, uses the environment variables supported by libpq (see Section 31.14).

Notes

The backup will include all files in the data directory and tablespaces, including the configuration files and any additional files placed in the directory by third parties. But only regular files and directories are copied. Symbolic links (other than those used for tablespaces) and special device files are skipped. (See Section 49.3 for the precise details.)

Tablespaces will in plain format by default be backed up to the same path they have on the server, unless the option `--tablespace-mapping` is used. Without this option, running a plain format base backup on the same host as the server will not work if tablespaces are in use, because the backup would have to be written to the same directory locations as the original tablespaces.

pg_basebackup works with servers of the same or an older major version, down to 9.1. However, WAL streaming mode (-X stream) only works with server version 9.3 and later.

Examples

To create a base backup of the server at `mydbserver` and store it in the local directory `/usr/local/pgsql/data`:

```
$ pg_basebackup -h mydbserver -D /usr/local/pgsql/data
```

To create a backup of the local server with one compressed tar file for each tablespace, and store it in the directory `backup`, showing a progress report while running:

```
$ pg_basebackup -D backup -Ft -z -P
```

To create a backup of a single-tablespace local database and compress this with bzip2:

```
$ pg_basebackup -D - -Ft | bzip2 > backup.tar.bz2
```

(This command will fail if there are multiple tablespaces in the database.)

To create a backup of a local database where the tablespace in `/opt/ts` is relocated to `./backup/ts`:

```
$ pg_basebackup -D backup/data -T /opt/ts=$(pwd)/backup/ts
```

See Also

pg_dump

pg_config

Name

pg_config — retrieve information about the installed version of PostgreSQL

Synopsis

pg_config [*option*...]

Description

The pg_config utility prints configuration parameters of the currently installed version of PostgreSQL. It is intended, for example, to be used by software packages that want to interface to PostgreSQL to facilitate finding the required header files and libraries.

Options

To use pg_config, supply one or more of the following options:

--bindir

Print the location of user executables. Use this, for example, to find the psql program. This is normally also the location where the pg_config program resides.

--docdir

Print the location of documentation files.

--htmldir

Print the location of HTML documentation files.

--includedir

Print the location of C header files of the client interfaces.

--pkgincludedir

Print the location of other C header files.

--includedir-server

Print the location of C header files for server programming.

--libdir

Print the location of object code libraries.

`--pkglibdir`

Print the location of dynamically loadable modules, or where the server would search for them. (Other architecture-dependent data files might also be installed in this directory.)

`--localedir`

Print the location of locale support files. (This will be an empty string if locale support was not configured when PostgreSQL was built.)

`--mandir`

Print the location of manual pages.

`--sharedir`

Print the location of architecture-independent support files.

`--sysconfdir`

Print the location of system-wide configuration files.

`--pgxs`

Print the location of extension makefiles.

`--configure`

Print the options that were given to the `configure` script when PostgreSQL was configured for building. This can be used to reproduce the identical configuration, or to find out with what options a binary package was built. (Note however that binary packages often contain vendor-specific custom patches.) See also the examples below.

`--cc`

Print the value of the `CC` variable that was used for building PostgreSQL. This shows the C compiler used.

`--cppflags`

Print the value of the `CPPFLAGS` variable that was used for building PostgreSQL. This shows C compiler switches needed at preprocessing time (typically, `-I` switches).

`--cflags`

Print the value of the `CFLAGS` variable that was used for building PostgreSQL. This shows C compiler switches.

`--cflags_sl`

Print the value of the `CFLAGS_SL` variable that was used for building PostgreSQL. This shows extra C compiler switches used for building shared libraries.

`--ldflags`

Print the value of the `LDFLAGS` variable that was used for building PostgreSQL. This shows linker switches.

`--ldflags_ex`

Print the value of the `LDFLAGS_EX` variable that was used for building PostgreSQL. This shows linker switches used for building executables only.

`--ldflags_sl`

> Print the value of the `LDFLAGS_SL` variable that was used for building PostgreSQL. This shows linker switches used for building shared libraries only.

`--libs`

> Print the value of the `LIBS` variable that was used for building PostgreSQL. This normally contains `-l` switches for external libraries linked into PostgreSQL.

`--version`

> Print the version of PostgreSQL.

`-?`
`--help`

> Show help about pg_config command line arguments, and exit.

If more than one option is given, the information is printed in that order, one item per line. If no options are given, all available information is printed, with labels.

Notes

The options `--docdir`, `--pkgincludedir`, `--localedir`, `--mandir`, `--sharedir`, `--sysconfdir`, `--cc`, `--cppflags`, `--cflags`, `--cflags_sl`, `--ldflags`, `--ldflags_sl`, and `--libs` were added in PostgreSQL 8.1. The option `--htmldir` was added in PostgreSQL 8.4. The option `--ldflags_ex` was added in PostgreSQL 9.0.

Example

To reproduce the build configuration of the current PostgreSQL installation, run the following command:

```
eval ./configure `pg_config --configure`
```

The output of `pg_config --configure` contains shell quotation marks so arguments with spaces are represented correctly. Therefore, using `eval` is required for proper results.

pg_dump

Name

pg_dump — extract a PostgreSQL database into a script file or other archive file

Synopsis

pg_dump [*connection-option*...] [*option*...] [*dbname*]

Description

pg_dump is a utility for backing up a PostgreSQL database. It makes consistent backups even if the database is being used concurrently. pg_dump does not block other users accessing the database (readers or writers).

Dumps can be output in script or archive file formats. Script dumps are plain-text files containing the SQL commands required to reconstruct the database to the state it was in at the time it was saved. To restore from such a script, feed it to psql. Script files can be used to reconstruct the database even on other machines and other architectures; with some modifications, even on other SQL database products.

The alternative archive file formats must be used with pg_restore to rebuild the database. They allow pg_restore to be selective about what is restored, or even to reorder the items prior to being restored. The archive file formats are designed to be portable across architectures.

When used with one of the archive file formats and combined with pg_restore, pg_dump provides a flexible archival and transfer mechanism. pg_dump can be used to backup an entire database, then pg_restore can be used to examine the archive and/or select which parts of the database are to be restored. The most flexible output file formats are the "custom" format (-Fc) and the "directory" format(-Fd). They allow for selection and reordering of all archived items, support parallel restoration, and are compressed by default. The "directory" format is the only format that supports parallel dumps.

While running pg_dump, one should examine the output for any warnings (printed on standard error), especially in light of the limitations listed below.

Options

The following command-line options control the content and format of the output.

dbname

> Specifies the name of the database to be dumped. If this is not specified, the environment variable PGDATABASE is used. If that is not set, the user name specified for the connection is used.

`-a`
`--data-only`

> Dump only the data, not the schema (data definitions). Table data, large objects, and sequence values are dumped.
>
> This option is similar to, but for historical reasons not identical to, specifying `--section=data`.

`-b`
`--blobs`

> Include large objects in the dump. This is the default behavior except when `--schema`, `--table`, or `--schema-only` is specified, so the `-b` switch is only useful to add large objects to selective dumps.

`-c`
`--clean`

> Output commands to clean (drop) database objects prior to outputting the commands for creating them. (Unless `--if-exists` is also specified, restore might generate some harmless error messages, if any objects were not present in the destination database.)
>
> This option is only meaningful for the plain-text format. For the archive formats, you can specify the option when you call `pg_restore`.

`-C`
`--create`

> Begin the output with a command to create the database itself and reconnect to the created database. (With a script of this form, it doesn't matter which database in the destination installation you connect to before running the script.) If `--clean` is also specified, the script drops and recreates the target database before reconnecting to it.
>
> This option is only meaningful for the plain-text format. For the archive formats, you can specify the option when you call `pg_restore`.

`-E` *encoding*
`--encoding=`*encoding*

> Create the dump in the specified character set encoding. By default, the dump is created in the database encoding. (Another way to get the same result is to set the `PGCLIENTENCODING` environment variable to the desired dump encoding.)

`-f` *file*
`--file=`*file*

> Send output to the specified file. This parameter can be omitted for file based output formats, in which case the standard output is used. It must be given for the directory output format however, where it specifies the target directory instead of a file. In this case the directory is created by `pg_dump` and must not exist before.

```
-F format
--format=format
```

Selects the format of the output. `format` can be one of the following:

```
p
plain
```

Output a plain-text SQL script file (the default).

```
c
custom
```

Output a custom-format archive suitable for input into pg_restore. Together with the directory output format, this is the most flexible output format in that it allows manual selection and reordering of archived items during restore. This format is also compressed by default.

```
d
directory
```

Output a directory-format archive suitable for input into pg_restore. This will create a directory with one file for each table and blob being dumped, plus a so-called Table of Contents file describing the dumped objects in a machine-readable format that pg_restore can read. A directory format archive can be manipulated with standard Unix tools; for example, files in an uncompressed archive can be compressed with the gzip tool. This format is compressed by default and also supports parallel dumps.

```
t
tar
```

Output a `tar`-format archive suitable for input into pg_restore. The tar-format is compatible with the directory-format; extracting a tar-format archive produces a valid directory-format archive. However, the tar-format does not support compression and has a limit of 8 GB on the size of individual tables. Also, the relative order of table data items cannot be changed during restore.

```
-i
--ignore-version
```

A deprecated option that is now ignored.

```
-j njobs
--jobs=njobs
```

Run the dump in parallel by dumping `njobs` tables simultaneously. This option reduces the time of the dump but it also increases the load on the database server. You can only use this option with the directory output format because this is the only output format where multiple processes can write their data at the same time.

pg_dump will open `njobs` + 1 connections to the database, so make sure your max_connections setting is high enough to accommodate all connections.

Requesting exclusive locks on database objects while running a parallel dump could cause the dump to fail. The reason is that the pg_dump master process requests shared locks on the objects that the worker processes are going to dump later in order to make sure that nobody deletes them and makes them go away while the dump is running. If another client then requests an exclusive lock on a table, that lock will not be granted but will be queued waiting for the shared lock of the master process to be released. Consequently any other access to the table will not be granted either and will queue after the exclusive lock request. This includes the worker process trying to dump the table. Without any precautions this would be a classic deadlock situation. To detect this conflict, the pg_dump worker process requests another shared lock using the NOWAIT option. If the worker process is not granted this shared lock, somebody else must have requested an exclusive lock in the meantime and there is no way to continue with the dump, so pg_dump has no choice but to abort the dump.

For a consistent backup, the database server needs to support synchronized snapshots, a feature that was introduced in PostgreSQL 9.2. With this feature, database clients can ensure they see the same data set even though they use different connections. pg_dump -j uses multiple database connections; it connects to the database once with the master process and once again for each worker job. Without the synchronized snapshot feature, the different worker jobs wouldn't be guaranteed to see the same data in each connection, which could lead to an inconsistent backup.

If you want to run a parallel dump of a pre-9.2 server, you need to make sure that the database content doesn't change from between the time the master connects to the database until the last worker job has connected to the database. The easiest way to do this is to halt any data modifying processes (DDL and DML) accessing the database before starting the backup. You also need to specify the --no-synchronized-snapshots parameter when running pg_dump -j against a pre-9.2 PostgreSQL server.

-n *schema*
--schema=*schema*

> Dump only schemas matching *schema*; this selects both the schema itself, and all its contained objects. When this option is not specified, all non-system schemas in the target database will be dumped. Multiple schemas can be selected by writing multiple -n switches. Also, the *schema* parameter is interpreted as a pattern according to the same rules used by psql's \d commands (see *Patterns*), so multiple schemas can also be selected by writing wildcard characters in the pattern. When using wildcards, be careful to quote the pattern if needed to prevent the shell from expanding the wildcards; see *Examples*.

> > **Note:** When -n is specified, pg_dump makes no attempt to dump any other database objects that the selected schema(s) might depend upon. Therefore, there is no guarantee that the results of a specific-schema dump can be successfully restored by themselves into a clean database.

> > **Note:** Non-schema objects such as blobs are not dumped when -n is specified. You can add blobs back to the dump with the --blobs switch.

-N *schema*
--exclude-schema=*schema*

> Do not dump any schemas matching the *schema* pattern. The pattern is interpreted according to the same rules as for -n. -N can be given more than once to exclude schemas matching any of several patterns.

When both -n and -N are given, the behavior is to dump just the schemas that match at least one -n switch but no -N switches. If -N appears without -n, then schemas matching -N are excluded from what is otherwise a normal dump.

-o

--oids

Dump object identifiers (OIDs) as part of the data for every table. Use this option if your application references the OID columns in some way (e.g., in a foreign key constraint). Otherwise, this option should not be used.

-O

--no-owner

Do not output commands to set ownership of objects to match the original database. By default, pg_dump issues ALTER OWNER or SET SESSION AUTHORIZATION statements to set ownership of created database objects. These statements will fail when the script is run unless it is started by a superuser (or the same user that owns all of the objects in the script). To make a script that can be restored by any user, but will give that user ownership of all the objects, specify -O.

This option is only meaningful for the plain-text format. For the archive formats, you can specify the option when you call pg_restore.

-R

--no-reconnect

This option is obsolete but still accepted for backwards compatibility.

-s

--schema-only

Dump only the object definitions (schema), not data.

This option is the inverse of --data-only. It is similar to, but for historical reasons not identical to, specifying --section=pre-data --section=post-data.

(Do not confuse this with the --schema option, which uses the word "schema" in a different meaning.)

To exclude table data for only a subset of tables in the database, see --exclude-table-data.

-S *username*

--superuser=*username*

Specify the superuser user name to use when disabling triggers. This is relevant only if --disable-triggers is used. (Usually, it's better to leave this out, and instead start the resulting script as superuser.)

-t *table*

--table=*table*

Dump only tables (or views or sequences or foreign tables) matching *table*. Multiple tables can be selected by writing multiple -t switches. Also, the *table* parameter is interpreted as a pattern according to the same rules used by psql's \d commands (see *Patterns*), so multiple tables can also be selected by writing wildcard characters in the pattern. When using wildcards, be careful to quote the pattern if needed to prevent the shell from expanding the wildcards; see *Examples*.

The −n and −N switches have no effect when −t is used, because tables selected by −t will be dumped regardless of those switches, and non-table objects will not be dumped.

> **Note:** When −t is specified, pg_dump makes no attempt to dump any other database objects that the selected table(s) might depend upon. Therefore, there is no guarantee that the results of a specific-table dump can be successfully restored by themselves into a clean database.

> **Note:** The behavior of the −t switch is not entirely upward compatible with pre-8.2 PostgreSQL versions. Formerly, writing −t tab would dump all tables named tab, but now it just dumps whichever one is visible in your default search path. To get the old behavior you can write −t '*.tab'. Also, you must write something like −t sch.tab to select a table in a particular schema, rather than the old locution of −n sch −t tab.

−T *table*

−−exclude-table=*table*

Do not dump any tables matching the *table* pattern. The pattern is interpreted according to the same rules as for −t. −T can be given more than once to exclude tables matching any of several patterns.

When both −t and −T are given, the behavior is to dump just the tables that match at least one −t switch but no −T switches. If −T appears without −t, then tables matching −T are excluded from what is otherwise a normal dump.

−v

−−verbose

Specifies verbose mode. This will cause pg_dump to output detailed object comments and start/stop times to the dump file, and progress messages to standard error.

−V

−−version

Print the pg_dump version and exit.

−x

−−no-privileges

−−no-acl

Prevent dumping of access privileges (grant/revoke commands).

−Z *0..9*

−−compress=*0..9*

Specify the compression level to use. Zero means no compression. For the custom archive format, this specifies compression of individual table-data segments, and the default is to compress at a moderate level. For plain text output, setting a nonzero compression level causes the entire output file to be compressed, as though it had been fed through gzip; but the default is not to compress. The tar archive format currently does not support compression at all.

−−binary-upgrade

This option is for use by in-place upgrade utilities. Its use for other purposes is not recommended or supported. The behavior of the option may change in future releases without notice.

`--column-inserts`
`--attribute-inserts`

> Dump data as INSERT commands with explicit column names (INSERT INTO *table* (*column*, ...) VALUES ...). This will make restoration very slow; it is mainly useful for making dumps that can be loaded into non-PostgreSQL databases. However, since this option generates a separate command for each row, an error in reloading a row causes only that row to be lost rather than the entire table contents.

`--disable-dollar-quoting`

> This option disables the use of dollar quoting for function bodies, and forces them to be quoted using SQL standard string syntax.

`--disable-triggers`

> This option is relevant only when creating a data-only dump. It instructs pg_dump to include commands to temporarily disable triggers on the target tables while the data is reloaded. Use this if you have referential integrity checks or other triggers on the tables that you do not want to invoke during data reload.

> Presently, the commands emitted for `--disable-triggers` must be done as superuser. So, you should also specify a superuser name with `-S`, or preferably be careful to start the resulting script as a superuser.

> This option is only meaningful for the plain-text format. For the archive formats, you can specify the option when you call `pg_restore`.

`--exclude-table-data=`*table*

> Do not dump data for any tables matching the *table* pattern. The pattern is interpreted according to the same rules as for `-t`. `--exclude-table-data` can be given more than once to exclude tables matching any of several patterns. This option is useful when you need the definition of a particular table even though you do not need the data in it.

> To exclude data for all tables in the database, see `--schema-only`.

`--if-exists`

> Use conditional commands (i.e. add an IF EXISTS clause) when cleaning database objects. This option is not valid unless `--clean` is also specified.

`--inserts`

> Dump data as INSERT commands (rather than COPY). This will make restoration very slow; it is mainly useful for making dumps that can be loaded into non-PostgreSQL databases. However, since this option generates a separate command for each row, an error in reloading a row causes only that row to be lost rather than the entire table contents. Note that the restore might fail altogether if you have rearranged column order. The `--column-inserts` option is safe against column order changes, though even slower.

`--lock-wait-timeout=`*timeout*

> Do not wait forever to acquire shared table locks at the beginning of the dump. Instead fail if unable to lock a table within the specified *timeout*. The timeout may be specified in any of the formats accepted by SET statement_timeout. (Allowed values vary depending on the server version you are dumping from, but an integer number of milliseconds is accepted by all versions since 7.3. This option is ignored when dumping from a pre-7.3 server.)

`--no-security-labels`

Do not dump security labels.

`--no-synchronized-snapshots`

This option allows running `pg_dump -j` against a pre-9.2 server, see the documentation of the `-j` parameter for more details.

`--no-tablespaces`

Do not output commands to select tablespaces. With this option, all objects will be created in whichever tablespace is the default during restore.

This option is only meaningful for the plain-text format. For the archive formats, you can specify the option when you call `pg_restore`.

`--no-unlogged-table-data`

Do not dump the contents of unlogged tables. This option has no effect on whether or not the table definitions (schema) are dumped; it only suppresses dumping the table data. Data in unlogged tables is always excluded when dumping from a standby server.

`--quote-all-identifiers`

Force quoting of all identifiers. This may be useful when dumping a database for migration to a future version that may have introduced additional keywords.

`--section=`*sectionname*

Only dump the named section. The section name can be `pre-data`, `data`, or `post-data`. This option can be specified more than once to select multiple sections. The default is to dump all sections.

The data section contains actual table data, large-object contents, and sequence values. Post-data items include definitions of indexes, triggers, rules, and constraints other than validated check constraints. Pre-data items include all other data definition items.

`--serializable-deferrable`

Use a `serializable` transaction for the dump, to ensure that the snapshot used is consistent with later database states; but do this by waiting for a point in the transaction stream at which no anomalies can be present, so that there isn't a risk of the dump failing or causing other transactions to roll back with a `serialization_failure`. See Chapter 13 for more information about transaction isolation and concurrency control.

This option is not beneficial for a dump which is intended only for disaster recovery. It could be useful for a dump used to load a copy of the database for reporting or other read-only load sharing while the original database continues to be updated. Without it the dump may reflect a state which is not consistent with any serial execution of the transactions eventually committed. For example, if batch processing techniques are used, a batch may show as closed in the dump without all of the items which are in the batch appearing.

This option will make no difference if there are no read-write transactions active when pg_dump is started. If read-write transactions are active, the start of the dump may be delayed for an indeterminate length of time. Once running, performance with or without the switch is the same.

```
--use-set-session-authorization
```

Output SQL-standard SET SESSION AUTHORIZATION commands instead of ALTER OWNER commands to determine object ownership. This makes the dump more standards-compatible, but depending on the history of the objects in the dump, might not restore properly. Also, a dump using SET SESSION AUTHORIZATION will certainly require superuser privileges to restore correctly, whereas ALTER OWNER requires lesser privileges.

```
-?
--help
```

Show help about pg_dump command line arguments, and exit.

The following command-line options control the database connection parameters.

```
-d dbname
--dbname=dbname
```

Specifies the name of the database to connect to. This is equivalent to specifying *dbname* as the first non-option argument on the command line.

If this parameter contains an = sign or starts with a valid URI prefix (postgresql:// or postgres://), it is treated as a conninfo string. See Section 31.1 for more information.

```
-h host
--host=host
```

Specifies the host name of the machine on which the server is running. If the value begins with a slash, it is used as the directory for the Unix domain socket. The default is taken from the PGHOST environment variable, if set, else a Unix domain socket connection is attempted.

```
-p port
--port=port
```

Specifies the TCP port or local Unix domain socket file extension on which the server is listening for connections. Defaults to the PGPORT environment variable, if set, or a compiled-in default.

```
-U username
--username=username
```

User name to connect as.

```
-w
--no-password
```

Never issue a password prompt. If the server requires password authentication and a password is not available by other means such as a .pgpass file, the connection attempt will fail. This option can be useful in batch jobs and scripts where no user is present to enter a password.

```
-W
--password
```

Force pg_dump to prompt for a password before connecting to a database.

This option is never essential, since pg_dump will automatically prompt for a password if the server demands password authentication. However, pg_dump will waste a connection attempt finding out

that the server wants a password. In some cases it is worth typing -W to avoid the extra connection attempt.

--role=*rolename*

Specifies a role name to be used to create the dump. This option causes pg_dump to issue a SET ROLE *rolename* command after connecting to the database. It is useful when the authenticated user (specified by -U) lacks privileges needed by pg_dump, but can switch to a role with the required rights. Some installations have a policy against logging in directly as a superuser, and use of this option allows dumps to be made without violating the policy.

Environment

PGDATABASE
PGHOST
PGOPTIONS
PGPORT
PGUSER

Default connection parameters.

This utility, like most other PostgreSQL utilities, also uses the environment variables supported by libpq (see Section 31.14).

Diagnostics

pg_dump internally executes SELECT statements. If you have problems running pg_dump, make sure you are able to select information from the database using, for example, psql. Also, any default connection settings and environment variables used by the libpq front-end library will apply.

The database activity of pg_dump is normally collected by the statistics collector. If this is undesirable, you can set parameter track_counts to false via PGOPTIONS or the ALTER USER command.

Notes

If your database cluster has any local additions to the template1 database, be careful to restore the output of pg_dump into a truly empty database; otherwise you are likely to get errors due to duplicate definitions of the added objects. To make an empty database without any local additions, copy from template0 not template1, for example:

CREATE DATABASE foo WITH TEMPLATE template0;

When a data-only dump is chosen and the option --disable-triggers is used, pg_dump emits commands to disable triggers on user tables before inserting the data, and then commands to re-enable them after the data has been inserted. If the restore is stopped in the middle, the system catalogs might be left in the wrong state.

Members of tar archives are limited to a size less than 8 GB. (This is an inherent limitation of the tar file format.) Therefore this format cannot be used if the textual representation of any one table exceeds that size. The total size of a tar archive and any of the other output formats is not limited, except possibly by the operating system.

The dump file produced by pg_dump does not contain the statistics used by the optimizer to make query planning decisions. Therefore, it is wise to run ANALYZE after restoring from a dump file to ensure optimal performance; see Section 23.1.3 and Section 23.1.6 for more information. The dump file also does not contain any ALTER DATABASE ... SET commands; these settings are dumped by pg_dumpall, along with database users and other installation-wide settings.

Because pg_dump is used to transfer data to newer versions of PostgreSQL, the output of pg_dump can be expected to load into PostgreSQL server versions newer than pg_dump's version. pg_dump can also dump from PostgreSQL servers older than its own version. (Currently, servers back to version 7.0 are supported.) However, pg_dump cannot dump from PostgreSQL servers newer than its own major version; it will refuse to even try, rather than risk making an invalid dump. Also, it is not guaranteed that pg_dump's output can be loaded into a server of an older major version — not even if the dump was taken from a server of that version. Loading a dump file into an older server may require manual editing of the dump file to remove syntax not understood by the older server.

Examples

To dump a database called mydb into a SQL-script file:

```
$ pg_dump mydb > db.sql
```

To reload such a script into a (freshly created) database named newdb:

```
$ psql -d newdb -f db.sql
```

To dump a database into a custom-format archive file:

```
$ pg_dump -Fc mydb > db.dump
```

To dump a database into a directory-format archive:

```
$ pg_dump -Fd mydb -f dumpdir
```

To dump a database into a directory-format archive in parallel with 5 worker jobs:

```
$ pg_dump -Fd mydb -j 5 -f dumpdir
```

To reload an archive file into a (freshly created) database named `newdb`:

```
$ pg_restore -d newdb db.dump
```

To dump a single table named `mytab`:

```
$ pg_dump -t mytab mydb > db.sql
```

To dump all tables whose names start with `emp` in the `detroit` schema, except for the table named `employee_log`:

```
$ pg_dump -t 'detroit.emp*' -T detroit.employee_log mydb > db.sql
```

To dump all schemas whose names start with `east` or `west` and end in `gsm`, excluding any schemas whose names contain the word `test`:

```
$ pg_dump -n 'east*gsm' -n 'west*gsm' -N '*test*' mydb > db.sql
```

The same, using regular expression notation to consolidate the switches:

```
$ pg_dump -n '(east|west)*gsm' -N '*test*' mydb > db.sql
```

To dump all database objects except for tables whose names begin with `ts_`:

```
$ pg_dump -T 'ts_*' mydb > db.sql
```

To specify an upper-case or mixed-case name in `-t` and related switches, you need to double-quote the name; else it will be folded to lower case (see *Patterns*). But double quotes are special to the shell, so in turn they must be quoted. Thus, to dump a single table with a mixed-case name, you need something like

```
$ pg_dump -t "\"MixedCaseName\"" mydb > mytab.sql
```

See Also

pg_dumpall, pg_restore, psql

pg_dumpall

Name

pg_dumpall — extract a PostgreSQL database cluster into a script file

Synopsis

pg_dumpall [*connection-option*...] [*option*...]

Description

pg_dumpall is a utility for writing out ("dumping") all PostgreSQL databases of a cluster into one script file. The script file contains SQL commands that can be used as input to psql to restore the databases. It does this by calling pg_dump for each database in a cluster. pg_dumpall also dumps global objects that are common to all databases. (pg_dump does not save these objects.) This currently includes information about database users and groups, tablespaces, and properties such as access permissions that apply to databases as a whole.

Since pg_dumpall reads tables from all databases you will most likely have to connect as a database superuser in order to produce a complete dump. Also you will need superuser privileges to execute the saved script in order to be allowed to add users and groups, and to create databases.

The SQL script will be written to the standard output. Use the [-flfile] option or shell operators to redirect it into a file.

pg_dumpall needs to connect several times to the PostgreSQL server (once per database). If you use password authentication it will ask for a password each time. It is convenient to have a ~/.pgpass file in such cases. See Section 31.15 for more information.

Options

The following command-line options control the content and format of the output.

-a
--data-only

Dump only the data, not the schema (data definitions).

-c
--clean

Include SQL commands to clean (drop) databases before recreating them. DROP commands for roles and tablespaces are added as well.

```
-f filename
--file=filename
```

Send output to the specified file. If this is omitted, the standard output is used.

```
-g
--globals-only
```

Dump only global objects (roles and tablespaces), no databases.

```
-i
--ignore-version
```

A deprecated option that is now ignored.

```
-o
--oids
```

Dump object identifiers (OIDs) as part of the data for every table. Use this option if your application references the OID columns in some way (e.g., in a foreign key constraint). Otherwise, this option should not be used.

```
-O
--no-owner
```

Do not output commands to set ownership of objects to match the original database. By default, pg_dumpall issues ALTER OWNER or SET SESSION AUTHORIZATION statements to set ownership of created schema elements. These statements will fail when the script is run unless it is started by a superuser (or the same user that owns all of the objects in the script). To make a script that can be restored by any user, but will give that user ownership of all the objects, specify -O.

```
-r
--roles-only
```

Dump only roles, no databases or tablespaces.

```
-s
--schema-only
```

Dump only the object definitions (schema), not data.

```
-S username
--superuser=username
```

Specify the superuser user name to use when disabling triggers. This is relevant only if --disable-triggers is used. (Usually, it's better to leave this out, and instead start the resulting script as superuser.)

```
-t
--tablespaces-only
```

Dump only tablespaces, no databases or roles.

```
-v
--verbose
```

Specifies verbose mode. This will cause pg_dumpall to output start/stop times to the dump file, and progress messages to standard error. It will also enable verbose output in pg_dump.

```
-V
--version
```

Print the pg_dumpall version and exit.

```
-x
--no-privileges
--no-acl
```

Prevent dumping of access privileges (grant/revoke commands).

```
--binary-upgrade
```

This option is for use by in-place upgrade utilities. Its use for other purposes is not recommended or supported. The behavior of the option may change in future releases without notice.

```
--column-inserts
--attribute-inserts
```

Dump data as INSERT commands with explicit column names (INSERT INTO *table* (*column*, ...) VALUES ...). This will make restoration very slow; it is mainly useful for making dumps that can be loaded into non-PostgreSQL databases.

```
--disable-dollar-quoting
```

This option disables the use of dollar quoting for function bodies, and forces them to be quoted using SQL standard string syntax.

```
--disable-triggers
```

This option is relevant only when creating a data-only dump. It instructs pg_dumpall to include commands to temporarily disable triggers on the target tables while the data is reloaded. Use this if you have referential integrity checks or other triggers on the tables that you do not want to invoke during data reload.

Presently, the commands emitted for --disable-triggers must be done as superuser. So, you should also specify a superuser name with -S, or preferably be careful to start the resulting script as a superuser.

```
--if-exists
```

Use conditional commands (i.e. add an IF EXISTS clause) to clean databases and other objects. This option is not valid unless --clean is also specified.

```
--inserts
```

Dump data as INSERT commands (rather than COPY). This will make restoration very slow; it is mainly useful for making dumps that can be loaded into non-PostgreSQL databases. Note that the restore might fail altogether if you have rearranged column order. The --column-inserts option is safer, though even slower.

```
--lock-wait-timeout=timeout
```

Do not wait forever to acquire shared table locks at the beginning of the dump. Instead, fail if unable to lock a table within the specified *timeout*. The timeout may be specified in any of the formats accepted by SET statement_timeout. Allowed values vary depending on the server version you are dumping from, but an integer number of milliseconds is accepted by all versions since 7.3. This option is ignored when dumping from a pre-7.3 server.

`--no-security-labels`

> Do not dump security labels.

`--no-tablespaces`

> Do not output commands to create tablespaces nor select tablespaces for objects. With this option, all objects will be created in whichever tablespace is the default during restore.

`--no-unlogged-table-data`

> Do not dump the contents of unlogged tables. This option has no effect on whether or not the table definitions (schema) are dumped; it only suppresses dumping the table data.

`--quote-all-identifiers`

> Force quoting of all identifiers. This may be useful when dumping a database for migration to a future version that may have introduced additional keywords.

`--use-set-session-authorization`

> Output SQL-standard `SET SESSION AUTHORIZATION` commands instead of `ALTER OWNER` commands to determine object ownership. This makes the dump more standards compatible, but depending on the history of the objects in the dump, might not restore properly.

`-?`

`--help`

> Show help about pg_dumpall command line arguments, and exit.

The following command-line options control the database connection parameters.

`-d connstr`

`--dbname=connstr`

> Specifies parameters used to connect to the server, as a connection string. See Section 31.1.1 for more information.

> The option is called `--dbname` for consistency with other client applications, but because pg_dumpall needs to connect to many databases, database name in the connection string will be ignored. Use `-l` option to specify the name of the database used to dump global objects and to discover what other databases should be dumped.

`-h host`

`--host=host`

> Specifies the host name of the machine on which the database server is running. If the value begins with a slash, it is used as the directory for the Unix domain socket. The default is taken from the `PGHOST` environment variable, if set, else a Unix domain socket connection is attempted.

`-l dbname`

`--database=dbname`

> Specifies the name of the database to connect to to dump global objects and discover what other databases should be dumped. If not specified, the `postgres` database will be used, and if that does not exist, `template1` will be used.

-p *port*

--port=*port*

> Specifies the TCP port or local Unix domain socket file extension on which the server is listening for connections. Defaults to the PGPORT environment variable, if set, or a compiled-in default.

-U *username*

--username=*username*

> User name to connect as.

-w

--no-password

> Never issue a password prompt. If the server requires password authentication and a password is not available by other means such as a .pgpass file, the connection attempt will fail. This option can be useful in batch jobs and scripts where no user is present to enter a password.

-W

--password

> Force pg_dumpall to prompt for a password before connecting to a database.

> This option is never essential, since pg_dumpall will automatically prompt for a password if the server demands password authentication. However, pg_dumpall will waste a connection attempt finding out that the server wants a password. In some cases it is worth typing -W to avoid the extra connection attempt.

> Note that the password prompt will occur again for each database to be dumped. Usually, it's better to set up a ~/.pgpass file than to rely on manual password entry.

--role=*rolename*

> Specifies a role name to be used to create the dump. This option causes pg_dumpall to issue a SET ROLE *rolename* command after connecting to the database. It is useful when the authenticated user (specified by -U) lacks privileges needed by pg_dumpall, but can switch to a role with the required rights. Some installations have a policy against logging in directly as a superuser, and use of this option allows dumps to be made without violating the policy.

Environment

PGHOST
PGOPTIONS
PGPORT
PGUSER

> Default connection parameters

This utility, like most other PostgreSQL utilities, also uses the environment variables supported by libpq (see Section 31.14).

Notes

Since pg_dumpall calls pg_dump internally, some diagnostic messages will refer to pg_dump.

Once restored, it is wise to run ANALYZE on each database so the optimizer has useful statistics. You can also run `vacuumdb -a -z` to analyze all databases.

pg_dumpall requires all needed tablespace directories to exist before the restore; otherwise, database creation will fail for databases in non-default locations.

Examples

To dump all databases:

```
$ pg_dumpall > db.out
```

To reload database(s) from this file, you can use:

```
$ psql -f db.out postgres
```

(It is not important to which database you connect here since the script file created by pg_dumpall will contain the appropriate commands to create and connect to the saved databases.)

See Also

Check pg_dump for details on possible error conditions.

pg_isready

Name

pg_isready — check the connection status of a PostgreSQL server

Synopsis

pg_isready [*connection-option*...] [*option*...]

Description

pg_isready is a utility for checking the connection status of a PostgreSQL database server. The exit status specifies the result of the connection check.

Options

-d *dbname*
--dbname=*dbname*

> Specifies the name of the database to connect to.
>
> If this parameter contains an = sign or starts with a valid URI prefix (postgresql:// or postgres://), it is treated as a conninfo string. See Section 31.1.1 for more information.

-h *hostname*
--host=*hostname*

> Specifies the host name of the machine on which the server is running. If the value begins with a slash, it is used as the directory for the Unix-domain socket.

-p *port*
--port=*port*

> Specifies the TCP port or the local Unix-domain socket file extension on which the server is listening for connections. Defaults to the value of the PGPORT environment variable or, if not set, to the port specified at compile time, usually 5432.

-q
--quiet

> Do not display status message. This is useful when scripting.

-t *seconds*
--timeout=*seconds*

> The maximum number of seconds to wait when attempting connection before returning that the server is not responding. Setting to 0 disables. The default is 3 seconds.

```
-U username
--username=username
```

Connect to the database as the user *username* instead of the default.

```
-V
--version
```

Print the pg_isready version and exit.

```
-?
--help
```

Show help about pg_isready command line arguments, and exit.

Exit Status

pg_isready returns 0 to the shell if the server is accepting connections normally, 1 if the server is rejecting connections (for example during startup), 2 if there was no response to the connection attempt, and 3 if no attempt was made (for example due to invalid parameters).

Environment

`pg_isready`, like most other PostgreSQL utilities, also uses the environment variables supported by libpq (see Section 31.14).

Notes

It is not necessary to supply correct user name, password, or database name values to obtain the server status; however, if incorrect values are provided, the server will log a failed connection attempt.

Examples

Standard Usage:

```
$ pg_isready
/tmp:5432 - accepting connections
$ echo $?
0
```

Running with connection parameters to a PostgreSQL cluster in startup:

```
$ pg_isready -h localhost -p 5433
localhost:5433 - rejecting connections
$ echo $?
1
```

Running with connection parameters to a non-responsive PostgreSQL cluster:

```
$ pg_isready -h someremotehost
someremotehost:5432 - no response
$ echo $?
2
```

pg_receivexlog

Name

`pg_receivexlog` — stream transaction logs from a PostgreSQL server

Synopsis

`pg_receivexlog [option...]`

Description

pg_receivexlog is used to stream transaction log from a running PostgreSQL cluster. The transaction log is streamed using the streaming replication protocol, and is written to a local directory of files. This directory can be used as the archive location for doing a restore using point-in-time recovery (see Section 24.3).

pg_receivexlog streams the transaction log in real time as it's being generated on the server, and does not wait for segments to complete like archive_command does. For this reason, it is not necessary to set archive_timeout when using pg_receivexlog.

The transaction log is streamed over a regular PostgreSQL connection, and uses the replication protocol. The connection must be made with a superuser or a user having `REPLICATION` permissions (see Section 20.2), and `pg_hba.conf` must explicitly permit the replication connection. The server must also be configured with max_wal_senders set high enough to leave at least one session available for the stream.

If the connection is lost, or if it cannot be initially established, with a non-fatal error, pg_receivexlog will retry the connection indefinitely, and reestablish streaming as soon as possible. To avoid this behavior, use the `-n` parameter.

Options

`-D directory`
`--directory=directory`

Directory to write the output to.

This parameter is required.

`-n`
`--no-loop`

Don't loop on connection errors. Instead, exit right away with an error.

`-s interval`
`--status-interval=interval`

Specifies the number of seconds between status packets sent back to the server. This allows for easier monitoring of the progress from server. A value of zero disables the periodic status updates completely, although an update will still be sent when requested by the server, to avoid timeout disconnect. The default value is 10 seconds.

`-S` *slotname*

`--slot=`*slotname*

> Require pg_receivexlog to use an existing replication slot (see Section 25.2.6). When this option is used, pg_receivexlog will report a flush position to the server, indicating when each segment has been synchronized to disk so that the server can remove that segment if it is not otherwise needed. When using this parameter, it is important to make sure that pg_receivexlog cannot become the synchronous standby through an incautious setting of synchronous_standby_names; it does not flush data frequently enough for this to work correctly.

`-v`

`--verbose`

> Enables verbose mode.

The following command-line options control the database connection parameters.

`-d` *connstr*

`--dbname=`*connstr*

> Specifies parameters used to connect to the server, as a connection string. See Section 31.1.1 for more information.
>
> The option is called `--dbname` for consistency with other client applications, but because pg_receivexlog doesn't connect to any particular database in the cluster, database name in the connection string will be ignored.

`-h` *host*

`--host=`*host*

> Specifies the host name of the machine on which the server is running. If the value begins with a slash, it is used as the directory for the Unix domain socket. The default is taken from the `PGHOST` environment variable, if set, else a Unix domain socket connection is attempted.

`-p` *port*

`--port=`*port*

> Specifies the TCP port or local Unix domain socket file extension on which the server is listening for connections. Defaults to the `PGPORT` environment variable, if set, or a compiled-in default.

`-U` *username*

`--username=`*username*

> User name to connect as.

`-w`

`--no-password`

> Never issue a password prompt. If the server requires password authentication and a password is not available by other means such as a `.pgpass` file, the connection attempt will fail. This option can be useful in batch jobs and scripts where no user is present to enter a password.

```
-W
--password
```

> Force pg_receivexlog to prompt for a password before connecting to a database.
>
> This option is never essential, since pg_receivexlog will automatically prompt for a password if the server demands password authentication. However, pg_receivexlog will waste a connection attempt finding out that the server wants a password. In some cases it is worth typing -W to avoid the extra connection attempt.

Other options are also available:

```
-V
--version
```

> Print the pg_receivexlog version and exit.

```
-?
--help
```

> Show help about pg_receivexlog command line arguments, and exit.

Environment

This utility, like most other PostgreSQL utilities, uses the environment variables supported by libpq (see Section 31.14).

Notes

When using pg_receivexlog instead of archive_command as the main WAL backup method, it is strongly recommended to use replication slots. Otherwise, the server is free to recycle or remove transaction log files before they are backed up, because it does not have any information, either from archive_command or the replication slots, about how far the WAL stream has been archived. Note, however, that a replication slot will fill up the server's disk space if the receiver does not keep up with fetching the WAL data.

Examples

To stream the transaction log from the server at `mydbserver` and store it in the local directory `/usr/local/pgsql/archive`:

```
$ pg_receivexlog -h mydbserver -D /usr/local/pgsql/archive
```

See Also

pg_basebackup

pg_recvlogical

Name

`pg_recvlogical` — control PostgreSQL logical decoding streams

Synopsis

`pg_recvlogical` [`option`...]

Description

`pg_recvlogical` controls logical decoding replication slots and streams data from such replication slots.

It creates a replication-mode connection, so it is subject to the same constraints as pg_receivexlog, plus those for logical replication (see Chapter 46).

Options

At least one of the following options must be specified to select an action:

`--create-slot`

Create a new logical replication slot with the name specified by `--slot`, using the output plugin specified by `--plugin`, for the database specified by `--dbname`.

`--drop-slot`

Drop the replication slot with the name specified by `--slot`, then exit.

`--start`

Begin streaming changes from the logical replication slot specified by `--slot`, continuing until terminated by a signal. If the server side change stream ends with a server shutdown or disconnect, retry in a loop unless `--no-loop` is specified.

The stream format is determined by the output plugin specified when the slot was created.

The connection must be to the same database used to create the slot.

`--create-slot` and `--start` can be specified together. `--drop-slot` cannot be combined with another action.

The following command-line options control the location and format of the output and other replication behavior:

-f *filename*

--file=*filename*

> Write received and decoded transaction data into this file. Use – for stdout.

-F *interval_seconds*

--fsync-interval=*interval_seconds*

> Specifies how often pg_recvlogical should issue fsync() calls to ensure the output file is safely flushed to disk.

> The server will occasionally request the client to perform a flush and report the flush position to the server. This setting is in addition to that, to perform flushes more frequently.

> Specifying an interval of 0 disables issuing fsync() calls altogether, while still reporting progress to the server. In this case, data could be lost in the event of a crash.

-I *lsn*

--startpos=*lsn*

> In --start mode, start replication from the given LSN. For details on the effect of this, see the documentation in Chapter 46 and Section 49.3. Ignored in other modes.

-n

--no-loop

> When the connection to the server is lost, do not retry in a loop, just exit.

-o *name*[=*value*]

--option=*name*[=*value*]

> Pass the option *name* to the output plugin with, if specified, the option value *value*. Which options exist and their effects depends on the used output plugin.

-P *plugin*

--plugin=*plugin*

> When creating a slot, use the specified logical decoding output plugin. See Chapter 46. This option has no effect if the slot already exists.

-s *interval_seconds*

--status-interval=*interval_seconds*

> This option has the same effect as the option of the same name in pg_receivexlog. See the description there.

-S *slot_name*

--slot=*slot_name*

> In --start mode, use the existing logical replication slot named *slot_name*. In --create-slot mode, create the slot with this name. In --drop-slot mode, delete the slot with this name.

-v

--verbose

> Enables verbose mode.

The following command-line options control the database connection parameters.

`-d` *database*
`--dbname=`*database*

> The database to connect to. See the description of the actions for what this means in detail. This can be a libpq connection string; see Section 31.1.1 for more information. Defaults to user name.

`-h` *hostname-or-ip*
`--host=`*hostname-or-ip*

> Specifies the host name of the machine on which the server is running. If the value begins with a slash, it is used as the directory for the Unix domain socket. The default is taken from the `PGHOST` environment variable, if set, else a Unix domain socket connection is attempted.

`-p` *port*
`--port=`*port*

> Specifies the TCP port or local Unix domain socket file extension on which the server is listening for connections. Defaults to the `PGPORT` environment variable, if set, or a compiled-in default.

`-U` *user*
`--username=`*user*

> Username to connect as. Defaults to current operating system user name.

`-w`
`--no-password`

> Never issue a password prompt. If the server requires password authentication and a password is not available by other means such as a `.pgpass` file, the connection attempt will fail. This option can be useful in batch jobs and scripts where no user is present to enter a password.

`-W`
`--password`

> Force pg_recvlogical to prompt for a password before connecting to a database.
>
> This option is never essential, since pg_recvlogical will automatically prompt for a password if the server demands password authentication. However, pg_recvlogical will waste a connection attempt finding out that the server wants a password. In some cases it is worth typing `-W` to avoid the extra connection attempt.

The following additional options are available:

`-V`
`--version`

> Print the pg_recvlogical version and exit.

`-?`
`--help`

> Show help about pg_recvlogical command line arguments, and exit.

Environment

This utility, like most other PostgreSQL utilities, uses the environment variables supported by libpq (see Section 31.14).

Examples

See Section 46.1 for an example.

See Also

pg_receivexlog

pg_restore

Name

pg_restore — restore a PostgreSQL database from an archive file created by pg_dump

Synopsis

pg_restore [*connection-option*...] [*option*...] [*filename*]

Description

pg_restore is a utility for restoring a PostgreSQL database from an archive created by pg_dump in one of the non-plain-text formats. It will issue the commands necessary to reconstruct the database to the state it was in at the time it was saved. The archive files also allow pg_restore to be selective about what is restored, or even to reorder the items prior to being restored. The archive files are designed to be portable across architectures.

pg_restore can operate in two modes. If a database name is specified, pg_restore connects to that database and restores archive contents directly into the database. Otherwise, a script containing the SQL commands necessary to rebuild the database is created and written to a file or standard output. This script output is equivalent to the plain text output format of pg_dump. Some of the options controlling the output are therefore analogous to pg_dump options.

Obviously, pg_restore cannot restore information that is not present in the archive file. For instance, if the archive was made using the "dump data as INSERT commands" option, pg_restore will not be able to load the data using COPY statements.

Options

pg_restore accepts the following command line arguments.

filename

> Specifies the location of the archive file (or directory, for a directory-format archive) to be restored. If not specified, the standard input is used.

-a
--data-only

> Restore only the data, not the schema (data definitions). Table data, large objects, and sequence values are restored, if present in the archive.

> This option is similar to, but for historical reasons not identical to, specifying --section=data.

`-c`
`--clean`

> Clean (drop) database objects before recreating them. (Unless `--if-exists` is used, this might generate some harmless error messages, if any objects were not present in the destination database.)

`-C`
`--create`

> Create the database before restoring into it. If `--clean` is also specified, drop and recreate the target database before connecting to it.

> When this option is used, the database named with `-d` is used only to issue the initial DROP DATABASE and CREATE DATABASE commands. All data is restored into the database name that appears in the archive.

`-d` *dbname*
`--dbname=`*dbname*

> Connect to database *dbname* and restore directly into the database.

`-e`
`--exit-on-error`

> Exit if an error is encountered while sending SQL commands to the database. The default is to continue and to display a count of errors at the end of the restoration.

`-f` *filename*
`--file=`*filename*

> Specify output file for generated script, or for the listing when used with `-l`. Default is the standard output.

`-F` *format*
`--format=`*format*

> Specify format of the archive. It is not necessary to specify the format, since pg_restore will determine the format automatically. If specified, it can be one of the following:

> `c`
> `custom`

> > The archive is in the custom format of pg_dump.

> `d`
> `directory`

> > The archive is a directory archive.

> `t`
> `tar`

> > The archive is a `tar` archive.

`-i`
`--ignore-version`

> A deprecated option that is now ignored.

-I *index*
--index=*index*

> Restore definition of named index only. Multiple indexes may be specified with multiple -I switches.

-j *number-of-jobs*
--jobs=*number-of-jobs*

> Run the most time-consuming parts of pg_restore — those which load data, create indexes, or create constraints — using multiple concurrent jobs. This option can dramatically reduce the time to restore a large database to a server running on a multiprocessor machine.

> Each job is one process or one thread, depending on the operating system, and uses a separate connection to the server.

> The optimal value for this option depends on the hardware setup of the server, of the client, and of the network. Factors include the number of CPU cores and the disk setup. A good place to start is the number of CPU cores on the server, but values larger than that can also lead to faster restore times in many cases. Of course, values that are too high will lead to decreased performance because of thrashing.

> Only the custom and directory archive formats are supported with this option. The input must be a regular file or directory (not, for example, a pipe). This option is ignored when emitting a script rather than connecting directly to a database server. Also, multiple jobs cannot be used together with the option --single-transaction.

-l
--list

> List the contents of the archive. The output of this operation can be used as input to the -L option. Note that if filtering switches such as -n or -t are used with -l, they will restrict the items listed.

-L *list-file*
--use-list=*list-file*

> Restore only those archive elements that are listed in *list-file*, and restore them in the order they appear in the file. Note that if filtering switches such as -n or -t are used with -L, they will further restrict the items restored.

> *list-file* is normally created by editing the output of a previous -l operation. Lines can be moved or removed, and can also be commented out by placing a semicolon (;) at the start of the line. See below for examples.

-n *namespace*
--schema=*schema*

> Restore only objects that are in the named schema. Multiple schemas may be specified with multiple -n switches. This can be combined with the -t option to restore just a specific table.

-O
--no-owner

> Do not output commands to set ownership of objects to match the original database. By default, pg_restore issues ALTER OWNER or SET SESSION AUTHORIZATION statements to set ownership of created schema elements. These statements will fail unless the initial connection to the database is made by a superuser (or the same user that owns all of the objects in the script). With -O, any user name can be used for the initial connection, and this user will own all the created objects.

`-P` *function-name(argtype [, ...])*
`--function=`*function-name(argtype [, ...])*

> Restore the named function only. Be careful to spell the function name and arguments exactly as they appear in the dump file's table of contents. Multiple functions may be specified with multiple `-P` switches.

`-R`
`--no-reconnect`

> This option is obsolete but still accepted for backwards compatibility.

`-s`
`--schema-only`

> Restore only the schema (data definitions), not data, to the extent that schema entries are present in the archive.

> This option is the inverse of `--data-only`. It is similar to, but for historical reasons not identical to, specifying `--section=pre-data --section=post-data`.

> (Do not confuse this with the `--schema` option, which uses the word "schema" in a different meaning.)

`-S` *username*
`--superuser=`*username*

> Specify the superuser user name to use when disabling triggers. This is relevant only if `--disable-triggers` is used.

`-t` *table*
`--table=`*table*

> Restore definition and/or data of named table only. Multiple tables may be specified with multiple `-t` switches. This can be combined with the `-n` option to specify a schema.

`-T` *trigger*
`--trigger=`*trigger*

> Restore named trigger only. Multiple triggers may be specified with multiple `-T` switches.

`-v`
`--verbose`

> Specifies verbose mode.

`-V`
`--version`

> Print the pg_restore version and exit.

`-x`
`--no-privileges`
`--no-acl`

> Prevent restoration of access privileges (grant/revoke commands).

`-1`
`--single-transaction`

Execute the restore as a single transaction (that is, wrap the emitted commands in `BEGIN`/`COMMIT`). This ensures that either all the commands complete successfully, or no changes are applied. This option implies `--exit-on-error`.

`--disable-triggers`

This option is relevant only when performing a data-only restore. It instructs pg_restore to execute commands to temporarily disable triggers on the target tables while the data is reloaded. Use this if you have referential integrity checks or other triggers on the tables that you do not want to invoke during data reload.

Presently, the commands emitted for `--disable-triggers` must be done as superuser. So you should also specify a superuser name with `-S` or, preferably, run pg_restore as a PostgreSQL superuser.

`--if-exists`

Use conditional commands (i.e. add an `IF EXISTS` clause) when cleaning database objects. This option is not valid unless `--clean` is also specified.

`--no-data-for-failed-tables`

By default, table data is restored even if the creation command for the table failed (e.g., because it already exists). With this option, data for such a table is skipped. This behavior is useful if the target database already contains the desired table contents. For example, auxiliary tables for PostgreSQL extensions such as PostGIS might already be loaded in the target database; specifying this option prevents duplicate or obsolete data from being loaded into them.

This option is effective only when restoring directly into a database, not when producing SQL script output.

`--no-security-labels`

Do not output commands to restore security labels, even if the archive contains them.

`--no-tablespaces`

Do not output commands to select tablespaces. With this option, all objects will be created in whichever tablespace is the default during restore.

`--section=`*sectionname*

Only restore the named section. The section name can be `pre-data`, `data`, or `post-data`. This option can be specified more than once to select multiple sections. The default is to restore all sections.

The data section contains actual table data as well as large-object definitions. Post-data items consist of definitions of indexes, triggers, rules and constraints other than validated check constraints. Pre-data items consist of all other data definition items.

`--use-set-session-authorization`

Output SQL-standard `SET SESSION AUTHORIZATION` commands instead of `ALTER OWNER` commands to determine object ownership. This makes the dump more standards-compatible, but depending on the history of the objects in the dump, might not restore properly.

```
-?
--help
```

Show help about pg_restore command line arguments, and exit.

pg_restore also accepts the following command line arguments for connection parameters:

```
-h host
--host=host
```

Specifies the host name of the machine on which the server is running. If the value begins with a slash, it is used as the directory for the Unix domain socket. The default is taken from the PGHOST environment variable, if set, else a Unix domain socket connection is attempted.

```
-p port
--port=port
```

Specifies the TCP port or local Unix domain socket file extension on which the server is listening for connections. Defaults to the PGPORT environment variable, if set, or a compiled-in default.

```
-U username
--username=username
```

User name to connect as.

```
-w
--no-password
```

Never issue a password prompt. If the server requires password authentication and a password is not available by other means such as a .pgpass file, the connection attempt will fail. This option can be useful in batch jobs and scripts where no user is present to enter a password.

```
-W
--password
```

Force pg_restore to prompt for a password before connecting to a database.

This option is never essential, since pg_restore will automatically prompt for a password if the server demands password authentication. However, pg_restore will waste a connection attempt finding out that the server wants a password. In some cases it is worth typing -W to avoid the extra connection attempt.

```
--role=rolename
```

Specifies a role name to be used to perform the restore. This option causes pg_restore to issue a SET ROLE *rolename* command after connecting to the database. It is useful when the authenticated user (specified by -U) lacks privileges needed by pg_restore, but can switch to a role with the required rights. Some installations have a policy against logging in directly as a superuser, and use of this option allows restores to be performed without violating the policy.

Environment

PGHOST
PGOPTIONS
PGPORT
PGUSER

Default connection parameters

This utility, like most other PostgreSQL utilities, also uses the environment variables supported by libpq (see Section 31.14). However, it does not read PGDATABASE when a database name is not supplied.

Diagnostics

When a direct database connection is specified using the -d option, pg_restore internally executes SQL statements. If you have problems running pg_restore, make sure you are able to select information from the database using, for example, psql. Also, any default connection settings and environment variables used by the libpq front-end library will apply.

Notes

If your installation has any local additions to the template1 database, be careful to load the output of pg_restore into a truly empty database; otherwise you are likely to get errors due to duplicate definitions of the added objects. To make an empty database without any local additions, copy from template0 not template1, for example:

```
CREATE DATABASE foo WITH TEMPLATE template0;
```

The limitations of pg_restore are detailed below.

- When restoring data to a pre-existing table and the option --disable-triggers is used, pg_restore emits commands to disable triggers on user tables before inserting the data, then emits commands to re-enable them after the data has been inserted. If the restore is stopped in the middle, the system catalogs might be left in the wrong state.

- pg_restore cannot restore large objects selectively; for instance, only those for a specific table. If an archive contains large objects, then all large objects will be restored, or none of them if they are excluded via -L, -t, or other options.

See also the pg_dump documentation for details on limitations of pg_dump.

Once restored, it is wise to run ANALYZE on each restored table so the optimizer has useful statistics; see Section 23.1.3 and Section 23.1.6 for more information.

Examples

Assume we have dumped a database called mydb into a custom-format dump file:

```
$ pg_dump -Fc mydb > db.dump
```

To drop the database and recreate it from the dump:

```
$ dropdb mydb
$ pg_restore -C -d postgres db.dump
```

The database named in the -d switch can be any database existing in the cluster; pg_restore only uses it to issue the CREATE DATABASE command for mydb. With -C, data is always restored into the database name that appears in the dump file.

To reload the dump into a new database called newdb:

```
$ createdb -T template0 newdb
$ pg_restore -d newdb db.dump
```

Notice we don't use -C, and instead connect directly to the database to be restored into. Also note that we clone the new database from template0 not template1, to ensure it is initially empty.

To reorder database items, it is first necessary to dump the table of contents of the archive:

```
$ pg_restore -l db.dump > db.list
```

The listing file consists of a header and one line for each item, e.g.:

```
;
; Archive created at Mon Sep 14 13:55:39 2009
;     dbname: DBDEMOS
;     TOC Entries: 81
;     Compression: 9
;     Dump Version: 1.10-0
;     Format: CUSTOM
;     Integer: 4 bytes
;     Offset: 8 bytes
;     Dumped from database version: 8.3.5
;     Dumped by pg_dump version: 8.3.8
;
;
; Selected TOC Entries:
;
3; 2615 2200 SCHEMA - public pasha
1861; 0 0 COMMENT - SCHEMA public pasha
1862; 0 0 ACL - public pasha
317; 1247 17715 TYPE public composite pasha
319; 1247 25899 DOMAIN public domain0 pasha
```

Semicolons start a comment, and the numbers at the start of lines refer to the internal archive ID assigned to each item.

Lines in the file can be commented out, deleted, and reordered. For example:

```
10; 145433 TABLE map_resolutions postgres
;2; 145344 TABLE species postgres
;4; 145359 TABLE nt_header postgres
6; 145402 TABLE species_records postgres
;8; 145416 TABLE ss_old postgres
```

could be used as input to pg_restore and would only restore items 10 and 6, in that order:

```
$ pg_restore -L db.list db.dump
```

See Also

pg_dump, pg_dumpall, psql

psql

Name

psql — PostgreSQL interactive terminal

Synopsis

psql [option...] [dbname [username]]

Description

psql is a terminal-based front-end to PostgreSQL. It enables you to type in queries interactively, issue them to PostgreSQL, and see the query results. Alternatively, input can be from a file. In addition, it provides a number of meta-commands and various shell-like features to facilitate writing scripts and automating a wide variety of tasks.

Options

-a
--echo-all

Print all nonempty input lines to standard output as they are read. (This does not apply to lines read interactively.) This is equivalent to setting the variable ECHO to all.

-A
--no-align

Switches to unaligned output mode. (The default output mode is otherwise aligned.)

-c command
--command=command

Specifies that psql is to execute one command string, command, and then exit. This is useful in shell scripts. Start-up files (psqlrc and ~/.psqlrc) are ignored with this option.

command must be either a command string that is completely parsable by the server (i.e., it contains no psql-specific features), or a single backslash command. Thus you cannot mix SQL and psql meta-commands with this option. To achieve that, you could pipe the string into psql, for example: echo '\x \\ SELECT * FROM foo;' | psql. (\\ is the separator meta-command.)

If the command string contains multiple SQL commands, they are processed in a single transaction, unless there are explicit BEGIN/COMMIT commands included in the string to divide it into multiple transactions. This is different from the behavior when the same string is fed to psql's standard input. Also, only the result of the last SQL command is returned.

Because of these legacy behaviors, putting more than one command in the -c string often has un-expected results. It's better to feed multiple commands to psql's standard input, either using echo as illustrated above, or via a shell here-document, for example:

```
psql <<EOF
\x
SELECT * FROM foo;
EOF
```

-d *dbname*

--dbname=*dbname*

>   Specifies the name of the database to connect to. This is equivalent to specifying *dbname* as the first non-option argument on the command line.

>   If this parameter contains an = sign or starts with a valid URI prefix (postgresql:// or postgres://), it is treated as a conninfo string. See Section 31.1.1 for more information.

-e

--echo-queries

>   Copy all SQL commands sent to the server to standard output as well. This is equivalent to setting the variable ECHO to queries.

-E

--echo-hidden

>   Echo the actual queries generated by \d and other backslash commands. You can use this to study psql's internal operations. This is equivalent to setting the variable ECHO_HIDDEN to on.

-f *filename*

--file=*filename*

>   Use the file *filename* as the source of commands instead of reading commands interactively. After the file is processed, psql terminates. This is in many ways equivalent to the meta-command \i.

>   If *filename* is - (hyphen), then standard input is read.

>   Using this option is subtly different from writing psql < *filename*. In general, both will do what you expect, but using -f enables some nice features such as error messages with line numbers. There is also a slight chance that using this option will reduce the start-up overhead. On the other hand, the variant using the shell's input redirection is (in theory) guaranteed to yield exactly the same output you would have received had you entered everything by hand.

-F *separator*

--field-separator=*separator*

>   Use *separator* as the field separator for unaligned output. This is equivalent to \pset fieldsep or \f.

-h *hostname*

--host=*hostname*

>   Specifies the host name of the machine on which the server is running. If the value begins with a slash, it is used as the directory for the Unix-domain socket.

`-H`

`--html`

> Turn on HTML tabular output. This is equivalent to `\pset format html` or the `\H` command.

`-l`

`--list`

> List all available databases, then exit. Other non-connection options are ignored. This is similar to the meta-command `\list`.

`-L` *filename*

`--log-file=`*filename*

> Write all query output into file *filename*, in addition to the normal output destination.

`-n`

`--no-readline`

> Do not use Readline for line editing and do not use the command history. This can be useful to turn off tab expansion when cutting and pasting.

`-o` *filename*

`--output=`*filename*

> Put all query output into file *filename*. This is equivalent to the command `\o`.

`-p` *port*

`--port=`*port*

> Specifies the TCP port or the local Unix-domain socket file extension on which the server is listening for connections. Defaults to the value of the `PGPORT` environment variable or, if not set, to the port specified at compile time, usually 5432.

`-P` *assignment*

`--pset=`*assignment*

> Specifies printing options, in the style of `\pset`. Note that here you have to separate name and value with an equal sign instead of a space. For example, to set the output format to LaTeX, you could write `-P format=latex`.

`-q`

`--quiet`

> Specifies that psql should do its work quietly. By default, it prints welcome messages and various informational output. If this option is used, none of this happens. This is useful with the `-c` option. This is equivalent to setting the variable `QUIET` to `on`.

`-R` *separator*

`--record-separator=`*separator*

> Use *separator* as the record separator for unaligned output. This is equivalent to the `\pset recordsep` command.

`-s`

`--single-step`

> Run in single-step mode. That means the user is prompted before each command is sent to the server, with the option to cancel execution as well. Use this to debug scripts.

```
-S
--single-line
```

Runs in single-line mode where a newline terminates an SQL command, as a semicolon does.

> **Note:** This mode is provided for those who insist on it, but you are not necessarily encouraged to use it. In particular, if you mix SQL and meta-commands on a line the order of execution might not always be clear to the inexperienced user.

```
-t
--tuples-only
```

Turn off printing of column names and result row count footers, etc. This is equivalent to the `\t` command.

```
-T table_options
--table-attr=table_options
```

Specifies options to be placed within the HTML `table` tag. See `\pset` for details.

```
-U username
--username=username
```

Connect to the database as the user *username* instead of the default. (You must have permission to do so, of course.)

```
-v assignment
--set=assignment
--variable=assignment
```

Perform a variable assignment, like the `\set` meta-command. Note that you must separate name and value, if any, by an equal sign on the command line. To unset a variable, leave off the equal sign. To set a variable with an empty value, use the equal sign but leave off the value. These assignments are done during a very early stage of start-up, so variables reserved for internal purposes might get overwritten later.

```
-V
--version
```

Print the psql version and exit.

```
-w
--no-password
```

Never issue a password prompt. If the server requires password authentication and a password is not available by other means such as a `.pgpass` file, the connection attempt will fail. This option can be useful in batch jobs and scripts where no user is present to enter a password.

Note that this option will remain set for the entire session, and so it affects uses of the meta-command `\connect` as well as the initial connection attempt.

```
-W
--password
```

Force psql to prompt for a password before connecting to a database.

This option is never essential, since psql will automatically prompt for a password if the server demands password authentication. However, psql will waste a connection attempt finding out that the server wants a password. In some cases it is worth typing -W to avoid the extra connection attempt.

Note that this option will remain set for the entire session, and so it affects uses of the meta-command \connect as well as the initial connection attempt.

-x

--expanded

Turn on the expanded table formatting mode. This is equivalent to the \x command.

-X,

--no-psqlrc

Do not read the start-up file (neither the system-wide psqlrc file nor the user's ~/.psqlrc file).

-z

--field-separator-zero

Set the field separator for unaligned output to a zero byte.

-0

--record-separator-zero

Set the record separator for unaligned output to a zero byte. This is useful for interfacing, for example, with xargs -0.

-1

--single-transaction

When psql executes a script, adding this option wraps BEGIN/COMMIT around the script to execute it as a single transaction. This ensures that either all the commands complete successfully, or no changes are applied.

If the script itself uses BEGIN, COMMIT, or ROLLBACK, this option will not have the desired effects. Also, if the script contains any command that cannot be executed inside a transaction block, specifying this option will cause that command (and hence the whole transaction) to fail.

-?

--help

Show help about psql command line arguments, and exit.

Exit Status

psql returns 0 to the shell if it finished normally, 1 if a fatal error of its own occurs (e.g. out of memory, file not found), 2 if the connection to the server went bad and the session was not interactive, and 3 if an error occurred in a script and the variable ON_ERROR_STOP was set.

Usage

Connecting to a Database

psql is a regular PostgreSQL client application. In order to connect to a database you need to know the name of your target database, the host name and port number of the server, and what user name you want to connect as. psql can be told about those parameters via command line options, namely -d, -h, -p, and -U respectively. If an argument is found that does not belong to any option it will be interpreted as the database name (or the user name, if the database name is already given). Not all of these options are required; there are useful defaults. If you omit the host name, psql will connect via a Unix-domain socket to a server on the local host, or via TCP/IP to localhost on machines that don't have Unix-domain sockets. The default port number is determined at compile time. Since the database server uses the same default, you will not have to specify the port in most cases. The default user name is your operating-system user name, as is the default database name. Note that you cannot just connect to any database under any user name. Your database administrator should have informed you about your access rights.

When the defaults aren't quite right, you can save yourself some typing by setting the environment variables PGDATABASE, PGHOST, PGPORT and/or PGUSER to appropriate values. (For additional environment variables, see Section 31.14.) It is also convenient to have a ~/.pgpass file to avoid regularly having to type in passwords. See Section 31.15 for more information.

An alternative way to specify connection parameters is in a conninfo string or a URI, which is used instead of a database name. This mechanism give you very wide control over the connection. For example:

```
$ psql "service=myservice sslmode=require"
$ psql postgresql://dbmaster:5433/mydb?sslmode=require
```

This way you can also use LDAP for connection parameter lookup as described in Section 31.17. See Section 31.1.2 for more information on all the available connection options.

If the connection could not be made for any reason (e.g., insufficient privileges, server is not running on the targeted host, etc.), psql will return an error and terminate.

If both standard input and standard output are a terminal, then psql sets the client encoding to "auto", which will detect the appropriate client encoding from the locale settings (LC_CTYPE environment variable on Unix systems). If this doesn't work out as expected, the client encoding can be overridden using the environment variable PGCLIENTENCODING.

Entering SQL Commands

In normal operation, psql provides a prompt with the name of the database to which psql is currently connected, followed by the string =>. For example:

```
$ psql testdb
psql (9.4.4)
Type "help" for help.

testdb=>
```

At the prompt, the user can type in SQL commands. Ordinarily, input lines are sent to the server when a command-terminating semicolon is reached. An end of line does not terminate a command. Thus commands can be spread over several lines for clarity. If the command was sent and executed without error, the results of the command are displayed on the screen.

Whenever a command is executed, psql also polls for asynchronous notification events generated by LISTEN and NOTIFY.

While C-style block comments are passed to the server for processing and removal, SQL-standard comments are removed by psql.

Meta-Commands

Anything you enter in psql that begins with an unquoted backslash is a psql meta-command that is processed by psql itself. These commands make psql more useful for administration or scripting. Meta-commands are often called slash or backslash commands.

The format of a psql command is the backslash, followed immediately by a command verb, then any arguments. The arguments are separated from the command verb and each other by any number of whitespace characters.

To include whitespace in an argument you can quote it with single quotes. To include a single quote in an argument, write two single quotes within single-quoted text. Anything contained in single quotes is furthermore subject to C-like substitutions for \n (new line), \t (tab), \b (backspace), \r (carriage return), \f (form feed), \digits (octal), and \xdigits (hexadecimal). A backslash preceding any other character within single-quoted text quotes that single character, whatever it is.

Within an argument, text that is enclosed in backquotes (`) is taken as a command line that is passed to the shell. The output of the command (with any trailing newline removed) replaces the backquoted text.

If an unquoted colon (:) followed by a psql variable name appears within an argument, it is replaced by the variable's value, as described in *SQL Interpolation*.

Some commands take an SQL identifier (such as a table name) as argument. These arguments follow the syntax rules of SQL: Unquoted letters are forced to lowercase, while double quotes (") protect letters from case conversion and allow incorporation of whitespace into the identifier. Within double quotes, paired double quotes reduce to a single double quote in the resulting name. For example, FOO"BAR"BAZ is interpreted as fooBARbaz, and "A weird"" name" becomes A weird" name.

Parsing for arguments stops at the end of the line, or when another unquoted backslash is found. An unquoted backslash is taken as the beginning of a new meta-command. The special sequence \\ (two backslashes) marks the end of arguments and continues parsing SQL commands, if any. That way SQL and psql commands can be freely mixed on a line. But in any case, the arguments of a meta-command cannot continue beyond the end of the line.

The following meta-commands are defined:

\a

> If the current table output format is unaligned, it is switched to aligned. If it is not unaligned, it is set to unaligned. This command is kept for backwards compatibility. See \pset for a more general solution.

`\c or \connect [ dbname [ username ] [ host ] [ port ] ] | conninfo`

Establishes a new connection to a PostgreSQL server. The connection parameters to use can be specified either using a positional syntax, or using `conninfo` connection strings as detailed in Section 31.1.1.

When using positional parameters, if any of `dbname`, `username`, `host` or `port` are omitted or specified as -, the value of that parameter from the previous connection is used; if there is no previous connection, the libpq default for the parameter's value is used. When using `conninfo` strings, no values from the previous connection are used for the new connection.

If the new connection is successfully made, the previous connection is closed. If the connection attempt failed (wrong user name, access denied, etc.), the previous connection will only be kept if psql is in interactive mode. When executing a non-interactive script, processing will immediately stop with an error. This distinction was chosen as a user convenience against typos on the one hand, and a safety mechanism that scripts are not accidentally acting on the wrong database on the other hand.

Examples:

```
=> \c mydb myuser host.dom 6432
=> \c service=foo
=> \c "host=localhost port=5432 dbname=mydb connect_timeout=10 sslmode=disa
=> \c postgresql://tom@localhost/mydb?application_name=myapp
```

`\C [ title ]`

Sets the title of any tables being printed as the result of a query or unset any such title. This command is equivalent to `\pset title title`. (The name of this command derives from "caption", as it was previously only used to set the caption in an HTML table.)

`\cd [ directory ]`

Changes the current working directory to `directory`. Without argument, changes to the current user's home directory.

> **Tip:** To print your current working directory, use `\!` `pwd`.

`\conninfo`

Outputs information about the current database connection.

`\copy { table [ ( column_list ) ] | ( query ) } { from | to } { 'filename' | program 'command' | stdin | stdout | pstdin | pstdout } [ [ with ] ( option [, ...] ) ]`

Performs a frontend (client) copy. This is an operation that runs an SQL COPY command, but instead of the server reading or writing the specified file, psql reads or writes the file and routes the data between the server and the local file system. This means that file accessibility and privileges are those of the local user, not the server, and no SQL superuser privileges are required.

When `program` is specified, `command` is executed by psql and the data passed from or to `command` is routed between the server and the client. Again, the execution privileges are those of the local user, not the server, and no SQL superuser privileges are required.

For \copy ... from stdin, data rows are read from the same source that issued the command, continuing until \. is read or the stream reaches EOF. This option is useful for populating tables in-line within a SQL script file. For \copy ... to stdout, output is sent to the same place as psql command output, and the COPY *count* command status is not printed (since it might be confused with a data row). To read/write psql's standard input or output regardless of the current command source or \o option, write from pstdin or to pstdout.

The syntax of this command is similar to that of the SQL COPY command. All options other than the data source/destination are as specified for COPY. Because of this, special parsing rules apply to the \copy command. In particular, psql's variable substitution rules and backslash escapes do not apply.

> **Tip:** This operation is not as efficient as the SQL COPY command because all data must pass through the client/server connection. For large amounts of data the SQL command might be preferable.

\copyright

Shows the copyright and distribution terms of PostgreSQL.

\d[S+] [*pattern*]

For each relation (table, view, index, sequence, or foreign table) or composite type matching the *pattern*, show all columns, their types, the tablespace (if not the default) and any special attributes such as NOT NULL or defaults. Associated indexes, constraints, rules, and triggers are also shown. For foreign tables, the associated foreign server is shown as well. ("Matching the pattern" is defined in *Patterns* below.)

For some types of relation, \d shows additional information for each column: column values for sequences, indexed expression for indexes and foreign data wrapper options for foreign tables.

The command form \d+ is identical, except that more information is displayed: any comments associated with the columns of the table are shown, as is the presence of OIDs in the table, the view definition if the relation is a view, a non-default replica identity setting.

By default, only user-created objects are shown; supply a pattern or the S modifier to include system objects.

> **Note:** If \d is used without a *pattern* argument, it is equivalent to \dtvsE which will show a list of all visible tables, views, sequences and foreign tables. This is purely a convenience measure.

\da[S] [*pattern*]

Lists aggregate functions, together with their return type and the data types they operate on. If *pattern* is specified, only aggregates whose names match the pattern are shown. By default, only user-created objects are shown; supply a pattern or the S modifier to include system objects.

\db[+] [*pattern*]

Lists tablespaces. If *pattern* is specified, only tablespaces whose names match the pattern are shown. If + is appended to the command name, each object is listed with its associated permissions.

`\dc[S+]` [*pattern*]

> Lists conversions between character-set encodings. If *pattern* is specified, only conversions whose names match the pattern are listed. By default, only user-created objects are shown; supply a pattern or the S modifier to include system objects. If + is appended to the command name, each object is listed with its associated description.

`\dC[+]` [*pattern*]

> Lists type casts. If *pattern* is specified, only casts whose source or target types match the pattern are listed. If + is appended to the command name, each object is listed with its associated description.

`\dd[S]` [*pattern*]

> Shows the descriptions of objects of type `constraint`, `operator class`, `operator family`, `rule`, and `trigger`. All other comments may be viewed by the respective backslash commands for those object types.

> `\dd` displays descriptions for objects matching the *pattern*, or of visible objects of the appropriate type if no argument is given. But in either case, only objects that have a description are listed. By default, only user-created objects are shown; supply a pattern or the S modifier to include system objects.

> Descriptions for objects can be created with the COMMENT SQL command.

`\ddp` [*pattern*]

> Lists default access privilege settings. An entry is shown for each role (and schema, if applicable) for which the default privilege settings have been changed from the built-in defaults. If *pattern* is specified, only entries whose role name or schema name matches the pattern are listed.

> The ALTER DEFAULT PRIVILEGES command is used to set default access privileges. The meaning of the privilege display is explained under GRANT.

`\dD[S+]` [*pattern*]

> Lists domains. If *pattern* is specified, only domains whose names match the pattern are shown. By default, only user-created objects are shown; supply a pattern or the S modifier to include system objects. If + is appended to the command name, each object is listed with its associated permissions and description.

`\dE[S+]` [*pattern*]
`\di[S+]` [*pattern*]
`\dm[S+]` [*pattern*]
`\ds[S+]` [*pattern*]
`\dt[S+]` [*pattern*]
`\dv[S+]` [*pattern*]

> In this group of commands, the letters E, i, m, s, t, and v stand for foreign table, index, materialized view, sequence, table, and view, respectively. You can specify any or all of these letters, in any order, to obtain a listing of objects of these types. For example, `\dit` lists indexes and tables. If + is appended to the command name, each object is listed with its physical size on disk and its associated description, if any. If *pattern* is specified, only objects whose names match the pattern are listed. By default, only user-created objects are shown; supply a pattern or the S modifier to include system objects.

`\des[+]` `[ pattern ]`

> Lists foreign servers (mnemonic: "external servers"). If `pattern` is specified, only those servers whose name matches the pattern are listed. If the form `\des+` is used, a full description of each server is shown, including the server's ACL, type, version, options, and description.

`\det[+]` `[ pattern ]`

> Lists foreign tables (mnemonic: "external tables"). If `pattern` is specified, only entries whose table name or schema name matches the pattern are listed. If the form `\det+` is used, generic options and the foreign table description are also displayed.

`\deu[+]` `[ pattern ]`

> Lists user mappings (mnemonic: "external users"). If `pattern` is specified, only those mappings whose user names match the pattern are listed. If the form `\deu+` is used, additional information about each mapping is shown.

>
> ## Caution
> `\deu+` might also display the user name and password of the remote user, so care should be taken not to disclose them.
>

`\dew[+]` `[ pattern ]`

> Lists foreign-data wrappers (mnemonic: "external wrappers"). If `pattern` is specified, only those foreign-data wrappers whose name matches the pattern are listed. If the form `\dew+` is used, the ACL, options, and description of the foreign-data wrapper are also shown.

`\df[antwS+]` `[ pattern ]`

> Lists functions, together with their arguments, return types, and function types, which are classified as "agg" (aggregate), "normal", "trigger", or "window". To display only functions of specific type(s), add the corresponding letters a, n, t, or w to the command. If `pattern` is specified, only functions whose names match the pattern are shown. By default, only user-created objects are shown; supply a pattern or the S modifier to include system objects. If the form `\df+` is used, additional information about each function is shown, including security classification, volatility, owner, language, source code and description.

> > **Tip:** To look up functions taking arguments or returning values of a specific type, use your pager's search capability to scroll through the `\df` output.

`\dF[+]` `[ pattern ]`

> Lists text search configurations. If `pattern` is specified, only configurations whose names match the pattern are shown. If the form `\dF+` is used, a full description of each configuration is shown, including the underlying text search parser and the dictionary list for each parser token type.

`\dFd[+]` `[ pattern ]`

> Lists text search dictionaries. If `pattern` is specified, only dictionaries whose names match the pattern are shown. If the form `\dFd+` is used, additional information is shown about each selected dictionary, including the underlying text search template and the option values.

`\dFp[+] [ pattern ]`

Lists text search parsers. If `pattern` is specified, only parsers whose names match the pattern are shown. If the form `\dFp+` is used, a full description of each parser is shown, including the underlying functions and the list of recognized token types.

`\dFt[+] [ pattern ]`

Lists text search templates. If `pattern` is specified, only templates whose names match the pattern are shown. If the form `\dFt+` is used, additional information is shown about each template, including the underlying function names.

`\dg[+] [ pattern ]`

Lists database roles. (Since the concepts of "users" and "groups" have been unified into "roles", this command is now equivalent to `\du`.) If `pattern` is specified, only those roles whose names match the pattern are listed. If the form `\dg+` is used, additional information is shown about each role; currently this adds the comment for each role.

`\dl`

This is an alias for `\lo_list`, which shows a list of large objects.

`\dL[S+] [ pattern ]`

Lists procedural languages. If `pattern` is specified, only languages whose names match the pattern are listed. By default, only user-created languages are shown; supply the S modifier to include system objects. If + is appended to the command name, each language is listed with its call handler, validator, access privileges, and whether it is a system object.

`\dn[S+] [ pattern ]`

Lists schemas (namespaces). If `pattern` is specified, only schemas whose names match the pattern are listed. By default, only user-created objects are shown; supply a pattern or the S modifier to include system objects. If + is appended to the command name, each object is listed with its associated permissions and description, if any.

`\do[S+] [ pattern ]`

Lists operators with their operand and result types. If `pattern` is specified, only operators whose names match the pattern are listed. By default, only user-created objects are shown; supply a pattern or the S modifier to include system objects. If + is appended to the command name, additional information about each operator is shown, currently just the name of the underlying function.

`\dO[S+] [ pattern ]`

Lists collations. If `pattern` is specified, only collations whose names match the pattern are listed. By default, only user-created objects are shown; supply a pattern or the S modifier to include system objects. If + is appended to the command name, each collation is listed with its associated description, if any. Note that only collations usable with the current database's encoding are shown, so the results may vary in different databases of the same installation.

`\dp [ pattern ]`

Lists tables, views and sequences with their associated access privileges. If `pattern` is specified, only tables, views and sequences whose names match the pattern are listed.

The GRANT and REVOKE commands are used to set access privileges. The meaning of the privilege display is explained under GRANT.

`\drds [ `*`role-pattern`*` [ `*`database-pattern`*` ] ]`

> Lists defined configuration settings. These settings can be role-specific, database-specific, or both. *role-pattern* and *database-pattern* are used to select specific roles and databases to list, respectively. If omitted, or if * is specified, all settings are listed, including those not role-specific or database-specific, respectively.
>
> The ALTER ROLE and ALTER DATABASE commands are used to define per-role and per-database configuration settings.

`\dT[S+] [ `*`pattern`*` ]`

> Lists data types. If *pattern* is specified, only types whose names match the pattern are listed. If + is appended to the command name, each type is listed with its internal name and size, its allowed values if it is an `enum` type, and its associated permissions. By default, only user-created objects are shown; supply a pattern or the `S` modifier to include system objects.

`\du[+] [ `*`pattern`*` ]`

> Lists database roles. (Since the concepts of "users" and "groups" have been unified into "roles", this command is now equivalent to `\dg`.) If *pattern* is specified, only those roles whose names match the pattern are listed. If the form `\du+` is used, additional information is shown about each role; currently this adds the comment for each role.

`\dx[+] [ `*`pattern`*` ]`

> Lists installed extensions. If *pattern* is specified, only those extensions whose names match the pattern are listed. If the form `\dx+` is used, all the objects belonging to each matching extension are listed.

`\dy[+] [ `*`pattern`*` ]`

> Lists event triggers. If *pattern* is specified, only those event triggers whose names match the pattern are listed. If + is appended to the command name, each object is listed with its associated description.

`\e` or `\edit [ `*`filename`*` ] [ `*`line_number`*` ]`

> If *filename* is specified, the file is edited; after the editor exits, its content is copied back to the query buffer. If no *filename* is given, the current query buffer is copied to a temporary file which is then edited in the same fashion.
>
> The new query buffer is then re-parsed according to the normal rules of psql, where the whole buffer is treated as a single line. (Thus you cannot make scripts this way. Use `\i` for that.) This means that if the query ends with (or contains) a semicolon, it is immediately executed. Otherwise it will merely wait in the query buffer; type semicolon or `\g` to send it, or `\r` to cancel.
>
> If a line number is specified, psql will position the cursor on the specified line of the file or query buffer. Note that if a single all-digits argument is given, psql assumes it is a line number, not a file name.

> **Tip:** See under *Environment* for how to configure and customize your editor.

`\echo` *text* `[ ... ]`

>Prints the arguments to the standard output, separated by one space and followed by a newline. This can be useful to intersperse information in the output of scripts. For example:
>
>`=>` **`\echo ‘date‘`**
>`Tue Oct 26 21:40:57 CEST 1999`
>If the first argument is an unquoted `-n` the trailing newline is not written.
>
>>**Tip:** If you use the `\o` command to redirect your query output you might wish to use `\qecho` instead of this command.

`\ef` `[` *function_description* `[` *line_number* `] ]`

>This command fetches and edits the definition of the named function, in the form of a CREATE OR REPLACE FUNCTION command. Editing is done in the same way as for `\edit`. After the editor exits, the updated command waits in the query buffer; type semicolon or `\g` to send it, or `\r` to cancel.
>
>The target function can be specified by name alone, or by name and arguments, for example `foo(integer, text)`. The argument types must be given if there is more than one function of the same name.
>
>If no function is specified, a blank CREATE FUNCTION template is presented for editing.
>
>If a line number is specified, psql will position the cursor on the specified line of the function body. (Note that the function body typically does not begin on the first line of the file.)
>
>>**Tip:** See under *Environment* for how to configure and customize your editor.

`\encoding` `[` *encoding* `]`

>Sets the client character set encoding. Without an argument, this command shows the current encoding.

`\f` `[` *string* `]`

>Sets the field separator for unaligned query output. The default is the vertical bar (|). See also `\pset` for a generic way of setting output options.

`\g` `[` *filename* `]`
`\g` `[` *|command* `]`

>Sends the current query input buffer to the server, and optionally stores the query's output in *filename* or pipes the output to the shell command *command*. The file or command is written to only if the query successfully returns zero or more tuples, not if the query fails or is a non-data-returning SQL command.
>
>A bare `\g` is essentially equivalent to a semicolon. A `\g` with argument is a "one-shot" alternative to the `\o` command.

`\gset [ prefix ]`

Sends the current query input buffer to the server and stores the query's output into psql variables (see *Variables*). The query to be executed must return exactly one row. Each column of the row is stored into a separate variable, named the same as the column. For example:

```
=> SELECT 'hello' AS var1, 10 AS var2
-> \gset
=> \echo :var1 :var2
hello 10
```

If you specify a *prefix*, that string is prepended to the query's column names to create the variable names to use:

```
=> SELECT 'hello' AS var1, 10 AS var2
-> \gset result_
=> \echo :result_var1 :result_var2
hello 10
```

If a column result is NULL, the corresponding variable is unset rather than being set.

If the query fails or does not return one row, no variables are changed.

`\h` or `\help [ command ]`

Gives syntax help on the specified SQL command. If *command* is not specified, then psql will list all the commands for which syntax help is available. If *command* is an asterisk (*), then syntax help on all SQL commands is shown.

> **Note:** To simplify typing, commands that consists of several words do not have to be quoted. Thus it is fine to type `\help alter table`.

`\H` or `\html`

Turns on HTML query output format. If the HTML format is already on, it is switched back to the default aligned text format. This command is for compatibility and convenience, but see `\pset` about setting other output options.

`\i` or `\include` *filename*

Reads input from the file *filename* and executes it as though it had been typed on the keyboard.

> **Note:** If you want to see the lines on the screen as they are read you must set the variable ECHO to `all`.

`\ir` or `\include_relative` *filename*

The `\ir` command is similar to `\i`, but resolves relative file names differently. When executing in interactive mode, the two commands behave identically. However, when invoked from a script, `\ir` interprets file names relative to the directory in which the script is located, rather than the current working directory.

\l[+] or \list[+] [*pattern*]

List the databases in the server and show their names, owners, character set encodings, and access privileges. If *pattern* is specified, only databases whose names match the pattern are listed. If + is appended to the command name, database sizes, default tablespaces, and descriptions are also displayed. (Size information is only available for databases that the current user can connect to.)

\lo_export *loid filename*

Reads the large object with OID *loid* from the database and writes it to *filename*. Note that this is subtly different from the server function lo_export, which acts with the permissions of the user that the database server runs as and on the server's file system.

Tip: Use \lo_list to find out the large object's OID.

\lo_import *filename* [*comment*]

Stores the file into a PostgreSQL large object. Optionally, it associates the given comment with the object. Example:

```
foo=> \lo_import '/home/peter/pictures/photo.xcf' 'a picture of me'
lo_import 152801
```
The response indicates that the large object received object ID 152801, which can be used to access the newly-created large object in the future. For the sake of readability, it is recommended to always associate a human-readable comment with every object. Both OIDs and comments can be viewed with the \lo_list command.

Note that this command is subtly different from the server-side lo_import because it acts as the local user on the local file system, rather than the server's user and file system.

\lo_list

Shows a list of all PostgreSQL large objects currently stored in the database, along with any comments provided for them.

\lo_unlink *loid*

Deletes the large object with OID *loid* from the database.

Tip: Use \lo_list to find out the large object's OID.

\o or \out [*filename*]
\o or \out [|*command*]

Arranges to save future query results to the file *filename* or pipe future results to the shell command *command*. If no argument is specified, the query output is reset to the standard output.

"Query results" includes all tables, command responses, and notices obtained from the database server, as well as output of various backslash commands that query the database (such as \d), but not error messages.

Tip: To intersperse text output in between query results, use \qecho.

\p or \print

> Print the current query buffer to the standard output.

\password [*username*]

> Changes the password of the specified user (by default, the current user). This command prompts for the new password, encrypts it, and sends it to the server as an ALTER ROLE command. This makes sure that the new password does not appear in cleartext in the command history, the server log, or elsewhere.

\prompt [*text*] *name*

> Prompts the user to supply text, which is assigned to the variable *name*. An optional prompt string, *text*, can be specified. (For multiword prompts, surround the text with single quotes.)
>
> By default, \prompt uses the terminal for input and output. However, if the -f command line switch was used, \prompt uses standard input and standard output.

\pset [*option* [*value*]]

> This command sets options affecting the output of query result tables. *option* indicates which option is to be set. The semantics of *value* vary depending on the selected option. For some options, omitting *value* causes the option to be toggled or unset, as described under the particular option. If no such behavior is mentioned, then omitting *value* just results in the current setting being displayed.
>
> \pset without any arguments displays the current status of all printing options.
>
> Adjustable printing options are:

> border
>
> > The *value* must be a number. In general, the higher the number the more borders and lines the tables will have, but this depends on the particular format. In HTML format, this will translate directly into the border=... attribute; in the other formats only values 0 (no border), 1 (internal dividing lines), and 2 (table frame) make sense. latex and latex-longtable also support a border value of 3 which adds a dividing line between each row.

> columns
>
> > Sets the target width for the wrapped format, and also the width limit for determining whether output is wide enough to require the pager or switch to the vertical display in expanded auto mode. Zero (the default) causes the target width to be controlled by the environment variable COLUMNS, or the detected screen width if COLUMNS is not set. In addition, if columns is zero then the wrapped format only affects screen output. If columns is nonzero then file and pipe output is wrapped to that width as well.

> expanded (or x)
>
> > If *value* is specified it must be either on or off, which will enable or disable expanded mode, or auto. If *value* is omitted the command toggles between the on and off settings. When expanded mode is enabled, query results are displayed in two columns, with the column name on the left and the data on the right. This mode is useful if the data wouldn't fit on the screen in the normal "horizontal" mode. In the auto setting, the expanded mode is used whenever the query output is wider than the screen, otherwise the regular mode is used. The auto setting is

only effective in the aligned and wrapped formats. In other formats, it always behaves as if the expanded mode is off.

fieldsep

Specifies the field separator to be used in unaligned output format. That way one can create, for example, tab- or comma-separated output, which other programs might prefer. To set a tab as field separator, type `\pset fieldsep '\t'`. The default field separator is `'|'` (a vertical bar).

fieldsep_zero

Sets the field separator to use in unaligned output format to a zero byte.

footer

If `value` is specified it must be either `on` or `off` which will enable or disable display of the table footer (the (`n rows`) count). If `value` is omitted the command toggles footer display on or off.

format

Sets the output format to one of `unaligned`, `aligned`, `wrapped`, `html`, `latex` (uses `tabular`), `latex-longtable`, or `troff-ms`. Unique abbreviations are allowed. (That would mean one letter is enough.)

`unaligned` format writes all columns of a row on one line, separated by the currently active field separator. This is useful for creating output that might be intended to be read in by other programs (for example, tab-separated or comma-separated format).

`aligned` format is the standard, human-readable, nicely formatted text output; this is the default.

`wrapped` format is like `aligned` but wraps wide data values across lines to make the output fit in the target column width. The target width is determined as described under the `columns` option. Note that psql will not attempt to wrap column header titles; therefore, `wrapped` format behaves the same as `aligned` if the total width needed for column headers exceeds the target.

The `html`, `latex`, `latex-longtable`, and `troff-ms` formats put out tables that are intended to be included in documents using the respective mark-up language. They are not complete documents! This might not be necessary in HTML, but in LaTeX you must have a complete document wrapper. `latex-longtable` also requires the LaTeX `longtable` and `booktabs` packages.

linestyle

Sets the border line drawing style to one of `ascii`, `old-ascii` or `unicode`. Unique abbreviations are allowed. (That would mean one letter is enough.) The default setting is `ascii`. This option only affects the `aligned` and `wrapped` output formats.

`ascii` style uses plain ASCII characters. Newlines in data are shown using a + symbol in the right-hand margin. When the `wrapped` format wraps data from one line to the next without a newline character, a dot (.) is shown in the right-hand margin of the first line, and again in the left-hand margin of the following line.

`old-ascii` style uses plain ASCII characters, using the formatting style used in PostgreSQL 8.4 and earlier. Newlines in data are shown using a : symbol in place of the left-hand column separator. When the data is wrapped from one line to the next without a newline character, a `;` symbol is used in place of the left-hand column separator.

`unicode` style uses Unicode box-drawing characters. Newlines in data are shown using a carriage return symbol in the right-hand margin. When the data is wrapped from one line to the next without a newline character, an ellipsis symbol is shown in the right-hand margin of the first line, and again in the left-hand margin of the following line.

When the `border` setting is greater than zero, this option also determines the characters with which the border lines are drawn. Plain ASCII characters work everywhere, but Unicode characters look nicer on displays that recognize them.

null

Sets the string to be printed in place of a null value. The default is to print nothing, which can easily be mistaken for an empty string. For example, one might prefer `\pset null '(null)'`.

numericlocale

If `value` is specified it must be either `on` or `off` which will enable or disable display of a locale-specific character to separate groups of digits to the left of the decimal marker. If `value` is omitted the command toggles between regular and locale-specific numeric output.

pager

Controls use of a pager program for query and psql help output. If the environment variable `PAGER` is set, the output is piped to the specified program. Otherwise a platform-dependent default (such as `more`) is used.

When the `pager` option is `off`, the pager program is not used. When the `pager` option is `on`, the pager is used when appropriate, i.e., when the output is to a terminal and will not fit on the screen. The `pager` option can also be set to `always`, which causes the pager to be used for all terminal output regardless of whether it fits on the screen. `\pset pager` without a `value` toggles pager use on and off.

recordsep

Specifies the record (line) separator to use in unaligned output format. The default is a newline character.

recordsep_zero

Sets the record separator to use in unaligned output format to a zero byte.

tableattr (or T)

In HTML format, this specifies attributes to be placed inside the `table` tag. This could for example be `cellpadding` or `bgcolor`. Note that you probably don't want to specify `border` here, as that is already taken care of by `\pset border`. If no `value` is given, the table attributes are unset.

In `latex-longtable` format, this controls the proportional width of each column containing a left-aligned data type. It is specified as a whitespace-separated list of values, e.g. `'0.2 0.2 0.6'`. Unspecified output columns use the last specified value.

title

Sets the table title for any subsequently printed tables. This can be used to give your output descriptive tags. If no `value` is given, the title is unset.

tuples_only (or t)

> If *value* is specified it must be either on or off which will enable or disable tuples-only mode. If *value* is omitted the command toggles between regular and tuples-only output. Regular output includes extra information such as column headers, titles, and various footers. In tuples-only mode, only actual table data is shown.

Illustrations of how these different formats look can be seen in the *Examples* section.

> **Tip:** There are various shortcut commands for \pset. See \a, \C, \H, \t, \T, and \x.

\q or \quit

> Quits the psql program. In a script file, only execution of that script is terminated.

\qecho *text* [...]

> This command is identical to \echo except that the output will be written to the query output channel, as set by \o.

\r or \reset

> Resets (clears) the query buffer.

\s [*filename*]

> Print psql's command line history to *filename*. If *filename* is omitted, the history is written to the standard output (using the pager if appropriate). This command is not available if psql was built without Readline support.

\set [*name* [*value* [...]]]

> Sets the psql variable *name* to *value*, or if more than one value is given, to the concatenation of all of them. If only one argument is given, the variable is set with an empty value. To unset a variable, use the \unset command.
>
> \set without any arguments displays the names and values of all currently-set psql variables.
>
> Valid variable names can contain letters, digits, and underscores. See the section *Variables* below for details. Variable names are case-sensitive.
>
> Although you are welcome to set any variable to anything you want, psql treats several variables as special. They are documented in the section about variables.
>
> **Note:** This command is unrelated to the SQL command SET.

\setenv *name* [*value*]

> Sets the environment variable *name* to *value*, or if the *value* is not supplied, unsets the environment variable. Example:
>
> ```
> testdb=> \setenv PAGER less
> testdb=> \setenv LESS -imx4F
> ```

\sf[+] *function_description*

> This command fetches and shows the definition of the named function, in the form of a CREATE OR REPLACE FUNCTION command. The definition is printed to the current query output channel, as set by \o.
>
> The target function can be specified by name alone, or by name and arguments, for example foo(integer, text). The argument types must be given if there is more than one function of the same name.
>
> If + is appended to the command name, then the output lines are numbered, with the first line of the function body being line 1.

\t

> Toggles the display of output column name headings and row count footer. This command is equivalent to \pset tuples_only and is provided for convenience.

\T *table_options*

> Specifies attributes to be placed within the table tag in HTML output format. This command is equivalent to \pset tableattr *table_options*.

\timing [*on* | *off*]

> Without parameter, toggles a display of how long each SQL statement takes, in milliseconds. With parameter, sets same.

\unset *name*

> Unsets (deletes) the psql variable *name*.

\w or \write *filename*
\w or \write |*command*

> Outputs the current query buffer to the file *filename* or pipes it to the shell command *command*.

\watch [*seconds*]

> Repeatedly execute the current query buffer (like \g) until interrupted or the query fails. Wait the specified number of seconds (default 2) between executions.

\x [*on* | *off* | *auto*]

> Sets or toggles expanded table formatting mode. As such it is equivalent to \pset expanded.

\z [*pattern*]

> Lists tables, views and sequences with their associated access privileges. If a *pattern* is specified, only tables, views and sequences whose names match the pattern are listed.
>
> This is an alias for \dp ("display privileges").

\! [*command*]

> Escapes to a separate shell or executes the shell command *command*. The arguments are not further interpreted; the shell will see them as-is. In particular, the variable substitution rules and backslash escapes do not apply.

\?

> Shows help information about the backslash commands.

Patterns

The various \d commands accept a *pattern* parameter to specify the object name(s) to be displayed. In the simplest case, a pattern is just the exact name of the object. The characters within a pattern are normally folded to lower case, just as in SQL names; for example, \dt FOO will display the table named foo. As in SQL names, placing double quotes around a pattern stops folding to lower case. Should you need to include an actual double quote character in a pattern, write it as a pair of double quotes within a double-quote sequence; again this is in accord with the rules for SQL quoted identifiers. For example, \dt "FOO""BAR" will display the table named FOO"BAR (not foo"bar). Unlike the normal rules for SQL names, you can put double quotes around just part of a pattern, for instance \dt FOO"FOO"BAR will display the table named fooFOObar.

Whenever the *pattern* parameter is omitted completely, the \d commands display all objects that are visible in the current schema search path — this is equivalent to using * as the pattern. (An object is said to be *visible* if its containing schema is in the search path and no object of the same kind and name appears earlier in the search path. This is equivalent to the statement that the object can be referenced by name without explicit schema qualification.) To see all objects in the database regardless of visibility, use *.* as the pattern.

Within a pattern, * matches any sequence of characters (including no characters) and ? matches any single character. (This notation is comparable to Unix shell file name patterns.) For example, \dt int* displays tables whose names begin with int. But within double quotes, * and ? lose these special meanings and are just matched literally.

A pattern that contains a dot (.) is interpreted as a schema name pattern followed by an object name pattern. For example, \dt foo*.*bar* displays all tables whose table name includes bar that are in schemas whose schema name starts with foo. When no dot appears, then the pattern matches only objects that are visible in the current schema search path. Again, a dot within double quotes loses its special meaning and is matched literally.

Advanced users can use regular-expression notations such as character classes, for example [0-9] to match any digit. All regular expression special characters work as specified in Section 9.7.3, except for . which is taken as a separator as mentioned above, * which is translated to the regular-expression notation .*, ? which is translated to ., and $ which is matched literally. You can emulate these pattern characters at need by writing ? for ., (R+|) for R*, or (R|) for R?. $ is not needed as a regular-expression character since the pattern must match the whole name, unlike the usual interpretation of regular expressions (in other words, $ is automatically appended to your pattern). Write * at the beginning and/or end if you don't wish the pattern to be anchored. Note that within double quotes, all regular expression special characters lose their special meanings and are matched literally. Also, the regular expression special characters are matched literally in operator name patterns (i.e., the argument of \do).

Advanced Features

Variables

psql provides variable substitution features similar to common Unix command shells. Variables are simply name/value pairs, where the value can be any string of any length. The name must consist of letters (including non-Latin letters), digits, and underscores.

To set a variable, use the psql meta-command \set. For example,

```
testdb=> \set foo bar
```

sets the variable foo to the value bar. To retrieve the content of the variable, precede the name with a colon, for example:

```
testdb=> \echo :foo
bar
```

This works in both regular SQL commands and meta-commands; there is more detail in *SQL Interpolation*, below.

If you call \set without a second argument, the variable is set, with an empty string as value. To unset (i.e., delete) a variable, use the command \unset. To show the values of all variables, call \set without any argument.

> **Note:** The arguments of \set are subject to the same substitution rules as with other commands. Thus you can construct interesting references such as \set :foo 'something' and get "soft links" or "variable variables" of Perl or PHP fame, respectively. Unfortunately (or fortunately?), there is no way to do anything useful with these constructs. On the other hand, \set bar :foo is a perfectly valid way to copy a variable.

A number of these variables are treated specially by psql. They represent certain option settings that can be changed at run time by altering the value of the variable, or in some cases represent changeable state of psql. Although you can use these variables for other purposes, this is not recommended, as the program behavior might grow really strange really quickly. By convention, all specially treated variables' names consist of all upper-case ASCII letters (and possibly digits and underscores). To ensure maximum compatibility in the future, avoid using such variable names for your own purposes. A list of all specially treated variables follows.

AUTOCOMMIT

> When on (the default), each SQL command is automatically committed upon successful completion. To postpone commit in this mode, you must enter a BEGIN or START TRANSACTION SQL command. When off or unset, SQL commands are not committed until you explicitly issue COMMIT or END. The autocommit-off mode works by issuing an implicit BEGIN for you, just before any command that is not already in a transaction block and is not itself a BEGIN or other transaction-control command, nor a command that cannot be executed inside a transaction block (such as VACUUM).

> > **Note:** In autocommit-off mode, you must explicitly abandon any failed transaction by entering ABORT or ROLLBACK. Also keep in mind that if you exit the session without committing, your work will be lost.

> > **Note:** The autocommit-on mode is PostgreSQL's traditional behavior, but autocommit-off is closer to the SQL spec. If you prefer autocommit-off, you might wish to set it in the system-wide psqlrc file or your ~/.psqlrc file.

COMP_KEYWORD_CASE

Determines which letter case to use when completing an SQL key word. If set to lower or upper, the completed word will be in lower or upper case, respectively. If set to preserve-lower or preserve-upper (the default), the completed word will be in the case of the word already entered, but words being completed without anything entered will be in lower or upper case, respectively.

DBNAME

The name of the database you are currently connected to. This is set every time you connect to a database (including program start-up), but can be unset.

ECHO

If set to all, all nonempty input lines are printed to standard output as they are read. (This does not apply to lines read interactively.) To select this behavior on program start-up, use the switch -a. If set to queries, psql prints each query to standard output as it is sent to the server. The switch for this is -e.

ECHO_HIDDEN

When this variable is set to on and a backslash command queries the database, the query is first shown. This feature helps you to study PostgreSQL internals and provide similar functionality in your own programs. (To select this behavior on program start-up, use the switch -E.) If you set the variable to the value noexec, the queries are just shown but are not actually sent to the server and executed.

ENCODING

The current client character set encoding.

FETCH_COUNT

If this variable is set to an integer value > 0, the results of SELECT queries are fetched and displayed in groups of that many rows, rather than the default behavior of collecting the entire result set before display. Therefore only a limited amount of memory is used, regardless of the size of the result set. Settings of 100 to 1000 are commonly used when enabling this feature. Keep in mind that when using this feature, a query might fail after having already displayed some rows.

> **Tip:** Although you can use any output format with this feature, the default aligned format tends to look bad because each group of FETCH_COUNT rows will be formatted separately, leading to varying column widths across the row groups. The other output formats work better.

HISTCONTROL

If this variable is set to ignorespace, lines which begin with a space are not entered into the history list. If set to a value of ignoredups, lines matching the previous history line are not entered. A value of ignoreboth combines the two options. If unset, or if set to any other value than those above, all lines read in interactive mode are saved on the history list.

> **Note:** This feature was shamelessly plagiarized from Bash.

HISTFILE

The file name that will be used to store the history list. The default value is ~/.psql_history. For example, putting:

\set HISTFILE ~/.psql_history- :DBNAME

in ~/.psqlrc will cause psql to maintain a separate history for each database.

Note: This feature was shamelessly plagiarized from Bash.

HISTSIZE

The number of commands to store in the command history. The default value is 500.

Note: This feature was shamelessly plagiarized from Bash.

HOST

The database server host you are currently connected to. This is set every time you connect to a database (including program start-up), but can be unset.

IGNOREEOF

If unset, sending an EOF character (usually **Control+D**) to an interactive session of psql will terminate the application. If set to a numeric value, that many EOF characters are ignored before the application terminates. If the variable is set but has no numeric value, the default is 10.

Note: This feature was shamelessly plagiarized from Bash.

LASTOID

The value of the last affected OID, as returned from an INSERT or \lo_import command. This variable is only guaranteed to be valid until after the result of the next SQL command has been displayed.

ON_ERROR_ROLLBACK

When set to on, if a statement in a transaction block generates an error, the error is ignored and the transaction continues. When set to interactive, such errors are only ignored in interactive sessions, and not when reading script files. When unset or set to off, a statement in a transaction block that generates an error aborts the entire transaction. The error rollback mode works by issuing an implicit SAVEPOINT for you, just before each command that is in a transaction block, and then rolling back to the savepoint if the command fails.

ON_ERROR_STOP

By default, command processing continues after an error. When this variable is set to on, processing will instead stop immediately. In interactive mode, psql will return to the command prompt; otherwise, psql will exit, returning error code 3 to distinguish this case from fatal error conditions, which are reported using error code 1. In either case, any currently running scripts (the top-level script, if any, and any other scripts which it may have in invoked) will be terminated immediately. If the top-level command string contained multiple SQL commands, processing will stop with the current command.

PORT

> The database server port to which you are currently connected. This is set every time you connect to a database (including program start-up), but can be unset.

PROMPT1
PROMPT2
PROMPT3

> These specify what the prompts psql issues should look like. See *Prompting* below.

QUIET

> Setting this variable to on is equivalent to the command line option -q. It is probably not too useful in interactive mode.

SINGLELINE

> Setting this variable to on is equivalent to the command line option -S.

SINGLESTEP

> Setting this variable to on is equivalent to the command line option -s.

USER

> The database user you are currently connected as. This is set every time you connect to a database (including program start-up), but can be unset.

VERBOSITY

> This variable can be set to the values default, verbose, or terse to control the verbosity of error reports.

SQL Interpolation

A key feature of psql variables is that you can substitute ("interpolate") them into regular SQL statements, as well as the arguments of meta-commands. Furthermore, psql provides facilities for ensuring that variable values used as SQL literals and identifiers are properly quoted. The syntax for interpolating a value without any quoting is to prepend the variable name with a colon (:). For example,

```
testdb=> \set foo 'my_table'
testdb=> SELECT * FROM :foo;
```

would query the table my_table. Note that this may be unsafe: the value of the variable is copied literally, so it can contain unbalanced quotes, or even backslash commands. You must make sure that it makes sense where you put it.

When a value is to be used as an SQL literal or identifier, it is safest to arrange for it to be quoted. To quote the value of a variable as an SQL literal, write a colon followed by the variable name in single quotes. To quote the value as an SQL identifier, write a colon followed by the variable name in double quotes. These constructs deal correctly with quotes and other special characters embedded within the variable value. The previous example would be more safely written this way:

```
testdb=> \set foo 'my_table'
```

```
testdb=> SELECT * FROM :"foo";
```

Variable interpolation will not be performed within quoted SQL literals and identifiers. Therefore, a construction such as `':foo'` doesn't work to produce a quoted literal from a variable's value (and it would be unsafe if it did work, since it wouldn't correctly handle quotes embedded in the value).

One example use of this mechanism is to copy the contents of a file into a table column. First load the file into a variable and then interpolate the variable's value as a quoted string:

```
testdb=> \set content `cat my_file.txt`
testdb=> INSERT INTO my_table VALUES (:'content');
```

(Note that this still won't work if `my_file.txt` contains NUL bytes. psql does not support embedded NUL bytes in variable values.)

Since colons can legally appear in SQL commands, an apparent attempt at interpolation (that is, `:name`, `:'name'`, or `:"name"`) is not replaced unless the named variable is currently set. In any case, you can escape a colon with a backslash to protect it from substitution.

The colon syntax for variables is standard SQL for embedded query languages, such as ECPG. The colon syntaxes for array slices and type casts are PostgreSQL extensions, which can sometimes conflict with the standard usage. The colon-quote syntax for escaping a variable's value as an SQL literal or identifier is a psql extension.

Prompting

The prompts psql issues can be customized to your preference. The three variables PROMPT1, PROMPT2, and PROMPT3 contain strings and special escape sequences that describe the appearance of the prompt. Prompt 1 is the normal prompt that is issued when psql requests a new command. Prompt 2 is issued when more input is expected during command input because the command was not terminated with a semicolon or a quote was not closed. Prompt 3 is issued when you run an SQL COPY command and you are expected to type in the row values on the terminal.

The value of the selected prompt variable is printed literally, except where a percent sign (%) is encountered. Depending on the next character, certain other text is substituted instead. Defined substitutions are:

%M

> The full host name (with domain name) of the database server, or [local] if the connection is over a Unix domain socket, or [local:/*dir/name*], if the Unix domain socket is not at the compiled in default location.

%m

> The host name of the database server, truncated at the first dot, or [local] if the connection is over a Unix domain socket.

%>

> The port number at which the database server is listening.

%n

The database session user name. (The expansion of this value might change during a database session as the result of the command SET SESSION AUTHORIZATION.)

%/

The name of the current database.

%~

Like %/, but the output is ~ (tilde) if the database is your default database.

%#

If the session user is a database superuser, then a #, otherwise a >. (The expansion of this value might change during a database session as the result of the command SET SESSION AUTHORIZATION.)

%R

In prompt 1 normally =, but ^ if in single-line mode, and ! if the session is disconnected from the database (which can happen if \connect fails). In prompt 2 the sequence is replaced by -, *, a single quote, a double quote, or a dollar sign, depending on whether psql expects more input because the command wasn't terminated yet, because you are inside a /* ... */ comment, or because you are inside a quoted or dollar-escaped string. In prompt 3 the sequence doesn't produce anything.

%x

Transaction status: an empty string when not in a transaction block, or * when in a transaction block, or ! when in a failed transaction block, or ? when the transaction state is indeterminate (for example, because there is no connection).

%*digits*

The character with the indicated octal code is substituted.

%:*name*:

The value of the psql variable *name*. See the section *Variables* for details.

%`*command*`

The output of *command*, similar to ordinary "back-tick" substitution.

%[... %]

Prompts can contain terminal control characters which, for example, change the color, background, or style of the prompt text, or change the title of the terminal window. In order for the line editing features of Readline to work properly, these non-printing control characters must be designated as invisible by surrounding them with %[and %]. Multiple pairs of these can occur within the prompt. For example:

testdb=> \set PROMPT1 '%[%033[1;33;40m%]%n@%/%R%[%033[0m%]%# '

results in a boldfaced (1;) yellow-on-black (33;40) prompt on VT100-compatible, color-capable terminals.

To insert a percent sign into your prompt, write %%. The default prompts are '%/%R%# ' for prompts 1 and 2, and '>> ' for prompt 3.

Note: This feature was shamelessly plagiarized from tcsh.

Command-Line Editing

psql supports the Readline library for convenient line editing and retrieval. The command history is automatically saved when psql exits and is reloaded when psql starts up. Tab-completion is also supported, although the completion logic makes no claim to be an SQL parser. The queries generated by tab-completion can also interfere with other SQL commands, e.g. SET TRANSACTION ISOLATION LEVEL. If for some reason you do not like the tab completion, you can turn it off by putting this in a file named .inputrc in your home directory:

```
$if psql
set disable-completion on
$endif
```

(This is not a psql but a Readline feature. Read its documentation for further details.)

Environment

COLUMNS

If \pset columns is zero, controls the width for the wrapped format and width for determining if wide output requires the pager or should be switched to the vertical format in expanded auto mode.

PAGER

If the query results do not fit on the screen, they are piped through this command. Typical values are more or less. The default is platform-dependent. The use of the pager can be disabled by using the \pset command.

PGDATABASE
PGHOST
PGPORT
PGUSER

Default connection parameters (see Section 31.14).

PSQL_EDITOR
EDITOR
VISUAL

Editor used by the \e and \ef commands. The variables are examined in the order listed; the first that is set is used.

The built-in default editors are vi on Unix systems and notepad.exe on Windows systems.

PSQL_EDITOR_LINENUMBER_ARG

When \e or \ef is used with a line number argument, this variable specifies the command-line argument used to pass the starting line number to the user's editor. For editors such as Emacs or vi, this is a plus sign. Include a trailing space in the value of the variable if there needs to be space between the option name and the line number. Examples:

```
PSQL_EDITOR_LINENUMBER_ARG='+'
PSQL_EDITOR_LINENUMBER_ARG='--line '
```

The default is + on Unix systems (corresponding to the default editor vi, and useful for many other common editors); but there is no default on Windows systems.

PSQL_HISTORY

Alternative location for the command history file. Tilde (~) expansion is performed.

PSQLRC

Alternative location of the user's .psqlrc file. Tilde (~) expansion is performed.

SHELL

Command executed by the \! command.

TMPDIR

Directory for storing temporary files. The default is /tmp.

This utility, like most other PostgreSQL utilities, also uses the environment variables supported by libpq (see Section 31.14).

Files

psqlrc and ~/.psqlrc

Unless it is passed an -X or -c option, psql attempts to read and execute commands from the system-wide startup file (psqlrc) and then the user's personal startup file (~/.psqlrc), after connecting to the database but before accepting normal commands. These files can be used to set up the client and/or the server to taste, typically with \set and SET commands.

The system-wide startup file is named psqlrc and is sought in the installation's "system configuration" directory, which is most reliably identified by running pg_config --sysconfdir. By default this directory will be ../etc/ relative to the directory containing the PostgreSQL executables. The name of this directory can be set explicitly via the PGSYSCONFDIR environment variable.

The user's personal startup file is named .psqlrc and is sought in the invoking user's home directory. On Windows, which lacks such a concept, the personal startup file is named %APPDATA%\postgresql\psqlrc.conf. The location of the user's startup file can be set explicitly via the PSQLRC environment variable.

Both the system-wide startup file and the user's personal startup file can be made psql-version-specific by appending a dash and the PostgreSQL major or minor release number to the file name, for example ~/.psqlrc-9.2 or ~/.psqlrc-9.2.5. The most specific version-matching file will be read in preference to a non-version-specific file.

.psql_history

The command-line history is stored in the file ~/.psql_history, or %APPDATA%\postgresql\psql_history on Windows.

The location of the history file can be set explicitly via the PSQL_HISTORY environment variable.

Notes

- In an earlier life psql allowed the first argument of a single-letter backslash command to start directly after the command, without intervening whitespace. As of PostgreSQL 8.4 this is no longer allowed.

- psql works best with servers of the same or an older major version. Backslash commands are particularly likely to fail if the server is of a newer version than psql itself. However, backslash commands of the \d family should work with servers of versions back to 7.4, though not necessarily with servers newer than psql itself. The general functionality of running SQL commands and displaying query results should also work with servers of a newer major version, but this cannot be guaranteed in all cases.

  If you want to use psql to connect to several servers of different major versions, it is recommended that you use the newest version of psql. Alternatively, you can keep a copy of psql from each major version around and be sure to use the version that matches the respective server. But in practice, this additional complication should not be necessary.

Notes for Windows Users

psql is built as a "console application". Since the Windows console windows use a different encoding than the rest of the system, you must take special care when using 8-bit characters within psql. If psql detects a problematic console code page, it will warn you at startup. To change the console code page, two things are necessary:

- Set the code page by entering **cmd.exe /c chcp 1252**. (1252 is a code page that is appropriate for German; replace it with your value.) If you are using Cygwin, you can put this command in /etc/profile.

- Set the console font to Lucida Console, because the raster font does not work with the ANSI code page.

Examples

The first example shows how to spread a command over several lines of input. Notice the changing prompt:

```
testdb=> CREATE TABLE my_table (
testdb(>  first integer not null default 0,
testdb(>  second text)
testdb-> ;
CREATE TABLE
```

Now look at the table definition again:

```
testdb=> \d my_table
```

```
            Table "my_table"
 Attribute |  Type   |     Modifier
-----------+---------+--------------------
 first     | integer | not null default 0
 second    | text    |
```

Now we change the prompt to something more interesting:

```
testdb=> \set PROMPT1 '%n@%m %~%R%# '
peter@localhost testdb=>
```

Let's assume you have filled the table with data and want to take a look at it:

```
peter@localhost testdb=> SELECT * FROM my_table;
 first | second
-------+--------
     1 | one
     2 | two
     3 | three
     4 | four
(4 rows)
```

You can display tables in different ways by using the \pset command:

```
peter@localhost testdb=> \pset border 2
Border style is 2.
peter@localhost testdb=> SELECT * FROM my_table;
+-------+--------+
| first | second |
+-------+--------+
|     1 | one    |
|     2 | two    |
|     3 | three  |
|     4 | four   |
+-------+--------+
(4 rows)

peter@localhost testdb=> \pset border 0
Border style is 0.
peter@localhost testdb=> SELECT * FROM my_table;
first second
----- ------
    1 one
    2 two
    3 three
    4 four
(4 rows)

peter@localhost testdb=> \pset border 1
Border style is 1.
peter@localhost testdb=> \pset format unaligned
Output format is unaligned.
peter@localhost testdb=> \pset fieldsep ","
Field separator is ",".
```

```
peter@localhost testdb=> \pset tuples_only
Showing only tuples.
peter@localhost testdb=> SELECT second, first FROM my_table;
one,1
two,2
three,3
four,4
```

Alternatively, use the short commands:

```
peter@localhost testdb=> \a \t \x
Output format is aligned.
Tuples only is off.
Expanded display is on.
peter@localhost testdb=> SELECT * FROM my_table;
-[ RECORD 1 ]-
first  | 1
second | one
-[ RECORD 2 ]-
first  | 2
second | two
-[ RECORD 3 ]-
first  | 3
second | three
-[ RECORD 4 ]-
first  | 4
second | four
```

reindexdb

Name

reindexdb — reindex a PostgreSQL database

Synopsis

reindexdb [*connection-option*...] [--table | -t *table*] ... [--index | -i *index*] ...
[*dbname*]

reindexdb [*connection-option*...] --all | -a

reindexdb [*connection-option*...] --system | -s [*dbname*]

Description

reindexdb is a utility for rebuilding indexes in a PostgreSQL database.

reindexdb is a wrapper around the SQL command REINDEX. There is no effective difference between reindexing databases via this utility and via other methods for accessing the server.

Options

reindexdb accepts the following command-line arguments:

-a
--all

> Reindex all databases.

[-d] *dbname*
[--dbname=]*dbname*

> Specifies the name of the database to be reindexed. If this is not specified and -a (or --all) is not used, the database name is read from the environment variable PGDATABASE. If that is not set, the user name specified for the connection is used.

-e
--echo

> Echo the commands that reindexdb generates and sends to the server.

-i *index*
--index=*index*

> Recreate *index* only. Multiple indexes can be recreated by writing multiple -i switches.

-q
--quiet

>   Do not display progress messages.

-s
--system

>   Reindex database's system catalogs.

-t *table*
--table=*table*

>   Reindex *table* only. Multiple tables can be reindexed by writing multiple -t switches.

-V
--version

>   Print the reindexdb version and exit.

-?
--help

>   Show help about reindexdb command line arguments, and exit.

reindexdb also accepts the following command-line arguments for connection parameters:

-h *host*
--host=*host*

>   Specifies the host name of the machine on which the server is running. If the value begins with a slash, it is used as the directory for the Unix domain socket.

-p *port*
--port=*port*

>   Specifies the TCP port or local Unix domain socket file extension on which the server is listening for connections.

-U *username*
--username=*username*

>   User name to connect as.

-w
--no-password

>   Never issue a password prompt. If the server requires password authentication and a password is not available by other means such as a .pgpass file, the connection attempt will fail. This option can be useful in batch jobs and scripts where no user is present to enter a password.

-W
--password

>   Force reindexdb to prompt for a password before connecting to a database.

>   This option is never essential, since reindexdb will automatically prompt for a password if the server demands password authentication. However, reindexdb will waste a connection attempt finding out

that the server wants a password. In some cases it is worth typing -W to avoid the extra connection attempt.

--maintenance-db=*dbname*

Specifies the name of the database to connect to discover what other databases should be reindexed. If not specified, the postgres database will be used, and if that does not exist, template1 will be used.

Environment

PGDATABASE
PGHOST
PGPORT
PGUSER

Default connection parameters

This utility, like most other PostgreSQL utilities, also uses the environment variables supported by libpq (see Section 31.14).

Diagnostics

In case of difficulty, see REINDEX and psql for discussions of potential problems and error messages. The database server must be running at the targeted host. Also, any default connection settings and environment variables used by the libpq front-end library will apply.

Notes

reindexdb might need to connect several times to the PostgreSQL server, asking for a password each time. It is convenient to have a ~/.pgpass file in such cases. See Section 31.15 for more information.

Examples

To reindex the database test:

```
$ reindexdb test
```

To reindex the table foo and the index bar in a database named abcd:

```
$ reindexdb --table foo --index bar abcd
```

See Also

REINDEX

vacuumdb

Name

vacuumdb — garbage-collect and analyze a PostgreSQL database

Synopsis

vacuumdb [*connection-option*...] [*option*...] [--table I -t *table* [(*column* [,...])]] ...
[*dbname*]

vacuumdb [*connection-option*...] [*option*...] --all I -a

Description

vacuumdb is a utility for cleaning a PostgreSQL database. vacuumdb will also generate internal statistics
used by the PostgreSQL query optimizer.

vacuumdb is a wrapper around the SQL command VACUUM. There is no effective difference between
vacuuming and analyzing databases via this utility and via other methods for accessing the server.

Options

vacuumdb accepts the following command-line arguments:

-a
--all

> Vacuum all databases.

[-d] *dbname*
[--dbname=]*dbname*

> Specifies the name of the database to be cleaned or analyzed. If this is not specified and -a (or
> --all) is not used, the database name is read from the environment variable PGDATABASE. If that is
> not set, the user name specified for the connection is used.

-e
--echo

> Echo the commands that vacuumdb generates and sends to the server.

-f
--full

> Perform "full" vacuuming.

```
-F
--freeze
```

Aggressively "freeze" tuples.

```
-q
--quiet
```

Do not display progress messages.

```
-t table [ (column [,...]) ]
--table=table [ (column [,...]) ]
```

Clean or analyze `table` only. Column names can be specified only in conjunction with the `--analyze` or `--analyze-only` options. Multiple tables can be vacuumed by writing multiple `-t` switches.

> **Tip:** If you specify columns, you probably have to escape the parentheses from the shell. (See examples below.)

```
-v
--verbose
```

Print detailed information during processing.

```
-V
--version
```

Print the vacuumdb version and exit.

```
-z
--analyze
```

Also calculate statistics for use by the optimizer.

```
-Z
--analyze-only
```

Only calculate statistics for use by the optimizer (no vacuum).

```
--analyze-in-stages
```

Only calculate statistics for use by the optimizer (no vacuum), like `--analyze-only`. Run several (currently three) stages of analyze with different configuration settings, to produce usable statistics faster.

This option is useful to analyze a database that was newly populated from a restored dump or by `pg_upgrade`. This option will try to create some statistics as fast as possible, to make the database usable, and then produce full statistics in the subsequent stages.

```
-?
--help
```

Show help about vacuumdb command line arguments, and exit.

vacuumdb also accepts the following command-line arguments for connection parameters:

`-h` *host*

`--host=`*host*

> Specifies the host name of the machine on which the server is running. If the value begins with a slash, it is used as the directory for the Unix domain socket.

`-p` *port*

`--port=`*port*

> Specifies the TCP port or local Unix domain socket file extension on which the server is listening for connections.

`-U` *username*

`--username=`*username*

> User name to connect as.

`-w`

`--no-password`

> Never issue a password prompt. If the server requires password authentication and a password is not available by other means such as a `.pgpass` file, the connection attempt will fail. This option can be useful in batch jobs and scripts where no user is present to enter a password.

`-W`

`--password`

> Force vacuumdb to prompt for a password before connecting to a database.
>
> This option is never essential, since vacuumdb will automatically prompt for a password if the server demands password authentication. However, vacuumdb will waste a connection attempt finding out that the server wants a password. In some cases it is worth typing `-W` to avoid the extra connection attempt.

`--maintenance-db=`*dbname*

> Specifies the name of the database to connect to discover what other databases should be vacuumed. If not specified, the `postgres` database will be used, and if that does not exist, `template1` will be used.

Environment

`PGDATABASE`
`PGHOST`
`PGPORT`
`PGUSER`

> Default connection parameters

This utility, like most other PostgreSQL utilities, also uses the environment variables supported by libpq (see Section 31.14).

Diagnostics

In case of difficulty, see VACUUM and psql for discussions of potential problems and error messages. The database server must be running at the targeted host. Also, any default connection settings and environment variables used by the libpq front-end library will apply.

Notes

vacuumdb might need to connect several times to the PostgreSQL server, asking for a password each time. It is convenient to have a ~/.pgpass file in such cases. See Section 31.15 for more information.

Examples

To clean the database test:

```
$ vacuumdb test
```

To clean and analyze for the optimizer a database named bigdb:

```
$ vacuumdb --analyze bigdb
```

To clean a single table foo in a database named xyzzy, and analyze a single column bar of the table for the optimizer:

```
$ vacuumdb --analyze --verbose --table 'foo(bar)' xyzzy
```

See Also

VACUUM

III. PostgreSQL Server Applications

This part contains reference information for PostgreSQL server applications and support utilities. These commands can only be run usefully on the host where the database server resides. Other utility programs are listed in Reference II, *PostgreSQL Client Applications*.

initdb

Name

initdb — create a new PostgreSQL database cluster

Synopsis

initdb [*option*...] [--pgdata | -D] *directory*

Description

initdb creates a new PostgreSQL database cluster. A database cluster is a collection of databases that are managed by a single server instance.

Creating a database cluster consists of creating the directories in which the database data will live, generating the shared catalog tables (tables that belong to the whole cluster rather than to any particular database), and creating the template1 and postgres databases. When you later create a new database, everything in the template1 database is copied. (Therefore, anything installed in template1 is automatically copied into each database created later.) The postgres database is a default database meant for use by users, utilities and third party applications.

Although initdb will attempt to create the specified data directory, it might not have permission if the parent directory of the desired data directory is root-owned. To initialize in such a setup, create an empty data directory as root, then use chown to assign ownership of that directory to the database user account, then su to become the database user to run initdb.

initdb must be run as the user that will own the server process, because the server needs to have access to the files and directories that initdb creates. Since the server cannot be run as root, you must not run initdb as root either. (It will in fact refuse to do so.)

initdb initializes the database cluster's default locale and character set encoding. The character set encoding, collation order (LC_COLLATE) and character set classes (LC_CTYPE, e.g. upper, lower, digit) can be set separately for a database when it is created. initdb determines those settings for the template1 database, which will serve as the default for all other databases.

To alter the default collation order or character set classes, use the --lc-collate and --lc-ctype options. Collation orders other than C or POSIX also have a performance penalty. For these reasons it is important to choose the right locale when running initdb.

The remaining locale categories can be changed later when the server is started. You can also use --locale to set the default for all locale categories, including collation order and character set classes. All server locale values (lc_*) can be displayed via SHOW ALL. More details can be found in Section 22.1.

To alter the default encoding, use the --encoding. More details can be found in Section 22.3.

Options

-A *authmethod*
--auth=*authmethod*

> This option specifies the authentication method for local users used in `pg_hba.conf` (`host` and `local` lines). Do not use `trust` unless you trust all local users on your system. `trust` is the default for ease of installation.

--auth-host=*authmethod*

> This option specifies the authentication method for local users via TCP/IP connections used in `pg_hba.conf` (`host` lines).

--auth-local=*authmethod*

> This option specifies the authentication method for local users via Unix-domain socket connections used in `pg_hba.conf` (`local` lines).

-D *directory*
--pgdata=*directory*

> This option specifies the directory where the database cluster should be stored. This is the only information required by `initdb`, but you can avoid writing it by setting the `PGDATA` environment variable, which can be convenient since the database server (`postgres`) can find the database directory later by the same variable.

-E *encoding*
--encoding=*encoding*

> Selects the encoding of the template database. This will also be the default encoding of any database you create later, unless you override it there. The default is derived from the locale, or `SQL_ASCII` if that does not work. The character sets supported by the PostgreSQL server are described in Section 22.3.1.

-k
--data-checksums

> Use checksums on data pages to help detect corruption by the I/O system that would otherwise be silent. Enabling checksums may incur a noticeable performance penalty. This option can only be set during initialization, and cannot be changed later. If set, checksums are calculated for all objects, in all databases.

--locale=*locale*

> Sets the default locale for the database cluster. If this option is not specified, the locale is inherited from the environment that `initdb` runs in. Locale support is described in Section 22.1.

--lc-collate=*locale*
--lc-ctype=*locale*
--lc-messages=*locale*
--lc-monetary=*locale*
--lc-numeric=*locale*
--lc-time=*locale*

> Like --locale, but only sets the locale in the specified category.

```
--no-locale
```

Equivalent to `--locale=C`.

```
-N
--nosync
```

By default, `initdb` will wait for all files to be written safely to disk. This option causes `initdb` to return without waiting, which is faster, but means that a subsequent operating system crash can leave the data directory corrupt. Generally, this option is useful for testing, but should not be used when creating a production installation.

```
--pwfile=filename
```

Makes `initdb` read the database superuser's password from a file. The first line of the file is taken as the password.

```
-S
--sync-only
```

Safely write all database files to disk and exit. This does not perform any of the normal initdb operations.

```
-T CFG
--text-search-config=CFG
```

Sets the default text search configuration. See default_text_search_config for further information.

```
-U username
--username=username
```

Selects the user name of the database superuser. This defaults to the name of the effective user running `initdb`. It is really not important what the superuser's name is, but one might choose to keep the customary name postgres, even if the operating system user's name is different.

```
-W
--pwprompt
```

Makes `initdb` prompt for a password to give the database superuser. If you don't plan on using password authentication, this is not important. Otherwise you won't be able to use password authentication until you have a password set up.

```
-X directory
--xlogdir=directory
```

This option specifies the directory where the transaction log should be stored.

Other, less commonly used, options are also available:

```
-d
--debug
```

Print debugging output from the bootstrap backend and a few other messages of lesser interest for the general public. The bootstrap backend is the program `initdb` uses to create the catalog tables. This option generates a tremendous amount of extremely boring output.

`-L` *directory*

> Specifies where `initdb` should find its input files to initialize the database cluster. This is normally not necessary. You will be told if you need to specify their location explicitly.

`-n`
`--noclean`

> By default, when `initdb` determines that an error prevented it from completely creating the database cluster, it removes any files it might have created before discovering that it cannot finish the job. This option inhibits tidying-up and is thus useful for debugging.

Other options:

`-V`
`--version`

> Print the initdb version and exit.

`-?`
`--help`

> Show help about initdb command line arguments, and exit.

Environment

`PGDATA`

> Specifies the directory where the database cluster is to be stored; can be overridden using the `-D` option.

`TZ`

> Specifies the default time zone of the created database cluster. The value should be a full time zone name (see Section 8.5.3).

This utility, like most other PostgreSQL utilities, also uses the environment variables supported by libpq (see Section 31.14).

Notes

`initdb` can also be invoked via `pg_ctl initdb`.

See Also

pg_ctl, postgres

pg_controldata

Name

pg_controldata — display control information of a PostgreSQL database cluster

Synopsis

pg_controldata [*option*] [*datadir*]

Description

pg_controldata prints information initialized during initdb, such as the catalog version. It also shows information about write-ahead logging and checkpoint processing. This information is cluster-wide, and not specific to any one database.

This utility can only be run by the user who initialized the cluster because it requires read access to the data directory. You can specify the data directory on the command line, or use the environment variable PGDATA. This utility supports the options -V and --version, which print the pg_controldata version and exit. It also supports options -? and --help, which output the supported arguments.

Environment

PGDATA

Default data directory location

pg_ctl

Name

pg_ctl — initialize, start, stop, or control a PostgreSQL server

Synopsis

pg_ctl init[db] [-s] [-D *datadir*] [-o *initdb-options*]

pg_ctl start [-w] [-t *seconds*] [-s] [-D *datadir*] [-l *filename*] [-o *options*] [-p *path*] [-c]

pg_ctl stop [-W] [-t *seconds*] [-s] [-D *datadir*] [-m s[mart] | f[ast] | i[mmediate]]

pg_ctl restart [-w] [-t *seconds*] [-s] [-D *datadir*] [-c] [-m s[mart] | f[ast] | i[mmediate]] [-o *options*]

pg_ctl reload [-s] [-D *datadir*]

pg_ctl status [-D *datadir*]

pg_ctl promote [-s] [-D *datadir*]

pg_ctl kill *signal_name process_id*

pg_ctl register [-N *servicename*] [-U *username*] [-P *password*] [-D *datadir*] [-S a[uto] | d[emand]] [-w] [-t *seconds*] [-s] [-o *options*]

pg_ctl unregister [-N *servicename*]

Description

pg_ctl is a utility for initializing a PostgreSQL database cluster, starting, stopping, or restarting the PostgreSQL database server (postgres), or displaying the status of a running server. Although the server can be started manually, pg_ctl encapsulates tasks such as redirecting log output and properly detaching from the terminal and process group. It also provides convenient options for controlled shutdown.

The init or initdb mode creates a new PostgreSQL database cluster. A database cluster is a collection of databases that are managed by a single server instance. This mode invokes the initdb command. See initdb for details.

In `start` mode, a new server is launched. The server is started in the background, and its standard input is attached to `/dev/null` (or `nul` on Windows). On Unix-like systems, by default, the server's standard output and standard error are sent to pg_ctl's standard output (not standard error). The standard output of pg_ctl should then be redirected to a file or piped to another process such as a log rotating program like rotatelogs; otherwise `postgres` will write its output to the controlling terminal (from the background) and will not leave the shell's process group. On Windows, by default the server's standard output and standard error are sent to the terminal. These default behaviors can be changed by using `-l` to append the server's output to a log file. Use of either `-l` or output redirection is recommended.

In `stop` mode, the server that is running in the specified data directory is shut down. Three different shutdown methods can be selected with the `-m` option. "Smart" mode (the default) waits for all active clients to disconnect and any online backup to finish. If the server is in hot standby, recovery and streaming replication will be terminated once all clients have disconnected. "Fast" mode does not wait for clients to disconnect and will terminate an online backup in progress. All active transactions are rolled back and clients are forcibly disconnected, then the server is shut down. "Immediate" mode will abort all server processes immediately, without a clean shutdown. This will lead to a crash-recovery run on the next restart.

`restart` mode effectively executes a stop followed by a start. This allows changing the `postgres` command-line options. `restart` might fail if relative paths specified were specified on the command-line during server start.

`reload` mode simply sends the `postgres` process a SIGHUP signal, causing it to reread its configuration files (`postgresql.conf`, `pg_hba.conf`, etc.). This allows changing of configuration-file options that do not require a complete restart to take effect.

`status` mode checks whether a server is running in the specified data directory. If it is, the PID and the command line options that were used to invoke it are displayed. If the server is not running, the process returns an exit status of 3. If an accessible data directory is not specified, the process returns an exit status of 4.

In `promote` mode, the standby server that is running in the specified data directory is commanded to exit recovery and begin read-write operations.

`kill` mode allows you to send a signal to a specified process. This is particularly valuable for Microsoft Windows which does not have a kill command. Use `--help` to see a list of supported signal names.

`register` mode allows you to register a system service on Microsoft Windows. The `-S` option allows selection of service start type, either "auto" (start service automatically on system startup) or "demand" (start service on demand).

`unregister` mode allows you to unregister a system service on Microsoft Windows. This undoes the effects of the `register` command.

Options

`-c`
`--core-file`

    Attempt to allow server crashes to produce core files, on platforms where this is possible, by lifting any soft resource limit placed on core files. This is useful in debugging or diagnosing problems by allowing a stack trace to be obtained from a failed server process.

-D *datadir*

--pgdata *datadir*

> Specifies the file system location of the database configuration files. If this is omitted, the environment variable PGDATA is used.

-l *filename*

--log *filename*

> Append the server log output to *filename*. If the file does not exist, it is created. The umask is set to 077, so access to the log file is disallowed to other users by default.

-m *mode*

--mode *mode*

> Specifies the shutdown mode. *mode* can be smart, fast, or immediate, or the first letter of one of these three. If this is omitted, smart is used.

-o *options*

> Specifies options to be passed directly to the postgres command.

> The options should usually be surrounded by single or double quotes to ensure that they are passed through as a group.

-o *initdb-options*

> Specifies options to be passed directly to the initdb command.

> The options should usually be surrounded by single or double quotes to ensure that they are passed through as a group.

-p *path*

> Specifies the location of the postgres executable. By default the postgres executable is taken from the same directory as pg_ctl, or failing that, the hard-wired installation directory. It is not necessary to use this option unless you are doing something unusual and get errors that the postgres executable was not found.

> In init mode, this option analogously specifies the location of the initdb executable.

-s

--silent

> Print only errors, no informational messages.

-t

--timeout

> The maximum number of seconds to wait when waiting for startup or shutdown to complete. The default is 60 seconds.

-V

--version

> Print the pg_ctl version and exit.

-w

> Wait for the startup or shutdown to complete. Waiting is the default option for shutdowns, but not startups. When waiting for startup, pg_ctl repeatedly attempts to connect to the server. When wait-

ing for shutdown, `pg_ctl` waits for the server to remove its PID file. This option allows the entry of an SSL passphrase on startup. `pg_ctl` returns an exit code based on the success of the startup or shutdown.

`-W`

Do not wait for startup or shutdown to complete. This is the default for start and restart modes.

`-?`
`--help`

Show help about pg_ctl command line arguments, and exit.

Options for Windows

`-N` *servicename*

Name of the system service to register. The name will be used as both the service name and the display name.

`-P` *password*

Password for the user to start the service.

`-S` *start-type*

Start type of the system service to register. start-type can be `auto`, or `demand`, or the first letter of one of these two. If this is omitted, `auto` is used.

`-U` *username*

User name for the user to start the service. For domain users, use the format `DOMAIN\username`.

Environment

`PGDATA`

Default data directory location.

`pg_ctl`, like most other PostgreSQL utilities, also uses the environment variables supported by libpq (see Section 31.14). For additional server variables, see postgres.

Files

`postmaster.pid`

The existence of this file in the data directory is used to help pg_ctl determine if the server is currently running.

`postmaster.opts`

> If this file exists in the data directory, pg_ctl (in `restart` mode) will pass the contents of the file as options to postgres, unless overridden by the `-o` option. The contents of this file are also displayed in `status` mode.

Examples

Starting the Server

To start the server:

```
$ pg_ctl start
```

To start the server, waiting until the server is accepting connections:

```
$ pg_ctl -w start
```

To start the server using port 5433, and running without `fsync`, use:

```
$ pg_ctl -o "-F -p 5433" start
```

Stopping the Server

To stop the server, use:

```
$ pg_ctl stop
```

The -m option allows control over *how* the server shuts down:

```
$ pg_ctl stop -m fast
```

Restarting the Server

Restarting the server is almost equivalent to stopping the server and starting it again, except that `pg_ctl` saves and reuses the command line options that were passed to the previously running instance. To restart the server in the simplest form, use:

```
$ pg_ctl restart
```

To restart the server, waiting for it to shut down and restart:

```
$ pg_ctl -w restart
```

To restart using port 5433, disabling fsync upon restart:

```
$ pg_ctl -o "-F -p 5433" restart
```

Showing the Server Status

Here is sample status output from pg_ctl:

```
$ pg_ctl status
pg_ctl: server is running (PID: 13718)
/usr/local/pgsql/bin/postgres "-D" "/usr/local/pgsql/data" "-p" "5433" "-B" "128"
```

This is the command line that would be invoked in restart mode.

See Also

initdb, postgres

www.ingramcontent.com/pod-product-compliance
Lightning Source LLC
LaVergne TN
LVHW060131070326

832902LV00018B/2750